Algorithms for Functional Programming

John David Stone

Algorithms for Functional Programming

 Springer

John David Stone
Department of Computer Science
Grinnell College
Grinnell, IA, USA

ISBN 978-3-662-58609-9   ISBN 978-3-662-57970-1   (eBook)
https://doi.org/10.1007/978-3-662-57970-1

This Springer imprint is published by the registered company Springer-Verlag GmbH, DE part of Springer Nature.
The registered company address is: Heidelberger Platz 3, 14197 Berlin, Germany

To ā̄: m.a.v.

Preface

The study of algorithms is motivated by the human desire for answers to questions. We prefer answers that are true and are arrived at by objective methods. The reasons for these preferences are practical. Our actions are more likely to have satisfactory results if we understand the world as it is, so we seek truth. It is easier to secure the agreement and cooperation of others towards common goals if they can confirm our answers independently, so in seeking truth we use methods that will give the same results when applied by others.

Sometimes we find that many questions have a similar structure and are instances of the same problem. Then there may be a single method by which one can answer any question of the common form. That is what an algorithm is: an effective, step-by-step, computational method for obtaining an answer to any instance of a general, formally stated problem.

Before computers, enacting an algorithm that required a large number of steps, or one that operated on a large quantity of data, called for extraordinary patience, care, and tenacity. Even so, the results were often flawed. For instance, from 1853 to 1873, a dedicated hobbyist named William Shanks devoted much of his free time to the computation of a high-precision value for π, obtaining 707 digits after the decimal point. This stood as a sort of record for a single computation until 1944, when it was discovered that Shanks had made a mistake that affected the 528th and all subsequent digits. The largest collection of related computations ever performed without mechanical aids was probably the 1880 census of the United States, which took seven or eight years to complete and was almost certainly riddled with incorrect results.

The invention and development of electronic stored-program computers largely eliminated these constraints on the complexity of computations. We can now compute 707 digits of π in a fraction of a second, while the 1880 census computations might take a minute. A long computation today would be something like computing five hundred billion digits of π, and we would expect the result to be completely correct. A large data set today might be measured in terabytes.

Another impediment to progress in the creation and use of algorithms, until the middle of the twentieth century, was the absence of any unambiguous general-purpose notation for recording them. When an algorithm is described in ordinary prose, it is often difficult to figure out exactly how to enact it. Such descriptions often omit details, fail to explain how to deal with exceptional cases, or require the performer to guess how to proceed at key points. For instance, if you learned the pencil-and-paper method for long division (in which the divisor has more than one digit), you may recall being obliged to estimate the next digit of the quotient and having to backtrack and revise if your initial guess was wrong.

The invention and development of high-level programming languages have largely removed this obstacle as well. It is now commonplace for the creator of an algorithm to express it exactly, completely, and unambiguously in the form of a computer program.

However, a human reader, encountering an algorithm for the first time, may have trouble recognizing the underlying structure of an algorithm in the source code for the computer program that enacts it. One of the difficulties for such a reader is that many high-level programming languages embody and enforce a model of computation in which programs work by repeatedly altering the state of an appropriately initialized storage device. We often find it difficult to grasp the interacting and cumulative effects of these alterations.

The solution to this difficulty is to use a different model of computation. In a pure functional programming language, one thinks of a computation as the application of a mathematical function to argument values, yielding result values. If the computation is long and intricate, it is convenient to define the mathematical function in terms of other, simpler functions, which in turn may be defined in terms of others that are simpler still. At each level, however, the functions are *stateless*, yielding the same results when given the same arguments. Once we have learned the rule by which a function derives its results from its arguments, we can treat the function as a reliable component with fixed and predictable behavior. This modularity makes it easier to design large programs, easier to construct them, and easier to reason about them.

In addition, functional programming languages make it easier to identify and abstract out general patterns of interaction among functions, so that one can describe and operate on those patterns within the language itself. Functions are themselves values that can be transmitted as arguments to other functions and returned as results by such functions. Using higher-order functions also makes it easier to formulate and understand common algorithms.

The plan of this book is to present a variety of widely used algorithms, expressing them in a pure functional programming language so as to make their structure and operation clearer to readers. Other advantages of the functional style will become apparent along the way.

We present the algorithms in a purely functional version of the Scheme programming language, implemented through the (afp primitives) library described in Appendix B. The code, which has been thoroughly tested under the Chibi-Scheme, Larceny, and Racket implementations of the *Revised*[7] *Report on the Algorithmic Language Scheme*, is available at the author's Web site:

http://unity.homelinux.net/afp/

It is licensed as free software under the GNU General Public License, version 3 or later (http://www.gnu.org/copyleft/gpl.html).

Acknowledgements

I am indebted to Grinnell College for providing me with the time and resources to write this book; to my colleagues Henry Walker, Samuel Rebelsky, Ben Gum, Janet Davis, Jerod Weinman, Peter-Michael Osera, and Charlie Curtsinger, for their patience and support; to Karen McRitchie and Jeff Leep for filling in for me; to Rice University, for providing a place to work during a sabbatical leave; to my editors at Springer-Verlag, Wayne Wheeler and Ronan Nugent; and to Matthias Felleisen and Shriram Krishnamurthi, who read a very early draft of this material and helped me climb out of some pitfalls and avoid some others. Thank you all.

Having corrected several thousand errors in the various drafts of this book, I am uncomfortably aware of the likelihood that many more remain. Accordingly, I extend my thanks in advance to the readers who will call them to my attention, so that I can make corrections at the Web site. Your e-mail to `reseda@grinnell.edu` will receive my prompt attention.

Contents

Chapter 1

Essential Notations

To express algorithms accurately and concisely, we need a formal notational system in which the meaning of each symbol and each identifier is accurately defined in advance. In this book, we'll use a variant of the Scheme programming language for this purpose, which gives us the additional advantage of being able to test and use the algorithms we develop by executing them on computers. This chapter introduces the specific notations that constitute our variant of Scheme.

1.1 Simple Values

We'll use the term *values* to describe the data that we operate on when we compute. For example, when we do some arithmetic and determine that the product of 17 and 33 is 561, the numbers 17, 33, and 561 are all values.

Not all values are numbers, however. Determining whether or not the letter M precedes the letter K in the alphabet is also a kind of computation, but the data in this case are letters rather than numbers. Also, the result of this computation is neither a number nor a letter, but a *Boolean* value—a yes-or-no answer to a yes-or-no question. Computation is not about numbers as such, but about values of any kind that we can operate on exactly and unambiguously.

The notation that we'll use in this book is a variant of the Scheme programming language. Scheme supplies built-in, unchangeable names—*literals*—for values of several kinds:

- **Booleans.** There are only two Boolean values. We'll use '#t' as a name for the affirmative answer to a yes-or-no question, '#f' as a name for the negative one. When spoken aloud, these names are pronounced "true" and "false."

- **Numbers.** We'll use everyday numerals, optionally preceded by a plus sign or a minus sign, as names for integers. A fraction (consisting of an

© Springer-Verlag GmbH Germany, part of Springer Nature 2018
J. D. Stone, *Algorithms for Functional Programming*,
https://doi.org/10.1007/978-3-662-57970-1_1

optionally signed integer numeral, a solidus, and an unsigned non-zero integer numeral) names a rational number: the ratio of the integer named before the solidus to the integer named after it.

For instance, '897' is the name for eight hundred ninety-seven, '-483' for negative four hundred eighty-three, and '+892/581' for the ratio of eight hundred ninety-two to five hundred eighty-one.

For our purposes, there is no difference between a ratio in which the denominator is 1 and the integer in the numerator of that ratio. For instance, '-17/1' and '-17' are different names for the same value. Thus values of the *integer* type also count as values of the *number* type.

It is sometimes convenient to distinguish non-negative integers, called *natural numbers*, from negative ones. Note that the *natural-number* type, under the convention we're adopting here, includes 0.

- **Characters.** The Unicode Consortium maintains a list that includes nearly all of the characters used in nearly all of the world's writing systems, past and present. To name any character on the Unicode list, we'll write a number sign, a reverse solidus, and the character itself. For instance, '#\M' is the name of the Latin capital letter M, '#\;' the name of the semicolon, and '#\ζ' the name of the Greek small letter zeta.

  Occasionally, programmers need to deal with characters that are difficult to write into the text of a program. The keyboard provides no way to input the character, or the text editor does not implement it correctly, or the display does not render it correctly. Some characters play such abstract roles in the writing systems to which they belong that there is no satisfactory way to represent them graphically in isolation. To accommodate such cases, Scheme provides additional names for some of the commonly used characters: #\newline for the newline character that one's operating system places at the end of each line of a text file, #\nul for the do-nothing character with which old-fashioned teletype machines used to fill up the text stream when the hardware needed to catch up, and so on.

  In addition, any character can be named by prefixing #\x to the base-sixteen numeral for the scalar value that Unicode assigns to it. For instance, if you don't have a Greek small letter zeta on your keyboard, you can write '#\x03b6' to name it.

- **Strings.** We'll sometimes treat a finite sequence of characters as a single value. To name such a value, we'll line up the characters of the sequence and enclose them in quotation marks. For instance, '"sample"' is the name of a string consisting entirely of Latin small letters—the letters s, a, m, p, l, and e, in that order.

  For some languages and writing systems, the relationship between characters and strings is more complicated, because characters can be joined or combined in non-linear ways that don't fit into the finite-sequence model.

The principle of forming a string literal by enclosing the string in quotation marks applies even in these cases, however.

There's an obvious difficulty with this simple naming convention for strings: What happens if the string we want to name contains a quotation mark among its component characters? To cope with this difficulty, we'll insert a reverse solidus (the character commonly known as "backslash") into the string literal, just before the internal quotation mark. For instance, '"\"Hi!\""' is the name of a five-character string consisting of a quotation mark, the Latin capital letter H, the Latin small letter i, an exclamation mark, and another quotation mark.

In programmers' jargon, the reverse solidus in string literals is an *escape character*. It is not itself part of the string, but instead acts as a conventional signal that the character that follows it should "escape" from the interpretation or role that it would otherwise have—in this case, the role of string terminator.

This convention, however, gives rise to a new difficulty of the same sort: What happens if the string we want to name contains a reverse solidus? Fortunately, we can apply the same solution to this difficulty: We'll insert an additional reverse solidus into the string literal, just before the "real" reverse solidus. For instance, '"\\a\\"' is the name of a three-character string consisting of a reverse solidus, the Latin small letter a, and another reverse solidus. In this case, by inserting an escape character, we signal that the character that follows it is *not* to be interpreted as an escape character!

- **Symbols.** A symbol is a value that has a name and an identity, but no other characteristics that can figure in a computation. In programming, symbols are convenient, neutral representations for real-world entities whose salient characteristics are not computational—colors, countries, sports teams, etc. To name a symbol, we'll place an apostrophe in front of an arbitrary identifier. For instance, ''midnight-blue' is the name of a symbol with the identifier 'midnight-blue', which might represent the color midnight blue in an inventory program for a company that makes shirts. Similarly, ''NZ' is the name of a symbol with the identifier 'NZ', which in turn designates New Zealand in the alpha-2 code adopted by the International Organization for Standardization (ISO 3166).

When spoken aloud, the apostrophe is pronounced "quote." Scheme processors treat the expression '(quote sample)' as interchangeable with ''sample' in most contexts, but the apostrophe notation is commoner and usually more convenient.

Since we won't use apostrophes or other potentially ambiguous characters in identifiers, no escape-character mechanism is needed in symbol literals.

Exercises

1.1–1   Write the literals for the negative Boolean value and the Latin small letter f.

1.1–2   Write two different literals that name the integer forty-two.

1.1–3   Do the literals '2/3' and '24/36' name the same value? What about the literals '+0/1' and '-0/1'?

1.1–4   Is '0/0' a literal? If so, what value does it name?

1.1–5 . Write the literals for the left parenthesis and the reverse solidus.

1.1–6   Write the literal for the string 'absolute value'.

1.1–7   Write the literal for the Latin capital letter A, the literal for a string that contains that letter as its one and only character, and the literal for a symbol with the identifier 'A'.

1.1–8   Is '""' a literal? If so, what value does it name?

1.1–9   Write the literal for the symbol with the identifier 'foo'.

1.2   Identifiers and Expressions

An *identifier* is a name that the programmer can associate with a value. Such an association is called a *binding*, and an identifier that stands in such an association is said to be *bound*.

In Scheme, any sequence of one or more letters and *extended alphabetic characters* can be used as an identifier. The extended alphabetic characters include the exclamation mark, the dollar sign, the percent sign, the ampersand, the asterisk, the solidus (/), the colon, the less-than sign, the equals sign, the greater-than sign, the question mark, the commercial at (@), the circumflex accent (^), the low line (_), and the tilde (~).

Decimal digits and the plus sign, the minus sign, and the full stop (.) can also be used in identifiers, but Scheme does not allow these to appear at the beginning of an identifier, since that would make it more difficult to distinguish identifiers from numerals. Three specific character sequences are exempted from this last rule, however: the plus sign by itself, '+', which is generally bound to Scheme's addition procedure; the minus sign by itself, '-', which is generally bound to Scheme's subtraction procedure; and the identifier '...'.

In the text of a program, every identifier is delimited at the beginning and end by characters that are not permitted in identifiers at all, usually parentheses, spaces, or newline characters. It is not permissible to juxtapose two identifiers with no delimiter between them. The Scheme processor treats such a construction as a single identifier or as an error.

The grammatical rules of Scheme provide a variety of ways of combining identifiers and other symbols into larger constructions, and the semantic rules of Scheme describe how to compute the values that those constructions denote or express. An *expression* is a language element or construction that expresses some number of values, and the process of determining what those values are is called *evaluation*.

Literals are expressions, but their evaluation rule is easy, because their values are permanently fixed: The numeral '1/3' always denotes the ratio of 1 to 3, for instance. Bound identifiers are expressions, but again their evaluation rule is almost trivial: During the execution of a program, the language processor keeps track of all the bindings that are in effect and can look up any identifier to determine the value to which it is bound. Unlike a literal, however, an identifier can be bound to different values at different times. The language processor keeps track of this, too.

A literal or a bound identifier always has one and only one value, but in general the evaluation of a Scheme expression can have any number of results, and collectively these are said to be the values of the expression.

Scheme sets aside a small number of identifiers as *syntactic keywords*, which are signals to the language processor, indicating how it should evaluate the expressions in which the keywords occur. Here is a complete list of the syntactic keywords used in the version of Scheme that we'll use in this book:

```
and
define
define-record-type
if
lambda
let
or
quote
rec
receive
sect
source
```

In principle, Scheme allows programs that change the bindings of syntactic keywords. Programmers should exercise extreme caution in using this language feature, which is apt to produce confusing results and unexpected errors that are difficult to diagnose. Accordingly, in this book, we'll refrain from rebinding any of these keywords.

Exercises

1.2–1 Is '1+' an identifier? What about '+1'?

1.2–2 Is '@@@' an identifier?

1.2–3 The previous section mentioned the identifier 'midnight-blue'. Since
'-' is a valid identifier in Scheme, what distinguishes 'midnight-blue' from a
sequence of three identifiers—'midnight', '-', 'blue'? How does the Scheme
language processor resolve this ambiguity?

1.3   Functions and Procedures

In functional programming, we regard functions as values. Higher-order functions can map values that are themselves functions to other values, or map other
values to functions, or map functions to functions. Our algorithms will construct
and operate on values that are functions dynamically, during execution, just as
they construct and compute with values that are numbers or strings.

In Scheme, functions are implemented as values of the *procedure* type. A
procedure is the form of a computation, abstracted from the particular values
with which that computation starts and on which it operates. Alternatively, one
can think of a procedure as a potential computation, deferred until the values
that it needs are available.

To *invoke* a procedure is to make the abstract computation real, the potential
computation actual. When invoking a procedure, we must therefore supply the
starting values that it needs—the *arguments* of the procedure. Once it receives
these arguments, the procedure carries out the computation. When and if the
computation ends, it yields some number of computed values—the *results* that
are *returned* by the procedure.

Scheme's procedure data type is just abstract enough to be compatible with
the mathematical concept of a function. However, Scheme is designed to support
several models of computation, not just the functional one. As a result, not all
Scheme procedures are functions, because some of them have internal states.
The results that such procedures return may depend on their internal states as
well as on the arguments they receive. Having to keep track of the internal states
of procedures tends to make it more difficult to understand algorithms, however,
so in this book we'll work exclusively with procedures that *are* functions, and
the notation that we'll use is a *purely functional* version of Scheme.

For the most part, we'll want to define and name our own procedures, but
there are some that can and should be implemented within the language processor that we use, for reasons of simplicity and efficiency. For example, we'll often
use addition as a step in algorithms that we define, but we don't need to write
our own definition of the addition function. The implementers of our language
processor (such as a Scheme compiler) have already figured out how to perform
addition very efficiently, using the capabilities of a computer's central processing
unit to best advantage. So we'll take addition as a *primitive*: a component that
we can use in the definition of other functions without needing to consider what
it looks like inside.

1.4 Arithmetic Functions

Let's start with a handful of primitive procedures that perform simple arithmetic. We'll inspect each one closely and summarize our findings at the end of the section.

Addition

The addition procedure is +. We usually think of addition as a function that maps two numbers, the *augend* and the *addend*, to their sum. But the designers of Scheme chose instead to have an extended version of addition that can receive any number of arguments, each of which must be a number, and returns their sum. For instance, we might give + the arguments 7, 4, 2, 6, and 3, and + would add them all up and return the value 22.

This generalization of the two-argument addition function illustrates a pattern that we'll use often. When a function of two arguments is commonly applied to many values in succession in order to accumulate a result, as addition is used to compute the sum of a collection of numbers, we'll implement it instead as a procedure that can receive any number of arguments to return that same final result.

This kind of generalization is particularly attractive and plausible when the two-argument function is associative. Associativity means that the order in which the intermediate results are produced does not affect the ultimate result. (Formally, an operation $\oplus$ is associative if $(x \oplus y) \oplus z = x \oplus (y \oplus z)$, for any choices of the operands x, y, and z.)

Addition is associative, which is why we expect to get the same sum for a column of numbers whether we add it up from top to bottom, from bottom to top, from the middle outwards in both directions, or in any other order. Simultaneously supplying all the values to be added up as arguments to + conveys our indifference to the order in which the implementation chooses to process them, since we know that we'll get the same answer in any case.

Scheme's + procedure can also receive *fewer* than two arguments. When it receives one argument, it returns that argument as its result. When it receives no arguments at all, it returns 0.

The reason for returning 0 in this last case is that 0 is the only number whose presence or absence has no effect on the sum of any collection of numbers. It is an *identity* for addition. Formally, this means that it satisfies the equations $0 + n = n$ and $n + 0 = n$, for any number n. If the + procedure returns 0 when given no arguments, we can find the sum of a collection of numbers by breaking it up into smaller sub-collections and adding together the sums of those sub-collections, without worrying about the special cases in which one of those sub-collections happens to be empty.

Subtraction

The subtraction procedure is -. Again, we usually think of subtraction as a function of two arguments, and the pattern that Scheme adopted for generalizing addition won't work here, because subtraction is not associative and does not have an identity. (There is no number v such that $v - n = n$ for every n.)

Instead, we'll generalize subtraction in a different way: If - receives more than two arguments, it will start with the first argument, the *minuend*, and successively subtract away each of the remaining arguments (the *subtrahends*), returning the result of the last subtraction. For instance, given the arguments 29, 4, 7, and 12, - returns 6, which is $((29-4)-7)-12$, the result of successively subtracting away 4, 7, and 12 from 29. (Thus multi-argument subtraction is said to "associate to the left.")

If - receives just one argument, it computes and returns the *additive inverse* of that argument, which is the number that produces 0 (the identity for addition) when added to the argument. For instance, if - receives the argument 8, it returns -8. If it receives -23, it returns 23. And if it receives 0, it returns 0.

The - procedure requires at least one argument and will balk if given none, reflecting the fact that no number is an identity for subtraction.

Multiplication

Multiplication is associative, and 1 is an identity for multiplication, so we extend the basic two-argument function as we do addition: The * procedure can receive any number of arguments and returns their product, or 1 if it receives no arguments at all.

Division

The term "division" is applied to two related but distinct operations in arithmetic. One of these operations determines the ratio between two given numbers. For instance, we divide 124 by 16 to determine the ratio between them, $31/4$. The operands may themselves be expressed as fractions: For instance, the ratio of $5/12$ to $9/14$ is $35/54$, and we compute this ratio by dividing $5/12$ by $9/14$.

The other operation determines the quotient and remainder of two integers. This is the kind of division that we perform when we compute that 16 "goes into" 124 seven times, with a remainder of 12.

When one integer evenly divides another, the two forms of division coincide, in a way. For instance, the ratio of 42 to its divisor 14 is $3/1$. That ratio is an integer, 3, which is also the quotient when 42 is divided by 14 in the second sense: 14 goes into 42 three times, with no remainder.

Despite this close relationship between the two kinds of division, Scheme provides different procedures, with different names, for them: the / procedure computes ratios, while the div-and-mod procedure computes quotients and remainders.[1]

Ratio computation is not associative, and there is no identity for it. The / procedure is therefore generalized on the model of the - procedure: Given more than two arguments, / takes the first argument as the *dividend* and successively divides by each of the remaining arguments (the *divisors*), returning the last result.

It is an error to supply 0 as a divisor when applying the / procedure, since the computation would have no intelligible result: No number correctly expresses the ratio of any number to 0. The Scheme language processor will balk and report this error if we mistakenly try to divide by 0 in a program.

A constraint of this kind is called a *precondition* for the correct use of the procedure. When we design and implement algorithms, it is our responsibility to make sure that the preconditions of the procedures we use are met whenever the language processor attempts to invoke those procedures. Sometimes it is easy to ensure this, but in other cases elaborate precautions will be needed.

If we give the / procedure only one argument, it computes and returns the *multiplicative inverse* of that argument, which is the ratio that 1 bears to it. For instance, given 5, / returns 1/5; given −3/8, it returns −8/3. Again, it is an error to supply 0 as the argument, since 1 does not bear any ratio to 0, and no number could correctly express such a ratio.

It is also an error to provide no arguments to /.

Since the div-and-mod procedure returns two results, the quotient and the remainder, there is no convenient way to generalize it. We'll always give it two arguments, no more and no fewer (and it is an error to try to invoke it with any other number of arguments).

The div-and-mod procedure can receive negative numbers as arguments as well as positive ones, but it deals with them in a somewhat unexpected way, known as *number-theoretic division*. Given a dividend n and a non-zero divisor d, div-and-mod computes the quotient q and remainder r that satisfy the conditions

$$0 \leq r < |d|,$$
$$q \cdot d + r = n.$$

When the dividend is negative and the divisor doesn't evenly divide it, the results of number-theoretic division may seem counterintuitive. For instance, given −42 as its first argument (the dividend) and 9 as its second (the divisor), div-and-mod returns the quotient −5 and the remainder 3. If you learned pencil-and-paper division in school and practiced the technique on examples with negative dividends, you probably anticipated different results: −4 as the quotient and −6 as the remainder. These values would satisfy the second of the conditions above, but not the first. The results of a number-theoretic division

---

[1]The *Revised*[7] *Report on the Algorithmic Language Scheme* actually provides several procedures for integer division, none of which exactly matches the number-theoretical definition described below. The (afp primitives) library defines div-and-mod in terms of the standard procedure floor/, adjusting the results as necessary.

are the unique values q and r that satisfy both conditions.

It is an error to supply 0 as the second argument to `div-and-mod`, since no number r can satisfy the condition that $0 \leq r < |d|$ when d is 0.

Exponentiation

The `expt` procedure performs the operation of raising a number to a power. For instance, given the numbers 3 and 4 as arguments, `expt` returns 3^4, which is 81. Either argument can be negative.

If the argument specifying the power is negative, the result is the multiplicative inverse of the corresponding positive power. For instance, given the arguments 2 and -3, `expt` returns the multiplicative inverse of 2^3, which is $1/8$. If the argument specifying the power is 0, `expt` always returns the identity for multiplication, 1.

Exponentiation is not associative, and there is no identity for it. The convention of grouping to the left, as in subtraction and division, doesn't fit very well here. It turns out that, when mathematicians write something like 'a^{b^c}', they invariably mean $a^{(b^c)}$ rather than $(a^b)^c$. The opposite convention would be superfluous, since the expression '$(a^b)^c$' can and ordinarily would be simplified, applying one of the laws of exponents, to $a^{b \cdot c}$. So if we need to perform successive exponentiation operations at all, we'd want to group to the right rather than to the left. Since successive exponentiations don't occur that frequently in the first place, and we'd have to adopt a new convention that doesn't match the one used by - and /, it's just as well to leave `expt` as a function that always receives exactly two arguments.

In principle, one can use Scheme's `expt` procedure to compute non-integer powers, returning irrational and even complex numbers as results. However, we'll have no need for these, so we'll observe the precondition that the second argument to `expt`, the exponent, is an integer.

A second precondition is that if the first argument, the base, is 0, the exponent must not be negative. As in the case of division by 0, the rationale for this restriction is that no conceivable numerical result would be correct, since 0 has no multiplicative inverse.

As a special case, `expt` returns 1 if both of its arguments are 0. This convention simplifies the statement of some of the laws of exponents.

Scheme also supports the `square` procedure, which receives any number and returns its square (the result of multiplying it by itself).

Procedure Summaries

In this book, we'll deal with about sixty of the procedures that Scheme provides as primitives, and a much larger number of procedures that we define for ourselves—so many that it may be difficult at times to remember how they all work. As a reference and an aid to memory, there is a summary at the end of each section of the procedures introduced in that section, in the following format:

---

div-and-mod   (afp primitives)
integer,   integer → *integer, natural-number*
dividend divisor
Divide dividend by divisor, returning the quotient and the remainder.
Precondition: divisor is not 0.

The first line gives the name of the procedure and indicates the library in which it is defined (in this case, the (afp primitives) library). The second line is a *type signature* for the procedure. The list on the left of the arrow indicates the types of the expected arguments, and the list on the right indicates the types of the results. The third line supplies names for the arguments that the procedure can receive, each positioned immediately underneath its type. The fourth line tells what the procedure does when it is invoked. If there are any preconditions other than type constraints on the invocation of the procedure, they are listed at the end of the summary.

The argument names are arbitrary, but they simplify the description of the procedure's preconditions and results.

When an ellipsis (. . .) appears after a type, it indicates "zero or more" values of that type. On the left of the arrow, this signals that the procedure has variable arity; on the right, it signals that the procedure has multiple results of the specified type. An argument name under a type with an ellipsis stands for a list of arguments of that type.

When an argument to a procedure can be of any type, we'll use lower-case Greek letters—'α' ("alpha"), 'β' ("beta"), 'γ' ("gamma"), or 'δ' ("delta") as *type variables*, to indicate the relationships among the types of the arguments and of the results. When there is no such relationship, we'll indicate this by writing the type variable '*any*' in place of an argument type.

Soon we'll encounter cases in which one procedure constructs another procedure and returns it as its result. In such cases, the preconditions of the constructed procedure are listed along with those of the one that carries out the construction.

We'll also see cases in which one procedure receives another procedure as one of its arguments. In summaries of such "higher-order" procedures, the name of such an argument (in the third line of the summary) is aligned exactly with the parenthesis that begins the specification of the type of that argument (in the line directly above the argument name). It's possible to get confused about the meaning of the identifier unless one studies the alignment carefully.

+   (scheme base)
number . . . → *number*
addends
Compute the sum of the elements of addends.

-   (scheme base)
number → *number*
negand

Compute the additive inverse of negand.

-   (scheme base)

number, number,   number ...   → *number*
minuend subtrahend other-subtrahends
Subtract the sum of subtrahend and the elements of other-subtrahends from minuend and return the difference.

*   (scheme base)

number ...   → *number*
multiplicands
Compute the product of the elements of multiplicands.

/   (scheme base)

number   → *number*
reciprocand
Compute the ratio of 1 to reciprocand.
Precondition: reciprocand is not 0.

/   (scheme base)

number, number, number ...   → *number*
dividend divisor other-divisors
Compute the ratio that dividend bears to the product of divisor and the elements of other-divisors.
Precondition: divisor is not 0.
Precondition: None of the elements of other-divisors is 0.

div-and-mod   (afp primitives)
integer,   integer → *integer, natural-number*
dividend divisor
Divide dividend by divisor, returning the number-theoretic quotient and remainder.
Precondition: divisor is not 0.

expt   (afp primitives)
number, integer   → *number*
base   exponent
Raise base to the power of exponent.
Precondition: If base is 0, then exponent is not negative.

square   (scheme base)
number   → *number*
quadrand
Square quadrand.

Exercises

1.4–1   What result or results does the - procedure return when it receives the arguments -13, 7, and -9, in that order?

1.4–2   What result or results does the div-and-mod procedure return when it receives the arguments 54 and -7, in that order?

1.4–3   What result or results does the div-and-mod procedure return when it receives the arguments -54 and -7, in that order?

1.4–4   Consider the function that receives two numbers, x and y, as arguments and computes their arithmetic mean, $(x + y)/2$. Is this function associative? Does it have an identity? Would it be reasonable to extend it into a general procedure that could receive any number of arguments? Justify your answers.

1.4–5 Consider the function that receives two integers as arguments and returns 1 if one of the arguments is even and the other odd, 0 if both are even or both are odd. Is this function associative? Does it have an identity? Would it be reasonable to extend it into a general procedure that could receive any number of arguments? Justify your answers.

1.5 Procedure Calls

A *procedure call* is an expression that, when evaluated, supplies arguments to a procedure and invokes it. The results of this computation are the values of the procedure call.

In Scheme, a procedure call consists of one or more expressions, lined up and enclosed in parentheses. Each of these expressions must have one and only one value, and the value of the first expression must be a procedure. Here's a simple example:

(expt 38 17)

In this case, there are three expressions between the parentheses, and we recognize all of them. The first is an identifier, 'expt', which is the name of our primitive procedure for computing powers of numbers. The second and third are numerals, naming the integers 38 and 17. In this call, then, we are supplying those integers as arguments to the expt procedure. When the call is evaluated, the expt procedure does all the computational work needed to raise 38 to the seventeenth power. The result of those calculations, 71832526622356959211539608, is the value of the procedure call.

In a procedure call, then, the value of the expression that immediately follows the left parenthesis (the *operator*) is the procedure to be invoked, and the values of all the other expressions (the *operands*) are its arguments. It is an error if the operator does not have a procedure as its value. For instance, attempting to evaluate the expression '(3 + 2)' causes an error, because the value of the operator expression, '3', is a number rather than a procedure. (On the other hand, the fact that the value of one of the *operands* is a procedure is not a problem.) To add 3 to 2, we have to remember to put the procedure first, writing '(+ 3 2)'.

The number of operands in the procedure call depends on the procedure. The expt procedure, for instance, raises a number to a power, so we have to give it two values—the number and the power that we want to raise it to—before the computation can proceed. Every call to expt therefore contains two operands (in addition to the operator).

If a procedure receives n arguments, no more and no fewer, so that a call to that procedure must contain n operand expressions, the procedure is said to be *of arity n*. (Thus expt is of arity 2.) A procedure of arity 1 is *unary*; a procedure of arity 2 is *binary*. Many Scheme procedures can receive different numbers of arguments in different invocations. They are said to be *of variable arity*.

An operand expression need not be a literal; it can be an identifier that names a primitive procedure, or one associated with its value by a definition (see §1.9), or even another procedure call. For example,

```
(expt 38 (+ 14 3))
```

is a procedure call containing another procedure call. The + procedure adds its arguments and returns their sum. Since the sum of 14 and 3 is 17, the value of the subexpression '(+ 14 3)' is 17. The value of the entire expression is the same as that of '(expt 38 17)'.

Note that when a procedure call contains another procedure call, as in this case, the inner call is evaluated first. The general principle is that all of the subexpressions in a procedure call must be evaluated before the procedure's internal computations can begin. The procedure operates on the values it receives, so it cannot start its work until after these values have been computed.

The operand expression in a procedure call is usually an identifier that names the procedure. However, the operand can be *any* expression that has a procedure as its value. Since our programs will frequently deal with procedures as data, receiving them as arguments, performing computations on them, and returning them as results, we'll sometimes see procedure calls like

```
((pipe div-and-mod expt) 63 12)
```

where the procedure to be called is itself computed as the result of a procedure call. (We haven't yet seen the pipe procedure. It will be introduced in Chapter 2.)

Exercises

1.5–1 Is the expression '+' a procedure call? If so, evaluate it.

1.5–2 Is the expression '(+)' a procedure call? If so, evaluate it.

1.5–3 Evaluate the procedure call '(div-and-mod (+ 7 8) (- 7 8))'.

1.5–4 The expression '(* (div-and-mod 32 9) 3)' looks like a procedure call, but cannot be evaluated. Explain what is wrong with it.

1.6   lambda-Expressions

Not all of the procedures that we'll need are provided as primitives. Another way to express a procedure is to use a lambda-expression, which sets out the details of the computation that the procedure performs and supplies an identifier for each of the values that have been abstracted from the computation. These identifiers are called the *parameters* of the procedure. When a procedure that has been expressed in this way is invoked, the call supplies an argument for each parameter, and the "placeholder" identifiers are bound to the corresponding argument values before the computation specified by the procedure body begins.

To assemble a `lambda`-expression, we collect three syntactic components and enclose them in parentheses.

- The first of these components is the keyword 'lambda'. Recall that keywords are not names for values, but act instead as signals to the Scheme processor. In this case, the significance of the keyword is that instead of treating the expression as a procedure call and trying to evaluate all of its pieces, the processor should construct the abstract form of a computation—a value of the *procedure* type.

- The second component consists of all of the parameters of the procedure, separated from one another by spaces or newlines and enclosed in parentheses. This component is the *parameter list*.

- The third component is an expression, the *procedure body*, which will be evaluated each time the procedure is invoked, and only when it is invoked. (Usually it would not even be *possible* to evaluate the procedure body when the `lambda`-expression that contains it is first encountered, because of the presence of parameters, which have no values until the procedure is invoked. But the language processor does not attempt any pre-invocation evaluation of the procedure body even when no parameters occur in it.) In any invocation, once the values of the procedure body have been determined, the procedure returns those values as its results.

For example, suppose that we need a procedure that computes the arithmetic mean of two numbers, by adding them together and dividing the sum by 2. In mathematical notation, we could write this function in the form of an equation, giving it the name m:

$$m(a, b) = \frac{a + b}{2}.$$

Alternatively, we could write it as a mapping rule:

$$(a, b) \mapsto \frac{a + b}{2}.$$

In Scheme, we use a `lambda`-expression to denote the procedure that computes this function:

```
(lambda (a b)
  (/ (+ a b) 2))
```

In this expression, '(a b)' is the parameter list (with 'a' and 'b' as the parameters), and the procedure body is '(/ (+ a b) 2)'.

Here's a call to this procedure that computes the arithmetic mean of 3/5 and 11/3:

```
((lambda (a b)
  (/ (+ a b) 2)) 3/5 11/3)
```

To determine the value of this call, we bind the name 'a' to the number 3/5 (the corresponding argument) and the name 'b' to 11/3. We then evaluate the body of the lambda-expression, recalling that we must evaluate the inner procedure call before the outer one:

$$
\begin{aligned}
\text{(/ (+ a b) 2)} &= \text{(/ (+ 3/5 11/3) 2)} \\
&= \text{(/ 64/15 2)} \\
&= \text{32/15.}
\end{aligned}
$$

The procedure denoted by the lambda-expression therefore returns 32/15 as its result, and this is the value of the procedure call.

Procedures of Variable Arity

In lambda-expressions like the one in the preceding example, the number of identifiers in the parameter list determines the arity of the procedure, and every call to the procedure supplies one and only one argument for each parameter. As we have seen in previous sections, however, Scheme also allows procedures of variable arity, such as +. How can we write lambda-expressions for such procedures?

If the procedure we want to express can receive any number of arguments, including none at all, we signal this by placing a single identifier, *not* enclosed in parentheses, in place of the second component of the lambda-expression. Such an identifier is called a *rest-parameter*. When the procedure is invoked, the argument values, no matter how many of them are provided, are assembled into a data structure called a *list*. The rest-parameter is bound to this data structure and then the body of the procedure is evaluated. The results of evaluating the procedure body become the values of the procedure call.

In writing the procedure body, then, we'll have to take account of the fact that the arguments arrive in the form of a list, rather than having individual names. Later on, we'll learn how to open up lists and to extract and name the values they contain (if any).

For now, however, let's look at just one primitive procedure for dealing with lists: apply. This procedure can receive two or more arguments, of which the first must be a procedure and the last a list. It extracts all of the values from the list and then invokes the procedure, supplying the now-unbundled values to it as arguments and returning the results of this invocation as its own results.

For instance, consider a variable-arity procedure that can receive any number of arguments, each of which must be a number, and returns the ratio of the sum of the numbers to their product. Here is a lambda-expression that denotes this procedure:

```
(lambda numbers
  (/ (apply + numbers) (apply * numbers)))
```

When this procedure is invoked, the rest-parameter 'numbers' is bound to a list containing all of the numbers that are supplied as arguments. When we evaluate the procedure call '(apply + numbers)', the apply procedure extracts all of these numbers from the list and passes them to the + procedure as arguments. The + procedure adds them all up and returns their sum, which apply then returns as its result. Similarly, when we evaluate '(apply * numbers)', apply invokes the * procedure, giving it all of the numbers as arguments, and returns the product that * computes. Now we have the values of the operands in the call to the / procedure, namely the sum of the given numbers and their product. The / procedure computes and returns the ratio of the sum to the product.

Note that it would be incorrect to write simply '(+ numbers)' to try to compute the sum. The syntax of the procedure call is correct, but the + procedure requires each of its arguments to be a number, and the value of the identifier 'numbers' is a list, not a number.

We can invoke this procedure by evaluating a procedure call in which the lambda-expression occupies the operator position. For instance, the value of the procedure call

```
((lambda numbers
   (/ (apply + numbers) (apply * numbers))) 3 5 8 2 6)
```

is 1/60, which is the ratio of the sum of the five given numbers, 24, to their product, 1440.

If the apply procedure receives more than two arguments, it supplies the extra values along with the values that it extracts from the list when invoking the procedure that it receives as its first argument. For instance, the procedure

```
(lambda numbers
  (apply + 23 14 6 numbers))
```

computes and returns the sum of 23, 14, 6, and all of the values that are supplied as arguments when it is invoked.

The apply procedure exemplifies another kind of variable arity: It would make no sense to invoke it without giving it at least two arguments, the procedure to be applied and the list containing the values to which it is to be applied. But it can receive any number of arguments beyond those two. In fact, we have already seen a similar case in the - procedure, which must receive at least one argument but can deal with any greater number of them.

We can write lambda-expressions for such procedures as well, by tinkering with the parameter list in a different way. As in a fixed-arity lambda-expression, we start by providing an identifier for each parameter position up to the minimum number required. At that point, we put in a full stop character (also called "dot" or "period"), standing by itself, with a space on each side. Finally, we add another identifier and enclose the entire sequence in parentheses. For instance, if a lambda-expression has

```
(alpha beta gamma . others)
```

as its parameter list, the procedure it expresses must receive at least three arguments, but can receive more.

When invoked, such a procedure begins by binding the identifiers that precede the full stop to the arguments it receives, one parameter to one argument. When the full stop is reached, however, the procedure collects all of the remaining arguments in a list and binds the identifier after the full stop to that list. In this case, too, the identifier after the full stop is a rest-parameter (the list to which it is bound contains the "rest" of the argument values).

For instance, the lambda-expression with the parameter list '(alpha beta gamma . others)' denotes a procedure that binds 'alpha' to the first argument it receives, 'beta' to the second, 'gamma' to the third, and 'others' to a list containing all of the remaining arguments.

Here's a call to such a procedure:

```
((lambda (alpha beta gamma . others)
   (* (+ alpha beta gamma) (apply + others))) 3 4 5 6 7 8)
```

The value of the expression '(+ alpha beta gamma)' is the sum of the first three arguments, which is 12 (the sum of 3, 4, and 5). The value of the identifier 'others' is a list containing the rest of the arguments (6, 7, and 8). The value of the expression '(apply + others)', therefore, is the sum of those three values, which is 21. So the value of the body of the procedure is the product of 12 and 21, which is 252, and this is also the value of the entire procedure call.

Building Lists

In the preceding examples, we relied on variable-arity procedures to construct lists, as part of the process of binding a rest-parameter. However, Scheme also provides a primitive procedure, list, that receives any number of values and returns a data structure that contains those values, in that order. Lists constructed in this way are indistinguishable from lists constructed as values for rest-parameters.

Even if the designers of Scheme had chosen not to provide list as a primitive, however, we could easily have written it for ourselves: It's simply (lambda arguments arguments)!

Like the simple values described in §1.1, lists can be passed as arguments to procedures and returned as results of procedures. In interactive Scheme sessions, the expression evaluator writes out a list by writing out the values it contains, separated by spaces and enclosed in parentheses:

```
> (list 3 8 7)
(3 8 7)
> (list)
()
```

Returning Multiple Values

The values of a procedure call are the results that the procedure computes. So far, each of the lambda-expressions that we have seen has denoted a procedure that returns one and only one value. How can we write a procedure that computes several results and returns all of them as values, as the primitive procedure div-and-mod does?

If the procedure body in a lambda-expression is a call to another procedure that itself returns multiple values, then the procedure that the lambda-expression denotes returns all of those values as well. For instance, consider the lambda-expression

```
(lambda (number)
  (div-and-mod number 3))
```

The procedure that this expression denotes receives just one argument, divides it by 3, and returns both the quotient and the remainder as results. Here's a call to this procedure:

```
((lambda (number)
  (div-and-mod number 3)) 7)
```

This procedure call has two values: 2 (the quotient) and 1 (the remainder).

If we want a procedure to perform two or more independent computations, each of which results in a single value, and then to return all of those results, we can use the primitive procedure values to collect those computed results for us. The values procedure can receive any number of arguments and returns all of those arguments, unchanged, as its results. Thus values, like list, doesn't really do any computations. Instead, a call to values is a conventional way of embedding several different single-valued expressions into one big expression, so that all of their values can be returned at once.

For instance, here is a lambda-expression for a procedure that can receive any number of arguments, each of which must be a number, and returns two results, the first of which is the sum of the arguments, the second their product:

```
(lambda numbers
  (values (apply + numbers) (apply * numbers)))
```

With the help of the values procedure, we can express the converse of the list procedure: an "unbundler" that receives one argument, a list, and returns all of the values in that list as results:

```
(lambda (ls)
  (apply values ls))
```

This procedure is included in the (afp primitives) library, under the name delist.

By applying the list and delist procedures at appropriate points, we can bundle and unbundle values to create whichever interfaces for arguments and results are best suited to the algorithm designs that we want to implement.

Computations Without Results

Sometimes a procedure fails to return when invoked, either because some step in the computation cannot be correctly performed (an attempt to divide by 0, for instance) or because each step in the computation requires a further step, so that the computation never reaches a point at which results could be returned.

As a short but twisted example of a non-terminating computation, consider the procedure call

```
((lambda (self-apply) (self-apply self-apply))
 (lambda (self-apply) (self-apply self-apply)))
```

The value of the lambda-expression is a procedure that receives one argument, binds the parameter 'self-apply' to that argument, and invokes it, giving it itself as an argument. In the call shown here, this procedure is applied to itself. So it takes itself, binds the name 'self-apply' to itself, and invokes itself, giving itself itself as an argument. When so invoked, it again takes itself, binds the name 'self-apply' to itself, and invokes itself, giving itself itself as an argument. When so invoked, ...

Each invocation of the procedure initiates another invocation, endlessly. None of the invocations ever returns any results, because none ever reaches the end of its computation. So the procedure call shown above, although it is syntactically correct, is useless. Attempting to evaluate it causes the Scheme processor to churn unproductively until some external interruption occurs.

It is usually an error in programming to initiate a computation that cannot be correctly completed. In formulating algorithms, therefore, we'll carefully consider situations in which a computation might not terminate and establish preconditions to forestall them.

```
apply                                                         (scheme base)
(α ..., β ... → γ ...),  α ...,      list(β)  → γ ...
procedure               arguments bundle
```
Invoke procedure, giving it the elements of arguments and the elements of bundle as its argu-
ments and returning the results.
Precondition: procedure can receive the elements of arguments and the elements of bundle.

```
list                                                          (scheme base)
α ...           → list(α)
arguments
```
Construct a list containing the elements of arguments.

```
values                                                        (scheme base)
α ...           → α ...
arguments
```
Return the elements of arguments.

```
delist                                                      (afp primitives)
list(α)  → α ...
bundle
```
Return the elements of bundle.

Exercises

1.6–1   Write a lambda-expression for a procedure that computes the cube
of a given number. This procedure has only one parameter, but you should
still enclose that parameter in parentheses when you construct the parameter
list. (Otherwise it would be mistaken for a rest-parameter in a variable-arity
procedure.)

1.6–2   To convert a temperature measured in degrees Celsius (°C) into degrees Fahrenheit (°F), multiply it by 9/5 and add 32 to the product. Write
a lambda-expression for a procedure that performs this conversion, taking the
temperature in °C as an argument and returning the temperature in °F. Then
write a procedure call in which this procedure is applied to −15 °C.

1.6–3   The sum of a finite arithmetic sequence $a, a + n, a + 2n, \ldots, a + kn$ is

$$(k + 1) \cdot \left(a + \frac{kn}{2} \right).$$

Write a lambda-expression that receives a, n, and k and returns the sum of the
finite arithmetic sequence shown above. Then write a procedure call with a
value equal to the sum of the finite arithmetic sequence 3, 10, 17, 24, 31.

1.6–4   Explain the difference between the "identity" procedure

```
(lambda (something)
  something)
```

and the list procedure

```
(lambda arguments
  arguments)
```

1.6–5   What is the arity of the procedure that the following lambda-expression denotes? What does it return when invoked?

```
(lambda (first . others)
 (* first first))
```

1.6–6   Write a lambda-expression that receives exactly three arguments and returns all of them as values, but in reverse order (so that the first argument is the third result, and vice versa).

1.6–7   Write a lambda-expression for a procedure that receives two lists of numbers as arguments, finds the sum of the values in each list, and constructs a list containing just those two sums.

1.7   Predicates

A *predicate* is a procedure that always returns exactly one Boolean value. A unary predicate determines whether its argument has some attribute. For instance, Scheme provides a primitive unary predicate even? that receives an integer and returns #t if that integer is even and #f if it is not. A predicate that receives two or more arguments determines whether some relation holds among them. For instance, the primitive predicate < can receive two or more arguments and determines whether they *increase monotonically*, that is, whether each argument (except the last) is less than the argument that follows it.

Scheme provides an excellent selection of primitive predicates for testing the attributes and relations of numbers. The ones we'll use are zero?, positive?, and negative? for testing the sign of a number, <, <=, =, >=, and > for comparing them, and even? and odd? for testing the parity of integers. The comparison predicates can receive more than two numbers as arguments, and test whether the specified relation holds between any two adjacent values. (For instance, the call '(= alpha beta gamma)' returns #t only if alpha is equal to beta *and* beta is equal to gamma.)

Conventionally, a question mark at the end of the name of a procedure indicates that it is a predicate, and the names for predicates that we define will conform to this practice.

To reverse the sense of a predicate, we can apply the not procedure to its result. Applying not to #f yields #t; applying not to #t (or, indeed, to any value other than #f) yields #f. For instance, the expression

```
(lambda (number)
 (not (negative? number)))
```

denotes a predicate that determines whether number is non-negative.

Classification Predicates

When the nature of a value is not known, we often need to determine whether it meets the precondition of some procedure. Scheme provides classification predicates for the types of its values: boolean?, number?, integer?, char?, string?, symbol?, and even procedure?.

We could also regard not as a uniquely specific classification predicate for detecting the Boolean value #f.

Many procedures impose type restrictions on their arguments as preconditions and will fail or deliver incorrect answers if these preconditions are not observed. Careful programmers often use classification predicates to make sure that the preconditions of a procedure are met before that procedure is invoked.

Equality Predicates

In addition to the equality predicate = for numbers, Scheme provides equality predicates for the other basic types of values, including boolean=? for Booleans, char=? for characters, string=? for strings, and symbol=? for symbols. Each of these predicates can receive two or more arguments of the specified type and returns #t if and only if all of those arguments are equal.

Scheme also provides a general-purpose predicate equal? that can receive values of any type, returning #f if the types of the arguments are incompatible. The equal? predicate is binary.

There is a conspicuous absence from this list of equality predicates. Where is the procedure=? predicate, for determining whether two given procedures are the same? The rationale for this omission is rather surprising. Theoretical computer scientists have shown that *there is no general algorithm for determining whether two procedures are the same*, even in the limited sense of returning the same values for any arguments they receive. In other words, it is impossible to implement a satisfactory equality predicate for procedures. Any predicate that we come up with will either fail to terminate in some cases or give incorrect answers in some cases!

Equality and Types

Since equal? can compare values of any type, it is natural to wonder whether there is any need for more specific equality predicates such as = and symbol=?. Aren't these all just special cases of the equal? predicate? If so, why don't we simply use equal? everywhere?

The answer is that the generality of equal? actually works against it in some of the applications that we'll encounter. For instance, when we define a data structure for sets, we'll want a set=? predicate that counts two sets as equal if they have the same members, regardless of the order in which they happen to be arranged. (For instance, in set theory, $\{1, 2, 3, 4\}$ is the same set as $\{2, 4, 3, 1\}$, because every member of either set is also a member of the other.) When `equal?` looks at values, however, it returns #f if it finds *any* difference between the values that it is given, even a difference that we intend to disregard, such as the order of the elements in a set. So the `equal?` predicate will *not* be a satisfactory substitute for `set=?`.

In general, the designer of a data type needs to consider carefully whether it is appropriate to provide an equality predicate and, if so, what criterion of "sameness" the equality predicate should express. The `equal?` predicate, though it is convenient and widely useful, is not always the right choice.

In addition, code that uses the type-specific equality predicate may be a little more readable and a little more efficient than code using `equal?`. We'll reserve `equal?`, therefore, for occasions on which we don't know what types of values we'll have to compare.

Since `equal?` tries to compare *any* values that it receives, it's natural to wonder how `equal?` deals with procedures. If there is no algorithm that can correctly determine, in every case, whether two given procedures are the same, how does `equal?` manage it? The answer is that `equal?` sometimes returns incorrect answers when it receives procedures as arguments. It avoids false positives (that is, it never claims that two procedures are the same when they are not), but it sometimes gives false negatives, returning #f even when it receives procedures that obviously *are* the same:

```
> (equal? div-and-mod (lambda (dividend divisor)
                        (div-and-mod dividend divisor)))
#f
> (equal? (lambda (number) (* number 2))
          (lambda (number) (* number 2)))
#f
```

There is no satisfactory remedy for this flaw. We'll just have to be careful not to trust the results of applying `equal?` to procedures.

---

zero?   (scheme base)
number → *Boolean*
number
Determine whether number is 0.

positive?   (scheme base)
number → *Boolean*
number
Determine whether number is positive.

negative?   (scheme base)
number → *Boolean*
number
Determine whether number is negative.

even?   (scheme base)
integer → *Boolean*
number

Determine whether number is even.

odd?   (scheme base)

integer → *Boolean*
number
Determine whether number is odd.

<   (scheme base)

number number number ... → *Boolean*
initial next   others
Determine whether initial, next, and the elements of others are monotonically increasing, from least to greatest.

<=   (scheme base)

number number number ... → *Boolean*
initial next   others
Determine whether initial, next, and the elements of others are monotonically non-decreasing, from least to greatest.

=   (scheme base)

number number number ... → *Boolean*
initial next   others
Determine whether initial, next, and the elements of others are all equal.

>=   (scheme base)

number number number ... → *Boolean*
initial next   others
Determine whether initial, next, and the elements of others are monotonically non-increasing, from greatest to least.

>   (scheme base)

number number number ... → *Boolean*
initial next   others
Determine whether initial, next, and the elements of others are monotonically decreasing, from greatest to least.

boolean?   (scheme base)

any → *Boolean*
something
Determine whether something is a Boolean value.

not   (scheme base)

any → *Boolean*
something
Determine whether something is #f.

number?   (scheme base)

any → *Boolean*
something
Determine whether something is a number.

integer?   (scheme base)

any → *Boolean*
something
Determine whether something is a whole number.

char?   (scheme base)

any → *Boolean*
something
Determine whether something is a character.

string?   (scheme base)

any → *Boolean*
something
Determine whether something is a string.

symbol?   (scheme base)

any   → *Boolean*
something
Determine whether something is a symbol.

procedure?   (scheme base)
any   → *Boolean*
something
Determine whether something is a procedure.

boolean=?   (scheme base)
Boolean Boolean Boolean ...   → *Boolean*
initial next   others
Determine whether initial, next, and the elements of others are all the same Boolean value.

char=?   (scheme base)
character character character ...   → *Boolean*
initial   next   others
Determine whether initial, next, and the elements of others are all the same character.

string=?   (scheme base)
string   string string ...   → *Boolean*
initial next   others
Determine whether initial, next, and the elements of others are all the same string.

symbol=?   (scheme base)
symbol   symbol symbol ...   → *Boolean*
initial next   others
Determine whether initial, next, and the elements of others are all the same symbol.

equal?   (scheme base)
any any   → *Boolean*
left right
Determine whether left and right are the same value.
Precondition: left and right are not procedures.

Exercises

1.7–1   Write a lambda-expression for a predicate that receives exactly two
arguments, both numbers, and determines whether they are unequal. (In other
words, the predicate should return #t if its arguments differ in value and #f if
they do not.)

1.7–2   Write a lambda-expression for a predicate that receives exactly two
arguments, both numbers, and determines whether they are multiplicative inverses, that is, whether their product is equal to 1.

1.7–3   Write a lambda-expression that has exactly four parameters (a, b, c, and
x), and denotes a predicate that determines whether x is a root of the quadratic
polynomial $ax^2 + bx + c$. In other words, the predicate should determine whether
the value of that polynomial, for the given value of x, is zero, returning #t if it
is and #f if it is not.

1.8   Conditional Expressions

Not every computation is a fixed sequence of operations on its parameters. In
many cases, we want to perform a test and take the computation in different

directions depending on the outcome.

Here's a small example. Suppose that we have counted the files in a directory and want to report the tally to an English-speaking user by returning an appropriate string. For instance, if the directory contains twenty-three files, the string will be `"23 files"`. When the directory contains only one file, we'd like to avoid the embarrassment of having our program report `"1 files"`, since the correct singular form of the word is 'file'. So part of our program will be a procedure that receives a natural number—the tally—and returns the string `"file"` if that number is 1 and `"files"` if it is anything else. The test, in other words, is to compare the tally with 1. Once we know the outcome of the test, the rest of the computation is, in this case, trivial.

A Scheme implementation of this algorithm uses an if-expression. To put together an if-expression, we line up the following components and enclose them in parentheses:

- The keyword 'if'. Like 'lambda', 'if' is not bound to a value. Think of it instead as a conventional signal to the Scheme processor that the subsequent expressions must be evaluated selectively.

- The *test expression*. The evaluation of an if-expression begins with the evaluation of the test expression. This evaluation must yield one and only one result (otherwise it is an error), and this result determines how the other components will be dealt with. Most often, the test expression is a procedure call in which the operator denotes a predicate, and its result is therefore either #t or #f. (Scheme allows test expressions to have non-Boolean values, all of which count as "truish," that is, as affirmative. In this book, however, every test expression has a Boolean value.)

- The *consequent*, an expression that is evaluated when the value of the test is affirmative, but skipped when the value of the test is #f.

- The *alternate*, an expression that is evaluated when the value of the test is #f, but skipped when the value of the test is #t (or any other "truish" value).

Thus either the consequent or the alternate is evaluated, but not both. The values of whichever of them is selected by the test expression are computed, and they become the values of the entire if-expression.

Here is an if-expression that has the value `"file"` if the value bound to the identifier 'file-tally' is 1 and the value `"files"` otherwise:

```
(if (= file-tally 1) "file" "files")
```

We can express the procedure we envisioned at the beginning of this section by situating this if-expression as the procedure body in a lambda-expression:

```
(lambda (file-tally)
  (if (= file-tally 1) "file" "files"))
```

and-Expressions and or-Expressions

Scheme provides convenient abbreviations for two special cases of the if-expression that occur frequently. In these cases, the test expression acts as a precondition for the evaluation of another Boolean expression. For instance, suppose we want to determine whether a value val, which may or may not be a number at all, is an even integer. Because the predicate even? can receive only integers, we must first test whether val is an integer, and invoke even? only if this precondition is satisfied:

```
(if (integer? val) (even? val) #f)
```

The and-expression

```
(and (integer? val) (even? val))
```

has exactly the same meaning and effect. When the Boolean expressions are long and complicated, an and-expression is often easier to read and understand than the equivalent if-expression.

In this example, the and-expression contains two Boolean subexpressions. In general, an and-expression can contain any number of Boolean subexpressions. They are evaluated one by one until either (1) one of them is found to be false (in which case the value of the entire and-expression is #f), or (2) all of them have been found to be true (in which case the value of the entire and-expression is #t). For instance, the value of

```
(and (integer? val)
     (even? val)
     (positive? val))
```

is #t just in case val is an even positive integer.

An or-expression is used in the case where the truth of the test expression makes it unnecessary to evaluate some other Boolean expression. For instance, the expression

```
(or (< number 0) (> number 100))
```

is true if number is *either* less than 0 or greater than 100. It is exactly equivalent to

```
(if (< number 0) #t (> number 100))
```

Like an and-expression, an or-expression can have any number of subexpressions, which are evaluated one by one. As soon as any of the subexpressions is found to be true, evaluation stops, and the value of the or-expression is #t. If none of the subexpressions is true, the value of the or-expression is #f.

Since and-expressions and or-expressions do not always evaluate all of their subexpressions, it is incorrect to think of them as procedure calls. Like 'lambda' and 'if', 'and' and 'or' are keywords, not names for procedures.

Exercises

1.8–1 The *absolute value* of a number is the number itself, if it is zero or positive, or the additive inverse of the number, if it is negative. Write a lambda-expression for a procedure that receives one argument, a number, and computes and returns its absolute value. (The procedure body in this lambda-expression will be an if-expression.)

1.8–2 Write a lambda-expression for a procedure that receives two numbers and returns the lesser of them. (If the arguments are equal, the procedure can return either one.)

1.8–3 Write a lambda-expression for a predicate that receives three numbers and determines whether the second of them is strictly between the first and third. In other words, the predicate should return #t if the sequence first, second, third is either monotonically increasing or monotonically decreasing; otherwise, the predicate should return #f.

1.8–4 Write a lambda-expression for a procedure that receives two integers and returns 1 if one of them is even and the other odd, 0 if they are both even or both odd. (Since the value that this procedure returns is not Boolean, you'll need at least one if-expression. But your test expression will be easier to understand if you use and- and or-expressions as well.)

1.9 Definitions

A definition binds an identifier to a value. Scheme provides a simple notation for definitions: Line up the keyword 'define', an identifier, and a single-valued expression and enclose them in parentheses.

For example, when a Scheme processor encounters the definition

```
(define meg 1048576)
```

it binds the identifier 'meg' to the number 1048576. Similarly, the definition

```
(define inches-in-a-mile (* 12 5280))
```

binds the identifier 'inches-in-a-mile' to the natural number 63360 (the product of 12 and 5280).

Procedure Definitions

Since procedures are expressible values in Scheme—specifically, the values of lambda-expressions—definitions can also bind identifiers to procedures. For instance, the definition

```
(define arithmetic-mean
  (lambda (a b)
    (/ (+ a b) 2)))
```

binds the identifier 'arithmetic-mean' to our procedure for computing the arithmetic mean of two numbers (from §1.6).

Because the need to bind an identifier to a procedure is so common, Scheme provides a "short form" syntax for such definitions. In this short form, the identifier that we want to bind to the procedure and the parameters of the lambda-expression are lined up and enclosed in parentheses, and this construction is placed after the keyword define. The body of the lambda-expression follows, and then the whole thing is enclosed in parentheses. Here is the short form of the definition of arithmetic-mean:

```
(define (arithmetic-mean a b)
  (/ (+ a b) 2))
```

The two forms of procedure definition are completely equivalent. In this book, we'll use short forms extensively from this point on, but this is a stylistic choice not affecting the meanings or effects of the definitions.

The body need not be a procedure call. Here is a definition for a procedure, lesser, that receives two numbers and returns the lesser of them, using a conditional expression:

```
(define (lesser left right)
  (if (< left right) left right))
```

(If lesser receives equal arguments, it makes no difference which one it returns. This implementation happens to return right, but it would make no difference if we changed '<' to '<=', so as to return left, when left and right are the same value.)

There are short-form definitions for variable-arity procedures as well. As with fixed-arity procedure definitions, the identifier that we want to bind and the parameters of the procedure to which we want to bind it are lined up and enclosed in parentheses. The variable arity of the procedure is signaled by the insertion of a full stop just before the rest-parameter:

```
(define (ratio-of-sum-to-product . numbers)
  (/ (apply + numbers) (apply * numbers)))

(define (fixed-sum-times-variable-sum alpha beta gamma . others)
  (* (+ alpha beta gamma) (apply + others)))
```

Recursive Definitions

In mathematics, it is sometimes convenient to define functions *recursively*, by stipulating the value of the function in some trivial case and describing how to compute the value for any other argument by showing how to reduce it to simpler cases.

Consider, for instance, the *factorial* function. For any natural number n, the factorial of n is the product of the integers from 1 through n. (The factorial of 0 is conventionally understood to be 1, the identity for multiplication.) Here's a mathematical definition of the factorial function—for the time being, let's call it f—using recursion:

$$f(n) = \begin{cases} 1, & \text{if } n = 0; \\ n \cdot f(n-1) & \text{otherwise.} \end{cases}$$

Even though the right-hand side of this definition contains the identifier f that is being defined, this definition is not circular, at least not in any way that makes it ambiguous or unsatisfactory. For any particular natural number n, the apparent circularity can be eliminated by repeated substitution:

$$\begin{aligned} f(5) &= 5 \cdot f(4) \\ &= 5 \cdot 4 \cdot f(3) \\ &= 5 \cdot 4 \cdot 3 \cdot f(2) \\ &= 5 \cdot 4 \cdot 3 \cdot 2 \cdot f(1) \\ &= 5 \cdot 4 \cdot 3 \cdot 2 \cdot 1 \cdot f(0) \\ &= 5 \cdot 4 \cdot 3 \cdot 2 \cdot 1 \cdot 1 \\ &= 120. \end{aligned}$$

Scheme's notation for procedure definitions allows them to be recursive, in a similar way. A procedure can be called, by name, in the body of the lambda-expression that supplies the value for that same name. Here is the definition of the factorial function in Scheme's notation. We'll use 'factorial' rather than 'f' and 'number' rather than 'n', since the mathematical convention of using only single-character identifiers quickly becomes confusing in programming.

```
(define (factorial number)
  (if (zero? number)
      1
      (* number (factorial (- number 1)))))
```

The test in the if-expression distinguishes the cases that are written on separate lines in the mathematical definition. The consequent of the if-expression is simply the numeral '1'. This ensures that when number is 0, the procedure returns 1. Finally, the alternate of the if-expression handles the case in which number is not 0, directing the processor to multiply number by the result that the factorial procedure returns when it is given an argument one less than number.

Calls to recursively defined procedures are just like calls to any other procedures, requiring no special syntax. For instance, to compute the factorial of 5, we can write '(factorial 5)'. The value of this expression is 120, the final result of the computation. In the course of this computation, factorial is invoked six times, receiving a different argument each time. Each invocation except the one in which the argument is 0 evaluates the procedure call '(factorial (- number 1))' again, thereby initiating another invocation.

Still, recursion may seem dangerously similar to the self-apply example at the end of §1.6, in which each invocation of a procedure led to another, and none of the invocations ever reached a result. To avoid such faults, we should provide every recursive procedure that we write with a *base case*, like the case of the factorial procedure in which number is 0, in which we can compute a result without invoking the procedure again.

Furthermore, we should ensure that each recursive invocation of a procedure gets us a step closer, in some sense, to the base case, and that the base case can always be reached through a finite number of such steps. In the definition of factorial, we achieve this by subtracting 1 from the argument in each successive invocation. Since any natural number can be reduced to 0 by subtracting 1 from it a finite number of times, the factorial procedure yields a result eventually no matter what natural number it receives.

---

arithmetic-mean   (afp arithmetic)
number, number → *number*
a   b
Compute the arithmetic mean of a and b.

lesser   (afp arithmetic)
number, number → *number*
left   right
Return left or right, whichever is lesser.

factorial   (afp arithmetic)
natural-number → *Boolean*
number
Compute the product of the positive integers up to and including number.

Exercises

1.9–1 Write a definition that binds the identifier 'star' to the asterisk character.

1.9–2 Write a lambda-expression for a unary procedure that multiplies its argument by 2 and returns the result. Then write a definition that binds the identifier 'double' to this procedure. Then, unless you used the short form of procedure definition in the preceding step, convert your definition to an equivalent short-form definition.

1.9–3 Modify the definition of lesser to define a procedure greater that receives two numbers and returns whichever of them is greater than the other.

1.9–4 Write a short-form definition for a predicate geo? that receives three numbers and determines whether they form a geometric sequence. (This will be the case if the square of the second is equal to the product of the other two.)

1.9–5 Define a procedure termial that receives one argument, a natural number, and determines the sum of all of the natural numbers less than or equal to its argument. For instance, given the argument 7, termial should compute and return $7 + 6 + 5 + 4 + 3 + 2 + 1 + 0$, or 28.

1.10 Local Bindings

A definition creates a binding that persists, so that later expressions and definitions can use the bound identifier to designate the corresponding value, just as if it were one of Scheme's predefined identifiers. Sometimes, however, we'll want to bind identifiers that do not persist in this way—*local* names, bound to values that are of interest during one short stretch of a computation but are not needed afterwards.

A let-expression is constructed by enclosing the following constituents in parentheses:

- The keyword 'let';

- a group of *binding specifications*, giving the local names and their values; and

- an expression (the *body* of the let-expression).

The values of a let-expression are the values of its body.

Each binding specification also has an internal structure. To construct a binding specification, we line up the identifier to be bound and an expression, which must have a single value, and enclose the identifier and the expression in parentheses. The idea is that the identifier is bound to the value of the expression for the duration of the evaluation of its body.

The entire group of binding specifications is enclosed in an additional pair of parentheses, even if it includes only one binding specification (or indeed none at all).

Here's a short let-expression that sets up and then uses two local bindings:

```
(let ((hours-in-a-day 24)
      (seconds-in-an-hour (* 60 60)))
  (* hours-in-a-day seconds-in-an-hour))
```

To evaluate this let-expression, we first evaluate the expressions that occur inside the binding specifications, '24' and '(* 60 60)', obtaining the values 24 and 3600. We then bind the identifiers in the binding specifications to
these respective values. Finally, we evaluate the body of the let-expression, '(*
hours-in-a-day seconds-in-an-hour)': The * procedure is invoked with the
values of the two identifiers as its arguments, and the result of the multiplication
operation, 86400, becomes the value of the entire let-expression.

When the value of the let-expression has been computed, the bindings for
the identifiers hours-in-a-day and seconds-in-an-hour are discarded.

Local Procedures

We can also bind identifiers to procedures locally, just like any other values. For
instance, the value of the expression

```
(let ((double (lambda (number)
                (+ number number))))
  (* (double 7) (double 12)))
```

is 336, the product of the doubles of 7 and 12. Again, once this value has been
computed, the binding of the identifier double to the procedure denoted by the
lambda-expression no longer exists. If we had wanted the binding to persist, we
would have written a definition instead:

```
(define (double number)
  (+ number number))
```

The syntax of let-expressions does not include a short form for associating
procedures with their local names. We must separate the identifier from the
lambda-expression to write the binding specification correctly.

Local Recursion

Since a binding created by a let-expression holds only inside the *body* of that
expression, there is a problem if we try to give a local name to a recursive
procedure using a let-expression. The name of the recursive procedure will
also occur inside the lambda-expression that denotes it. But at that point the
name of the recursive procedure is not yet bound, and so the attempt to call it
recursively will not succeed. In an interactive Scheme session, the failure looks
something like this:

```
> (let ((factorial (lambda (number)
                      (if (zero? number)
                          1
                          (* number (factorial (- number 1)))))))
    (factorial 5))
```

Error: variable factorial is not bound.

One solution to this difficulty is a `rec`-expression, which resembles a procedure definition syntactically, but binds the name to the procedure only inside the expression itself instead of creating a global binding that any caller can use. Here, for instance, is a `rec`-expression that has the factorial procedure as its value:

```
(rec factorial
  (lambda (number)
    (if (zero? number)
        1
        (* number (factorial (- number 1))))))
```

Now the identifier 'factorial' in the procedure call '(factorial (- number 1))' is correctly bound to the recursively defined procedure. The binding is formed before the procedure is ever actually invoked, so it is in place by the time it is needed in the evaluation of a procedure call.

Indeed, since now the identifier 'factorial' is bound *only* inside the rec-expression, it's not immediately obvious how to invoke the procedure! One way is to put the `rec`-expression itself in the operator position of the procedure call:

```
> ((rec factorial
    (lambda (number)
      (if (zero? number)
          1
          (* number (factorial (- number 1))))))
   5)
120
```

Another approach is to place the `rec`-expression into a binding specification inside a `let`-expression, so that `let`-expression manages the "external" binding and the `rec`-expression manages the "internal" one:

```
> (let ((fact (rec factorial
                (lambda (number)
                  (if (zero? number)
                      1
                      (* number (factorial (- number 1))))))))
    (fact 5))
120
```

In this example, the identifier that is bound by the let-expression, fact, is different from the identifier that is bound by the rec-expression, factorial, even though they denote the same procedure. We could use the same identifier in both places, however—the two uses would not interfere with one another. (Scheme actually provides another kind of expression, the letrec-expression, that combines the effects of let and rec, but we won't need it.)

There are also short-form rec-expressions, which are syntactically similar to short-form procedure definitions. For instance, we could also write the rec-expression for the procedure that computes factorials as

```
(rec (factorial number)
  (if (zero? number)
      1
      (* number (factorial (- number 1)))))
```

receive-Expressions

In let-expressions, it is an error if any expression in a binding specification has more than one value. Frequently, however, we want to have local names for the values of a multiple-valued expression. A third local-binding construction, the receive-expression, provides for this possibility.

To construct a receive-expression, we line up the following components and enclose them in parentheses:

- The keyword 'receive';

- a *formals list*, which is analogous to the parameter list in a lambda-expression and can have any of the structures that a parameter list can have;

- an expression (the producer); and

- another expression (the body).

To evaluate a receive-expression, we first evaluate the producer expression, which may (and usually does) yield several values. These are matched against the formals list to create local bindings, exactly as the arguments to a procedure are matched against its parameter list:

- If the formals list is a parenthesis-enclosed collection of identifiers, the number of identifiers must be equal to the number of values of the producer expression, and the identifiers are bound respectively to those values.

- If the formals list is a single identifier, not enclosed in parentheses, then the values of the producer expression are collected in a list, and the identifier is bound to that list.

- If the formals list is a parenthesis-enclosed list of two or more identifiers, with a full stop inserted before the last of them, then the number of identifiers before the full stop must be less than or equal to the number of values of the producer expression, and those identifiers are bound respectively to those values until they run out. At that point, any remaining values of the producer expression are collected into a list, and the identifier after the full stop is bound to that list.

Once all the local bindings are in place, we evaluate the body of the `receive`-expression, and its values are the values of the entire `receive`-expression.

Let's look at a couple of examples. Here is a `receive`-expression that performs a division using `div-and-mod`, binds identifiers to the quotient and remainder, and uses those identifiers in a computation:

```
(receive (quotient remainder) (div-and-mod 2759 100)
  (if (< remainder 50)
      (* quotient 100)
      (* (+ quotient 1) 100)))
```

The division is performed first. Its results are 27 and 59. So the identifier 'quotient' is bound to 27 and the identifier 'remainder' to 59. Then the body of the `receive`-expression is evaluated. It is an `if`-expression, so we start with the test expression, which is a procedure call. The < procedure receives the values 59 and 50 and determines that 59 is not less than 50, so it returns #f. So we ignore the consequent of the `if`-expression and evaluate the alternate, '(* (+ quotient 1) 100)', to get 2800. This becomes the value of the `if`-expression, and hence of the entire `receive`-expression.

The following `receive`-expression has two values, the sum and product of several numbers:

```
(receive numbers (values 3 8 5 6 2 9 7)
  (values (apply + numbers) (apply * numbers)))
```

The first call to the `values` procedure returns all of the numbers as its values. Since the formals list is an unparenthesized identifier, the `receive`-expression makes a list of those numbers and binds the identifier to them. In the body of the `receive`-expression, the sum and product are computed and provided to the `values` procedure, which simply returns them. These two values then become the values of the `receive`-expression.

---

double   (afp arithmetic)
number → *number*
number
Compute the double of number.

Exercises

1.10–1   Write a `let`-expression that binds the identifiers 'mu' and 'prod' respectively to the arithmetic mean of 1/3 and 3/2 and to their product, then (in the body) determines whether the mean is less than the product. The Boolean result of that determination should be the value of the entire `let`-expression.

1.10–2   To compute the number of seconds in a week, we might try the `let`-expression

```
(let ((seconds-in-a-minute 60)
      (seconds-in-an-hour (* seconds-in-a-minute 60))
      (seconds-in-a-day (* seconds-in-an-hour 24)))
  (* seconds-in-a-day 7))
```

When we attempt to evaluate this expression, however, an "unbound identifier" error occurs. Explain why, and suggest a way of working around this problem. (Hint: The body of a `let`-expression can be another `let`-expression.)

1.10–3   Define a procedure `halve`, which receives an integer and divides it by 2, returning the quotient. Use number-theoretic division. (For instance, the value of '(halve 39)' should be 19, and the value of '(halve -39)' should be −20.)

1.10–4   To find the greatest odd divisor of a positive integer n (as, for instance, 35 is the greatest odd divisor of 280), we might begin with two observations:

- If n is odd, then it is its own greatest odd divisor, since no larger number can divide it.

- If n is even, then its greatest odd divisor is the greatest odd divisor of $n/2$.

Write a `rec`-expression in which the identifier 'greatest-odd-divisor' is bound to a recursive procedure that uses these observations as the basis for a strategy. The procedure should receive a positive integer and return the greatest odd divisor of that integer. Invoke the procedure to determine the greatest odd divisor of 702464.

1.10–5   Define a unary procedure `reverse-digits` that can receive any integer in the range from 10 to 99 and returns the integer expressed by the numeral that results from reversing the digits in the numeral for the argument. For instance, the value of the call '(reverse-digits 74)' should be the integer 47. (Hint: Use a `receive`-procedure to name the quotient and remainder obtained by dividing the given integer by 10.)

Chapter 2

The Tool Box

In functional programming, we adapt and combine functions in a variety of ways. Sometimes a pattern of adaptation and combination appears again and again, in different contexts, expressing the same underlying programming idea and design. Scheme provides names for only a few of these patterns, but we can define and name the others ourselves, using the notations that we learned in Chapter 1. This chapter introduces many of the simpler and more general patterns.

2.1 List Mapping

The map Procedure

One functional-programming pattern that Scheme provides as a primitive procedure is map, which applies a single-valued procedure to each of the values in a list and collects the results of these applications in another list. As an illustration of the use of map, consider the following procedure, which can receive any number of arguments, each of which must be a number, and returns the sum of their squares:

```
(define (sum-of-squares . numbers)
  (apply + (map square numbers)))
```

The inner procedure call, '(map square numbers)', applies the square procedure to each item in the list numbers, collecting the results in a list, which it returns. The call to apply then invokes the + procedure to add up all the squares, returning the sum.

The map procedure can receive any positive number of lists as arguments. If it is given two or more lists, it applies the procedure that it receives as its first argument to values in corresponding positions in those lists. For instance, here

© Springer-Verlag GmbH Germany, part of Springer Nature 2018
J. D. Stone, *Algorithms for Functional Programming*,
https://doi.org/10.1007/978-3-662-57970-1_2

is a procedure that can receive any number of arguments, each of which is a number, and returns the sum of their cubes:

```
(define (sum-of-cubes . numbers)
  (apply + (map * numbers numbers numbers)))
```

In effect, map opens up each list (or, in this case, the same list three times), takes the first item from each list, and applies the * procedure to those first items, keeping the result for its own result-list; takes the second item from each list, applies the procedure, keeps the result; and so on.

As you might expect, this won't work if the lists differ in size. There is also a constraint on the arity of the procedure that map calls repeatedly: It must be able to receive as many arguments as there are lists from which map pulls values. For instance, in sum-of-squares, the fact that square is unary corresponds significantly to the fact that map received only one list. It would be an error to put a binary procedure such as expt in that position. Similarly, in sum-of-cubes, the presence of three lists in the call to map implies that the * procedure must be able to receive three arguments.

The procedure that map applies can be constructed or computed, if we don't already have a name for it. Here is an alternative definition of the sum-of-cubes procedure, using a lambda-expression to denote the operation of computing the cube of a number:

```
(define (sum-of-cubes . numbers)
  (apply + (map (lambda (number)
                  (* number number number))
                numbers)))
```

---

map   (scheme base)
$(\alpha, \beta \ldots \rightarrow \gamma)$, $list(\alpha)$, $list(\beta) \ldots$ $\rightarrow list(\gamma)$
procedure   initial-list other-lists
Apply procedure to corresponding elements of initial-list and of the elements of other-lists, collecting the results in a list.
Precondition: procedure can receive any element of initial-list and the corresponding elements of elements of other-lists.
Precondition: The length of initial-list is equal to the length of each element of other-lists.

Exercises

2.1–1   Use map to define a procedure toggle-list that receives one argument, a list of Boolean values, and returns a similar list, but with each value replaced by its negation. (In other words, the result-list should have #f in each position where the given list has #t, and vice versa.)

2.1–2   Define a procedure unbundled-products that receives two arguments, each of which is a list of numbers, and returns the products of corresponding elements of those lists, as separate values. (For instance, the procedure call '(unbundled-products (list 7 3 4) (list 2 9 8))' has the three values 14, 27, and 32—the product of 7 and 2, the product of 3 and 9, and the product of 4 and 8).

2.1–3 Define a procedure wrap-each that can receive any number of arguments and returns, for each argument, a list containing just that one argument. (For instance, the values of the procedure call '(wrap-each 4 #f 'egg)' should be a list containing 4, another list containing #f, and a third list containing the symbol egg. Each of these three lists should be returned as a separate value.)

2.2 Constant Procedures

A *constant procedure* is one that essentially ignores its arguments, returning the same results no matter what values it receives. We can create a constant procedure for any value or values that we want it to return. For instance, the predicate

```
(define (values? . ignored)
  #t)
```

can receive any number of arguments, which can be any values whatever, but it invariably returns #t.

Building a constant procedure to return some particular value or values is such a routine process that it is easy to write a higher-order procedure that automates it. The constant procedure can receive any number of arguments and returns a constant procedure in which those arguments are in effect stored up for later use. When invoked, the constant procedure ignores the arguments it receives and returns the stored-up values.

```
(define (constant . fixed-values)
  (lambda ignored
    (delist fixed-values)))
```

Thus values? could also be defined as (constant #t).

Here's another instance: In an interactive Scheme processor, we could use the procedure (constant "Why?") to simulate the verbal behavior of an annoying kid brother:

```
> (define hey-kid (constant "Why?"))
> (hey-kid "Don't put your gum in the electrical outlet.")
"Why?"
> (hey-kid "It's gross, and you'll get a shock.")
"Why?"
> (hey-kid "The gum is wet. There's an electrical current.")
"Why?"
```

```
> (hey-kid "Just don't do it, okay?")
"Why?"
```

Since the procedure that `constant` returns ignores all of its arguments, it is not necessary to provide that procedure with any arguments to begin with, so that it simply produces its values "out of nothing." We'll use the name 'create' for a variant of `constant` that produces only nullary (zero-argument) procedures:

```
(define (create . fixed-values)
  (lambda ()
    (delist fixed-values)))
```

It is also possible for a procedure to return no values at all. This is not an error or a non-terminating computation, but simply a computation that produces nothing when it finishes, like a committee that decides not to issue a report (which is sometimes the most useful thing a committee can do). We can even imagine a `black-hole` procedure that can receive any number of arguments and just swallows them up, returning no values. This procedure would combine, in a slightly comic way, the notions of variable arity and multiple results.

If you think about it, the definition of `black-hole` is trivial: It's the procedure that `constant` returns when you give it no arguments!

```
(define black-hole (constant))
```

Here's a more representative example illustrating the use of a constant function. Given a list, we can find out how many elements it has by mapping each of those elements to 1 and adding up the results:

```
(lambda (ls)
  (apply + (map (constant 1) ls)))
```

The call to the `map` procedure constructs and returns a list similar to `ls`, except that each value has been replaced by a 1. So the sum of that list is the number of elements in `ls`. (In this case, it happens that Scheme provides an equivalent procedure as a primitive, under the name `length`.)

---

values?   (afp constant-procedures)
any ... → *Boolean*
ignored
Return #t, regardless of the elements of ignored.

constant   (afp constant-procedures)
α ...   → (*any* ...   → α ...)
fixed-values   ignored
Construct a procedure that returns the elements of fixed-values, regardless of the elements of ignored.

create   (afp constant-procedures)
α ...   → (→ α ...)
fixed-values
Construct a nullary procedure that returns the elements of fixed-values.

black-hole   (afp constant-procedures)
any ... →
ignored
Return no values, regardless of the elements of ignored.

Exercises

2.2–1 Define a constant procedure that can receive any number of arguments, but always returns the two Boolean values, #t and #f, as its results. Then, if you didn't use constant in your definition, write an alternative definition of the same procedure using constant.

2.2–2 Define a procedure argument-count that can receive any number of arguments and returns a natural number indicating how many arguments it received.

2.3 Procedure Sections

One of the limitations of procedure calls as a building block for programs is that, to invoke a procedure, we must have all of the arguments on hand simultaneously. This can be awkward in cases where we have fully computed some of those arguments long before the others become available. For instance, we might want to invoke a procedure many times, varying some of the arguments while keeping others fixed. In such cases, it is usually more efficient to compute the fixed values just once, before any of the procedure invocations takes place.

To keep the calls short and simple, however, what we'd really like to do in such a case is to build a specialized variant of the procedure, with the fixed arguments hardwired into it, so that only the varying arguments are needed in each invocation.

For instance, a computation might involve raising the number 2 to several different powers. Although we have a general expt procedure, there is no primitive Scheme procedure specifically for computing powers of 2. Of course, it's easy to write a lambda-expression that denotes such a procedure:

```
(lambda (power)
  (expt 2 power))
```

A more elegant approach, however, is to derive this procedure from expt by "filling in" its first argument with the fixed value 2. Such a partially filled-in procedure is called a *procedure section*.

To construct procedure sections, we'll use sect-expressions. A sect-expression comprises the following constituents, enclosed in a pair of parentheses:

- the keyword 'sect';

- one or more single-valued expressions, interspersed with any number of occurrences of the identifier '<>' (which, in this context, is pronounced like the word 'slot' when spoken aloud); and

- optionally, at the end, the identifier '<...>' ("dotted slot").

The value of a sect-expression is always a procedure. The arity of this procedure is equal to the number of occurrences of the open-slot identifier '<>' in the sect-expression. If '<...>' is present, the procedure has variable arity and can receive any number of additional arguments. The body of the procedure is a procedure call, constructed from the subexpressions of the sect-expression, but with slots replaced (in order) by parameters. If '<...>' is present, it is replaced by a rest-parameter, and the body of the resulting procedure becomes a call to apply, so that all of the arguments corresponding to the rest-parameter are unbundled and used.

Here, then, is the definition of the procedure to raise 2 to a given power:

```
(define power-of-two (sect expt 2 <>))
```

Note also that '(sect expt <> 2)' is another way to express the square procedure.

We'll use sect-expressions extensively, since they are syntactically simpler than the lambda-expressions that they replace, and make it unnecessary to invent names for parameters that we'll only use once.

Some procedure sections come up so frequently that it will be helpful to have even shorter names for them:

```
(define add1 (sect + <> 1))
(define sub1 (sect - <> 1))
(define double (sect * <> 2))
```

The invoke Procedure

It is occasionally useful to have a name for the abstract form of a procedure invocation as such—that is, for just the computational process of transmitting arguments to a procedure and launching it. Our name for this form is invoke, and we can use an extreme sect-expression to define it:

```
(define invoke (sect <> <...>))
```

The first slot is in the position that is usually occupied by the procedure that we want to section. The sect-expression is so general that the operator position in a procedure call can also be parameterized. The identifier '<...>' then signals that any further arguments will be bound to a rest-parameter.

In case the preceding definition is too obscure, here is a more conventional presentation of the invoke procedure:

```
(define (invoke procedure . arguments)
  (apply procedure arguments))
```

It would be a little pointless to write a direct procedure call with 'invoke' as its operator, since one would get exactly the same results more efficiently by simply crossing out 'invoke'! However, invoke is sometimes useful as an argument to other procedures. I have included it here because the situations in which it is used are similar to those in which sectioning is needed: A procedure to be invoked and the arguments to be given to it arrive from different sources or at different points in the computation, and invoke is needed to combine them correctly.

Currying

If we're going to be taking sections of a multi-argument procedure frequently, we may find that it is simpler to adapt the interface of the procedure so that it receives only one argument and returns the corresponding section—a process called *currying*, in honor of the logician Haskell Curry.

For instance, a curried version of expt receives one argument, the base, and returns a procedure that receives the exponent as *its* argument and returns the result of the exponentiation:

```
(define (curried-expt base)
  (sect expt base <>))
```

For instance, the value of the procedure call '(curried-expt 2)' is the power-of-two procedure.

Naturally, we don't want to have to define a curried version of every multi-argument procedure that we might want to section in this way. Once we recognize the pattern that transforms expt into curried-expt, we can abstract that pattern and give it a name. The curry procedure receives any procedure of arity 2 (or higher) and returns a curried version of it:

```
(define (curry procedure)
  (lambda (initial)
    (lambda remaining
      (apply procedure initial remaining))))
```

Then, instead of pausing to define curried-expt, we can compute it as needed, as the value of the call '(curry expt)'.

One procedure that we'll frequently use in curried form is equal?. The unary equal-to? procedure can receive any value and returns a unary predicate that tests whether another value is equal? to it.

```
(define equal-to? (curry equal?))
```

---

power-of-two   (afp arithmetic)
integer   → *number*
exponent
Raise 2 to the power of exponent.

add1   (afp arithmetic)
number   → *number*
increscend
Add 1 to increscend.

sub1   (afp arithmetic)
number   → *number*
decrescend
Subtract 1 from decrescend.

double   (afp arithmetic)
number   → *number*
duplicand
Multiply duplicand by 2.

invoke   (afp procedure-sections)
$(\alpha \ldots \to \beta \ldots)$, $\alpha \ldots$ $\to \beta \ldots$
procedure   arguments
Apply procedure to the elements of arguments, returning the results.
Precondition: procedure can receive the elements of arguments.

curry   (afp procedure-sections)
$(\alpha, \beta \ldots \to \gamma \ldots) \to (\alpha \to (\beta \ldots \to \gamma \ldots))$
procedure   initial   remaining
Construct a unary procedure that constructs a procedure that, in turn, applies procedure to
initial and the elements of remaining and returns the results.
Precondition: procedure can receive initial and the elements of remaining.

equal-to   (afp procedure-sections)
any   → (*any*   → *Boolean)*
left   right
Construct a unary predicate that determines whether left and right are the same value.

Exercises

2.3–1   Define a procedure `reciprocal-of-product` that can receive any number of arguments and returns the result of dividing 1 by all of those arguments in succession. For instance, the value of the call

```
(reciprocal-of-product 2 3 5)
```

should be 1/30—the result of dividing 1 by 2, dividing the result by 3, and dividing the result of that second division by 5. (Hint: Using a sect-expression, it is possible to give an extremely concise definition of this procedure.)

2.3–2   The value of the procedure call '(curry div-and-mod)' is a procedure. Describe that procedure. What is its arity? How many results does it return? Specifically, what does the call '((curry div-and-mod) 60)' return?

2.4   Couplers

A *coupler* is a tool that links two or more procedures together to produce a new one.

Procedure Composition

The most common pattern of procedure linkage is composition. To *compose* two procedures is to arrange for one of them to receive the results of the other as its arguments. For example, we could compose the `integer?` and `/` procedures, using the number returned by `/` as the argument to `integer?`:

```
(lambda (dividend divisor)
  (integer? (/ dividend divisor)))
```

This predicate can be used to test whether its first argument is evenly divisible by its second, assuming that both arguments are integers and that the second is not 0.

The composition pattern occurs quite frequently, so it's useful to abstract it as a coupler. The coupler receives the two procedures and returns the composite procedure. It manages internally the mechanical process of collecting any results produced by the procedure that is invoked first and supplying them as arguments to the other procedure.

When defining this coupler, we have to decide which of the component procedures should be the first argument and which should be the second. There are good arguments for each arrangement:

1. It seems logical for the procedure that is invoked first to be the first argument. Also, it seems natural, given the left-to-right, top-to-bottom order in which we usually read Scheme code, to think of the intermediate results as flowing from the procedure on the left into the procedure on the right, or from the upper procedure to the lower one.

2. On the other hand, it also seems natural for the component procedures to be arranged in the same order as in the nested procedure call that the composition tool abstracts. Since we write '(integer? (/ dividend divisor))' to apply `integer?` to the result returned by `/`, 'integer?' should also precede '/' when we apply the composition tool to them.

   Some authors bolster this observation with an appeal to ordinary language. In English, at least, it is natural to read an expression like '(square (* 5 3))' as "the square of the product of 5 and 3," and to choose a compound name reflecting the same order for the composite procedure. (For instance, it would be natural to give the name 'square-of-product' to a composition of `square` and `*`.) Just as the procedure invoked first is named last in these constructions, it should be the second argument in a call to the higher-order composition tool.

Since these opposing arguments are almost equally compelling, I'll try to accommodate everyone's stylistic preferences by defining two variants. I prefer arrangement (1) and use it exclusively in this book. As consolation to those who prefer (2), however, I'll use the name compose for their version and present its definition first.

The definition is slightly more complicated than the examples we've looked at so far might suggest, because of the possibility that the component procedure that is invoked first might have several results. We'll take it as a precondition of the use of the composition tool that the arity of the other procedure is consistent with the number of these intermediate results. The added complication is that we have to use a receive-expression in order to make sure that all of the results are transmitted:

```
(define (compose outer inner)
  (lambda arguments
    (receive intermediates (apply inner arguments)
      (apply outer intermediates))))
```

The alternative to compose, using arrangement (1) of the arguments, is pipe. This name continues the hydraulic metaphor in which values flow from one procedure through the coupler into the other:

```
(define (pipe earlier later)
  (lambda arguments
    (receive intermediates (apply earlier arguments)
      (apply later intermediates))))
```

So, for instance, the divisibility predicate mentioned above can be computed either as (compose integer? /) or as (pipe / integer?). If one of these formulations seems much more natural to you than the other, I recommend that you use it exclusively. Code that switches back and forth between pipe and compose is harder to understand than code that consistently uses just one of the two.

Parallel Application

In a procedure composition, the component procedures apply *in sequence*, with the results of one becoming the arguments of the other. Another way to combine procedures is to think of them as applying in parallel, each performing a computation that is independent of the others and arriving at its own result. ("Parallel," in this context, does not imply that the implementation actually executes the computations simultaneously, on separate processors, but only that the computations are conceptually independent.)

The higher-order procedure cross receives n unary procedures (where n can be any natural number), each of which produces a single result, and constructs from them a procedure that receives n arguments, applies each of the procedures to the corresponding argument, and returns all n of the results. Here's a simple example of its use:

```
(define transfer-unit (cross sub1 add1))
```

The `transfer-unit` procedure receives two arguments and returns two results. Since `sub1` is a procedure that subtracts 1 from its argument, the first result of a call to `transfer-unit` is a number one less than its first argument. Similarly, the second result is one greater than the second argument (since `add1` adds one to its argument). So, for instance, the call '(transfer-unit 861 19)' has the values 860 and 20.

The definition of the `cross` procedure is simple but subtle:

```
(define (cross . procedures)
  (lambda arguments
    (delist (map invoke procedures arguments))))
```

Recall that when the `map` procedure is given a binary procedure and two lists of equal size, it applies the binary procedure to corresponding items in the two lists. In this case, one bundle contains unary procedures and the other contains the arguments to which those procedures are to be applied; `invoke` can receive two arguments, so `map` correctly applies it in turn to each of the unary procedures and the corresponding argument. The `map` returns a list of the results, so we use `delist` to break them out as separate values.

Dispatching

A *dispatcher* is a procedure that combines a number of single-result procedures, applying each one to *all* of the arguments supplied to the combined procedure. Each such application returns one result; the dispatcher returns the results of those individual applications as multiple values.

The `dispatch` tool can receive any number of procedures and constructs a dispatcher from them:

```
(define (dispatch . procedures)
  (lambda arguments
    (delist (map (sect apply <> arguments) procedures))))
```

For instance, consider the predicate (pipe (dispatch + *) <); applied to any number of arguments, each of which is a number, this predicate determines whether the sum of the numbers is less than their product.

---

compose   (afp couplers)

$(\alpha \ldots \to \beta \ldots), (\gamma \ldots \to \alpha \ldots) \to (\gamma \ldots \quad \to \beta \ldots)$
outer   inner   arguments

Construct a procedure that applies outer to the results of applying inner to the elements of

arguments, returning the results.
Precondition: `outer` can receive the results of any invocation of `inner`.
Precondition: `inner` can receive the elements of `arguments`.

pipe   (afp couplers)
$(\alpha \ldots \rightarrow \beta \ldots), (\beta \ldots \rightarrow \gamma \ldots) \rightarrow (\alpha \ldots \qquad \rightarrow \gamma \ldots)$
earlier   later   arguments
Construct a procedure that applies `later` to the results of applying `earlier` to the elements
of `arguments`, returning the results.
Precondition: `earlier` can receive the elements of `arguments`.
Precondition: `later` can receive the results of any invocation of `earlier`.

cross   (afp couplers)
$(\alpha \rightarrow \beta) \ldots \rightarrow (\alpha \ldots \qquad \rightarrow \beta \ldots)$
procedures   arguments
Construct a procedure that applies each element of `procedures` to the corresponding element
of `arguments` and returns the results.
Precondition: Each element of `procedures` can receive the corresponding element of `arguments`.

dispatch   (afp couplers)
$(\alpha \ldots \rightarrow \beta) \rightarrow (\alpha \ldots \qquad \rightarrow \beta \ldots)$
procedures   arguments
Construct a procedure that applies each of the elements of `procedures` to the elements of
`arguments`, returning the results.
Precondition: Each element of `procedures` can receive the elements of `arguments`.

Exercises

2.4–1   Define a ternary (three-argument) analogue of `pipe`: a procedure that
receives three procedures as arguments and returns a procedure that applies
the first of those three to its own arguments, the second to the results of that
application, and the third to the results of that second application, returning
the results of the third application as its own results.

(If you prefer working with `compose`, define its ternary analogue instead.)

2.4–2   If you used `pipe` or `compose` in your solution to the preceding exercise, redefine the same procedure using `receive`-expressions instead. If you
used `receive`-expressions, redefine the procedure using calls to `pipe` or `compose`
instead.

2.4–3   Using the appropriate coupler, define the `sum-of-reciprocals` procedure: Given any number of arguments, each of which is a non-zero number,
`sum-of-reciprocals` returns the sum of their multiplicative inverses.

2.4–4   Using appropriate couplers, define the `harmonic-mean` procedure: Given
two positive rational numbers a and b, `harmonic-mean` returns their harmonic
mean, $\frac{2ab}{a+b}$.

2.5   Adapters

Besides the issue of timing that we addressed in §2.3, a procedure call can
encounter other kinds of obstacles: The procedure being invoked may not need

all of the arguments that the caller finds it convenient to provide, and may not even be able to receive all of them (because of its arity), or it may expect to receive the arguments in a different order. Similar problems can arise in connection with the values that the procedure returns to the caller.

One way to address such mismatches is to compose the procedure to be invoked with an *adapter*: a procedure that selects, rearranges, or duplicates the values it receives as arguments and returns the results. An adapter can be placed between the caller and the procedure being called to fix argument mismatches, or between the procedure being called and the caller to fix result mismatches, or both.

Almost all such mismatches fit into a few easily identified categories. This section presents the adapters that address them.

Selection

For instance, we might want to invoke the square procedure in a context that would require it to receive, say, three arguments, returning the square of the first and ignoring the others completely. The fact that the arity of square is fixed at 1 prevents such a use.

If we were interested only in immediate results, we could write a lambda-expression to take the place of square in the invocation:

```
(lambda (number . ignored)
  (square number))
```

A more general approach, however, is to use an adapter that we'll call >initial. (In this context, the character '>' is pronounced "keep" when said aloud: "keep initial.")

```
(define (>initial initial . ignored)
  initial)
```

So, for instance, we can write '(pipe >initial square)' to compute the procedure denoted by the lambda-expression shown above. Similarly, we could write '(pipe >initial zero?)' to get a procedure that can receive one or more arguments and determines whether the first of them is 0.

The same adapter can be attached at the other end of the procedure, to select and return the first of several results. For instance, we often need only the quotient of a number-theoretic division, so we might write the definition

```
(define div (pipe div-and-mod >initial))
```

to perform the division and select just the first result.

A similar adapter, >next, can receive any number of arguments and selects and returns the second of them:

```
(define (>next initial next . ignored)
  next)
```

For instance, the mod procedure returns just the remainder of a number-theoretic division:

```
(define mod (pipe div-and-mod >next))
```

It is straightforward to continue this series of positional adapters, but only the first two appear often enough in this book to need separate names.

The >initial and >next adapters single out one of their arguments and discard the rest. Sometimes, though, we want the adapter to discard one of its arguments and keep all of the remaining ones. The >all-but-initial adapter deals with the most common of these cases, in which the value to be discarded is the initial argument:

```
(define (>all-but-initial initial . others)
  (delist others))
```

Among the procedures that we've already encountered, two can be regarded as adapters that make extreme selections: values, which keeps all of its arguments, and black-hole, which keeps none of them. Another procedure that belongs in this category is identity:

```
(define (identity something)
  something)
```

There is seldom a reason to invoke identity explicitly, since in any context such a call could be replaced by its operand expression without affecting the rest of the computation. However, like invoke, identity is occasionally useful as an argument to other procedures.

Rearrangement

Another kind of mismatch occurs when we want to invoke a procedure and have all of its arguments on hand, but the larger computation supplies them in the wrong order. In the simplest and most frequent case, the procedure is binary, and we just want to swap the positions of its arguments. The >exch adapter performs this operation (and also handles the more general case in which we want to reverse the first two of many arguments):

```
(define (>exch initial next . others)
  (apply values next initial others))
```

The *converse* of a binary procedure is the result of swapping its arguments around. Using >exch, we can write a higher-order procedure that converts any binary procedure into its converse:

```
(define converse (sect pipe >exch <>))
```

For instance, (converse expt) is a "backwards" version of expt that receives the exponent as its first argument and the number to be raised to that power as its second argument, so that the value of the call '((converse expt) 3 5)' is 5^3, or 125. Take care when applying converse to variable-arity procedures, however: The result of the call '(converse <=)' is not the same procedure as >=, and the difference shows up when three or more arguments are provided. (The >exch adapter swaps only the first two, instead of reversing the entire argument list, as some might expect.)

Preprocessing and Postprocessing

A third kind of adapter, a *preprocessor*, can be interposed when a procedure is invoked. The idea is that the arguments are *almost* right as they stand—it's just that one of them has to be tweaked a little bit before it is ready to be sent on to the procedure that we actually want to call. Often we can come up with a unary, single-valued procedure to perform this tweak. Each of our next three procedures receives a tweaking procedure as its argument and returns an adapter that applies it in just the right place.

The ~initial procedure builds and returns an adapter that tweaks the first of the arguments it receives and returns the result along with all of its other arguments:

```
(define (~initial procedure)
  (lambda (initial . others)
    (apply values (procedure initial) others)))
```

For instance, (~initial (sect * <> 3)) is an adapter that receives one or more arguments and returns all of them, except that the first argument, which must be a number, is replaced in the results by its triple.

Similarly, the ~next procedure builds and returns an adapter that tweaks the *second* of the arguments it receives and returns the result along with all of its other arguments:

```
(define (~next procedure)
  (lambda (initial next . others)
    (apply values initial (procedure next) others)))
```

If *all* of the arguments to a procedure need to be preprocessed in the same way, we can use the ~each procedure:

```
(define (~each procedure)
  (lambda arguments
    (delist (map procedure arguments))))
```

For instance, the value of the expression '(pipe (~each square) +)' is the
procedure that we defined under the name sum-of-squares in §2.1.

Quite commonly, the ~each adapter is used to preprocess values so that
a predicate can determine whether they are related in a particular way. For
instance, if we want to find out whether two integers have the same parity (that
is, whether they are both even or both odd), we could write

```
(define same-in-parity? (pipe (~each even?) boolean=?))
```

Attaching the adapter to the predicate converts boolean=? into a new predicate that compares integers by their evenness. Let's give the name compare-by
to this frequently occurring pattern:

```
(define (compare-by pre comparer)
  (pipe (~each pre) comparer))
```

So, for instance, we could define same-in-parity? thus:

```
(define same-in-parity? (compare-by even? boolean=?))
```

Adapters constructed by ~initial, ~next, and ~each can also be placed
in the other position in a composition, so that they *postprocess* the results of
a procedure invocation instead of preprocessing the arguments. For instance,
(pipe div-and-mod (~each (sect * <> 2))) receives two arguments, divides
the first by the second, doubles the quotient and the remainder, and returns the
results of those doublings (as separate values).

>initial   (afp adapters)
$\alpha,$ *any* ... $\rightarrow \alpha$
initial ignored
Return initial.

div   (afp arithmetic)
integer,   *integer* $\rightarrow$ *integer*
dividend divisor
Divide dividend by divisor and return the (number-theoretic) quotient, discarding any remainder.
Precondition: divisor is not 0.

>next   (afp adapters)
any, $\alpha,$ *any* ... $\rightarrow \alpha$
initial next ignored
Return next.

mod   (afp arithmetic)
integer,   *integer* $\rightarrow$ *natural-number*
dividend divisor
Divide dividend by divisor and return the (number-theoretic) remainder, discarding the quotient.
Precondition: divisor is not 0.

>all-but-initial   (afp adapters)
any, α ... $\rightarrow \alpha$ ...
initial others
Return the elements of others.

identity   (afp adapters)
α $\rightarrow \alpha$
something
Return something.

>exch   (afp adapters)
$\alpha,$ $\beta,$ $\gamma \ldots$ $\rightarrow \beta, \alpha, \gamma \ldots$
initial next others
Return next, initial, and the elements of others, in that order.

converse   (afp adapters)
$(\alpha, \beta \rightarrow \gamma \ldots)$ $\rightarrow (\beta,$ α $\rightarrow \gamma \ldots)$
procedure   left right
Construct a binary procedure that applies procedure to right and left and returns the results.
Precondition: procedure can receive right and left.

~initial   (afp adapters)
$(\alpha \rightarrow \beta)$ $\rightarrow (\alpha,$ $\gamma \ldots$ $\rightarrow \beta, \gamma \ldots)$
procedure   initial others
Construct a procedure that applies procedure to initial and returns the result of that application and the elements of others.
Precondition: procedure can receive initial.

~next   (afp adapters)
$(\alpha \rightarrow \beta)$ $\rightarrow (\gamma,$ $\alpha,$ $\delta \ldots$ $\rightarrow \gamma, \beta, \delta \ldots)$
procedure   initial next others
Construct a procedure that applies procedure to next and returns initial, the result of the application, and the elements of others.
Precondition: procedure can receive next.

~each   (afp adapters)
$(\alpha \rightarrow \beta)$ $\rightarrow (\alpha \ldots$ $\rightarrow \beta \ldots)$
procedure   arguments
Construct a procedure that applies procedure to each element of arguments, returning the results.
Precondition: procedure can receive each element of arguments.

compare-by   (afp adapters)
$(\alpha \rightarrow \beta), (\beta \ldots \rightarrow Boolean)$ $\rightarrow (\alpha \ldots$ $\rightarrow Boolean)$
pre   comparer   comparands
Construct a predicate that applies pre to each element of comparands and applies comparer to the results, returning the result.
Precondition: pre can receive each element of comparands.
Precondition: comparer can receive the results of any invocation of pre.

same-in-parity?   (afp adapters)
integer, integer $\rightarrow Boolean$
left   right
Determine whether the parity of left and the parity of right are the same—that is, whether both are even or both are odd.

Exercises

2.5–1 Define an adapter >initial-and-next that can receive two or more arguments and returns only its first two (as separate results).

2.5–2 Is (converse (converse expt)) the same procedure as expt? Justify your answer.

2.5–3 Define an adapter >rotate that can receive three or more arguments and returns them all as separate results, but with the first argument as the third result, the second argument as the first result, and the third argument as the second result. (For instance, the call '(>rotate 1 2 3 4 5)' should return the values 2, 3, 1, 4, and 5, in that order.)

2.5–4   Define an adapter >duplicate that receives one argument and returns that argument twice, as separate values. Using this adapter, propose an alternative definition for the square procedure.

2.6   Recursion Managers

The tools presented in this section abstract common patterns of recursion.

The recur Procedure

In a narrow sense, the term "recursion" is used to describe a computational structure in which the solution to any but the simplest instances of a problem requires, as an initial step, the solution of one or more subproblems of the same sort. Recursive procedure invocations are used to obtain the results for these subproblems, which are then brought together and postprocessed. The results of the postprocessing are returned as the results of the original invocation of the recursive procedure.

The factorial procedure presented in §1.9 has this form: In order to compute, say, (factorial 8), we first compute (factorial 7) and then multiply the result by 8. Of course, to compute (factorial 7), we must first compute (factorial 6), which requires us first to compute (factorial 5), and so on. The recursion bottoms out when we reach (factorial 0)—the simplest instance of the problem—for which the result 1 is returned immediately. It is only when the computation reaches this point that the multiplications begin. Each of them operates on the result of the most recently completed invocation of the recursive procedure and completes an invocation that began earlier.

The first tool that we'll develop in this section, the higher-order procedure recur, creates such *singly recursive* procedures, in which the solution to a given instance of a problem depends on at most one subproblem, so that only one recursive call appears in the definition. The recur procedure receives four arguments, corresponding to the four points at which singly recursive procedures differ:

- We must be able to detect the base cases of the recursion—the instances for which a solution can be returned immediately, without further recursion. The first argument to recur is a predicate that returns #t in a base case, #f if a further invocation of the recursive procedure is needed.

- When we reach a base case of the recursion, we must be able to construct the solution, using only the values supplied as arguments in the final invocation of the recursive procedure. The second argument to recur is a procedure expressing the computation that constructs the solution in a base case.

- When we have not yet reached a base case, we must be able to simplify or reduce the instance of the problem that we're currently working on, to obtain a smaller subproblem that is at least one step closer to the base cases. The third argument to recur is a simplification procedure that transforms the current instance of the problem into two values: a local, "current" component that can be dealt with in the current invocation of the recursive procedure, and a simpler instance of the problem for the next invocation.

- Finally, when we receive the results of an invocation of a recursive procedure, we must be able to combine them with the "current" component of the problem instance before we can return the results of the current invocation. The fourth argument to recur is an integration procedure that performs this processing.

For instance, we could define the factorial procedure as

```
(recur zero? (constant 1) (dispatch identity sub1) *)
```

which corresponds reasonably well to a description of the algorithm in English prose: "Given any natural number n, determine whether it is 0. If so, ignore n and return 1; otherwise, subtract 1 from n, recur on the result to get the factorial of $n - 1$, and multiply n by the value of the recursive invocation."

Here is the definition of recur:

```
(define (recur base? terminal simplify integrate)
  (rec (recurrer guide)
    (if (base? guide)
        (terminal guide)
        (receive (current next) (simplify guide)
          (receive recursive-results (recurrer next)
            (apply integrate current recursive-results)))))))
```

The internal recurrer procedure receives a single argument to guide the recursion.

We can use a similar but slightly more complicated recursion manager, build, when the basic recursive procedure (in this case builder) needs two or more arguments:

```
(define (build base? terminal derive simplify integrate)
  (rec (builder . guides)
    (if (apply base? guides)
        (apply terminal guides)
        (receive recursive-results
                 (apply (pipe simplify builder) guides)
          (apply integrate (apply derive guides) recursive-results)))))
```

The `derive` procedure, which must be single-valued, performs the computation that can be done "locally," that is, within the current invocation of `builder`, while the `simplify` procedure transforms the guide values to prepare them for the recursive call.

Recursive Predicates

When recursion is used to define a predicate, there are often two base cases— one in which the final result is known to be #t, and another in which it is known to be #f—and, naturally, the conditions used to detect these base cases are different.

As an example of this frequently encountered pattern, consider the predicate `power-of-two?`, which determines whether a given positive integer `candidate` is an exact power of 2. The algorithm is surprisingly simple and illustrates the power of recursion. It's based on the observation that an odd positive integer is a power of 2 if and only if it is 1, while an even positive integer is a power of 2 if and only if the result of dividing it by 2 is a power of 2. We can conveniently express the operation of dividing a number by 2 as a procedure section:

```
(define halve (sect div <> 2))
```

Now let's turn the observation made above into an algorithm:

```
(define (power-of-two? candidate)
  (or (= candidate 1)
      (and (even? candidate)
           (power-of-two? (halve candidate)))))
```

For instance, the value of '(power-of-two? 2048)' is #t, because 2048 is 2^{11}; but the value of '(power-of-two? 4860)' is #f, because 4860 is not an exact power of two.

The recursion manager `check` abstracts the general pattern, leaving three parameters to be supplied by the caller:

```
(define (check stop? continue? step)
  (rec (checker . arguments)
    (or (apply stop? arguments)
        (and (apply continue? arguments)
             (apply (pipe step checker) arguments)))))
```

In a predicate constructed and returned by `check`, applying the `stop?` predicate to the arguments determines whether we can immediately return #t, without additional recursive calls, and applying the `continue?` predicate determines whether we can immediately return #f (if the arguments do not satisfy `continue?`) or must proceed to recursive invocation. The `step` procedure transforms the current arguments into values appropriate for the next level of recursion.

The `power-of-two?` predicate, for instance, could also be defined thus:

```
(define power-of-two? (check (sect = <> 1) even? halve))
```

"If the argument is equal to 1, stop and return #t; otherwise, if it is even, divide it by 2 and continue with the quotient; otherwise, stop and return #f."

Any invocation of the power-of-two? predicate terminates eventually, if it respects the precondition that the argument be a positive integer. The result of applying halve to any integer n except 1 is a positive integer that is strictly less than n. So each successive invocation of the recursive procedure receives a lesser positive integer as its argument than the preceding invocation. The supply of positive integers less than the original argument is finite. After repeated halving, therefore, we eventually reach 1 (or some other odd number) no matter what positive integer we started with.

Iteration

Another common pattern for designing recursive procedures is to perform some operation repeatedly, with the results of each invocation becoming the arguments for the next one. The process stops when some condition, tested before each repetition, is at last satisfied. The recursive procedure then returns the results of the last invocation. This pattern is called *iteration*.

The iterate procedure is a tool that constructs and returns recursive procedures according to this pattern. It receives two arguments:

- The *termination predicate* determines whether to terminate the iteration, returning the current values, or to continue for at least one more round.

- The *step procedure* performs the basic operation once, returning new values that will take the place of its arguments if and when the operation is performed again.

Here is the definition of the iterate procedure:

```
(define (iterate stop? step)
  (rec (iterator . arguments)
    (if (apply stop? arguments)
        (apply values arguments)
        (apply (pipe step iterator) arguments))))
```

As an example of the use of iterate, let's consider the determination of the greatest odd divisor of a given positive integer—a problem that you've already encountered in the exercises for §1.10. If the integer is itself odd, then it is its own greatest odd divisor (since it obviously divides itself, and no greater integer can evenly divide it). On the other hand, if the given integer is even, we can simplify the problem by halving that integer. All of the odd divisors of the original number, including the greatest one, will also divide the quotient, so finding the greatest odd divisor of the quotient solves the original problem.

If the quotient resulting from this first division is still even, we can halve it again without losing any odd divisors. If the quotient of the second division is again even, we can halve it again, and so on. Since we obtain a lesser positive integer at each step, the divisions cannot go on forever—eventually one of the quotients is odd. Since this quotient still has all of the odd divisors of the original number, it is itself the greatest odd divisor of that number.

In this example, the only numerical value that we need to keep track of is the most recent quotient. The test that determines whether we should stop is the primitive predicate odd?. So we can define the `greatest-odd-divisor` procedure concisely:

```
(define greatest-odd-divisor (iterate odd? halve))
```

In `greatest-odd-divisor`, the internal recursive procedure needs only one argument. In a more typical case, we might need to build up a result and at the same time keep track of some other values that figure in the intermediate computation. In such cases, both the termination predicate and the step procedure receive two or more arguments. The step procedure must therefore produce two or more values, to be used as arguments in the recursive call.

For instance, suppose that we want to know how many times we can apply a doubling operation, starting from 1, before the result equals or exceeds a given positive integer. If the integer is, say, 23, we can do this by hand or even in our heads: $1 \mapsto 2 \mapsto 4 \mapsto 8 \mapsto 16 \mapsto 32$, which exceeds 23. We had to perform five doublings, so the answer in this case is 5. But if the integer is much larger, we want the computer both to perform the doubling operations and, at the same time, to count them.

In mathematical terminology, the number we want is the ceiling of the base-two logarithm of the given positive integer. So let's call the Scheme procedure that carries out this computation `ceiling-of-log-two`. It should receive the given positive integer—let's call it bound—as its argument and return the number of doubling operations required, starting from 1, to reach a number that equals or exceeds bound.

The iterative procedure at the core of `ceiling-of-log-two` should keep track both of the number of doublings that have been performed so far and of the result of the most recent doubling, just as we did above in working out the special case of 23. We arrange this by making both the termination predicate and the step procedure binary, in each case taking the result of the most recent doubling as the first argument and the number of doublings so far as the second.

In each step of the iteration, we want to double the first argument and add 1 to the second (recording the fact that we've done one more doubling), so our step procedure is (`cross double add1`).

Now let's consider the termination predicate. To determine whether some number equals or exceeds a given positive integer bound, we apply the procedure section (`sect >= <> bound`) to it. However, this section is a unary predicate, and the termination predicate has to be binary. Specifically, it should ignore its second argument and apply this procedure section to just the first one. The solution to this mismatch is to apply the >initial adapter as a preprocessor, since that adapter does precisely what we want: It discards the second argument and passes the first one along to a unary predicate that we already know how to write.

The core iteration, then, is

```
(iterate (pipe >initial (sect >= <> bound))
         (cross double add1))
```

Two difficulties remain, both involving mismatches between the interface that this iteration provides and the original problem that we're trying to solve. One is that, when the iteration finishes, it returns two values: the result of the final doubling operation (32, in our example above) and the count of the number of doublings performed. Once we've completed the iteration, we're interested only in the second of these, which is the only value we want our ceiling-of-log-two procedure to return. Again, the solution is to attach an adapter, this time as a postprocessor. The adapter >next selects the second of the two results and returns it.

The other problem is how to get the iteration started. The caller provides a value for the parameter bound when it invokes the ceiling-of-log-two procedure, but it wouldn't make sense to pass that value along to the core iteration procedure, because bound is fixed throughout the computation. We need it to stay the same throughout all the recursive calls so that we can tell when the result of the most recent doubling meets the termination condition. But then what values *should* the core iteration start from, and how do we provide it with those values?

Looking back at the original statement of the problem, we see that the initial value of the argument that is doubled at each step should be 1. And at the outset, before we've done any doubling operations, the number of doublings "so far" should be 0. So, no matter what bound is, we always want the core iteration to receive 1 and 0 as its initial arguments. To arrange this, all we need to do is *invoke* the procedure that iterate constructs for us, giving it 1 and 0 as arguments. That procedure will do all the rest of the work.

Assembling the pieces, we obtain the definition of ceiling-of-log-two:

```
(define (ceiling-of-log-two bound)
  ((pipe (iterate (pipe >initial (sect >= <> bound))
                  (cross double add1))
         >next)
   1 0))
```

As a matter of style, if the procedure call seems unpleasantly top-heavy or awkward, we could use create to generate the initial values for the recursion:

```
(define (ceiling-of-log-two bound)
  ((pipe (create 1 0)
         (pipe (iterate (pipe >initial (sect >= <> bound))
                        (cross double add1))
               >next))))
```

Of course, there are also many other ways to write a procedure like
ceiling-of-log-two in Scheme, and some Scheme programmers would be more
comfortable coding in a style that places less emphasis on the apparatus of
functional programming, like this:

```
(define (ceiling-of-log-two bound)
  ((rec (doubler most-recent-double count)
     (if (>= most-recent-double bound)
         count
         (doubler (double most-recent-double) (add1 count))))
   1 0))
```

The explicit use of iterate in our first definition identifies the design pattern
at the core of the algorithm, and thus exposes its relationship to other iterative
procedures, which is harder to perceive in the second version. Our definition
also suggests a view of programming as assembling structures by joining modular components according to fixed and well-understood patterns, while the
alternative definition implies a more fluid view of programming in which each
problem presents unique opportunities for optimization. Both approaches have
merits, and in subsequent chapters we'll use both of them freely.

---

recur   (afp recursion-managers)
$(\alpha \to Boolean)$, $(\alpha \to \beta \ldots)$, $(\alpha \to \gamma, \alpha)$, $(\gamma, \beta \ldots \to \beta \ldots)$ →
base?   terminal   simplify   integrate

$$(\alpha \qquad \to \beta \ldots)$$
guide

Construct a singly recursive procedure that applies base? to guide to determine whether the
base case has been reached, applies terminal to guide to obtain the results to be returned in the
base case, applies simplify to guide to separate the values needed for the local computation
from those needed for the recursive invocation, invokes itself recursively, and applies integrate
to the locally needed values and the results of the recursive invocation to obtain the results
to be returned.
Precondition: base? can receive guide.
Precondition: base? can receive the second result of any invocation of simplify.
Precondition: If guide satisfies base?, then terminal can receive it.
Precondition: If the second result of an invocation of simplify satisfies base?, then terminal
can receive it.
Precondition: If guide does not satisfy base?, then simplify can receive it.
Precondition: If the second result of an invocation of simplify does not satisfy base?, then
simplify can receive it.
Precondition: integrate can receive the first result of an invocation of simplify and the results
of an invocation of terminal.
Precondition: integrate can receive the first result of an invocation of simplify and the results
of an invocation of integrate.

build   (afp recursion-managers)
$(\alpha \ldots \to Boolean)$, $(\alpha \ldots \to \beta \ldots)$, $(\alpha \ldots \to \gamma)$, $(\alpha \ldots \to \alpha \ldots)$,
base?   terminal   derive   simplify

$$(\gamma, \beta \ldots \rightarrow \beta \ldots) \rightarrow (\alpha \ldots \rightarrow \beta)$$

integrate   guides

Construct a simply recursive procedure that applies base? to the elements of guides to determine whether the base case has been reached, applies terminal to the elements of guides to obtain the results to be returned in the base case, applies derive to the elements of guides to obtain the value needed for the local computation, applies simplify to the elements of guides to obtain the values needed for the recursive invocation, invokes itself recursively, and applies integrate to the locally needed value and the results of the recursive invocation to obtain the results to be returned in the recursive case.

Precondition: base? can receive the elements of guides.

Precondition: base? can receive the results of any invocation of simplify.

Precondition: If the elements of guides satisfy base?, then terminal can receive them.

Precondition: If the results of an invocation of simplify satisfy base?, then terminal can receive them.

Precondition: If the elements of guides do not satisfy base?, then derive can receive them.

Precondition: If the results of an invocation of simplify do not satisfy base?, then derive can receive them.

Precondition: If the elements of guides do not satisfy base?, then simplify can receive them.

Precondition: If the results of an invocation of simplify do not satisfy base?, then simplify can receive them.

Precondition: integrate can receive the result of any invocation of derive and the results of any invocation of terminal.

Precondition: integrate can receive the result of any invocation of derive and the results of any invocation of integrate.

power-of-two?   (afp arithmetic)

natural-number $\rightarrow$ *Boolean*

candidate

Determine whether candidate is a power of 2.

Precondition: candidate is positive.

check   (afp recursion-managers)

$(\alpha \ldots \rightarrow Boolean), (\alpha \ldots \rightarrow Boolean), (\alpha \ldots \rightarrow \alpha \ldots) \rightarrow$

stop?   continue?   step

$$(\alpha \ldots \rightarrow Boolean)$$

arguments

Construct a predicate that is satisfied if either the elements of arguments satisfy stop?, or they satisfy continue? and the results of applying step to them satisfy the constructed predicate.

Precondition: stop? can receive the elements of arguments.

Precondition: stop? can receive the results of any invocation of step.

Precondition: If the elements of arguments do not satisfy stop?, then continue? can receive them.

Precondition: If the results of an invocation of step do not satisfy stop?, then continue? can receive them.

Precondition: If the elements of arguments do not satisfy stop? but do satisfy continue?, then step can receive them.

Precondition: If the results of an invocation of step do not satisfy stop? but do satisfy continue?, then step can receive them.

iterate   (afp recursion-managers)

$(\alpha \ldots \rightarrow Boolean), (\alpha \ldots \rightarrow \alpha \ldots) \rightarrow (\alpha \ldots \rightarrow \alpha \ldots)$

stop?   step   arguments

Construct a singly recursive procedure that applies stop? to the elements of arguments to determine whether the base case has been reached (in which case it returns the elements of arguments) and applies step to the elements of arguments to obtain the values needed for the recursive invocation (returning the results of that recursive invocation).

Precondition: stop? can receive the elements of arguments.

Precondition: stop? can receive the results of any invocation of step.

Precondition: If the elements of arguments do not satisfy stop?, then step can receive them.

Precondition: If the results of an invocation of step do not satisfy stop?, then step can receive them.

halve   (afp arithmetic)
number   → *number*
dividend
Divide dividend by 2 and return the quotient, discarding any remainder.

greatest-odd-divisor   (afp arithmetic)
natural-number   → *natural-number*
number
Compute the greatest odd natural number that evenly divides number.
Precondition: number is positive.

ceiling-of-log-two   (afp arithmetic)
natural-number   → *natural-number*
bound
Compute the ceiling of the base-two logarithm of bound.
Precondition: bound is positive.

Exercises

2.6–1   Define a procedure next-power-of-ten that receives one argument, a
natural number, and returns the least integer that is a power of ten and is
greater than the given number. For instance, the value of '(next-power-of-ten
954)' is 1000, and the value of '(next-power-of-ten 10000)' is 100000. Note
also that, under this specification, the value of '(next-power-of-ten 0)' is 1.

2.6–2   Explain the precondition on the power-of-two? predicate. What would
happen if we supplied 0 as the argument when invoking this procedure? What
would happen if we supplied a negative integer? Why?

2.6–3   The *sideways sum* of a natural number is the number of 1 bits in its
base-two numeral (or, equivalently, the sum of the values of the bits in that
numeral). For instance, the base-two numeral for 53 is '110101', so the sideways
sum of 53 is 4. Define a unary procedure sideways-sum that receives any natural
number as argument and returns its sideways sum, by repeatedly halving the
given number and tallying the number of odd results.

2.6–4   Define a predicate equal-after-transfer? that receives two natural
numbers, returning #t if they are equal and #f if the first argument is 0 and
the second is positive. If neither one of these conditions holds, the predicate
should apply the transfer-unit procedure (from §2.4) to the arguments and
repeat the process on the results. Thus equal-after-transfer? will determine
whether any number of unit transfers from the first given number to the second
will make the results equal before the first is reduced to 0.

2.7   Euclid's Algorithm

To illustrate some of the tools we've developed, let's design an algorithm for
finding the greatest common divisor of two positive integers.

We'll begin by defining the key terms: An integer n is *evenly divisible* by a non-zero integer d if there is an integer q such that $n/d = q$. Since d is non-zero, we can write the same condition as $n = dq$. It's also easy to express this relationship as a Scheme predicate:

```
(define divisible-by? (pipe mod zero?))
```

A positive integer d is the *greatest common divisor* of two positive integers m and n if both m and n are evenly divisible by d, but not by any positive integer greater than d. So, for instance, the greatest common divisor of 30 and 42 is 6, because both of these numbers are evenly divisible by 6, but no integer greater than 6 evenly divides both.

The definition suggests a brute-force approach to the problem of finding the greatest common divisor of two given positive integers m and n: Starting with the lesser of m and n, count downwards through the positive integers, testing each one to see whether it evenly divides both m and n. The first one that passes this test is the greatest common divisor.

```
(define (greatest-common-divisor left right)
  (let ((divides-both? (lambda (candidate)
                  (and (divisible-by? left candidate)
                       (divisible-by? right candidate)))))
    ((iterate divides-both? sub1) (lesser left right))))
```

Correct answers can be obtained with this approach, but it's not an elegant solution. When m and n are both large (which is when it is most useful to automate the computation) and the greatest common divisor is small (as it usually is), most of the computation is wasted, in the sense that almost all of the divisions result in non-zero remainders. With a little more mathematical insight, we can get the same answers with much less effort even in these difficult cases. We can borrow the insight from the geometer Euclid, who first proposed a version of the algorithm presented below.

Our first observation about divisibility is that if either of two positive integers evenly divides the other, then it is their greatest common divisor (since obviously it evenly divides itself, and no greater integer can evenly divide it). This suggests that it might make sense to begin our algorithm by dividing the greater of the given numbers by the lesser. If the remainder is 0, we have our answer immediately.

What happens, though, if we divide, say, m by n and get a non-zero remainder r? Even though we don't have an immediate solution in this case, r turns out to be a useful piece of information. Euclid's insight was that, even though we don't know yet what the greatest common divisor of m and n is, we can prove that it evenly divides r.

Here's the proof: Let d be any positive integer that evenly divides both m and n. Then there are positive integers a and b such that $m = ad$ and $n = bd$. When we divide m by n, we get a quotient q and a remainder r such that

$m = qn + r$, by the definition of number-theoretic division. Hence, substituting equals for equals, $ad = qbd + r$. So $r = ad - qbd = d(a - qb)$. Since a, q, and b are all integers, so is $a - qb$. Therefore, by the definition of "evenly divides," d evenly divides r.

So far we have shown that *every* integer that evenly divides both m and n evenly divides r as well. In particular, then the greatest common divisor of m and n, whatever it is, evenly divides r. Moreover, any integer d' that evenly divides both r and n also evenly divides m (because $m = qn + r = qa'd' + b'd' = d'(qa' + b')$, for some integers a' and b'). So the greatest common divisor of n and r is the same as the greatest common divisor of m and n, because both pairs of numbers have exactly the same common divisors.

This observation gives us a way to transform one instance of the greatest-common-divisor problem into another, which is a useful thing to do if the new instance of the problem is easier to solve. And in this case it *is* easier to solve, because n and r are less, respectively, than m and n. (The remainder left over in a division by n must be in the range from 0 to $n - 1$, so clearly r is less than n; and n is less than m because we started by dividing the greater of our two given positive integers by the lesser one.)

Now we can use recursion to implement the better algorithm that we've been looking for: Iterate the transformation that replaces m and n with n and r, obtaining lesser numbers each time, until one of the divisions yields a remainder of 0. At that point, we can conclude that the most recent divisor is the greatest common divisor. Since all the instances of the problem that are generated along the way have the same answer, we solve them all, including the original instance, in one stroke.

We can be sure that this algorithm reaches a solution, no matter what positive integers we begin with, because r is reduced at each step. There are only a finite number of integer values that it can run through before being reduced to 0, at which point the termination predicate is satisfied and no further recursive calls are made.

The computation that we have described fits the pattern that the `iterate` procedure captures. In the termination predicate, we want to test whether the first argument is evenly divisible by the second. For the step procedure, we want to receive m and n and return n and r, which is the remainder when m is divided by n. Obviously `>next` selects n from m and n, and `mod` computes the desired remainder r given m and n. To get both results, we need only dispatch m and n to `>next` and `mod`. Thus the recursion at the heart of the algorithm is

```
(iterate divisible-by? (dispatch >next mod))
```

The earlier reasoning about Euclid's algorithm began with the assumption that in the first step we divided the greater number by the lesser one. We should therefore establish the precondition that m is greater than n before starting the principal recursion. We can do this by composing the iterator with a preprocessing procedure that can receive any two positive integers and returns them with the greater one as the first result and the lesser one as the second. If you defined the `greater` procedure in the exercises for §1.9, you could write this preprocessor as (`dispatch greater lesser`). Alternatively, we could define the necessary adapter directly:

```
(define (greater-and-lesser left right)
  (if (< left right)
      (values right left)
      (values left right)))
```

Like `div-and-mod`, this implementation has the advantage that the key computation (in this case, the comparison of `left` and `right`) is performed only once.

At the other end of the iteration, we wind up with two results, of which the first is evenly divisible by the second. As we saw above, the second of those results is the greatest common divisor, so in postprocessing we select it out (using `>next`) and return it.

Now we can assemble the pieces:

```
(define greatest-common-divisor
  (pipe greater-and-lesser
        (pipe (iterate divisible-by? (dispatch >next mod)) >next)))
```

This algorithm finds the greatest common divisor very quickly, even if the arguments it receives are gigantic.

---

divisible-by?   (afp arithmetic)
integer, integer $\rightarrow$ *Boolean*
dividend candidate
Determine whether `dividend` is evenly divisible by `candidate`.
Precondition: `candidate` is not 0.

greater-and-lesser   (afp arithmetic)
number number $\rightarrow$ *number, number*
left   right
Return both arguments, the greater one first.

greatest-common-divisor   (afp arithmetic)
natural-number natural-number $\rightarrow$ *natural-number*
left   right
Compute the greatest positive integer that is a divisor of both `left` and `right`.
Precondition: `left` is positive.
Precondition: `right` is positive.

Exercises

2.7–1 Use Euclid's algorithm to compute the greatest common divisor of 1152 and 1280 without the use of a computer.

2.7–2 How many times is the `mod` procedure invoked during the determination of the greatest common divisor of 1152 and 1280 using the brute-force procedure from the beginning of this section? How many times is it invoked if Euclid's algorithm is used?

2.7–3 Show that the preprocessing adapter in our implementation of Euclid's algorithm is superfluous, in the sense that we would always get the same result using the simpler definition

```
(define greatest-common-divisor
  (pipe (iterate divisible-by? (dispatch >next mod)) >next))
```

(Hint: If we don't observe the precondition that the first argument to the iterator be greater than or equal to the second, what happens during the first division, when a lesser number is divided by a greater one?)

2.8   Raised Boolean Procedures

Operating on Booleans and on Predicates

Since there are only two Boolean values, the repertoire of useful basic operations on them is small. We'll need only the not and boolean=? procedures introduced in §1.7, both of which are predefined in the Scheme base library.

Often, however, we'll have occasion to use analogues of Boolean operations "one level up," applying them to predicates to form new predicates. For instance, we can write a higher-level procedure, analogous to the not procedure on Boolean values, that receives a predicate and returns a reversed-polarity predicate, satisfied by exactly those values that do not satisfy the original predicate:

```
(define (^not condition-met?)
  (pipe condition-met? not))
```

For instance, (^not zero?) is a predicate that tests whether a number is non-zero, and (^not odd?) is the same procedure as even?. (Note that the preconditions of the reversed predicate are the same as those of the original predicate. It is just as nonsensical to apply (^not zero?) to a value that is not a number at all as to apply zero? itself to such a value.)

Although and and or are syntactic keywords rather than names for procedures, we can write procedures to implement the analogous operations on predicates. Initially, we'll write only the binary versions, ^et and ^vel (*et* and *vel* are the Latin words for "and" and "or," respectively). In §3.7, we'll see how to extend these binary procedures to variable-arity versions.

```
(define (^et left-condition-met? right-condition-met?)
  (lambda arguments
    (and (apply left-condition-met? arguments)
         (apply right-condition-met? arguments))))
```

```
(define (^vel left-condition-met? right-condition-met?)
  (lambda arguments
    (or (apply left-condition-met? arguments)
        (apply right-condition-met? arguments))))
```

The ^if Procedure

We can similarly raise the structure of an if-expression to an ^if procedure. The ^if procedure receives three arguments, of which the first is a predicate and the other two are procedures; let's call the predicate condition-met? and the procedures consequent and alternate. The value that ^if returns is a procedure that, when invoked, applies condition-met? to the arguments it receives and uses the result to select one of the two procedures, consequent or alternate, to apply to those same arguments.

```
(define (^if condition-met? consequent alternate)
  (lambda arguments
    (if (apply condition-met? arguments)
        (apply consequent arguments)
        (apply alternate arguments))))
```

For instance, we can define a procedure to find the *disparity* between two real numbers—the distance along the number line from the lesser to the greater:

```
(define disparity (^if < (converse -) -))
```

Given the arguments 588 and 920, for instance, disparity invokes the < predicate and determines that 588 is indeed less than 920. Since the result of the test is #t, the consequent procedure, which in this case is (converse -), is selected and applied to the same arguments. The converse procedure arranges for them to be submitted to - in the opposite order, so that the lesser value is subtracted from the greater one.

A more restricted but frequently encountered variation of ^if modifies a given procedure of one or more arguments by making its operation conditional on some condition that the first argument must satisfy. If the condition is not satisfied, the first argument is ignored and the remaining arguments are returned unchanged.

```
(define (conditionally-combine combine? combiner)
  (lambda (initial . others)
    (if (combine? initial)
        (apply combiner initial others)
        (delist others))))
```

For instance, the value of the procedure call '(conditionally-combine positive? +)' is a procedure that returns the sum of two numbers, on condition that the first one is positive. If the condition fails, the procedure bypasses the addition and returns the second argument unchanged.

---

^not   (afp predicate-operations)
$(\alpha \ldots \rightarrow Boolean) \rightarrow (\alpha \ldots \rightarrow Boolean)$
condition-met?   arguments
Construct a predicate that the elements of arguments satisfy if and only if they do not satisfy condition-met?.
Precondition: condition-met? can receive the elements of arguments.

^et   (afp predicate-operations)
$(\alpha \ldots \rightarrow Boolean), (\alpha \ldots \rightarrow Boolean) \rightarrow (\alpha \ldots \rightarrow Boolean)$
left-condition-met? right-condition-met?   arguments
Construct a predicate that the elements of arguments satisfy if and only if they satisfy both left-condition-met? and right-condition-met?.
Precondition: left-condition-met? can receive the elements of arguments.
Precondition: right-condition-met? can receive the elements of arguments.

^vel   (afp predicate-operations)
$(\alpha \ldots \rightarrow Boolean), (\alpha \ldots \rightarrow Boolean) \rightarrow (\alpha \ldots \rightarrow Boolean)$
left-condition-met? right-condition-met?   arguments
Construct a predicate that the elements of arguments satisfy if and only if they satisfy either left-condition-met? or right-condition-met? (or both).
Precondition: left-condition-met? can receive the elements of arguments.
Precondition: right-condition-met? can receive the elements of arguments.

^if   (afp predicate-operations)
$(\alpha \ldots \rightarrow Boolean), (\alpha \ldots \rightarrow \beta \ldots), (\alpha \ldots \rightarrow \beta \ldots) \rightarrow (\alpha \ldots \rightarrow \beta \ldots)$
condition-met?   consequent   alternate   arguments
Construct a procedure that first applies condition-met? to the elements of arguments. If they satisfy it, then the constructed procedure applies consequent to the elements of arguments and returns the results; if not, then the constructed procedure applies alternate to the elements of arguments and returns the results.
Precondition: condition-met? can receive the elements of arguments.
Precondition: If the elements of arguments satisfy condition-met?, then consequent can receive them.
Precondition: If the elements of arguments do not satisfy condition-met?, then alternate can receive them.

conditionally-combine   (afp predicate-operations)
$(\alpha \rightarrow Boolean), (\alpha, \beta \ldots \rightarrow \beta \ldots) \rightarrow (\alpha, \beta \ldots \rightarrow \beta \ldots)$
combine?   combiner   initial others
Construct a procedure that first applies combine? to initial. If initial satisfies combine?, then the constructed procedure applies combiner to initial and the elements of others and returns the results; if not, the constructed procedure returns the elements of others.
Precondition: combine? can receive initial.
Precondition: If initial satisfies combine?, then combiner can receive initial and the elements of others.

Exercises

2.8–1 Define a unary predicate that can receive any integer and determines whether that integer is divisible by 2, by 3, and by 5, but not by 7. (For instance, 2490 satisfies this predicate, but 2510 and 2520 do not.)

2.8–2 Is there an analogue of disparity that uses division in place of subtraction? Suggest a name for that procedure.

2.8–3 Using ^if, define a procedure safe-expt that can receive two arguments, a number and an integer, and raises the first to the power of the second, just as expt does. However, if the first argument to safe-expt is zero and the second is negative, safe-expt should return the symbol domain-error (unlike expt, which signals an error that interrupts the execution of the program).

2.8–4 Now that we have ^if, we might be tempted to reconsider the definition of iterate (in §2.6), rewriting it more concisely as

```
(define (iterate final? step)
  (rec iterator (^if final? values (pipe step iterator)))))
```

However, this definition fails when iterate is actually invoked, resulting in some cryptic error message such as "#<void> is not a procedure." What's wrong with this definition? (Hint: Think about the conditions under which a rec-expression can establish a recursive local binding, and when that binding becomes available.)

2.9 Natural Numbers and Recursion

Natural numbers occur frequently in descriptions and definitions of algorithms. We use them, for example, to count the number of times some step in a computation is performed, to measure the sizes of data structures, and to enumerate the components of such structures.

The unary predicate natural-number?, which we'll take to be a primitive, determines whether its argument is a natural number. (It is defined in the (afp primitives) library.)

Mathematical Induction

The central importance of this class of numbers derives from the fact that it can be defined recursively. It is the least inclusive class C that satisfies two conditions:

- 0 is a member of C.

- The successor of any member of C is also a member of C.

As an immediate consequence of this definition, we get a *principle of mathematical induction*: If 0 is a member of some class C', and every successor of a member of C' is also a member of C', then every natural number is a member of C'.

Mathematical induction is the organizing principle in the proofs of many theorems about algorithms, theorems that can be formulated as generalizations about natural numbers. To prove that such a theorem holds universally, we prove two lemmas: a *base case* asserting that the theorem holds in the special case of 0, and an *induction step* asserting that if the theorem holds for some natural number k, then it also holds for the successor of k. The principle of mathematical induction links these lemmas to the unconditional conclusion that the theorem holds for every natural number.

For instance, we can use mathematical induction to prove that when the `factorial` procedure (§1.9) is given a natural number n as its argument, it correctly computes the product of the first n positive integers, as advertised:

- *Base case.* Given the argument 0, `factorial` returns 1. By convention, the product of an empty collection of numbers is the identity for multiplication, which is 1. So '(`factorial 0`)' is evaluated correctly.

- *Induction step.* Let k be a natural number, and suppose that the `factorial` procedure correctly computes the product of the first k positive integers. Then, given the successor $k + 1$ as an argument, `factorial` multiplies $k + 1$ by the product of the first k positive integers and returns the result of the multiplication. But $k+1$ times the product of the integers from 1 to k is the product of the integers from 1 to $k + 1$, so `factorial` correctly computes this product as well.

The base case shows that 0 belongs to the class C' of values for which `factorial` computes the correct result. The induction step shows that the successor of any member of C' is also a member of C'. So, by the principle of mathematical induction, every natural number is a member of C'. Thus `factorial` returns the correct answer whenever its argument is a natural number.

Managing Recursion with Natural Numbers

Because of the power of mathematical induction as an organizing principle for proofs, we'll often want to use natural numbers to manage recursions. This section introduces some convenient tools for this purpose.

The most natural way to use the recursive structure of natural numbers as a guide in functional programming is to think of 0 as being mapped to some "base values" that serve as the starting points for the computation and to think of the successor operation as being mapped to a step procedure, which transforms the values in some systematic way to yield an equal number of results. If `base` is a nullary procedure that generates and returns the base values and `step` is a step procedure of the appropriate arity, the general structure will be this:

```
(define (natural-number-mapper nat)
  (if (zero? nat)
      (base)
```

```
(receive recursive-results (natural-number-mapper (sub1 nat))
  (apply step recursive-results))))
```

For instance, if `base` is `(create 1)` and `step` is `double`, the resulting
`natural-number-mapper` procedure is `power-of-two`: It maps 0 to 1, and, for
each step by which we advance from a natural number to its successor, the
`natural-number-mapper` procedure performs another doubling operation.

Abstracting out the `base` and `step` procedures gives us a higher-order procedure that we'll call `fold-natural`:

```
(define (fold-natural base step)
  (rec (natural-number-mapper nat)
    (if (zero? nat)
        (base)
        (receive recursive-results (natural-number-mapper (sub1 nat))
          (apply step recursive-results)))))
```

The structure of the definition of the `fold-natural` procedure may seem
familiar, since it is quite similar to the definition of `recur` (§2.6). In fact, we
could also define `fold-natural` thus:

```
(define (fold-natural base step)
  (recur zero?
    (pipe black-hole base)
    (dispatch identity sub1)
    (pipe >all-but-initial step)))
```

Here `zero?` is the predicate that determines whether we have reached the
base case of the recursion, `(pipe black-hole base)` generates the values to be
returned in the base case, `sub1` is the procedure for "simplifying" any natural
number other than 0, and `(pipe >all-but-initial step)` "integrates" that
natural number with the results of the recursive call to solve the simplified
problem.

For any natural number n, the `natural-number-mapper` procedure that
`fold-natural` constructs returns the results of applying the `step` procedure
n times in succession, starting from the results of invoking the `base` procedure:

- *Base case.* When `natural-number-mapper` receives 0 as its argument,
  it discovers this immediately and invokes `base`, which returns the
  starting values. These are the correct results when the argument to
  `natural-number-mapper` is 0, since the `step` procedure is not supposed
  to be applied to them even once.

- *Induction step.* Let k be a natural number, and suppose, as the hypothesis
  of induction, that when `natural-number-mapper` is given k as its argument,
  it applies the `step` procedure k times in succession, as specified.

Now consider what happens when `natural-number-mapper` is applied to the argument $k + 1$. Since this argument is not 0, the alternative in the `if`-expression is evaluated: 1 is subtracted from the argument, giving k, and `natural-number-mapper` is applied recursively to k. By the hypothesis of induction, the results of this recursive call are the results of k successive applications of `step`. Finally, `natural-number-mapper` applies `step` once more to these intermediate results. Thus `step` is applied $k + 1$ times in succession, as specified.

One of the benefits of using higher-order procedures as tools is that proofs like this one have extraordinary breadth and power. Although it would be possible to give a separate proof by mathematical induction of the correctness of each use of `fold-natural`, as it is invoked to repeat various step procedures, such proofs are really only special cases of the general proof that we have just given. The correctness of an application of `fold-natural` is a corollary of the general proof.

We get a similar advantage in proving that computations eventually terminate and return results. One of the dangers of using `recur`, for instance, is that even if we can guarantee that each invocation of `base?`, `terminal`, `simplify`, and `integrate` eventually finishes its work and returns, we can't immediately conclude that the composite procedure that `recur` constructs is similarly well-behaved. We have to show, in addition, that any possible value of the guide can be reduced, by a finite number of successive applications of `simplify`, to a value that satisfies `base?`. The computation initiated by a call to `fold-natural`, because it conforms to the structure of the natural numbers, can encounter no such problem. If we know that the `base` and `step` procedures always return, then we know that any `natural-number-mapper` does too, by the principle of mathematical induction:

- *Base case.* When `natural-number-mapper` receives 0 as an argument, it need only evaluate (`base`), which (by hypothesis) always returns.

- *Induction step.* Suppose, as the hypothesis of induction, that the `natural-number-mapper` procedure returns when it is given the natural number k as its argument. Now consider what happens when its argument is $k + 1$. The `natural-number-mapper` procedure invokes itself recursively, with k as the argument; by the hypothesis of induction, this call eventually returns values. The `natural-number-mapper` procedure forwards these values to the `step` procedure, which (by hypothesis) also returns. So `natural-number-mapper` returns in this case as well.

In calls to `fold-natural`, the natural number that guides the recursion is a pure counter, playing no other role in the central computation, which may have nothing at all to do with numbers. This is why the `black-hole` and `>all-but-initial` adapters are needed in the second definition of `fold-natural` above: The `base` and `step` procedures have no use for the guide value that `recur` wants to supply, so the adapters discard it.

However, there are cases in which the step procedure needs the value of the counter in some of its computations. The `ply-natural` tool is a recursion manager in which the step procedure receives the counter as an additional argument—its first argument. (In an invocation of `ply-natural`, therefore, we must supply a step procedure that returns one fewer value than it receives.)

```
(define (ply-natural base step)
  (recur zero? (pipe black-hole base) (dispatch identity sub1) step))
```

For instance, the `factorial` procedure can be expressed concisely as

```
(ply-natural (create 1) *)
```

In other words: Taking 1 as the starting value, perform the specified number of multiplications on it, counting as you go and using the counter as the first argument in each multiplication.

Note that no multiplication by 0 occurs in the computation of any factorial, since the `step` procedure is not invoked at all when the value of the counter is 0. The number that is "multiplied in" at each recursive step is always positive, ranging from 1 up to, and including, the argument in the initial call to the recursively defined procedure.

Sometimes it is more convenient for the values supplied to the step procedure to range instead from 0 up to, but *not* including, the initial guide argument. We can achieve this by tweaking that argument with `sub1`:

```
(define (lower-ply-natural base step)
  (ply-natural base (pipe (~initial sub1) step)))
```

The recursions over natural numbers constructed by the `fold-natural`, `ply-natural`, and `lower-ply-natural` procedures correspond to such mathematical notations as the summation operator:

$$\sum_{i=m}^{n} f(i) = f(m) + f(m+1) + \cdots + f(n).$$

To reflect this correspondence more exactly, we can define a higher-order Scheme procedure that receives f, m, and n and computes the sum of the values of f for every natural-number argument from m up to and including n, under the precondition that $m \leq n$. Let's work it out, one piece at a time.

The base case for this recursion occurs when $m = n$, so that the summation covers only one function value, $f(m)$. In that case, we just want to return that function value. Switching over to Scheme so that we can use full identifiers ('function' for f, 'lower-bound' for m, 'upper-bound' for n), the nullary procedure that generates the base-case value will be (create (function lower-bound)).

For the step function, we want to transform the value such as $\sum_{i=m}^{j-1} f(i)$ into the value of $\sum_{i=m}^{j} f(i)$, for any value of j in the range from $m+1$ up to and including n. Looking at the definition of the summation operator, we see that we can do this by adding $f(j)$. The fact that we need the value of a counter in this computation indicates that we should use `ply-natural` or `lower-ply-natural` rather than `fold-natural` as our recursion manager.

However, there's a mismatch in the range of the counter: The one we need is supposed to start at $m+1$, whereas the one that `ply-natural` uses starts at 1 and the one that `lower-ply-natural` uses starts at 0. To accommodate this difference, we'll attach an adapter that adds m (that is, `lower-bound`) to the value of the counter before it is used. It's easy to write the adapter, since we know that the counter will be the first argument to the step procedure: It's `(~initial (sect + <> lower-bound))`.

Once this tweak has been carried out, the step procedure applies f to the (tweaked) value of the counter and adds the result to the result of the recursive call. We could write a one-of-a-kind `lambda`-expression to express this operation:

```
(lambda (tweaked-counter recursive-result)
  (+ (function tweaked-counter) recursive-result))
```

But this is a familiar pattern of nested invocation. In fact, it's the `~initial` pattern again: `(pipe (~initial function) +)`. Another way of looking at the overall structure is to think of `ply-natural`'s implicit counter as needing two tweaks in succession: the first to add m to it, and the second to apply f to the result. So the overall step procedure will be

```
(pipe (~initial (sect + <> lower-bound))
      (pipe (~initial function) +))
```

Since we have our base and step procedures, we can now proceed to construct the recursive procedure that we need with `ply-natural`:

```
(ply-natural (create (function lower-bound))
             (pipe (~initial (sect + <> lower-bound))
                   (pipe (~initial function) +)))
```

The remaining component in the definition of a `summation` procedure is to use n to work out how many function values have to be added in (or, in other words, how many times the step procedure needs to be invoked). When $n = m$, the answer is 0 (the base value $f(m)$ is returned immediately, and the step procedure is never invoked at all); when $n = m + 1$, the number of invocations of the step procedure is 1, and so on. So the guide argument that controls the number of step invocations is simply $n - m$.

We can now assemble these pieces to get the definition of `summation`:

```
(define (summation function lower-bound upper-bound)
  ((ply-natural (create (function lower-bound))
                (pipe (~initial (sect + <> lower-bound))
                      (pipe (~initial function) +)))
   (- upper-bound lower-bound)))
```

Expanding the calls to those higher-level procedures, one could also write essentially the same definition in the more fluid style discussed in §2.6, thus:

```
(define (summation function lower-bound upper-bound)
  ((rec (summer counter)
     (if (zero? counter)
         (function lower-bound)
         (+ (function (+ counter lower-bound)) (summer (sub1 counter)))))
   (- upper-bound lower-bound)))
```

This is not quite as concise as our definition, and it obliges the programmer to think up two additional local names ('summer' and 'counter'), but it seems "grounded" in comparison, since most of the operations work on numbers rather than on functions. From the *programmer's* point of view, what are the advantages of using the higher-order constructions?

The answer begins with the fact, mentioned in the earlier discussion of the functional style, that the first definition is more modular than the second. It separates out the parts of the code that deal with managing the recursion, testing the counter, and adjusting it for the recursive call, allowing us to program and test these components separately. Having once written any of those pieces of code, we don't need to write them again every time the same pattern appears.

More importantly, however, we don't have to *prove it correct* all over again every time we use it. With fold-natural or ply-natural managing the recursion, the task of proving that our procedure terminates and returns the specified results reduces to the relatively easy task of showing that our base and step procedures terminate with correct results.

Tallying

The recursion managers in the preceding section used a given natural number to guide the recursion, reflecting in the code the recursive structure of the natural numbers. Sometimes, however, we want a natural number as the *result* of a procedure, and we take advantage of the recursive structure of the natural numbers in *constructing* this result, returning 0 in some base case and the successor of the result of a recursive call otherwise. The idea is that the value returned by such a procedure constitutes a *tally* of the steps traversed before the base case is reached.

A tallying procedure therefore depends on two other procedures: a predicate that distinguishes the base cases from those in which a recursive call is needed, and a step procedure that transforms any additional arguments in the currently

executing procedure into the appropriate arguments to be submitted to that
recursive call.

```
(define (tally final? step)
  (rec (tallier .  arguments)
    (if (apply final? arguments)
        0
        (add1 (apply (pipe step tallier) arguments)))))
```

The `tallier` procedure that `tally` returns can receive any number of arguments. If these arguments satisfy `final?`, `tallier` immediately returns 0. If
not, it applies the `step` procedure to those arguments and feeds the results into
a recursive call to itself. The successor of whatever natural number the recursive
call returns becomes the result of the original call to `tallier`.

In a way, `tally` is the opposite of `fold-natural`: Where `fold-natural` constructs and returns procedures that map natural numbers to the results of applying a step procedure the specified number of times, the `tally` procedure
constructs and returns procedures that map results of the step procedure to
natural numbers, counting the number of applications of the step procedure it
took to produce those results.

Unlike `fold-natural` and its variants, `tally` may fail to terminate, if the
`step` procedure never produces results that satisfy `final?`. The principle of
mathematical induction does not guarantee that a procedure that tries to construct a natural number by building *upwards from 0* will ever complete its work.
Nevertheless, the `tally` procedure is quite useful, because we can often prove
in some other way that the `step` procedure must eventually produce results
satisfying `final?`.

For instance, the `ceiling-of-log-two` procedure from §2.6 is a tallying procedure, counting the number of times `double` can be applied, starting from 1,
before it produces a result that equals or exceeds `bound`. We can use `tally` to
define it thus:

```
(define (ceiling-of-log-two bound)
  ((tally (sect <= bound <>) double) 1))
```

No matter what `bound` is, repeated doubling (starting from 1) eventually generates a result that exceeds it, so this particular tallier always terminates.

Just as `fold-natural` can be defined concisely using `recur`, we can define
`tally` concisely using `build`:

```
(define (tally final? step)
  (build final? (constant 0) values? step (pipe >next add1)))
```

"If the arguments satisfy `final?`, return 0; otherwise, add 1 to the result of the
recursive call on the results of applying `step` to the arguments." (In this case,
no "local" processing is needed, so the `values?` procedure is used to generate a
dummy value, which (pipe >next add1) ignores.)

Sometimes, instead of tallying the steps that the recursive procedure takes before reaching the base case, we wish to find out how many times some particular condition is satisfied along the way. If we can formulate the condition as a predicate, it's easy to adapt the code for `tally` to get a *conditional tallier*:

```
(define (conditionally-tally final? condition-met? step)
  (build final?
         (constant 0)
         condition-met?
         step
         (conditionally-combine identity (pipe >next add1))))
```

This time, when the tallier receives the result of a recursive call, it does not automatically return the successor of that result. Instead, it applies `condition-met?`, and increments the count only if the predicate is satisfied.

Bounded Generalization

Another common application of recursion over natural numbers starts with a predicate that expresses a property of natural numbers taken singly and *generalizes* that predicate. The result of this generalization is a new predicate that tests whether *all* of the natural numbers up to (but not including) some upper bound satisfy the original predicate:

```
(define (for-all-less-than condition-met?)
  (lambda (exclusive-upper-bound)
    ((check (sect = <> exclusive-upper-bound) condition-met? add1) 0)))
```

An alternative generalization tests whether *any* of the natural numbers less than the upper bound satisfies the given predicate, returning #t if there is even one such number. The strategy is to build on `for-all-less-then`, using ^not to reverse the polarity of the given predicate going in. The `for-all-less-than` checks whether all of the lesser natural numbers *fail* to satisfy the original predicate, returning #t if they *all* fail). We can then reverse the polarity of the constructed predicate again at the end of the process, so that the finished predicate returns #f if all the natural numbers fail to satisfy the given predicate, #t if any one of them succeeds.

```
(define exists-less-than (pipe ^not (pipe for-all-less-than ^not)))
```

---

fold-natural   (afp natural-numbers)
$(\rightarrow \alpha \ldots), (\alpha \ldots \rightarrow \alpha \ldots) \rightarrow (natural\text{-}number \rightarrow \alpha \ldots)$
base   step   nat
Construct a procedure that returns the results of invoking base if nat is 0. If nat is non-zero, the constructed procedure applies itself recursively to the predecessor of nat and returns the results of applying step to nat and the results of the recursive invocation.

Precondition: step can receive the results of an invocation of base.
Precondition: step can receive the results of any invocation of step.

ply-natural   (afp natural-numbers)
$(\rightarrow \alpha \ldots)$, $(natural\text{-}number, \alpha \ldots \rightarrow \alpha \ldots)$ $\rightarrow$ $(natural\text{-}number \rightarrow \alpha \ldots)$
base   step   nat
Construct a procedure that returns the results of invoking base if nat is 0. If nat is non-zero,
the constructed procedure applies itself recursively to the predecessor of nat and returns the
results of applying step to the results of the recursive invocation.
Precondition: step can receive 1 and the results of an invocation of base.
Precondition: step can receive any natural number greater than 1 and the results of any
invocation of step.

lower-ply-natural   (afp natural-numbers)
$(\rightarrow \alpha \ldots)$, $(natural\text{-}number, \alpha \ldots \rightarrow \alpha \ldots)$ $\rightarrow$ $(natural\text{-}number \rightarrow \alpha \ldots)$
base   step   nat
Construct a procedure that returns the results of invoking base if nat is 0. If nat is non-zero,
the constructed procedure applies itself recursively to the predecessor of nat and returns the
results of applying step to the results of the recursive invocation.
Precondition: step can receive 0 and the results of an invocation of base.
Precondition: step can receive any positive integer and the results of any invocation of step.

summation   (afp natural-numbers)
$(integer \rightarrow number)$, $integer$, $integer \rightarrow number$
function   lower   upper
Compute the sum of the results of applying function to all of the integers from lower up to
and including upper.
Precondition: function can receive any integer in the range from lower up to and including
upper.
Precondition: lower is less than or equal to upper.

tally   (afp natural-numbers)
$(\alpha \ldots \rightarrow Boolean)$, $(\alpha \ldots \rightarrow \alpha \ldots)$ $\rightarrow$ $(\alpha \ldots \rightarrow natural\text{-}number)$
final?   step   arguments
Construct a procedure that returns 0 if the elements of arguments satisfy final?; otherwise, the
constructed procedure applies step to those elements, applies itself recursively to the results,
and returns the successor of the result.
Precondition: final? can receive the elements of arguments.
Precondition: final? can receive the results of any invocation of step.
Precondition: If the elements of arguments do not satisfy final?, then step can receive them.
Precondition: If the results of an invocation of step do not satisfy final?, then step can
receive them.

conditionally-tally   (afp natural-numbers)
$(\alpha \ldots \rightarrow Boolean)$, $(\alpha \ldots \rightarrow Boolean)$, $(\alpha \ldots \rightarrow \alpha \ldots)$ $\rightarrow$
final?   condition-met?   step

$(\alpha \ldots \rightarrow natural\text{-}number)$
arguments
Construct a procedure that returns 0 if the elements of arguments satisfy final?; otherwise,
the constructed procedure checks whether those elements satisfy condition-met?, then applies
step to those elements, applies itself recursively to the results, and returns either the successor
of the result (if the elements satisfied condition-met?) or the result itself (if they did not).
Precondition: final? can receive the elements of arguments.
Precondition: final? can receive the results of any invocation of step.
Precondition: If the elements of arguments do not satisfy final?, then condition-met? can
receive them.
Precondition: If the results of an invocation of step do not satisfy final?, then condition-met?
can receive them.
Precondition: If the elements of arguments do not satisfy final?, then step can receive them.
Precondition: If the results of an invocation of step do not satisfy final?, then step can
receive them.

for-all-less-than   (afp natural-numbers)
(natural-number → *Boolean)* → *(natural-number* → *Boolean)*
condition-met?   exclusive-upper-bound
Construct a predicate that determines whether every natural number strictly less than
exclusive-upper-bound satisfies condition-met?.
Precondition: condition-met? can receive any natural number less than exclusive-upper-bound.

exists-less-than   (afp natural-numbers)
(natural-number → *Boolean)* → *(natural-number* → *Boolean)*
condition-met?   exclusive-upper-bound
Construct a predicate that determines whether at least one natural number less than
exclusive-upper-bound satisfies condition-met?.
Precondition: condition-met? can receive any natural number less than exclusive-upper-bound.

Exercises

2.9–1   Define a unary procedure divisibility-tester that receives a natural number as its argument and determines how many natural numbers less than the given natural number are evenly divisible by 3 and 7 but not by 5.

2.9–2   Find the sum of all the odd natural numbers less than 2^{16}.

2.9–3   Define a recursion manager repeat that receives a procedure and a natural number and returns a procedure that applies the given procedure to its argument or arguments repeatedly, with the natural number determining the number of successive applications. (For instance, (repeat square 3) should be a procedure that computes the square of the square of the square of its argument, that is, its eighth power, and (repeat >all-but-initial 5) should be an adapter that discards its first five arguments and returns all of the others as separate results.)

2.9–4   Define a unary predicate prime? that determines whether a given integer greater than or equal to 2 is prime, that is, whether none of the integers greater than 1 and less than itself evenly divides it. (For instance, 11 is prime, because none of the integers $2, 3, \ldots, 10$ is a divisor of 11; but 221 is not prime, because 13 is a divisor of 221.)

Chapter 3

Data Structures

In addition to the simple values that we've encountered so far, many of the algorithms that we'll study operate on composite values, data structures, that contain other values as components and provide specific kinds of access to those other values. Scheme provides a few kinds of data structures as primitive (including lists, which we have also encountered above). We'll use these to build the others that we need. This approach will enable us to be sure that the structures always meet certain side conditions, called *invariants*, that are needed in proofs of correctness.

3.1   Modeling

In designing data structures and the procedures that operate on them, we'll develop an elementary type theory to describe the new values. Type theory often prescribes or suggests design patterns to simplify programs that operate with values that belong to the same type.

To *model* a type is to establish a correspondence between values of that type and values of types that are simpler or better understood, either because they are directly supported in our programming language or because we have previously, in turn, modeled them. The goal of modeling is again to simplify and clarify programs and correctness proofs, by relating novel types of data to ones that we already know how to talk about and program with.

Often a model takes the form of a collection of procedures that correspond to primitive procedures for operating on values of the modeled type. Once these definitions are in place, we can subsequently use them as if we were operating with the actual values of the modeled type. To make this pretense even minimally plausible, however, we have to ensure that our contrived pseudo-primitives satisfy axioms that describe how the primitives of the modeled type are supposed to interact, converting those axioms into theorems about the actual values that we're using to implement them.

© Springer-Verlag GmbH Germany, part of Springer Nature 2018
J. D. Stone, *Algorithms for Functional Programming*,
https://doi.org/10.1007/978-3-662-57970-1_3

The pseudo-primitives in a model for a data structure type generally include one or more *constructors*, for creating values that represent the values of the modeled type; one or more *selectors*, for recovering components from the structure; a *classification predicate* that distinguishes the values that represent values of the modeled type from those that do not; and an *equality predicate*, a binary predicate that determines whether its arguments represent the same value of the modeled type.

A programmer who uses models is sometimes tempted to break the pretense, writing a procedure that exploits her knowledge of the correspondence in order to take a short cut around the limited repertoire of operations provided by the pseudo-primitives. There is a trade-off between the greater reliability and maintainability of code that respects the model and the greater speed and more economical use of resources that one can sometimes achieve by breaking it. Both in theory and in practice, however, it is imprudent to break the model on the basis of the *speculation* that the short-cut code will be faster or consume less memory, since such speculations are often incorrect. The would-be model-breaker should be prepared to support his proposal with evidence as well as reasoning.

Exercises

3.1–1   If a type is not supported as a primitive in a particular programming language, it is almost always possible to built a suitable model for it.   But the values that such a model provides typically have implementation-specific characteristics that don't reflect or represent any characteristics of values of the type being modeled. (For instance, such a value may satisfy not only the type predicate defined for the data type that is being modeled but also the type predicate for the value that models it in the implementation.) How should programmers who wish to use such models accommodate this disparity? How, if at all, does this disparity affect the utility and power of the model?

3.1–2   If a type is not supported as a primitive in a particular programming language, it is almost always possible to built several different models for it, inconsistent with one another but each internally consistent as a representation for values of the type being modeled. How should a programmer choose among different models for the same type?

3.2   The Null Value

Let's begin with an extremely simple type, a type that has only one value in it. In order to develop algorithms with this type, we'll need only the most basic operations: a way to construct or name its unique value (which might be a literal, a predefined name, or a nullary procedure that returns it), and a way to distinguish this value from values of any other type.

Scheme provides a "null" data type that fits this description. The Scheme literal for the unique value of the null data type is ''()'. However, since this notation is neither readable nor intuitive, we'll use the identifier 'null' to express it instead. (I've defined this name in the (afp primitives) library.) The primitive classification predicate null? returns #t if its argument is null and #f if its argument is any other value.

The null type needs no selectors, since it has no internal structure. In this case, it would be pointless to provide an equality predicate: Since null is always equal to itself, the predicate would always return #t.

Conventionally, null indicates absence or emptiness inside some larger data structure—a list with no elements, for instance.

---

null   (afp primitives)
null
The null value.

null?   (scheme base)
any   → *Boolean*
something
Determine whether something is null.

Exercises

3.2–1 If Scheme did not provide a null value, we could model it with a symbol, say 'nil. Write definitions for two procedures to implement this model: a nullary constructor make-new-null and a classification predicate new-null?.

3.2–2 For Scheme programmers: The standard library (scheme base) supplies another type that contains only one value, the *end-of-file object*. How can the programmer name or express this value? How can she distinguish it from values of any other type?

3.3 Sum Types

Enumerations

If the number of values in a type is finite, and the values themselves have no internal structure, one simple way to define the type is to produce a roster (called an *enumeration* of the values), each of which must have its own name. For instance, an enumeration of the four suits in a deck of playing cards defines a "suit" type:

$$suit \ = \ clubs \mid diamonds \mid hearts \mid spades$$

To implement this type in Scheme, we might use a symbol to stand for each suit, and supply a classification predicate suit? for the type:

```
(define (suit? something)
  (and (symbol? something)
       (or (symbol=? something 'clubs)
           (symbol=? something 'diamonds)
           (symbol=? something 'hearts)
           (symbol=? something 'spades))))
```

Constructors and selectors for enumerations are unnecessary, but we could use an equality predicate:

```
(define suit=? symbol=?)
```

Scheme's built-in Boolean and character types are also, in effect, enumerations:

$$Boolean = \text{\#f} \mid \text{\#t}$$
$$character = \text{\#\textbackslash null} \mid \text{\#\textbackslash x1} \mid \ldots \mid \text{\#\textbackslash x10ffff}$$

(The roster of characters comprises more than a million values, so I haven't shown it in full here.)

Discriminated Union

If we think of each of the individual values in an enumeration as having a unique type of its own, on the analogy of null, then the enumeration is the *discriminated union* of those types, that is, a set comprising all of the values from the types that it collects, together with a way to determine which of the types so collected each value belongs to. In enumerations, the discrimination step is trivial: Each value has its own unique type, so knowing the value uniquely determines the original type.

However, the operation of taking a discriminated union (symbolized in the type equations above by the vertical bar, '|') can be applied to any types, not just to one-element types like *diamonds* or the null type. For instance, we might form a *character-or-Boolean* type as a discriminated union:

$$character\text{-}or\text{-}Boolean = character \mid Boolean$$

In this case, we can simply use the character and Boolean values to implement themselves inside this new type, and the primitive char? and boolean? predicates to determine which of the source types a given value comes from. The classification and equality predicates for the type are also easy to define:

```
(define character-or-Boolean? (^vel char? boolean?))
(define (character-or-Boolean=? left right)
  (or (and (char? left)
           (char? right)
           (char=? left right))
```

```
      (and (boolean? left)
           (boolean? right)
           (boolean=? left right))))
```

This simple strategy won't work unless the types that are being collected into the discriminated union are disjoint. For instance, suppose that we wanted to have a type somewhat similar to Booleans, but with the possibility of expressing either a confident, strongly held answer (which might be either affirmative or negative) or a tentative, weakly held answer (which might also be either affirmative or negative). The "confident" values are Boolean, and so are the "diffident" ones, but we want them to be *different kinds* of Booleans in our new data type:

$$survey\text{-}response \; = \; Boolean \mid Boolean$$

In a model for the *survey-response* type, we won't be able to use the Booleans just to stand for themselves, because we wouldn't be able to distinguish #t that belongs to the "confident" Boolean type on the left-hand side of the vertical bar from #t that belongs to the "diffident" Boolean type on the right-hand side. One way to implement this type would be to choose completely different values as representations—the natural numbers 0, 1, 2, and 3, perhaps, with 0 and 1 standing for the confident negative and affirmative answers, respectively, and 2 and 3 for the diffident ones. The construction procedures would then convert values of the source type (in each case, Boolean) into the representations of values of the *survey-response* type:

```
(define (make-confident-survey-response b)
  (if b 1 0))
(define (make-diffident-survey-response b)
  (if b 3 2))
```

The classification and equality predicates are straightforward:

```
(define survey-response? (^et natural-number? (sect < <> 4)))
(define survey-response=? =)
```

In this model, the *discrimination predicates* for distinguishing values of the confident Boolean type from values of the diffident Boolean type perform numeric comparisons:

```
(define confident? (sect < <> 2))
(define diffident? (sect <= 2 <>))
```

To complete the model, we'll also want *projections* that map values of the *survey-response* type back into the underlying Boolean values. In this case, we've cleverly chosen the numeric representations so that the same procedure can be used to project either a confident or a diffident value:

```
(define survey-response->Boolean odd?)
```

As an example of the application of these procedures, let's define a procedure negate, which turns any value of the *survey-response* type into the opposite value at the same confidence level:

```
(define negate
  (let ((reverse-polarity (pipe survey-response->Boolean not)))
    (^if confident?
         (pipe reverse-polarity make-confident-survey-response)
         (pipe reverse-polarity make-diffident-survey-response))))
```

A type that is constructed by forming a discriminated union of types is called a *sum type*. In §3.4, we'll see a more systematic way to implement sum types.

Recursive Type Equations

In the preceding examples, our descriptions of types have taken the form of *type equations* in which the name of the type to be specified appears on the left of the equals sign and an expression describing the construction of the type appears on its right.

We can also think of type equations in which arbitrary expressions occur on both sides of the equals sign, formulating conditions that the type that we're trying to specify should meet. In general, it is possible for such equations to impose inconsistent conditions that no type could meet, or conditions so weak that any type could meet them. Sometimes, however, a type equation captures the structure of a type, even a type that has infinitely many values and so could not be specified by enumeration.

For instance, the natural numbers, as a type, constitute a solution to the type equation

$$nn \;=\; z \mid nn,$$

where z is a type that includes only 0 and we distinguish each of the values on the right-hand side of the discriminated union by adding 1 to it! The type equation then says, in effect, that every natural number is either 0 or the result of adding 1 to a natural number—which is essentially how we defined the class of natural numbers in §2.9. Our natural-number? predicate is the classification predicate for this type, = is the equality predicate, the zero? and positive? predicates distinguish the source types in the discriminated union, and sub1 is the projection that maps any positive natural number back into the nn type on the right-hand side of the discriminated union.

Exercises

3.3–1 A typical traffic signal lamp operating in the United States displays one of three colored lights: red, amber, or green. Write the type equation for an enumeration that includes these three colors, and implement a type predicate for the enumeration in Scheme.

3.3–2 Alternative implementations of the *survey-response* type might use different values to stand for values of that type. For instance, one might use the symbols yes! and no! for the confident values and maybe-so and maybe-not for the diffident ones, or the integers 2 and −2 for the confident values and 1 and −1 for the diffident ones. Choose one of these implementations, or contrive your own, and implement the pseudo-primitive procedures:

```
make-confident-survey-response
make-diffident-survey-response
survey-response?
survey-response=?
confident?
diffident?
survey-response->Boolean
```

If you do this correctly, it won't be necessary to define negate again—the definition given above will work without modification.

3.3–3 Show that negative integers, as a type, can also model the type equation for *nn*. What is the model for the *z* type in this interpretation?

3.4 Pairs

Scheme also supports the *pair* type. A pair is a data structure that consists of exactly two values. A pair is often depicted as a rectangle with a vertical partition in the middle, separating the value in the left-hand compartment from the value in the right-hand compartment. The compartments are distinguishable, and so Scheme's pairs are ordered. No restrictions are imposed on the nature of the values that pairs contain. In particular, either or each of them may itself be a pair.

The primitive classification predicate pair? determines whether its argument is a pair.

The primitive procedure cons receives two arguments and returns a pair containing them. The name cons is short for "construct," reflecting the fact that cons is the constructor for pairs.

There are two primitive selectors for pairs: The car selector returns the value in the left compartment of a given pair, and the cdr selector returns the one in the right compartment.[1]

---

[1]The processor in the machine on which these procedures were first implemented contained a register of which the left half was often used for the hardware addresses of memory locations, and the right half for quantities to be subtracted from addresses, called *decrements*. The register as a whole was also large enough to contain (on other occasions) a pair, with each

Scheme does not provide a selector that returns *both* of the components of a pair, but we can easily define one:

```
(define decons (dispatch car cdr))
```

We'll also need a predicate that determines whether two given pairs are the same, in the sense that their components are the same and occur in the same order. Since the components of pairs can be of any type, we'll use equal? to compare them. Our equality predicate for pairs, then, will be

```
(define pair=? (^et (compare-by car equal?) (compare-by cdr equal?)))
```

As we noted in §1.7, there is no algorithm for testing whether two procedure values are the same. Our use of equal? implies that pair=? is just as unreliable when applied to pairs containing procedures as equal? itself is when applied to procedures.

Naming Pairs

Most interactive environments for Scheme display pairs by enclosing text representations of their components in parentheses and placing a full stop between them. For instance, a pair with the integer 425 as its car and the integer 50 as its cdr would appear as '(425 . 50)'. To refer to pairs in this text, however, we'll use expressions that, in Scheme programs, would be calls to their constructors—'(cons 425 50)' to refer to the pair just mentioned, for instance. The rationale for this decision is that constructor expressions are more readable and better suited to expository prose than the dotted-pair syntax. There is a surprising amount of disagreement among implementers of Scheme about how data structures should be displayed, so readers should in any case be prepared to adjust to different conventions in different contexts.

We'll also use constructor expressions for other data structures, without worrying about how interactive Scheme implementations would display those values.

Product Types

A *product type* is formed by combining values of its source types by packing them into structures rather than as alternatives in a union, as sum types do. For instance, each value in the product type formed from the character and Boolean types contains a character *and* a Boolean. (Recall that, in the sum type, each value was a character *or* a Boolean.) In type equations, the symbol

---

half containing the hardware address at which one of the pair's components was stored. The names car and cdr are acronyms for "contents of address register" and "contents of decrement register." Now steeped in tradition, these names are so widely used that we'll retain them, as Scheme's designers did, in spite of their artificiality.

'×' expresses the operation of forming a product type. For instance, we might write

$$character\text{-}and\text{-}Boolean = character \times Boolean$$

to specify the type just described.

In fact, the *pair* data type is the most general of all product types. It behaves as if it were specified by a type equation

$$pair = any \times any,$$

where *any* is a sum type that encompasses all of the values that can be expressed in Scheme:

$$any = Boolean \mid number \mid character \mid symbol \mid string \mid procedure \mid \ldots$$

The second of these isn't really a valid type equation, since its right-hand side is incomplete, and so it doesn't really specify an *any* type. Recall that we use '*any*' as a type variable, implying compatibility with any value that we can name or compute. The idea is that any value can appear as either component of a pair.

Thus Scheme pairs are flexible enough to implement any product type, and if we like we can use the pair constructors and selectors as pseudo-primitives for any such type, although we may want to give them more specialized names:

```
(define make-character-and-Boolean cons)
(define select-character car)
(define select-Boolean cdr)
```

Pairs also provide straightforward implementations of the classification and equality predicates in a product type:

```
(define character-and-Boolean? (^et pair? (^et (pipe car char?)
                                               (pipe cdr boolean?))))
(define character-and-Boolean=? (^et (compare-by car char=?)
                                     (compare-by cdr boolean=?)))
```

Discriminated Unions Reconsidered

Using pairs, we can also provide a more systematic and general way to implement discriminated unions in Scheme, even when the types that we are trying to bring together overlap: The values of the sum type can be pairs, with the cdr of each pair containing a value from one of the source types and the car containing some value that identifies which source type it was. This distinguishing value could be a symbol, perhaps, or even a Boolean if there are only two source types. Under this approach, the values of the *survey-response* type from §3.3 would be implemented as pairs, with the car being a symbol—confident or diffident, say—as the distinguishing value, and the cdr being the actual value from the source type, which in this case is Boolean:

```
(define make-confident-survey-response (sect cons 'confident <>))
(define make-diffident-survey-response (sect cons 'diffident <>))
(define survey-response?
  (^et pair? (^et (pipe car (^et symbol?
                              (^vel (sect symbol=? <> 'confident)
                                    (sect symbol=? <> 'diffident))))
                  (pipe cdr boolean?))))
(define survey-response=? (^et (compare-by car symbol=?)
                               (compare-by cdr boolean=?)))
(define confident? (pipe car (sect symbol=? <> 'confident)))
(define diffident? (pipe car (sect symbol=? <> 'diffident)))
(define survey-response->Boolean cdr)
```

Since it uses the model's primitives without relying on any features of the implementation, the definition of the negate procedure from §3.3 works under the new model without modification.

Reimplementing Natural Numbers

Similarly, if Scheme did not provide natural numbers as primitives, we could construct a suitable implementation using pairs, following the type equation $nn = z \mid nn$. This time we need two constructors, a nullary one to create the base value (representing the natural number 0) and a unary one that receives any of our artificial natural numbers and returns its successor:

```
(define make-new-zero (create (cons 'z 'z)))
(define make-new-successor (sect cons 'nn <>))
```

It doesn't make any difference what the second component of the pair that represents 0 is, so I've arbitrarily used the symbol z both in the car (to indicate the source type z) and in the cdr (to signify the one and only value of that source type).

Thus our replacement for 0 is (cons 'z 'z), 1 is (cons 'nn (cons 'z 'z)), 2 is (cons 'nn (cons 'nn (cons 'z 'z))), 3 is (cons 'nn (cons 'nn (cons 'nn (cons 'z 'z)))), and so on. In practice, this is an inefficient way to represent natural numbers. Nevertheless, it is instructive to see how straightforward it would be to implement the basic arithmetic operations and the recursion managers that we developed in §2.9. Let's look at a few of the definitions.

In place of the primitive natural-number? predicate, we'd need one that makes sure that we have a pair that is correctly structured:

```
(define (new-natural-number? something)
  (and (pair? something)
       (symbol? (car something))
       (or (and (symbol=? (car something) 'z)
                (symbol=? (cdr something) 'z))
```

```
          (and (symbol=? (car something) 'nn)
               (new-natural-number? (cdr something))))))
```

Note that we use a recursive call to make sure that the cdr of a non-"zero" value is itself a valid natural-number replacement.

The primitives zero? and positive? have simple reimplementations, as discriminator predicates for the sum type:

```
(define new-zero? (pipe car (sect symbol=? <> 'z)))
(define new-positive? (pipe car (sect symbol=? <> 'nn)))
```

The new add1 is just our make-new-successor constructor, and the new sub1 procedure is the projection procedure for the right-hand side of the sum type. This implies that the replacement for the sub1 procedure has a precondition: Its argument must be "positive."

```
(define new-add1 make-new-successor)
(define new-sub1 cdr)
```

We can use the recursion manager check to define the equality predicate for our representations of natural numbers:

```
(define new-= (check (^et (pipe >initial new-zero?)
                          (pipe >next new-zero?))
                     (^et (pipe >initial new-positive?)
                          (pipe >next new-positive?))
                     (~each new-sub1)))
```

With new-zero? and new-sub1 as drop-in replacements for zero? and sub1, it's trivial to adapt fold-natural:

```
(define (new-fold-natural base step)
  (rec (natural-mapper nat)
    (if (new-zero? nat)
        (base)
        (receive recursive-results (natural-mapper (new-sub1 nat))
          (apply step recursive-results)))))
```

Note that, when we call a recursive procedure that new-fold-natural has constructed, we must give it one of our replacement natural numbers as its argument. It can't receive ordinary natural numbers even if they are available.

We can construct replacements for the remaining arithmetic primitives using new-fold-natural. Here are a few examples:

```
(define (new-+ augend addend)
  ((new-fold-natural (create augend) new-add1) addend))
(define new-even? (new-fold-natural (create #t) not))
(define (new-div-and-mod dividend divisor)
  ((new-fold-natural (create (make-new-zero) (make-new-zero))
                  (^if (pipe >next (pipe new-add1
                                         (sect new-= <> divisor)))
                       (cross new-add1 (constant (make-new-zero)))
                       (cross identity new-add1)))
   dividend))
```

Our new-+ and new-= procedures have fixed arity 2. In §3.7, we'll see how to extend them to variable-arity procedures, so that they too can act as drop-in replacements.

---

pair?   (scheme base)
any   → *Boolean*
something
Determine whether something is a pair.

cons   (scheme base)
α, β → *pair(α, β)*
left right
Construct a pair with left and right as its components.

car   (scheme base)
pair(α, any) → α
pr
Return the left component of pr.

cdr   (scheme base)
pair(any, α) → α
pr
Return the right component of pr.

decons   (afp pairs)
pair(α, β) → α, β
pr
Return both components of pr.

pair=?   (afp pairs)
pair(any, any), *pair(any, any)* → *Boolean*
left   right
Determine whether left and right have the same components, arranged in the same order.

Exercises

3.4–1 Propose an implementation for the *map-coordinate* type defined by

$$map\text{-}coordinate = character \times integer$$

(Think of a map with letters down the side to indicate vertical positions and numbers across the top to indicate horizontal positions. A map coordinate, such as M14, tells you where to look on the map for a feature, such as a town, a campground, or an airport.)

Provide a constructor, appropriate selectors, a classification predicate, and an equality predicate for the implementation that you choose.

3.4–2   Using pairs, implement a data structure that can contain any *three* given values, with a classification predicate `triple?`, an equality predicate `triple=?`, a three-argument constructor `make-triple`, and selectors `fore`, `mid`, and `aft`, as well as a selector `detriple` that returns all three values as separate results.

3.4–3   The × operation by which product types are formed is not commutative. Illustrate this fact by explaining how the values of the product type *character* × *Boolean* differ from those of the product type *Boolean* × *character*.

3.4–4   Is the | operation by which sum types are formed commutative? Justify your answer.

3.4–5   Continue the implementation of the "new" natural-number type by defining the analogues of `odd?`, * (for two arguments), `expt`, `double`, and `square`.

3.4–6   Define a procedure `old->new` that can receive any natural number as argument and returns the corresponding "new" natural number. Define a procedure `new->old` that can receive any "new" natural number and returns the corresponding natural number.

3.4–7   Using the procedures that you defined in the preceding exercise, prove that the result of applying the procedure

```
(pipe (~each old->new) (pipe new-+ new->old))
```

to any natural numbers m and n is $m + n$.

3.5   Boxes

A *box* is a data structure that holds exactly one value. We'll define our own procedures for creating and operating on boxes, taking the opportunity to give another example of the idea of implementation by modeling in a simple and straightforward case.

Using Pairs to Model Boxes

Our model for boxes consists of four procedures: a classification predicate `box?` that distinguishes boxes from other values, an equality predicate `box=?` that determines whether two boxes have the same contents, a constructor `box` that can receive any value and returns a box containing it, and a selector `debox` that can receive any box and returns the value it contains. To count as successful, our model should meet the following conditions:

- The box? procedure can receive any value.

- The box procedure can receive any value.

- Every value returned by box satisfies box?.

- Every value that satisfies box? can be constructed by box, given an appropriate argument.

- The debox procedure can receive any value that satisfies box?.

- For any value v, v is the result of applying debox to the result of applying box to v.

- If each of the values b_0 and b_1 is the result of applying box to the same value, then the result of applying box=? to b_0 and b_1 is #t.

- For any boxes b_0 and b_1, if the result of applying box=? to b_0 and b_1 is #t, then the result of applying debox to b_0 is the same as the result of applying debox to b_1.

We'll often use boxes as results of procedures that can either achieve some intended goal, returning some useful value, or fail in the attempt, returning some indication of the failure. To distinguish successful results from failure indicators, we'll pack the former in boxes before returning them.

If this plan is to work, however, we'll need to be able to distinguish boxes from other values that might be used as failure indicators, such as symbols, numbers, and Booleans. For this reason, we'll add a practical constraint to the list of axioms above:

- No box is a symbol, a number, or a Boolean value.

Without this constraint, it would be trivial to model boxes by simply identifying them with the values they contain, or equivalently imagining that every value carries an invisible box around with it. Then box? could be defined as (lambda (something) #t), box as identity, debox also as identity, and box=? as equal?. This model satisfies all of the other axioms and is computationally efficient, but it's also useless, since it makes everything a box.

We'll avoid this trivialization by choosing a different model, in which the box containing the value v is implemented as a pair in which the car is v and the cdr is null. We can define the basic box procedures thus:

```
(define box (sect cons <> null))

(define box? (^et pair? (pipe cdr null?)))

(define box=? (compare-by car equal?))

(define debox car)
```

The choice of the null value is not of any particular importance here. It is a conventional signal that the right component of the pair is unused.

In the definition of box=?, we again use equal? to compare the contents of two boxes, since boxes can contain values of any type.

---

box   (afp boxes)
$\alpha \qquad \to box(\alpha)$
contents
Construct a box containing contents.

box?   (afp boxes)
any $\qquad \to$ *Boolean*
something
Determine whether something is a box.

box=?   (afp boxes)
box(any), box(any) $\to$ *Boolean*
left   right
Determine whether left and right contain the same value.

debox   (afp boxes)
box(α) $\to \alpha$
bx
Return the contents of bx.

Exercises

3.5–1 Confirm that our implementation of boxes satisfies the itemized specification at the beginning of the section.

3.5–2 Define a safe-reciprocal procedure that receives one argument, a number, and returns #f if the argument is 0, and a box containing the multiplicative inverse of the argument if it is non-zero.

3.5–3 Define an embox-null procedure that receives a natural number as argument and returns the result of applying box the specified number of times in succession, starting with null. (So, for instance, the value of the call '(embox-null 0)' is null, and the value of the call '(embox-null 3)' is (box (box (box null))).

3.5–4 The procedure defined in the preceding exercise suggests another model for the natural numbers, with null representing 0 and box taking the place of the make-successor procedure. How would the other primitive procedures for natural numbers be implemented in this model?

3.6 Lists

It would not be difficult to continue upwards through the possible sizes for linear data structures, describing one for each fixed size and defining the associated type predicate, constructor, selectors, and equality predicate. For instance, one of the exercises in §3.4 is to implement the *triple* type, a three-component analogue of *pair*, and by modifying and extending that design we could successively implement *quadruple*, *quintuple*, and so on.

A better idea, however, is to use a data structure that can hold *any* finite number of values. Scheme has built-in support for such a type, under the name of *list*. We've already seen some of the procedures for lists, in connection with Scheme's mechanism for bundling arguments to variable-arity procedures: the constructor, list, which can receive any number of arguments and returns a list containing them; the selector delist, which receives a list and returns its elements as separate values; and the map procedure, which applies a procedure to corresponding elements of one or more lists and collects the results in a list. Scheme also provides a classification predicate for the *list* type, list?.

In working with these procedures, we can think of *list* as a *sequence type*, defined by the use of a third type operator, *, meaning *all finite sequences of values* of the type on which it operates. For instance, the *natural-number-sequence* type defined by the equation

$$natural\text{-}number\text{-}sequence \quad = \quad natural\text{-}number^*$$

includes all finite sequences of natural numbers, and similarly the values of the type *survey-response** are finite sequences of *survey-response* values. The *list* type is the most general sequence type, and its elements can be of any type, as if specified by the type equation

$$list \quad = \quad any^*$$

However, there is a second way of looking at the *list* type, using a model expressed in the type equation

$$list \quad = \quad null \mid (any \times list)$$

Correspondingly, in the implementation that Scheme supports, a list is either null or a pair in which the second component is also a list.

This structure turns out to be equivalent to the sequence type *any**, because of the universality of pairs. The one and only sequence of length 0 is adequately represented by null. A sequence of length 1 is adequately represented by a box: a pair in which the first component is the element of the sequence and the second component is null. The fundamental idea is to continue this mode of construction: A two-element list is a pair in which the second component is a one-element list; a three-element list is a pair in which the second component is a two-element list; and in general a $(k+1)$-element list is a pair in which the second component is a k-element list. To make room for one more element, we pair it with the list of all the other elements to get a list one size larger.

Since the second type equation provides a way to implement lists using only null and pairs, the *list* type that Scheme provides is not primitive. Instead, most Scheme programmers use the primitive procedures provided for the null value and pairs to work with lists as well. For instance, they use null? to determine whether a given list is the *empty list* (that is, whether it has no elements), car to select the first element of a non-empty list, and so on. For clarity, we'll provide different names for these procedures for use in connection with lists. As we'll sometimes want to think of lists as being defined by the first of the type equations above and sometimes as being defined by the second, a more neutral vocabulary for list procedures is preferable in any case.

The second type equation for *list* is recursive, and reflects a recursive definition of the class of lists, closely analogous to the definition of the class of natural numbers. The class of lists is the least inclusive class C that meets two requirements:

- The value null is a member of C.

- Any pair in which the cdr is a member of C is also a member of C.

Note that a pair is not a list unless its cdr is a list. The value of the expression '(cons 483 379)' is a pair and contains two components, but it is not a two-element list. A two-element list would have a one-element list, not a number, as its cdr. We could construct such a list in either of two ways in Scheme: with nested calls to cons to create the pairs separately, as in '(cons 483 (cons 379 null))', or all at once, with a call to list, as in '(list 483 379)'. These expressions have the same value.

Selection Procedures

When we think of *list* as a sequence type, it is natural to regard each of its elements as equal in status, regardless of its position in the list. Any of the elements should be equally available for selection, by a uniform mechanism. To make it possible for programmers to adopt this view, Scheme provides a selector, list-ref, that receives a list and a natural number and returns the list element at the position denoted by the natural number.

When designating a position in a data structure, a natural number conventionally refers to the number of elements preceding the position designated. In other words, the index of the initial element is 0 (the position is preceded by no others), and that of the final element is the natural number one less than the number of elements in the entire container (its position is preceded by all but one of the container's elements). Giving list-ref a natural number greater than or equal to the number of elements in its list argument is nonsensical, so observing this upper bound on the index is a precondition for invoking list-ref.

However, experienced Scheme programmers tend to avoid calling the list-ref procedure. There are two reasons for this. One is that, in practice, the fact that non-empty lists are really pair-structures affects the performance of the procedure. Recovering the hundredth element of a hundred-element list takes much more computation than recovering its first element, because there is no way to get the hundredth element except by taking the car of the cdr of the cdr of the cdr of ... of the cdr of the pair that represents the list, counting off ninety-nine cdr operations altogether. Pretending that a list is a random-access structure is likely to lead to slow programs unless all the lists that we operate on are short.

A more important consideration, however, is that it is easier to reason about procedures that operate on lists—to prove that such procedures meet their specifications, for instance—if we can take advantage of the recursive structure provided by the pair model. In particular, we can give general inductive arguments, analogous to the mathematical inductions in §2.9, for higher-order operations guided by the structure of a list.

We'll therefore arrange most of our computations on lists so that we inspect and perform computations preferentially on the element at the beginning of a non-empty list. The selector that we'll use most often, therefore, is first, which receives a non-empty list and returns the element at index 0. (It is an error to apply first to the empty list.)

We already had the resources to define first back in Chapter 2:

```
(define first (pipe delist >initial))
```

However, since Scheme represents all non-empty lists as pairs, there is an even simpler definition, which we'll use in practice:

```
(define first car)
```

In other words, first is an alias for car that we use when we're thinking of the value to which we apply it as a list.

Similarly, when we apply cdr to a list, we'll use the alias rest to remind ourselves that we're computing the "rest" of a list, a sublist lacking only the first element.

```
(define rest cdr)
```

The first and rest procedures presuppose that their argument is a list of one or more elements. We therefore need a predicate to distinguish the empty list from lists to which first and rest can be applied. Since the pair model treats *list* as a sum type in which the underlying values from the *null* and *pair* types are brought in unchanged (and the *Revised*[7] *Report on the Algorithmic Language Scheme* guarantees that these types are disjoint), we can use the classification predicates from those underlying types, null? and pair?, as our discriminators:

```
(define empty-list? null?)
```

```
(define non-empty-list? pair?)
```

To complete the series, let's give cons and decons aliases that we can use when applying them as list constructors and selectors, as described in the recursive definition of the class of lists:

```
(define prepend cons)
```

```
(define deprepend decons)
```

Scheme does not provide the equality predicate, list=?, which is a little more complicated. Two lists are equal if (1) both are empty, or (2) both are non-empty, the same value is the first element of both, and their "rest" lists are equal. As with pairs and boxes, we'll rely on equal? as a general-purpose test for sameness of value. Here's the definition:

```
(define (list=? left right)
  (or (and (empty-list? left)
           (empty-list? right))
      (and (non-empty-list? left)
           (non-empty-list? right)
           (equal? (first left) (first right))
           (list=? (rest left) (rest right)))))
```

Homogeneous Lists

The type equation defining *list* places no constraint on the elements of a list. Sometimes, however, we'd like to require that a list be *homogeneous*—that is, that all of the elements of the list belong to a specified type. For instance, it should be possible to indicate somehow that a list that we're dealing with is specifically a list *of numbers* or a list *of characters*.

In our type equations, we'll signal this by enclosing the type of the list elements in parentheses, after the name *list*. For instance, we could specify the "list of numbers" type with the equation

$$list(number) \;=\; null \,|\, (number \times list(number))$$

We'll use similar notation when we want to constrain the types of the components of boxes, pairs, and other structures. For instance, *box(string)* is the type of boxes that contain strings, *pair(character, symbol)* is the type of pairs in which the car is a character and the cdr is a symbol, and so on.

Most of the primitive procedures for lists are defined the same way regardless of the intended type of the elements, but we should provide different classification and equality predicates for homogeneous lists:

```
(define list-of-numbers?
  (check null? (^et pair? (pipe car number?)) cdr))
(define (list-of-numbers=? left right)
  (or (and (empty-list? left)
           (empty-list? right))
      (and (non-empty-list? left)
           (non-empty-list? right)
           (= (first left) (first right))
           (list-of-numbers=? (rest left) (rest right)))))
```

To automate the process of constructing such classification and equality predicates for the various kinds of homogeneous lists that we'll need, let's introduce higher-order procedures that abstract out their common structure, leaving the only thing that varies (the classification or equality predicate for the elements) as a parameter:

```
(define (list-of right-type-of-element?)
  (check null? (^et pair? (pipe car right-type-of-element?)) cdr))
(define (list-of= element=?)
  (rec (equivalent? left right)
    (or (and (empty-list? left)
             (empty-list? right))
        (and (non-empty-list? left)
             (non-empty-list? right)
             (element=? (first left) (first right))
             (equivalent? (rest left) (rest right))))))
```

Using these definitions, `list-of-numbers?` is simply (`list-of number?`), and `list-of-numbers=?` is (`list-of= =`).

In retrospect, we could regard unconstrained lists as having the type *list(any)*. Correspondingly, the general `list?` predicate could alternatively be defined as (`list-of values?`), and `list=?` as (`list-of= equal?`).

Recursive Procedures for Lists

Let's work through a few examples to get a sense of how to take advantage of the recursive structure of lists.

One of the basic characteristics of a list is its *length*—the number of elements in it, counting duplicates as separate elements. As we noted in §2.2, Scheme provides `length` as a primitive procedure. Nevertheless, let's look at how it might be defined as a list recursion.

The recursive type equation for lists suggests the following plan: Use an if-expression to separate the case in which `ls` is the empty list from the case in which it has one or more elements. In the consequent of the if-expression, compute and return the appropriate value for the empty list—in this case, 0. In the alternate, split off the first element of `ls`, use a recursive call to get the length of the rest of `ls`, and add 1 to the result of that recursive call to compute the length of `ls` itself:

```
(define (length ls)
  (if (empty-list? ls)
      0
      (add1 (length (rest ls)))))
```

Here's a second example. Suppose that we want to determine the sum of the elements of a list `ls` of numbers, but we are working in an incomplete implementation of Scheme that supports + only as a binary procedure, so that we can't just write `(apply + ls)`. Once more, we can take advantage of the recursive structure of lists to break up the problem: An `if`-expression distinguishes the empty list from non-empty ones. We can return 0 as the sum of the empty list. For non-empty lists, we split off the first element, invoke the procedure recursively to get the sum of the rest of the list, and add the first element to the result of that recursive invocation to get the sum for the entire list.

```
(define (sum ls)
  (if (empty-list? ls)
      0
      (+ (first ls) (sum (rest ls)))))
```

As a third example, let's develop a procedure `catenate` that receives two lists (`left` and `right`) as arguments and returns a combined list, which begins with all of the elements of `left`, in their original order, and continues with all of the elements of `right`, in their original order. So, for instance, the value of the call '(catenate (list 'alpha 'beta 'gamma) (list 'delta 'epsilon))' is a five-element list comprising the symbols `alpha`, `beta`, `gamma`, `delta`, and `epsilon`, in that order.

Since both arguments to `catenate` are lists, it is perhaps not obvious which one we should use to guide the recursion. If we start taking `right` apart, however, we'll be working in the middle of the list that we eventually want to return. It is better to apply the recursion to `left`, so that we'll be working at the front of the result list, where the elements are more accessible.

If `left` is the empty list, we can immediately return the answer—the catenation of the empty list with any list `right` is obviously just `right` itself. If `left` is not empty, we'll separate off its first element, use a recursive call to `catenate` to attach the rest of `left` to the whole of `right`, and finally invoke `prepend` to place the first element of `left` at the front of the result:

```
(define (catenate left right)
  (if (empty-list? left)
      right
      (prepend (first left) (catenate (rest left) right))))
```

The Principle of List Induction

As we have seen, one of the advantages of designing our algorithms so that they start at the beginning of a list whenever possible is that, when we follow this rule, we can take advantage of the recursive structure of lists. Just as there is a principle of mathematical induction for natural numbers, we can formulate and prove a *principle of list induction* that serves as an organizing principle for computations involving lists: If null is a member of some class C', and every pair in which the cdr is a member of C' is also a member of C', then every list is a member of C'. This principle is an immediate consequence of the definition of lists presented at the beginning of this section. Since the class of lists is included in every class C that contains null and also contains all pairs in which the cdr is a member of C, finding such a class C is enough to ensure that all lists are in it.

Allowing the pair model to fade away again now, let's restate the principle in list terminology: If the empty list is a member of some class C', and a non-empty list is a member of C' whenever its rest is a member of C', then every list is a member of C'.

As a simple example of the use of this principle, let's prove that the length procedure that we developed above is correct—that it always returns the number of elements of its argument.

- *Base case.* Given the empty list, length immediately returns 0. The empty list has no elements, so this answer is correct.

- *Induction step.* Suppose that length returns the correct answer when given the rest of some non-empty list ls. Given ls itself, then, length determines the number of elements in the rest of ls and adds 1 to the result. This yields the correct answer, since ls has one more element than the rest of ls—its first element.

These two lemmas implicitly define a class C' of arguments for which length computes the correct result. The base case shows that the empty list is a member of C', and the induction step shows that if the rest of a list is a member of C', so is the entire list. Hence, by the principle of list induction, every list is a member of C', and length returns the correct value no matter what list it is given.

Managing Recursion with Lists

The recursive procedures length, sum, and catenate follow a common plan that can often be used when one of the arguments to a procedure is a list: Determine whether the list has any elements. If it has none, return some base values; if it has at least one, separate the first element from the rest of the list, apply the procedure being defined to the rest of the list by means of a recursive call, and somehow combine the first element with the results of the recursive call.

Recall that we defined the fold-natural tool by taking the recursive structure of the natural numbers as a guide, providing a base procedure to generate the values to which 0 would be mapped and a step procedure to transform the values to which k would be mapped into the values to which $k + 1$ would be mapped. Since lists have a similar recursive structure, we can define a `fold-list` tool that uses a `base` procedure to generate the values to which the empty list should be mapped and a `combiner` procedure that somehow synthesizes the values to which a non-empty list should be mapped, given the first element of the list and the results of the recursive call that deals with the rest of the list.

Abstracting the pattern of recursion over lists, we can define `fold-list` as follows:

```
(define (fold-list base combiner)
  (rec (folder ls)
    (if (empty-list? ls)
        (base)
        (receive recursive-results (folder (rest ls))
          (apply combiner (first ls) recursive-results)))))
```

To accommodate the possibility of multiple return values, we use a `receive`-expression to transmit the results of the recursive call, instead of the nested procedure calls that we used in the definition of `sum`.

We can now define our three examples quite concisely:

```
(define length (fold-list (create 0) (pipe >next add1)))
(define sum (fold-list (create 0) +))
(define (catenate left right)
  ((fold-list (create right) cons) left))
```

Since `fold-list` is singly recursive and uses a single value, the list, to guide the recursion, it is also possible to define `fold-list` concisely using `recur`:

```
(define (fold-list base combiner)
  (recur empty-list? (pipe black-hole base) deprepend combiner))
```

In processing a long list, a procedure that `fold-list` constructs invokes itself recursively until it reaches the base case (in which the list is empty). It then applies the `base` procedure first, and subsequently processes the elements of the list from right to left as it emerges from the recursive invocations, applying `combiner` to integrate each element in turn with the results of the invocation just completed. This processing order is a natural one, considering the definition of lists as a product type, because it reflects the right-to-left order in which a long list is built up, starting from an empty list and applying `prepend` repeatedly. The first element to be prepended is the one that ends up in the last position of the finished list, and vice versa.

When the actual values of the elements are ignored, as in `length`, or when the `combiner` procedure is commutative, as in `sum`, the order of processing makes no difference. In other cases, however, it is much more convenient to write the combining operation so that it associates to the left, so that we get the results we want by applying the combiner to the elements of a list in left-to-right order. We can achieve this ordering by using iteration to manage the list explicitly.

The `process-list` procedure provides the same interface as `fold-list`, taking a `base` procedure that creates the values to be returned when the given list is empty and a `combiner` procedure that integrates each element of the list in turn into the result. Behind the scenes, however, the iterator at the core of a procedure constructed by `process-list` manages an extra argument, which keeps track of the part of the given list that has not yet been processed. An adapter at the beginning of the iteration adds this extra argument, which initially is the entire list, to the values that `base` supplies when invoked. The adapter is

```
(lambda (ls)
  (receive starters (base)
    (apply values ls starters)))
```

Now the iterator can use `ls` explicitly in its processing, along with the rest of the base values.

The step procedure for the iterator receives as its first argument the part of the list that has not yet been processed. The rest of the arguments are the results of integrating the elements that *have* been processed, one by one, with the base values. The step procedure breaks the list that it receives into its first element and the rest of the list, and applies `combiner` to integrate the element with the results of the previous steps. It then returns as values the rest of the list (i.e., the unprocessed part) and the results of the call to `combiner`. In other words, the step procedure is

```
(lambda (sublist . results-so-far)
  (receive new-results (apply combiner (first sublist) results-so-far)
    (apply values (rest sublist) new-results)))
```

The iteration stops when no elements remain to be processed, that is, when the first argument to the iterator is an empty list. Thus the iterator's `stop?` predicate is

```
(pipe >initial empty-list?)
```

Once the iteration is over, we no longer need the empty list that the iterator returns as its first result. We can discard it by attaching the adapter `>all-but-initial` as a postprocessor.

Assembling the pieces yields the following definition of `process-list`:

```
(define (process-list base combiner)
  (pipe (lambda (ls)
          (receive starters (base)
            (apply values ls starters)))
        (pipe (iterate (pipe >initial empty-list?)
                       (lambda (sublist . results-so-far)
                         (receive new-results
                                  (apply combiner (first sublist)
```

```
                                              results-so-far)
                   (apply values (rest sublist) new-results))))
        >all-but-initial)))
```

One simple example of the use of process-list is the reverse procedure, which constructs a list comprising the elements of a given list, but arranges those elements in the reverse order. Scheme provides reverse as a primitive procedure, but let's consider how we might define it ourselves if we needed to. One algorithm that is easy to find, but inefficient, builds up the result list by adding each new item at the far end:

```
(define (postpend new ls)
  ((fold-list (create (list new)) prepend) ls))
(define reverse (fold-list list postpend))
```

Since each such addition involves getting past all of the previously added items (in another invocation of fold-list), the number of steps required to reverse a list is a quadratic function of the length of the list. For applications that use long lists, we'd prefer to have the running time of the reverse procedure increase only as a linear function of the length of the list. Managing the recursion with process-list accomplishes this goal:

```
(define reverse (process-list list prepend))
```

The element at the beginning of the given list is the first to be prepended and so winds up at the end of the result list, and the element at the end of the given list is the last to be prepended and so appears at the beginning of the result list. The point of process-list is to manage the behind-the-scenes mechanics of making the elements available for processing in the correct order. Each item is processed only once, and each step in the processing takes constant time, so this is indeed a linear-time algorithm.

Unfolding

To fold a list is to process its elements one by one while constructing some results; to *unfold* a list is to construct its elements one by one while processing some given values. The completed list is the result of the unfolding procedure. Again, there is a rough analogy to natural numbers: Unfolding a list is like tallying, in that we build up the result one element at a time, by successive invocations of prepend, just as a tally is built up by successive invocations of add1. (One could argue that 'unfold-natural' would be a better name for the tally procedure, or at least one that expresses this analogy more clearly.)

Looking back at the definition of a list as either a null value or a pair containing a datum and another list, we see that an unfolder procedure naturally depends on three other procedures, each of which operates on the (still unspecified) givens:

- final?, which determines whether the result list should be empty;

- producer, which generates the initial element of the result list when it is not empty; and

- step, which, when the result list is not empty, transforms the givens into arguments appropriate for the recursive call that unfolds the rest of the list.

Naturally, the producer and step procedures are invoked only if the givens do not satisfy final?.

We didn't need a producer procedure in the definition of tally, because add1 doesn't need any information other than the previous value of the counter to work out the next value, whereas prepend needs the new value to put at the front of the part of the list that has already been constructed.

Here, then, is the definition of the unfold-list tool:

```
(define (unfold-list final? producer step)
  (build final? (constant (list)) producer step prepend))
```

To illustrate its use, let's define pairs-with-given-sum, a procedure that constructs and returns a list of all the pairs of natural numbers that add up to a given natural number partiend. For instance, the value of the call '(pairs-with-given-sum 6)' should be (list (cons 0 6) (cons 1 5) (cons 2 4) (cons 3 3) (cons 4 2) (cons 5 1) (cons 6 0)) (or some other list with the same elements).

To build up this list one pair at a time, we can start with two counters, an upwards counter beginning at 0 and a downwards counter beginning at partiend. The unfolder manages these counters as its generates the elements of the list: At each step, we'll apply add1 to the upwards counter and sub1 to the downwards counter (and so our step procedure is (cross add1 sub1)). Also, at each step, we can form a suitable pair from the values of the two counters (and so our producer procedure is cons). The list will be complete when the first counter exceeds partiend, so the stop predicate should select out that first counter with >initial and compare it to partiend. Assembling the pieces yields the definition

```
(define (pairs-with-given-sum partiend)
  ((unfold-list (pipe >initial (sect < partiend <>))
                cons
                (cross add1 sub1))
   0 partiend))
```

Here is another example: Given a list ls with at least one element, the adjacent-pairs procedure returns a list of pairs, each pair consisting of two adjacent elements of ls. So, for instance, the value of the call '(adjacent-pairs (list 2 5 7 9))' would be (list (cons 2 5) (cons 5 7) (cons 7 9)).

This time, our only given is `ls` itself, and we form each element of the result list by pairing off two elements from `ls`, applying `cdr` to advance step by step down the list, and stopping when the source list has been reduced to a single element:

```
(define adjacent-pairs
  (unfold-list (pipe rest empty-list?)
               (pipe (dispatch first (pipe rest first)) cons)
               cdr))
```

Often one can arrive at superficially different solutions to a problem by looking at it from opposite directions, either as an input-driven problem to be addressed by folding with respect to one of the arguments, or as an output-driven problem to be addressed by unfolding the desired result a little at a time. For instance, to define a procedure that receives a natural number n as argument and returns a list of the squares of the first n positive integers, in descending order, we might choose to fold with respect to the natural number, providing an empty list in the base case and prepending the next square at each step forward:

```
(ply-natural list (pipe (~initial square) prepend))
```

Alternatively, we could unfold the desired list, using `square` as the producer and `sub1` as the step procedure, thus:

```
(unfold-list zero? square sub1)
```

The difference between these alternative approaches is more apparent than real. Comparing the operations of `ply-natural` and `unfold-list` reveals that the same recursive pattern underlies both formulations. If we set aside the constructions that deal with multiple values, which aren't needed in this particular case, the internal structure of the computation in each case boils down to this:

```
(rec (helper counter)
  (if (zero? counter)
      (list)
      (prepend (square counter) (helper (sub1 counter)))))
```

The `ply-natural` procedure supplies the calls to `zero?` and `sub1` as part of its structure, but needs to be told about the roles of `list` and `prepend`. With the `unfold-list` procedure, it's the other way around—`list` and `prepend` are internal, `zero?` and `sub1` arrive as arguments. But we get essentially the same procedure using either approach.

A common variation on unfolding is to omit the generation of an element when the givens fail to satisfy some condition, returning the result of the recursive call without change. This variant bears the same relation to `unfold-list` that `conditionally-tally` bears to `tally`, so we'll call it `conditionally-unfold-list`. Like `conditionally-tally`, it receives an extra argument, `condition-met?`:

```
(define (conditionally-unfold-list final? condition-met? producer step)
  (build final?
         (constant (list))
         (^if condition-met? (pipe producer box) (constant #f))
         step
         (conditionally-combine box? (pipe (~initial debox) prepend)))))
```

This design uses the convention proposed in §3.5 for signalling the success or
failure of a value-producing operation. When the arguments to the unfolder
satisfy condition-met?, it applies producer to those arguments and boxes the
result; otherwise it constructs an unboxed failure indicator, #f. The integration
procedure then checks whether the local computation resulted in a boxed value.
If so, it unboxes the value and prepends it to the list resulting from the recursive call; otherwise, the integration procedure discards the failure indicator and
returns that list without changing it.

For instance, one could construct a descending list of the squares of the *odd*
natural numbers less than 10 by writing

```
((conditionally-unfold-list zero? odd? square sub1) 10)
```

When the value of the counter is even, the test fails, square is not invoked, and
nothing is added to the list resulting from the recursive invocation.

---

list?   (scheme base)
any   → *Boolean*
something
Determine whether something is a list.

list-ref   (scheme base)
list(α), natural-number → *α*
ls   position
Return the element at (zero-based) position position in ls.
Precondition: position is less than the length of ls.

first   (afp lists)
list(α) → *α*
ls
Return the initial element of ls.
Precondition: ls is not empty.

rest   (afp lists)
list(α) → *list(α)*
ls
Return a list similar to ls, but lacking its initial element.
Precondition: ls is not empty.

empty-list?   (afp lists)
list(any) → *Boolean*
ls
Determine whether ls is empty.

non-empty-list?   (afp lists)
list(any) → *Boolean*
ls
Determine whether ls is non-empty.

prepend (afp lists)
$\alpha, \qquad list(\alpha) \rightarrow list(\alpha)$
something ls
Construct a list with something as its initial element and the elements of ls, in order, as its remaining elements.

deprepend (afp lists)
$list(\alpha) \rightarrow \alpha, list(\alpha)$
ls
Return the initial element of ls and a list similar to ls, but lacking its initial element.
Precondition: ls is not empty.

list=? (afp lists)
$list(any), list(any) \rightarrow Boolean$
left right
Determine whether the elements of left and right are equal in number and whether corresponding elements are the same.

list-of (afp lists)
$(any \rightarrow Boolean) \qquad \rightarrow (any \qquad \rightarrow Boolean)$
right-type-of-element? something
Construct a predicate that determines whether something is a list, every element of which satisfies right-type-of-element?.
Precondition: right-type-of-element? can receive any value.

list-of= (afp lists)
$(\alpha, \beta \rightarrow Boolean), \rightarrow (list(\alpha), list(\beta) \rightarrow Boolean)$
element=? left right
Construct a predicate that determines whether the elements of left and right are equal in number and whether corresponding elements satisfy element=?.
Precondition: element=? can receive any element of left and any element of right.

length (scheme base)
$list(any) \rightarrow natural\text{-}number$
ls
Compute the number of elements of ls.

sum (afp lists)
$list(number) \rightarrow number$
ls
Compute the sum of the elements of ls.

catenate (afp lists)
$list(\alpha), list(\alpha) \rightarrow list(\alpha)$
left right
Construct a list that contains all of the elements of left, in their original order, followed by all of the elements of right, in their original order.

fold-list (afp lists)
$(\rightarrow \alpha \ldots), (\beta, \alpha \ldots \rightarrow \alpha \ldots) \rightarrow (list(\beta) \rightarrow \alpha \ldots)$
base ·combiner ls
Construct a procedure that returns the results of invoking base if ls is empty. If ls is non-empty, the constructed procedure applies itself recursively to the rest of ls and returns the results of applying combiner to the first of ls and the results of the recursive invocation.
Precondition: If ls is non-empty, then combiner can receive the last element of ls and the results of an invocation of base.
Precondition: If ls is non-empty, then combiner can receive any but the last element of ls and the results of an invocation of combiner.

process-list (afp lists)
$(\rightarrow \alpha \ldots), (\beta, \alpha \ldots \rightarrow \alpha \ldots) \rightarrow (list(\beta) \rightarrow \alpha \ldots)$
base combiner ls
Construct a procedure that iteratively applies combiner to an element of ls and the results of the previous iteration (or to the results of invoking base, if there was no previous iteration). The constructed procedure returns the results of the last application of combiner.

Precondition: If ls is non-empty, then combiner can receive the initial element of ls and the results of an invocation of base.

Precondition: If ls is non-empty, combiner can receive any but the initial element of ls and the results of an invocation of combiner.

reverse   (scheme base)
$list(\alpha) \ \rightarrow list(\alpha)$
ls
Construct a list containing the elements of ls, in reverse order.

unfold-list   (afp lists)
$(\alpha \ldots \rightarrow Boolean), \ (\alpha \ldots \rightarrow \beta), \ (\alpha \ldots \rightarrow \alpha \ldots) \ \rightarrow (\alpha \ldots \quad \rightarrow list(\beta))$
final?   producer   step   arguments
Construct a procedure that first determines whether the elements of arguments satisfy final?. If so, the constructed procedure returns the empty list. Otherwise, it returns a non-empty list in which the initial element is the result of applying producer to the elements of arguments, and the remainder of the list is the result of first applying step to the elements of arguments and then applying the constructed procedure recursively to the results.

Precondition: final? can receive the elements of arguments.

Precondition: final? can receive the results of any invocation of step.

Precondition: If the elements of arguments do not satisfy final?, then producer can receive them.

Precondition: If the results of an invocation of step do not satisfy final?, then producer can receive them.

Precondition: If the elements of arguments do not satisfy final?, then step can receive them.

Precondition: If the results of an invocation of step do not satisfy final?, then step can receive them.

adjacent-pairs   (afp lists)
$list(\alpha) \ \rightarrow list(pair(\alpha, \alpha))$
ls
Construct a list containing pairs of adjacent elements of ls.

Precondition: ls is not empty.

conditionally-unfold-list   (afp lists)
$(\alpha \ldots \rightarrow Boolean), \ (\alpha \ldots \rightarrow \beta), \ (\beta \rightarrow Boolean), \ (\alpha \ldots \rightarrow \alpha \ldots) \ \rightarrow$
final?   producer   condition-met?   step

$(\alpha \ldots \quad \rightarrow list(\beta))$
arguments

Construct a procedure that first determines whether the elements of arguments satisfy final?. If so, the constructed procedure returns the empty list. Otherwise, it applies producer to those arguments and determines whether the result satisfies condition-met?. If so, the constructed procedure returns a non-empty list in which the initial element is the result of the invocation of producer, and the remainder of the list is the result of first applying step to the elements of arguments and then applying the constructed procedure recursively to the results. If the result of the invocation of producer does not satisfy condition-met?, then the constructed procedure simply returns the result of the recursive invocation described above.

Precondition: final? can receive the elements of arguments.

Precondition: final? can receive the results of any invocation of step.

Precondition: If the elements of arguments do not satisfy final?, then producer can receive them.

Precondition: If the results of an invocation of step do not satisfy final?, then producer can receive them.

Precondition: condition-met? can receive the result of any invocation of producer.

Precondition: If the elements of arguments do not satisfy final?, then step can receive them.

Precondition: If the results of an invocation of step do not satisfy final?, then step can receive them.

Exercises

3.6–1 Using `fold-list`, define a procedure `count-evens` that receives any list of integers and returns a natural number indicating how many of the integers on the list are even. (For instance, the call '(count-evens (list 7 3 12 9 4 1 5))' has the value 2.)

3.6–2 The *alternating sum* of a list of numbers is the result of alternately adding elements to and subtracting them from a running total, beginning with an addition (the initial element of the list is added to 0). For instance, the alternating sum of (list 7 2 4 6 1) is $7 - 2 + 4 - 6 + 1$, or 4. The alternating sum of an empty list is 0. Define the procedure `alternating-sum` that receives any list of numbers and returns its alternating sum. (Hint: Consider how to define the alternating sum recursively.)

3.6–3 If the `list?` predicate were not provided as a primitive, we could define it for ourselves. Propose a definition, using `check`.

3.6–4 If the `list-ref` procedure were not provided as a primitive, we could define it for ourselves. Propose a definition, using either `recur` or `fold-natural`.

3.6–5 Define a `make-list` procedure that receives two arguments, of which the first is a natural number, and returns a list comprising the specified number of copies of the second argument. For instance, the value of the call '(make-list 7 'foo)' is (list 'foo 'foo 'foo 'foo 'foo 'foo 'foo).

3.6–6 If you used `unfold-list` in your solution to the preceding exercise, write an alternative definition of the same procedure, using a call to `fold-natural`. Otherwise, write an alternative definition, using a call to `unfold-list`.

3.6–7 Define a procedure (traditionally called `iota`) that receives a natural number as argument and returns a list of all the lesser natural numbers, in ascending order. For instance, the value of the call '(iota 5)' is (list 0 1 2 3 4), and the value of the call '(iota 0)' is the empty list.

3.7 List Algorithms

Lists are exceptionally flexible and convenient structures. With the tools developed in the previous sections, we can express a great variety of common algorithms.

Arity Extension

The `fold-list` procedure can be used for arity extension, to convert any single-valued binary procedure into a variable-arity procedure. For instance, with

fold-list and catenate, it's easy to define the variable-arity catenator append.[2]
This procedure can receive any number of arguments, each of which must be a
list, and catenates all of them to form one long list, which it returns:

```
(define append (pipe list (fold-list (create (list)) catenate)))
```

Here the list procedure is used in two ways: first, as an adapter, to collect the
arguments to the variable-arity procedure into a list of lists, and second, to generate the base case for the fold (the empty list). The procedure that fold-list
returns folds over that list of lists, successively catenating the arguments onto
the initially empty result.

The append procedure has the same relation to catenate as our variable-
arity addition procedure + to the two-argument addition operation found in
most programming languages. If we start with any binary procedure that has
an identity, we can use fold-list to turn it into a variable-arity procedure. For
example, the ^et procedure from §2.8 is a binary procedure with values? as its
identity, and so we can define a procedure that forms the conjunction of *any*
number of predicates by folding over the list of arguments:

```
(define ^and (pipe list (fold-list (create values?) ^et)))
```

Let's abstract this arity-extension pattern and give it a name:

```
(define (extend-to-variable-arity id combiner)
  (pipe list (fold-list (create id) combiner)))
```

Here id is the identity of the operation (like the empty list for catenate and
values? for ^et) and combiner is the operation itself.

So, for instance, we can derive ^or from ^vel as we derived ^and from ^et,
though it may take a few moments' thought to figure out the identity for ^vel:

```
(define ^or (extend-to-variable-arity (constant #f) ^vel))
```

Similarly, we can extend the arity of the pipe procedure to get a higher-
order tool that can receive any number of procedures as arguments and returns
a single procedure that combines their effects, piping the results of each one into
the parameters of the next. To continue the hydraulic metaphor, let's call this
procedure run, as in "a run of pipe":

```
(define run (extend-to-variable-arity values pipe))
```

---

[2]Scheme provides append as a primitive procedure.

We can actually use the `extend-to-variable-arity` procedure even in cases where the base value is not an identity for the binary procedure that we're extending. If it makes sense to return that value when the extended-arity procedure receives no arguments, and if it can serve as the second argument in a call to the binary procedure to start the computation when the extended-arity procedure *does* receive arguments, then the extended-arity procedure is likely to generalize the binary procedure in some potentially useful way.

In each of the preceding examples, too, the binary procedure involved (`catenate`, `^et`, `^vel`, `pipe`) was associative; but this restriction is also unnecessary, provided that it is acceptable for the extended-arity procedure to associate its arguments to the right. For instance, if we changed our mind about the variable-arity version of `expt` that we considered and rejected in §1.4, we could now define it after all as (`extend-to-variable-arity 1 expt`), and it would group the exponents the way mathematicians prefer, starting from the right:

```
> ((extend-to-variable-arity 1 expt) 2 3 3)
134217728    ;; = 2^27 = (expt 2 (expt 3 (expt 3 1))),
             ;;              not (expt (expt (expt 2 3) 3) 1),
             ;;              not (expt (expt (expt 1 2) 3) 3)
```

There are some cases in which the procedure that we want to define really makes sense only when there is at least one argument. For instance, we'd like to extend the binary `lesser` procedure from §1.9, creating a procedure `min` that can receive one or more numbers as arguments and returns the least of them. It would make no sense to invoke such a procedure without giving it any arguments at all—there is no identity for `lesser`, and no value that would be an obvious candidate to return in such a case.

We can define a variant of `extend-to-variable-arity`, adjusting the interface to give us the tool we need. We'll use the same preprocessing adapter, `list`, to collect all of the given arguments into a list. Then we'll use that list as the guide value in a simple recursion, as constructed by `recur`. To detect the base case (a single argument value), we naturally use (`pipe rest empty-list?`); we'll assume that, when the recursive procedure is invoked with just one argument, it should return that argument unchanged as its result, so our terminal procedure is `first`. To deal with the non-base cases, the simplifier for the guide value, which splits it into a value for local use and a value for the recursive call, is obviously `deprepend`, and the integration procedure that combines the first argument with the result of the recursive call is the binary procedure that we're generalizing.

Here, then, is the definition of `extend-to-positive-arity`:

```
(define (extend-to-positive-arity combiner)
  (pipe list (recur (pipe rest empty-list?) first deprepend combiner)))
```

For instance, min is (extend-to-positive-arity lesser).[3]

We saw in §1.4 that the primitive arithmetic procedures – and / use variable arity in a different way: They require at least one argument. They express different operations when given a single argument than when given two or more. Finally, the variable-arity operations that they express implicitly associate the arguments to the left rather than to the right. We can write a higher-order procedure that captures this pattern as well. Since fold-list has a bias towards right-associative operations, we'll use process-list instead to manage the left association.

Given a unary procedure (to handle the single-argument case) and a binary procedure (to be applied repeatedly in the multiple-argument cases), extend-like-subtraction generates a procedure that can receive one or more arguments. If it receives just one (so that the value of the rest-parameter others is the empty list), it applies the unary procedure to the initial argument. Otherwise, it processes the entire list iteratively, taking the initial argument as the starting value and successively applying the binary procedure to combine the accumulated result so far with the next element of others.

There is one more slightly awkward point, which becomes evident when the binary procedure is not commutative: The pattern of left-to-right association presupposes that "the accumulated result so far" will appear as the *first* argument to the binary procedure, and the new operand from others as the second. The process-list recursion manager, however, presupposes the opposite order. So we need an adapter: We'll use the *converse* of the binary operation, rather than the binary operation itself, as the combiner procedure when we invoke process-list.

Writing the definition of the extend-like-subtraction procedure is now just a matter of assembling the pieces:

```
(define (extend-like-subtraction unary binary)
  (lambda (initial . others)
    (if (empty-list? others)
        (unary initial)
        ((process-list (create initial) (converse binary)) others))))
```

For instance, if we were working with an incomplete implementation of Scheme that provided only a binary procedure for dividing ratios, we could create our own variable-arity division operator with the call

```
(extend-like-subtraction (sect / 1 <>) /)
```

Filtering and Partitioning

To *filter* a list is to select the elements that satisfy some condition, making a new list from them. For instance, given the list comprising the natural numbers 918,

---

[3]Scheme provides min, and the corresponding procedure max for finding the greatest of one or more numbers, as primitives.

653, 531, 697, 532, and 367, we could filter it to select even numbers. The result would be a list comprising just 918 and 532. In general, filtering procedures that preserve the relative order of the elements are particularly useful. With the resources that we have developed, particularly `fold-list`, we can define a variety of filtering operations. Let's look at a few of the definitions.

The `filter` procedure receives a predicate that expresses the condition to be satisfied and a list from which to select the elements that satisfy it. It returns the filtered list:

```
(define (filter keep? ls)
  ((fold-list list (conditionally-combine keep? prepend)) ls))
```

The idea is to fold over the original list, adding each element to the result list if it satisfies the predicate. (Recall that the procedure constructed by `conditionally-combine`, from §2.8, applies `prepend` to add the element only if `keep?` is satisfied.)

Sometimes we'll want to filter *out* list elements that meet a given condition, retaining the ones that do not meet it. The `remp` procedure accomplishes this by inverting the test before filtering:

```
(define remp (pipe (~initial ^not) filter))
```

In still other cases, we'll want to recover *both* lists—the one with the elements that satisfy the test predicate (the "ins" list), and the one with the elements that fail to satisfy it (the "outs" list). We can still fold down the given list. In the base case, `ins` and `outs` are both empty. At each step, we prepend an element from the source list either to `ins` or to `outs`, depending on whether it satisfies the test predicate. So the step procedure looks like this:

```
(lambda (candidate ins outs)
  (if (condition-met? candidate)
      (values (prepend candidate ins) outs)
      (values ins (prepend candidate outs))))
```

Assembling the pieces, we get the following definition for `partition`:

```
(define (partition condition-met? ls)
  ((fold-list (create (list) (list))
              (lambda (candidate ins outs)
                (if (condition-met? candidate)
                    (values (prepend candidate ins) outs)
                    (values ins (prepend candidate outs)))))
   ls))
```

Filtering or partitioning a list collects *all* of the list elements that satisfy a given predicate. In some cases, we want to take out only one such element—the first one we encounter as we traverse the list. If that's the only result we need, we could use the construction (`pipe filter first`). However, under that strategy, we'd traverse the entire list, even if the element we're looking for is near the beginning. It would be better to avoid the superfluous computation. Also, it's frequently useful to obtain two results—the element we're looking for, and a list of all the other elements of the given list. So we'll look for a different approach.

Another complication is that, in some cases, *none* of the elements of the given list will satisfy the given predicate. (This is not a problem for `filter`, which simply returns the empty list.) What should our procedure (let's call it `extract`) return if that happens? One solution would be to adopt the convention that when `extract` cannot find any list element that satisfies the predicate, it should instead return some arbitrary value, such as #f or null, as its first result. However, this convention leads to an ambiguity: Whatever value we choose to indicate the failure of the search could, in other cases, be the result of a *successful* search.

Instead, we'll use the convention envisioned in §3.5: When `extract` succeeds in finding a value that satisfies the predicate, it puts that value into a box before returning it. When the search fails, `extract` instead returns #f, unboxed, as its first result. In either case, the second result is a list containing all the unselected values in the given list. (In other words, if the search fails, `extract` returns the given list unchanged as its second result.)

This convention causes no ambiguity even when the result of a successful search is itself a box. The `extract` procedure just puts that box in another box before returning it. The caller can determine that the search was successful, because it receives a box as its first result, and the caller also knows to discard the outer box in order to get at the actual list element (once it has determined that the search was successful). From the caller's end, the result is processed in the same way, regardless of the kind of value that the box contains (even if it turns out to be another box).

Here, then, is the implementation of the `extract` procedure:

```
(define (extract condition-met? ls)
  ((rec (extracter sublist)
     (if (empty-list? sublist)
         (values #f sublist)
         (receive (chosen others) (deprepend sublist)
           (if (condition-met? chosen)
               (values (box chosen) others)
               (receive (sought relicts) (extracter others)
                 (values sought (cons chosen relicts)))))))
   ls))
```

Sublists

One way of generalizing the first and rest operations is to think of splitting the list farther down, specifying by means of a natural number how many elements should be taken from the beginning of the list. The take and drop procedures implement this idea. Both receive a list and a natural number as arguments; take returns a list of the elements that precede the split (a *prefix* of the given list), drop the list of elements that follow the split (a *suffix* of the given list).

The definition of the drop procedure is quite simple: The natural-number argument tells us how many times to apply the rest procedure to the list argument. The fold-natural tool is the obvious choice to manage the recursion:

```
(define (drop ls count)
  ((fold-natural (create ls) rest) count))
```

It would be possible to use fold-natural to define take as well (and this option is explored in the exercises), but we get a simpler definition if we start from the result that we want take to produce and consider how to construct it one element at a time, using unfold-list. Again the arguments are the list ls and the natural number count. There are three things to consider, then:

- Under what conditions should we return the empty list? That is, what is our stop? predicate?

- If we need to unfold an element for the result list, how do we compute it from the given arguments? That is, what is our producer procedure?

- Having unfolded an element, how do we transform the given values, to prepare them for the recursive call that generates the rest of the elements for the result list? That is, what is our step procedure?

The natural-number argument count is the guide for the recursion, indicating the number of elements to be generated as we produce the result list. So the stop? predicate is obvious: It should test whether the count is 0. Since the count is the second of the arguments, we can write this predicate as (pipe >next zero?).

If the count isn't 0, we need to unfold an element for the result list. The first element of a non-empty result list is the same as the first element of the given list. So the producer is (pipe >initial first).

Finally, to prepare the list and the count for the recursive call, we need to subtract 1 from the count (since the number of elements remaining to be generated is one smaller), and we need to strip the first element away from the list, so that the remaining elements for the result list come from the rest of the original list. The step procedure, therefore, is (cross rest sub1).

No preprocessing or postprocessing is needed, so the definition of take is:

```
(define take (unfold-list (pipe >next zero?)
                          (pipe >initial first)
                          (cross rest sub1)))
```

It is a precondition of each of these procedures that the length of the list
argument is greater than or equal to the value of the natural-number argument.
(If the length is equal to the natural number, then take returns the entire list
and drop returns the empty list.)

Using take and drop, we can define a sublist procedure that breaks a list
at two positions, start and finish, and returns a list of the elements between
the breaks:

```
(define (sublist ls start finish)
  (take (drop ls start) (- finish start)))
```

Once again, there are preconditions: start and finish are natural numbers,
with start less than or equal to finish and finish less than or equal to the
length of the list.

Positional Selection

As mentioned in §3.6, Scheme programmers generally avoid accessing list elements by position. However, when the lists are known to be short or the
alternative methods of computation very cumbersome, list-ref may be the
best tool available. Scheme provides it as a primitive, though it would be quite
easy to define it:

```
(define list-ref (pipe drop first))
```

As an example of appropriate use of list-ref, let's create a procedure for
building custom adapters that can select, permute, and duplicate their arguments in more intricate ways than the ones we defined in §2.5. The idea is to
provide the adapter-building procedure with natural numbers that serve as indices into the arguments of the desired adapter. Given these position numbers,
the adapter can use list-ref to pick out the results one by one.

Here's the definition of the adapter-building procedure, which we'll call
adapter:

```
(define (adapter . positions)
  (lambda arguments
    (delist (map (sect list-ref arguments <>) positions))))
```

Since list-ref uses zero-based positions, (adapter 0) is the adapter that
we've been calling >initial, and (adapter 1) is >next. The converse procedure is rather like (adapter 1 0), except that converse passes any additional

arguments through as results, while (adapter 1 0) returns only the first two, in reverse order.

To build an adapter that selects some of its arguments and excludes others, we supply adapter with the positions of the arguments that we want to keep. For instance, the values of the call

```
((adapter 0 3 5) 'alpha 'beta 'gamma 'delta 'epsilon 'zeta)
```

are the symbols alpha, delta, and zeta.

If we want the adapter to rearrange its arguments, we describe the permutation that we want to achieve in the call to adapter, rearranging the natural numbers less than the length of the argument list to reflect the rearrangement that we want the adapter to perform. For instance, the values of the call

```
((adapter 1 3 0 2) 'alpha 'beta 'gamma 'delta)
```

are beta, delta, alpha, and gamma, in that order.

Finally, if we want the adapter to repeat one or more of its arguments as duplicate results, we give it the same natural number more than once. For instance, the call

```
((adapter 2 2 0 0) 'alpha 'beta 'gamma 'delta)
```

has four values: gamma, gamma, alpha, and alpha.

Extending Predicates from List Elements to Lists

Suppose that we want to write a procedure all-even? that determines whether all of the elements of a given list of natural numbers are even. There is a temptation to use list mapping to obtain a list of Boolean results, and then to try to combine them somehow with and:

```
(define all-even? (run (sect map even? <>) delist and))
```

However, this approach is unworkable and unsatisfactory, for two related reasons. One is that 'and' is a keyword, not the name of a procedure; an and-expression is not a procedure call, and its subexpressions are not operands. The other reason is that, even if and were a procedure, a definition like the preceding one would be inefficient in cases where the given list is long and contains an odd number near the beginning. We'd prefer to traverse the list a step at a time, stopping and returning #f as soon as we find an odd number, so as not to waste time pointlessly testing the numbers farther along in the list.

A better approach, then, is to use check to manage the recursion:

```
(define all-even? (check empty-list? (pipe first even?) rest))
```

That is: If the given list is empty, return #t at once. Otherwise, determine whether its first element is even; if not, return #f at once. Otherwise, check whether the rest of the list is all-even (by issuing a recursive call).

This pattern occurs quite frequently in practice, so it's useful to abstract it out as a higher-order procedure that builds (and immediately applies) a "raised" version of any given predicate—that is, one that efficiently determines whether every element of a list satisfies that predicate, like this:

```
(define (for-all? condition-met? ls)
  ((check empty-list? (pipe first condition-met?) rest) ls))
```

So, for instance, all-even? could be defined as (sect for-all? even? <>).

We can also define a dual procedure, exists?, with the same interface. It returns #t if even one element of a given list satisfies the predicate and #f if all of them fail. To achieve this, we complement the predicate, apply for-all, and negate the result. (The list contains a value that satisfies the predicate if and only if not every value in the list satisfies its complement.)

```
(define exists? (pipe (~initial ^not) (pipe for-all? not)))
```

We'll find more use for a variation on this theme that extends unary predicates in a more direct way. Given a unary predicate, the every procedure returns a variable-arity predicate that returns #t if and only if each of its arguments satisfies the given predicate:

```
(define (every condition-met?)
  (lambda arguments
    (for-all? condition-met? arguments)))
```

For instance, the value of the call '((every even?) 6 2 0 4 8)' is #t, because 6, 2, 0, 4, and 8 all satisfy even?. But the value of '((every positive?) 6 2 0 4 8)' is #f, since 0 is not positive.

The dual procedure, at-least-one, constructs a variable-arity predicate that determines whether at least one of its arguments satisfies a given predicate:

```
(define (at-least-one condition-met?)
  (lambda arguments
    (exists? condition-met? arguments)))
```

Transposing, Zipping, and Unzipping

When the elements of a non-empty list are themselves lists, and they all have the same length, one can sometimes usefully imagine the elements of the elements as being arranged in rows and columns:

```
(list (list #\o #\m #\e #\n)    ; row 0
      (list #\r #\a #\v #\e)    ; row 1
      (list #\a #\r #\e #\a)    ; row 2
      (list #\l #\e #\n #\t))   ; row 3
; column    0   1   2   3
```

To *transpose* a list of this sort is to turn its columns into rows, and vice versa. To pick up column 0, we take the first element of each row and make a list of them; this list becomes row 0 of the result, and so on. For instance, the result of transposing the list shown above is

```
(list (list #\o #\r #\a #\l)
      (list #\m #\a #\r #\e)
      (list #\e #\v #\e #\n)
      (list #\n #\e #\a #\t))
```

The definition of the `transpose` procedure is surprisingly simple: We apply `list` to groups of elements in corresponding positions in the rows, thus forming column lists, and collect those column lists in one big list:

```
(define transpose (sect apply map list <>))
```

To *zip* one or more lists of equal length is to construct a list of lists from them, making them the columns in a structure like the ones shown above. Each element of the result is a list of corresponding elements of the original list. It may be easier to grasp the idea from an example: The value of the call

```
(zip (list 0 1 2 3) (list 4 5 6 7) (list 8 9 10 11))
```

is `(list (list 0 4 8) (list 1 5 9) (list 2 6 10) (list 3 7 11))`.

The `unzip` procedure performs the inverse operation of splitting a list of lists into its columns—one or more lists of equal length, which it returns as separate values. For instance, the call

```
(unzip (list (list 1 4 7) (list 2 5 8) (list 3 6 9)))
```

returns three values: `(list 1 2 3)`, `(list 4 5 6)`, and `(list 7 8 9)`.

It is easy to recognize that `zip` is just `transpose`, with a preprocessor attached to bundle up the lists:

```
(define zip (pipe list transpose))
```

More surprisingly, `unzip` is also just `transpose` with a postprocessor attached to unbundle the columns so that they can be returned as separate values:

```
(define unzip (pipe transpose delist))
```

Aggregating Multiple Results

The map procedure that Scheme provides as a primitive requires the procedure that it applies to be single-valued, because of the way it constructs the result list. It could be defined as

```
(define (map procedure initial-list . other-lists)
  (if (null? initial-list)
      (list)
      (prepend (apply procedure (first initial-list)
                                (map first other-lists))
               (apply map procedure (rest initial-list)
                                    (map rest other-lists)))))
```

The call to the prepend procedure is the source of the restriction. As in any procedure call, all of its subexpressions must be single-valued.

However, we are now in a position to define an analogous higher-order procedure collect-map, which assembles into one large list *all* of the results obtained when a multiple-valued procedure is mapped along one or more lists:

```
(define collect-map
  (run (~initial (sect pipe <> list)) map delist append))
```

The adapter (~initial (sect pipe <> list)) converts the first argument to collect-map from a multiple-valued procedure into one that collects its results into a list, which it returns. The map procedure can now apply this list-returning version of the given procedure to corresponding values from the list arguments, returning a list of the resulting lists. The delist procedure breaks out the separate lists, and the append procedure combines them into a single list.

The collect-map procedure can be used even in cases where the mapped procedure returns different numbers of elements for different arguments.

Similarly, we can define a version of dispatch that constructs dispatchers that return *all* of the results of applying given procedures to whatever arguments they are given, and an analogous version of cross that applies a different unary procedure to each of the arguments it receives and returns all of the results of the applications:

```
(define dispatch-return-all
  (run (~each (sect pipe <> list)) dispatch (sect run <> append delist)))

(define cross-return-all
  (run (~each (sect pipe <> list)) cross (sect run <> append delist)))
```

In each case, the preprocessor (~each (sect pipe <> list)) converts each of the given multiple-valued procedures into a single-valued procedure returning a list, and the postprocessor (sect run <> append delist) combines the result lists and then breaks out the values into separate results.

---

append   (scheme base)
$list(\alpha) \ldots \rightarrow list(\alpha)$
lists
Construct a list containing every element of every element of lists, retaining both the relative order of the elements and the relative order of the elements within each element.

^and   (afp lists)
$(\alpha \ldots \rightarrow Boolean) \ldots \rightarrow (\alpha \ldots \rightarrow Boolean)$
predicates   arguments
Construct a predicate that determines whether the elements of arguments satisfy every element of predicates.
Precondition: Every element of predicates can receive the elements of arguments.

extend-to-variable-arity   (afp lists)
$\alpha, (\beta, \alpha \rightarrow \alpha), \rightarrow (\beta \ldots \rightarrow \alpha)$
id combiner   arguments
Construct a procedure of variable arity that returns id if arguments has no elements and otherwise returns the result of applying combiner to the initial element of arguments and the result of applying itself recursively to the remaining elements of arguments.
Precondition: combiner can receive any element of arguments as its first argument.
Precondition: combiner can receive id as its second argument.
Precondition: combiner can receive any result of combiner as its second argument.

^or   (afp lists)
$(\alpha \ldots \rightarrow Boolean) \ldots \rightarrow (\alpha \ldots \rightarrow Boolean)$
predicates   arguments
Construct a predicate that determines whether the elements of arguments satisfy at least one element of predicates.
Precondition: Every element of predicates can receive the elements of arguments.

run   (afp lists)
$(\alpha \ldots \rightarrow \alpha \ldots) \ldots \rightarrow (\alpha \ldots \rightarrow \alpha \ldots)$
sequence   arguments
Construct a procedure that returns the elements of arguments if sequence has no elements, and otherwise applies itself recursively to all but the initial element of sequence, applies the procedure resulting from that recursive invocation to the results of applying the initial element of sequence to the elements of arguments, and returns the results of that final invocation.
Precondition: If sequence has any elements, then its initial element can receive the elements of arguments.
Precondition: If sequence has any elements, then every element of sequence except the initial one can receive the results of any invocation of the preceding element of sequence.

extend-to-positive-arity   (afp lists)
$(\alpha, \alpha \rightarrow \alpha) \rightarrow (\alpha, \alpha \ldots) \rightarrow \alpha$
combiner   initial others
Construct a procedure that returns initial if given one argument and otherwise returns the result of applying combiner to initial and the results of applying itself recursively to others.
Precondition: If others is not empty, then combiner can receive initial as its first argument.
Precondition: If others is not empty, then combiner can receive any element of others except the last as its first argument.
Precondition: If others is not empty, then combiner can receive the last element of others as its second argument.
Precondition: combiner can receive the result of any invocation of combiner as its second argument.

extend-like-subtraction   (afp lists)
$(\alpha \rightarrow \alpha), (\alpha, \beta \rightarrow \alpha) \rightarrow (\alpha, \beta \ldots \rightarrow \alpha)$
unary   binary   initial others
Construct a procedure that, given one argument, applies unary to that argument and returns the result; given two or more arguments, the constructed procedure applies binary iteratively, operating at each step on the result of the previous iteration (or on initial, if there was no

previous iteration) and the next-element of others.

Precondition: If others has no elements, then unary can receive initial.

Precondition: If others has at least one element, then binary can receive initial as its first argument.

Precondition: If others has at least one element, then binary can receive the result of any invocation of binary as its first argument.

Precondition: If others has at least one element, then binary can receive any element of others as its second argument.

min   (scheme base)
number, number ... → number
initial others
Return the least of initial and the elements of others.

max   (scheme base)
number, number ... → number
initial others
Return the greatest of initial and the elements of others.

filter   (afp lists)
(α → Boolean), list(α) → list(α)
keep?   ls
Construct a list comprising the elements of ls that satisfy keep?.

Precondition: keep? can receive any element of ls.

remp   (afp lists)
(α → Boolean), list(α) → list(α)
exclude?   ls
Construct a list comprising the elements of ls that do not satisfy exclude?.

Precondition: exclude? can receive any element of ls.

partition   (afp lists)
(α → Boolean), list(α) → list(α), list(α)
condition-met? ls
Construct a list comprising the elements of ls that satisfy condition-met? and a list comprising those that do not.

Precondition: condition-met? can receive any element of ls.

extract   (afp lists)
(α → Boolean), list(α) → box(α) | Boolean, list(α)
condition-met? ls
Search ls for an element that satisfies condition-met?. If and when such an element is found, return a box containing that element and a list of the other elements of ls; otherwise, return #f and ls.

Precondition: condition-met? can receive any element of ls.

drop   (afp lists)
list(α), natural-number → list(α)
ls   count
Return a list similar to ls, but with the first count elements removed.

Precondition: count is less than or equal to the length of ls.

take   (afp lists)
list(α), natural-number → list(α)
ls   count
Construct a list comprising the first count elements of ls, in order.

Precondition: count is less than or equal to the length of ls.

sublist   (afp lists)
list(α), natural-number, natural-number → list(α)
ls   start   finish
Construct the sublist of ls that starts at the (zero-based) position specified by start and leaves off before the position specified by finish.

Precondition: start is less than or equal to finish.

Precondition: finish is less than or equal to the length of ls.

adapter   (afp lists)

natural-number ... → *(α ...*   → *α ...)*
positions   arguments

Construct an adapter procedure that returns the values that appear in the (zero-based) positions of arguments specified by the elements of positions.
Precondition: The number of elements of arguments is greater than every element of positions.

for-all?   (afp lists)

(α → Boolean), list(α) → *Boolean*
condition-met?   ls

Determine whether every element of ls satisfies condition-met?.
Precondition: condition-met? can accept any element of ls.

exists?   (afp lists)

(α → Boolean), list(α) → *Boolean*
condition-met?   ls

Determine whether at least one element of ls satisfies condition-met?.
Precondition: condition-met? can accept any element of ls.

every   (afp lists)

(α → Boolean) → *(α ...*   → *Boolean)*
condition-met?   arguments

Construct a predicate that determines whether every element of arguments satisfies condition-met?.
Precondition: condition-met? can receive any element of arguments.

at-least-one   (afp lists)

(α → Boolean) → *(α ...*   → *Boolean)*
condition-met?   arguments

Construct a predicate that determines whether at least one element of arguments satisfies condition-met?.
Precondition: condition-met? can receive any element of arguments.

transpose   (afp lists)

list(list(α)) → *list(list(α))*
ls

Construct the transpose of ls.
Precondition: ls is not empty.
Precondition: The lengths of the elements of ls are equal.

zip   (afp lists)

list(α), list(α) ... → *list(list(α))*
initial others

Construct a list of lists, each comprising corresponding elements of initial and of the elements of others.
Precondition: The length of initial is equal to the length of every element of others.

unzip   (afp lists)

list(list(α)) → *list(α), list(α) ...*
ls

Precondition: ls is not empty.
Precondition: The lengths of the elements of ls are equal.

collect-map   (afp lists)

(α, β ... → γ ...), list(α), list(β) ... → *list(γ)*
procedure   initial others

Apply procedure to corresponding elements of one or more lists (initial and the elements of others), collecting all of the results in a list.
Precondition: The length of initial and the lengths of the elements of others are equal.
Precondition: procedure can receive corresponding elements of initial and of the elements of others.

```
dispatch-return-all                                                          (afp lists)
(α ... → β ...) ...   → (α ...      → β ...)
procedures                   arguments
```
Construct a procedure that applies every element of procedures to the elements of arguments,
returning all of the results.
Precondition: Every element of procedures can receive the elements of arguments.

```
cross-return-all                                                             (afp lists)
(α → β ...)  → (α ...      → β ...)
procedures         arguments
```
Construct a procedure that applies each element of procedures to the corresponding element
of arguments, returning all of the results.
Precondition: Every element of procedures can receive the corresponding element of
arguments.

Exercises

3.7–1   Design and implement variable-arity versions of the new-+ and new-=
procedures defined in §3.4.

3.7–2   Design and implement a variable-arity gcd procedure that finds the
greatest natural number that evenly divides all of its arguments (which must
be positive integers). (Scheme provides this as a primitive procedure. For this
exercise, you don't get to use that one!)

3.7–3   What procedure is the value of the call '(extend-to-variable-arity
null cons)'?

3.7–4   Define a procedure multidiv that can receive one or more arguments,
each of which must be an integer, and all but the first of which must be non-zero,
and successively divides the first by all of the others, using number-theoretic
division and discarding remainders. So, for instance, the value of the call
'(multidiv 360 5 3 2)' is 12, because 360 divided by 5 is 72, 72 divided by 3
is 24, and 24 divided by 2 is 12. Again, the value of the call '(multidiv 17016
7 11 13 17)' is 0, the last of the quotients of the successive number-theoretic
divisions. If multidiv receives only one argument, it should return it unchanged.

3.7–5   Define a procedure double-divisors that receives two arguments, the
first a list of positive integers and the second a natural number, and returns
a list of the elements of the given list whose squares are divisors of the given
natural number. (The rationale for the name is that an element of the list that
results from this procedure not only evenly divides the given natural number,
but also evenly divides the quotient from the first division.) For instance, the
value of the call '(double-divisors (list 2 5 8 11 14 17 20) 3628800)' is
(list 2 5 8 20), because the squares of 2, 5, 8, and 20 (namely 4, 25, 64, and
400) are divisors of 3628800, while the squares of 11, 14, and 17 are not.

3.7–6   It is a common programming pattern for the result of an invocation of
map to be used immediately as an argument to filter. For instance, if we had
a list 1s of pairs of integers and wanted to draw up a list of their cdrs, but only
the negative ones, we could write

```
(filter negative? (map cdr ls))
```

to do the job.

However, implementing this pattern as shown, with explicit calls to filter and map, can be rather inefficient. The map procedure has to build up the entire list of cdrs even if only a few of them are negative, and filter has to build up its result list all over again. The whole process would be faster if filter and map were combined into a single procedure that could build up the result list just once, by deciding whether to include each of the results of the mapped procedure as soon as it is generated.

Define a filtermap procedure that implements this more efficient strategy. It should receive a unary predicate, a single-valued procedure, and one or more lists, with the arity of the procedure matching the number of lists. It should apply the procedure to corresponding elements of the lists, just as map does, but should then apply the unary predicate to each result of that application, returning a list of those that satisfy the predicate.

3.7–7 Define an unshuffle procedure that receives a list and returns two lists (as separate results), respectively comprising the elements in even-numbered positions in the given list and the elements in odd-numbered positions. Preserve the relative order of the elements within each result.

3.7–8 Here is an unsuccessful attempt to define take using fold-natural:

```
(define (take ls count)
  ((pipe (fold-natural (create (list) ls)
                       (dispatch (pipe (~next first) prepend)
                                 (pipe >next rest)))
         >initial)
   count))
```

The idea is that the recursive procedure that fold-natural constructs returns two lists each time it is invoked, specifically, a "result list" of elements that have been taken from the beginning of ls, and a "remainder list" of elements of ls that have not yet been examined. When count is 0, the base procedure generates the starting values: an empty result list, and ls as the remainder list. When count is positive, it indicates the number of times that we want to transfer an element from the remainder list to the result list. The step procedure performs one such transfer.

Test this definition and determine how the procedure it defines differs in behavior from the take procedure defined in the text (using unfold-list). Diagnose the flaw in the plan and suggest a possible remedy.

3.7–9 Define an adapter that receives three arguments and returns the last and the first of them, in that order.

3.7–10 Suggest an alternative definition of at-least-one, based on the observation that at least one of a group of values satisfies a predicate condition-met?

if and only if it is not the case that every value in the group satisfies the complementary predicate (`^not condition-met?`).

3.7–11   Define a procedure `matrix-map` that receives two arguments, a unary procedure and a non-empty list of non-empty lists of equal length, and returns a similarly structured non-empty list of non-empty lists in which each element is the result of applying the unary procedure to the element in the corresponding row and column of the given list of lists.

3.8   Sources

Lists are so general and so flexible that they can serve as models for almost all of the data structures that we consider. However, they have two limitations that are occasionally awkward and restrictive:

- All of the elements of a list are actually present in the list, so that they must be computed even if it turns out that the intended application needs only a few of them.

- Every list is finite, containing a certain number of elements and no more.

The first of these limitations implies the second, since if a data structure contained infinitely many values, all actually present, no algorithm could construct it and no physical storage device could hold it.

Consider what would happen if we tried, for instance, to construct a list comprising all the natural numbers, in ascending order. Here's one plausible-looking attempt:

```
(define natural-number-list
  ((unfold-list (constant #f) identity add1) 0))
```

The unfolder first determines that 0 does not satisfy (`constant #f`)—nothing does, of course—and concludes that it should return a non-empty list. It applies `identity` to 0 to get the first element, 0. To generate the rest of the list, it applies the step procedure `add1` to 0 and invokes itself recursively on the result, 1. Since 1 does not satisfy (`constant #f`), we get another element, (`identity 1`) or simply 1, and another recursive invocation, this one receiving (`add1 1`), or 2, as its argument ... and so on, forever. Each invocation of the unfolder launches another, and none of the invocations ever returns a value because none of them ever finishes building a list.

Since algorithms must terminate, this definition does not express an algorithm. In practice, if we submit the definition of `natural-number-list` to a Scheme processor, it will continue invoking the unfolder over and over again until it exhausts either the available storage, at which point it will crash, or the patience of the observer, at which point she will interrupt it. In neither case will a useful result be obtained.

A *source* is a data structure that *implicitly* contains infinitely many elements. No algorithm can generate or use all of the elements of a source (because a process that requires an infinite number of steps is not an algorithm), but at the same time there is no fixed upper bound on the number of elements that an algorithm *can* generate and use, as there would be with a list.

But how can a data structure of any kind contain its elements "implicitly"? The answer is that, in place of the element itself, the data structure contains a way to generate or construct that element when it is needed. It is natural to implement the generator as a nullary procedure that computes the desired element when it is invoked.

However, if each element were replaced by a separate generation procedure of this sort, and each of these generation procedures were actually present in the data structure, we would have made no progress: A procedure also takes some time to construct and occupies storage, so we can't have infinitely many of them actually present in a data structure.

The solution to this problem is to use procedures that bear the same kind of relation to sources that pairs bear to lists. A source implicitly contains both its first element and another source, which in turn implicitly contains another element and yet another source, and so on.

Now we can see a more useful strategy for implementing sources: We'll represent a source as a nullary procedure that, when invoked, returns two values, of which the first is the initial element of the source and the second is another source—the "rest" of the given source. To support this strategy, the (afp primitives) library provides a new keyword, source. A source-expression consists of this keyword and one subexpression, with parentheses enclosing these components. The subexpression, when evaluated, should produce two values, of which the second is a source.

For instance, if all-zeroes is a source, then the value of the expression

```
(source (values 0 all-zeroes))
```

is the procedure

```
(lambda ()
  (values 0 all-zeroes))
```

which is also a source.

Note that the source keyword itself does not designate a procedure and that evaluating a source-expression does not immediately result in the evaluation of the subexpression that becomes the body of the nullary procedure. This makes it possible to write recursive definitions like

```
(define all-zeroes (source (values 0 all-zeroes)))
```

without getting an "unbound identifier" error: The value of the identifier
`all-zeroes` in the body of the definition is not needed until the nullary procedure is actually invoked, which can't happen until after the definition is complete.

To hide the implementation, let's use `tap` as an alias for `invoke` in cases
where the argument is a source:

```
(define tap invoke)
```

For instance, the call '`(tap all-zeroes)`' has two values: 0 and the source
`all-zeroes`. It may be helpful to think of `tap` as the analogue for sources of
the `deprepend` procedure for lists.

Note that there is no guarantee that the `tap` operation runs in a constant
amount of time. Unlike a list, a source does not have its first element ready and
waiting in a storage location, and there is no upper bound on the amount of
computation that a source may have to do in order to compute its first element.

We can now define `natural-number-source` in a way that pleasantly reflects
the definition of the *natural-number* type:

```
(define natural-number-source
  ((rec (up-from nat)
     (source (values nat (up-from (add1 nat)))))
   0))
```

The `up-from` procedure gives us a source containing the natural numbers
starting with `nat`. Tapping that source gives us `nat` and a source that starts
from (`add1 nat`) and carries on forever from there. The value to which this definition binds the identifier '`natural-number-source`' is the source that `up-from`
constructs when `nat` is 0.

One disadvantage of using procedures to model sources is that there is no
satisfactory classification predicate. One might be tempted to write something
like

```
(define (source? something)
  (and (procedure? something)
       (receive results (something)
         (and (= (length results) 2)
              (source? (first (rest results)))))))
```

However, this procedure does not return `#t` when given a source, because it
does not return at all. Each recursive invocation of `source?` leads to another,
and none of them ever returns a result. (Another problem is that this procedure
crashes instead of returning `#f` when `something` happens to be a procedure that
requires at least one argument.)

Similarly, the fact that sources have infinitely many elements makes it impossible to define an equality predicate for them. An attempt might look like
this:

```
(define (source=? left right)
  (receive (left-starter left-followers) (tap left)
    (receive (right-starter right-followers) (tap right)
      (and (equal? left-starter right-starter)
           (source=? left-followers right-followers)))))
```

This procedure taps the two sources repeatedly until a difference shows up, at which point it returns #f. The problem is that it runs forever if the two sources are indeed the same (in the sense of having equal elements at every position).

So our collection of primitives for sources is extremely limited: just source-expressions (which act as constructors) and the tap procedure (a selector). The surprise is how much we can do with these resources. Many operations on lists have analogues using sources instead.

For instance, it is easy to define the source-ref procedure, which selects the element at a given position in a given source. (The position can be any natural number.)

```
(define (source-ref src position)
  (receive (initial others) (tap src)
    (if (zero? position)
        initial
        (source-ref others (sub1 position)))))
```

The source->list procedure collects a specified number of elements from a source and assembles them into a list, returning both the list and a source containing the rest of the elements of the original source:

```
(define (source->list src number)
  (if (zero? number)
      (values (list) src)
      (receive (initial others) (tap src)
        (receive (rest-of-list depleted)
                 (source->list others (sub1 number))
          (values (prepend initial rest-of-list) depleted)))))
```

A simpler version is possible if we just want to discard elements from the beginning of a source: We tap the source repeatedly, using number to count the taps, and return the source that results from the last one.

```
(define (source-drop src number)
  ((fold-natural (create src) (pipe tap >next)) number))
```

Given any value, we can construct a source that implicitly contains that value as each of its elements, as all-zeroes implicitly contains infinitely many zeroes. The constant-source procedure generalizes the process:

```
(define (constant-source element)
  (rec repeater (source (values element repeater))))
```

Still more generally, the `cyclic-source` procedure constructs a source that
cycles through one or more given values:

```
(define (cyclic-source initial . others)
  ((rec (cycler ls)
     (source (if (empty-list? ls)
                 (values initial (cycler others))
                 (values (first ls) (cycler (rest ls))))))
   (prepend initial others)))
```

For instance, the call '`(cyclic-source 1 2 3)`' returns a source with the elements 1, 2, 3, 1, 2, 3, 1, ..., indefinitely. Each time the values supplied as
arguments run out, the cycle starts over again.

We can interleave the elements of two given sources, taking them alternately
from one and then from the other:

```
(define (interleave left right)
  (source (receive (initial new-right) (tap left)
            (values initial (interleave right new-right)))))
```

For instance, we can interleave the natural numbers with the negative integers
to get a source that has all the integers as elements:

```
(define integer-source
  (interleave natural-number-source
              ((rec (down-from number)
                 (source (values number (down-from (sub1 number)))))
               -1)))
```

Conversely, we can split a source into two, putting the elements occupying
even-numbered positions in the given source into one and those occupying odd-
numbered positions into the other. As a warmup, let's define an `alternator`
procedure that transforms a given source by discarding the elements in odd
positions:

```
(define (alternator src)
  (source (receive (initial others) (tap src)
            (receive (next still-others) (tap others)
              (values initial (alternator still-others))))))
```

To split a source, then, we construct two alternating sources, one starting with
the first element of the given source, the other starting with the second:

```
(define (disinterleave src)
  (values (alternator src)
          (source (tap (alternator (source-drop src 1))))))
```

The mechanics of the `disinterleave` procedure illustrate one of the serious limitations of using sources. Suppose that we take the two sources that `disinterleave` returns (let's call them `evens` and `odds`). If we proceed to compute, say, (`source->list evens 7`), the computation that recovers the first seven elements of `evens` actually involves computing the first thirteen elements of the source from which `evens` was obtained, discarding almost half of them. And if we also compute, say, (`source->list odds 9`), all of those elements from the original source will be computed all over again, along with five more (although this time we keep the elements that we discarded in the earlier computation, and discard the ones that we kept then).

Thus each element of `evens` and `odds`, except for the first element of `evens`, requires as much computation as two elements of `src`. Moreover, each of the two sources has to do essentially the same underlying computation. Creating a lot of duplicates and derivatives of the same underlying source and using them in such as way as to compute the same elements from that same underlying source over and over again loses most of the advantages of using sources in the first place: Anything we might gain by not having to compute elements we don't need, we could easily lose back by repeatedly computing the ones we do need. It would be smarter to compute them once and save them.[4]

We'll therefore avoid the use of source splitters like `disinterleave`, and arrange most of our computations so that we never tap twice for the same element: Having once asked a source to compute its first element, we discard it and continue instead with the source that we get back as the second result of `tap`. Similarly, if we use `source->list` to get several elements at once, we'll refrain from using the source again, so that we never recompute those elements, and go on instead with the source that `source->list` returns as its second result.

If we follow this policy strictly, there are almost no appropriate occasions for using the `source-ref` procedure, since to recover the element in position n we have to tap our way through all of the elements in lower-numbered positions. Also, we'll have to take care while writing the source analogues of procedures like `map`. A `map-source` procedure should not actually do any tapping at all when it is invoked, but should rather build and return a source that defers the tapping until it itself is tapped. Even then, tapping the source that `map-source` returns should do only enough computation to produce its first element and the source that will compute the rest of the elements.

Let's see how this can work in practice. Given an n-ary procedure and n sources, `map-source` returns a new source in which each element is the result of applying the given procedure to corresponding elements of those sources. The idea is to compute each element of the new source, *when it is tapped*, by tapping

---

[4]There are data structures known as *streams*, which are similar in some ways to sources, but automate the process of saving elements as they are computed. A full implementation of streams can be found in Scheme Request for Implementation 41 (http://srfi.schemers.org/srfi-41/), by Philip L. Bewig. I have avoided introducing streams here because the structures that implement them have mutable state: Tapping a stream for the first time has a side effect on it, overwriting some of the values that the underlying data structure formerly contained with new values.

all of the given sources once, collecting the elements that they return, and applying procedure. However, each tap on one of the given sources produces not only an element but another source, and we'll need to keep those returned sources around, so that we can provide them as arguments when we're ready to do the recursive call.

This suggests that we need to build a data structure to hold the results of all the taps: a list of pairs, one pair for each of the given sources, in which the car is the first element of that source and the cdr is the source containing the rest of the elements. The following definition of map-source shows how this data structure (let's call it tap-pairs) is built up pair by pair and then unzipped to separate the cars from the cdrs:

```
(define (map-source procedure . sources)
  ((rec (mapper srcs)
     (source (let ((tap-pairs (map (pipe tap cons) srcs)))
               (values (apply procedure (map car tap-pairs))
                       (mapper (map cdr tap-pairs))))))
   sources))
```

For instance, the result of the call

```
(map-source + (cyclic-source 0 1)
              (cyclic-source 0 0 2 2)
              (cyclic-source 0 0 0 0 4 4 4 4))
```

is a source that runs cyclically through the integers from 0 to 7, computed as $0 + 0 + 0$, $1 + 0 + 0$, $0 + 2 + 0$, $1 + 2 + 0$, $0 + 0 + 4$, and so on.

Notice the placement of the keyword source in the definition of the map-source procedure. None of the operations on srcs actually take place when mapper is invoked, because the body of the source-expression is not evaluated at that point. The mapper procedure simply builds a source (a nullary procedure, remember) with that body and returns it. The actual computation and use of tap-pairs is deferred until the source that map-source returns is tapped. And the same is true on each recursive invocation of mapper: No substantial computation is done at the time of the invocation. It's all deferred until the source that the invocation *returns* is tapped, presumably because another element is needed.

To illustrate the power of map-source, here is an alternative definition of natural-number-source. The first element of this source is 0, and each subsequent element is the result of adding 1 to a natural number. To obtain the source that contains all the non-zero natural numbers, then, we can map add1 along the very source we're constructing!

```
(define natural-number-source
  (source (values 0 (map-source add1 natural-number-source))))
```

This definition is recursive, but not viciously circular, because the use of a source-expression once more means that the identifier `natural-number-source` will not be evaluated until after it has been defined.

There is no analogue of `fold-list` for sources, both because no algorithm can fold an infinite number of elements together to produce a result and because there is no base case for the recursion—*every* source produces another source when it is tapped. However, it is possible to process elements of a source from left to right, releasing the resulting values one by one, through a new source. For this to work, the `base` and `combiner` procedures must both be single-valued. The first element of the new source is the result of invoking `base`; the second element is the result of applying `combiner` to that base value and the first element of the given source; the third element is the result of applying `combiner` to *that* result and the second element of the given source; and so on:

```
(define (process-source base combiner)
  (lambda (src)
    (source (let ((base-value (base)))
              (values
                base-value
                ((rec (processor src previous)
                    (source (receive (initial others) (tap src)
                              (let ((new (combiner initial previous)))
                                (values new (processor others new))))))
                 src base-value))))))
```

For instance, the call '`(process-source (create 1) *)`' returns a procedure that transforms any source of numbers into a source of the cumulative partial products of those numbers. Applying this procedure to `(constant-source 7)` would give a source containing the powers of 7; applying it to `(map-source add1 natural-number-source)`, which is the source of positive integers, yields a source containing the factorials, in ascending order!

Sources can also be unfolded. Since a source never runs out, there is no need for a `final?` predicate in `unfold-source`, but the `producer` and `step` procedures operate as in `unfold-list`:

```
(define (unfold-source producer step)
  (rec (unfolder . arguments)
    (source (values (apply producer arguments)
                    (apply (pipe step unfolder) arguments)))))
```

For instance, the value of the call '`(unfold-source square add1)`' is a procedure that receives an integer as a starting point and returns a source containing the squares of successive integers, beginning with the one specified.

As the examples suggest, many infinite sequences are conveniently represented by sources. For instance, there are several ways to construct the *Fibonacci sequence* 0, 1, 1, 2, 3, 5, 8, 13, 21, ..., in which every term after the first two is the sum of the two terms that precede it. One straightforward approach is to unfold the sequence. We supply the first two values of the sequence explicitly. To produce an element, the source simply returns the first of the two values, and the step procedure generates the values for the next source by promoting the second of the two values it receives to the first position and adding those two values to generate the next element of the sequence:

```
(define Fibonacci
  ((unfold-source >initial (dispatch >next +)) 0 1))
```

The unfold-source procedure supplies the mechanism for deferring the computation of new elements until they are needed.

Finite Sources

One of the reasons for preferring sources to lists is that an application can tap a source for the elements that it needs and no more, never computing any elements that aren't actually used in the computation. This rationale also applies in some cases where the number of elements is finite but large. Also, even in applications where it would be possible to use a list, we might prefer to use a source because it occupies less storage than a long list, since it contains its elements implicitly rather than explicitly.

There are several ways to adapt sources so that they can represent finite sequences as well as infinite ones. The key design decision is how to represent a sequence that has run out of elements to return, that is, an empty source. If we continue to use procedures to implement sources, what should an empty source return when we invoke it?

One possibility is to have the procedure that represents an empty source return zero values rather than two, which would unambiguously show that it can provide no more information from its store. Alternatively, we could use the convention of signalling the failure of a normally successful operation by returning an unboxed #f, and revising the other source operations so that non-empty sources return their elements in boxed form.

However, neither of these designs meshes very well with our existing design for infinite sources. There is a third design that enables us to use the procedures developed above almost without change: An empty source can signal that it has no more elements by returning a *sentinel*—a conventional, designated value that is used only for this single purpose, rather like the null value that terminates a list. The (afp primitives) library provides such a value, the one and only value of the *end-of-source* type, and two primitive procedures for working with it: the nullary procedure end-of-source, which constructs it, and the classification predicate end-of-source?, which distinguishes it from other values.

Any source that returns the sentinel when it is tapped counts as empty, so we can determine whether a given source is empty by tapping it and testing the first result:

```
(define empty-source? (run tap >initial end-of-source?))
```

However, this is another of those procedures that it would be imprudent to use in most cases. If we discover that the source is not empty, we'd usually want to tap it again to get its first element—the same element that `empty-source?` has already computed once in order to be able to see whether it was an end-of-source value. A better approach is to tap the source without first testing whether it is empty, preparing to take appropriate action later on if we have gone too far.

A carelessly or deviously written application might construct a source that has the end-of-source value as its first element, but other values concealed behind it. Indeed, it's trivial to construct such a source:

```
(source (values (end-of-source) natural-number-source))
```

We will treat such sources as empty, and in general we will regard a source as finite if any of its elements is the end-of-source value, ignoring all subsequent elements no matter what they are. The definition of `empty-source?`, above, is consistent with this convention.

The `list->finite-source` procedure converts a list into a finite source with the same elements. It uses `unfold-source`. The producer procedure obtains the first element of the given list and makes it the first element of the source; the step procedure hands the rest of the list over to the recursion to build the source containing the rest of its elements. If the given list is empty, the producer instead returns the end-of-source value and the step procedure does nothing (so that the sentinel occupies all of the subsequent positions in the resulting source):

```
(define list->finite-source
  (unfold-source (^if empty-list? (constant (end-of-source)) first)
                 (^if empty-list? identity rest)))
```

With `list->finite-source`, it is trivial to define a finite-source constructor that can receive any number of arguments and constructs a source that has those arguments as its elements:

```
(define (finite-source . elements)
  (list->finite-source elements))
```

Going in the other direction, the `finite-source->list` procedure computes all of the elements in a finite source and assembles them into a list. Instead of using `unfold-list` or one of the other stock patterns of recursion, we arrange the computation so that the tap comes before the test that determines whether the source is empty:

```
(define (finite-source->list src)
  (receive (initial others) (tap src)
    (if (end-of-source? initial)
        (list)
        (prepend initial (finite-source->list others)))))
```

The analogues of `catenate` and `append` are not very useful for infinite sources, because no amount of tapping would ever get us past the first source into the second! If we're working with finite sources, however, we can switch over to the second source when the first one produces the sentinel value:

```
(define (catenate-sources left right)
  ((rec (advancer rest-of-left)
     (source (receive (initial others) (tap rest-of-left)
               (if (end-of-source? initial)
                   (tap right)
                   (values initial (advancer others))))))
   left))
```

It is not *necessarily* an error to give `catenate-sources` arguments that are not finite when invoking it, provided that your application can accommodate the behavior just mentioned (unless `left` is finite, the elements of `right` will never be reached).

We can obtain an `append-sources` procedure by extending the arity of `catenate-sources`, with an empty source as the right identity:

```
(define append-sources
  (extend-to-variable-arity (constant-source (end-of-source))
                            catenate-sources))
```

We saw above that folding wouldn't make sense for infinite sources. On the other hand, we can treat finite sources like lists, with empty sources constituting the base case. Since we want to tap the source once and only once for each element, the recursive procedure is slightly different in structure from the one we used to define `fold-list`, in that the tap is placed ahead of the test for the base case:

```
(define (fold-finite-source base combiner)
  (rec (folder src)
    (receive (initial others) (tap src)
      (if (end-of-source? initial)
          (base)
          (receive recursive-results (folder others)
            (apply combiner initial recursive-results))))))
```

Although we could use the `map-source` procedure defined above with finite sources as well, it is convenient to define a separate `map-finite-source` procedure that does not attempt to apply the mapping procedure to the end-of-source object:

```
(define (map-finite-source procedure src)
  ((rec (mapper subsource)
     (source (receive (chosen others) (tap subsource)
```

```
                (if (end-of-source? chosen)
                    (values (end-of-source) subsource)
                    (values (procedure chosen) (mapper others)))))))
   src))
```

---

tap   (afp sources)
source(α) $\rightarrow$ α, *source(α)*
src
Return the initial element of src and a source containing the remaining elements of src.

natural-number-source   (afp sources)
source(natural-number)
A source implicitly containing the natural numbers, in ascending order.

source->list   (afp sources)
source(α), natural-number $\rightarrow$ *list(α), source(α)*
src   number
Construct a list of the first number elements of src, returning both the list and a source
containing the rest of the elements of src.

source-drop   (afp sources)
source(α), natural-number $\rightarrow$ *source(α)*
src   number
Discard number elements from src and return a source containing the rest of the elements of
src.

constant-source   (afp sources)
α $\rightarrow$ *source(α)*
element
Construct a source with element as each of its elements.

cyclic-source   (afp sources)
α, α ... $\rightarrow$ *source(α)*
initial others
Construct a source with initial and the elements of others as its elements, starting over with
initial after each has appeared.

interleave   (afp sources)
source(α), source(α) $\rightarrow$ *source(α)*
left   right
Construct a source whose elements are taken alternately from left and right.

integer-source   (afp sources)
source(integer)
A source implicitly containing the integers, in ascending order by absolute value.

map-source   (afp sources)
(α ... $\rightarrow$ β), source(α) ... $\rightarrow$ *source(β)*
procedure   sources
Construct a source in which each element is the result of applying procedure to corresponding
elements of sources.
Precondition: procedure can receive corresponding elements of sources.

process-source   (afp sources)
($\rightarrow$ α), (β, α $\rightarrow$ α) $\rightarrow$ *(source(β) $\rightarrow$ source(α))*
base   combiner   src
Construct a procedure that iteratively applies combiner to an element of src and the result of
the previous iteration (or to the result of invoking base, if there was no previous iteration).
The constructed procedure returns a source containing the results of successive iterations.
Precondition: combiner can receive the initial element of src and the result of an invocation
of base.
Precondition: combiner can receive any but the initial element of src and the result of any
invocation of combiner.

unfold-source   (afp sources)
$(\alpha \ldots \to \beta), (\alpha \ldots \to \alpha \ldots) \to (\alpha \ldots \qquad \to source(\beta))$
producer   step   arguments
Construct a procedure that, in turn, constructs a source in which the initial element is the
result of applying producer to the elements of arguments, and the remainder of the source is the
result of first applying step to the elements of arguments and then applying the constructed
procedure recursively to the results.
Precondition: producer can receive the elements of arguments.
Precondition: producer can receive the results of any invocation of step.
Precondition: step can receive the elements of arguments.
Precondition: step can receive the results of any invocation of step.

end-of-source   -   (afp primitives)
$\to end\text{-}of\text{-}source$
Return the end-of-source sentinel value.

end-of-source?   (afp primitives)
$any \qquad \to Boolean$
something
Determine whether something is the end-of-source sentinel value.

list->finite-source   (afp sources)
$list(\alpha) \to source(\alpha)$
ls
Construct a finite source with the elements of ls as its elements.

finite-source   (afp sources)
$\alpha \ldots \qquad \to source(\alpha)$
elements
Construct a finite source with the elements of elements as its elements.

finite-source->list   (afp sources)
$source(\alpha) \to list(\alpha)$
src
Construct a list with the elements of src as its elements.
Precondition: src is a finite source.

catenate-sources   (afp sources)
$source(\alpha), source(\alpha) \to source(\alpha)$
left   right
Construct a source containing the (pre-sentinel) elements of left, in order, followed by the
elements of right, in order.

append-sources   (afp sources)
$source(\alpha) \ldots \to source(\alpha)$
sources
Construct a source containing the elements of the elements of sources, retaining both the
relative order of the elements and the relative order of the elements within each element.

fold-finite-source   (afp sources)
$(\to \alpha \ldots), (\beta, \alpha \ldots \to \alpha \ldots) \to (source(\beta) \to \alpha \ldots)$
base   combiner   src
Construct a procedure that returns the results of invoking base if src is empty. If src is
non-empty, the constructed procedure applies itself recursively to the source that results from
tapping src and returns the results of applying combiner to the first result of tapping src and
the results of the recursive invocation.
Precondition: combiner can receive the last (pre-sentinel) element of src and the results of an
invocation of base.
Precondition: combiner can receive any but the last (pre-sentinel) element of src and the
results of any invocation of combiner.
Precondition: src is a finite source.

map-finite-source   (afp sources)

$(\alpha \to \beta),\ source(\alpha)\ \to\ source(\beta)$
procedure src
Construct a source (a finite source, if src is finite) comprising the results applying procedure to successive elements of src.
Precondition: procedure can receive any element of src.

Exercises

3.8–1 Define a source containing the negative powers of two, in descending order. (The first element should be 1/2, the second 1/4, and so on.)

3.8–2 Define a procedure merge-sources that receives two sources each containing numbers in monotonically non-decreasing order, and constructs a single source containing all of the elements from both sources, also in monotonically non-decreasing order. (If a number is duplicated in either of the given sources, or if the same number is an element of both, it should also be duplicated in the constructed source.) Assume than neither source is finite.

3.8–3 Define a procedure finite-source-length that determines how many elements a finite source has (not including the sentinel or any of the elements that follow it).

3.8–4 Define a procedure conditionally-unfold-source, bearing the same relation to unfold-source that conditionally-unfold-list bears to unfold-list: The conditionally-unfold-source procedure should receive an additional argument, a predicate, and arrange for an element to be produced by a source only when that predicate is satisfied by the guide arguments.

3.8–5 Define a procedure unfold-finite-source, similar to the unfold-source procedure defined above, except that it receives a final? predicate in addition to the producer and step procedures, and constructs a procedure that returns an empty finite source when the guide arguments satisfy final?.

3.9 Tuples

A slightly different way to think about product types is to think of each component as having a different significance and role. The elements of a list are usually alike in some way, or at least differ in ways that are independent of their positions in the list. By contrast, the significance of each component of a *tuple* depends at least partly on its position in the tuple. To mark this significance, each position in the tuple is given a name, and selection procedures that apply to tuples use these names.

For instance, in an astronomy program, one might design a tuple to hold various kinds of information about a star. Let's say that the tuple has as its components a string giving the name of the star, a number indicating its apparent magnitude (that is, its brightness, as seen from the earth); another number indicating its distance from the Sun in parsecs, and a symbol indicating its spectral class. The type-theoretical view of the *star* type, then, is summarized in the equations

$$
\begin{aligned}
name &= string \\
magnitude &= number \\
distance &= number \\
spectral\text{-}class &= symbol \\
star &= star\text{-}name \times magnitude \times distance \times spectral\text{-}class
\end{aligned}
$$

The constructor for values of the *star* type receives these four separate values and returns a four-component tuple containing them. Four separate selector procedures are needed, each taking a star-tuple as its argument and returning a specific component; in addition, it would be useful to have a selection procedure that returns *all* of the components as separate values, disaggregating the structure. Since we'll also want a classification predicate and an equality predicate, the repertoire of basic procedures for star-tuples comprises eight procedures:

```
(define (make-star name magnitude distance spectral-class) ...)
(define (star-name star) ...)
(define (star-magnitude star) ...)
(define (star-distance star) ...)
(define (star-spectral-class star) ...)
(define (destar star) ...)
(define (star? something) ...)
(define (star=? star-0 star-1) ...)
```

On the foundation provided by these basic procedures, we can build procedures that the astronomy program might use, such as these:

```
(define brighter? (compare-by star-magnitude <))
(define (filter-by-spectral-class sc catalog)
  (filter (pipe star-spectral-class (sect symbol=? <> sc)) catalog))
(define nearest-star
  (extend-to-positive-arity (^if (compare-by star-distance <=)
                             >initial
                             >next)))
```

Building the Model

One way to model the *star* type is to implement its values as four-element lists. Everything is straightforward: The constructor invokes `list` to build the star from its components. The component selectors invoke `list-ref`, each giving it the appropriate index, and the selector that returns all of the components invokes `delist`. The classification predicate checks whether the value it is given is a list and, if so, whether it has the right number of elements and whether the type of each element is correct. The equality predicate goes through the fields, checking whether they match up and returning #f if it finds a mismatch and #t if it finds none:

```
(define make-star (sect list <> <> <> <>))
(define star-name (sect list-ref <> 0))
(define star-magnitude (sect list-ref <> 1))
(define star-distance (sect list-ref <> 2))
(define star-spectral-class (sect list-ref <> 3))
(define destar delist)
(define star? (^and list?
                    (pipe length (sect = <> 4))
                    (pipe star-name string?)
                    (pipe star-magnitude number?)
                    (pipe star-distance number?)
                    (pipe star-spectral-class symbol?)))
(define star=? (^and (compare-by star-name string=?)
                     (compare-by star-magnitude =)
                     (compare-by star-distance =)
                     (compare-by star-spectral-class symbol=?)))
```

Writing similar definitions for any kind of tuples that one needs is a matter of routine.

Record Types

Alternatively, Scheme provides a way for programmers to create new tuple types, making it unnecessary to model them. The idea is to describe the tuple that you want in a special form called define-record-type, which will then build the constructor, classification predicate, and selectors for you, like this:

```
(define-record-type star
  (make-star name magnitude distance spectral-class)
  proto-star?
  (name star-name)
  (magnitude star-magnitude)
  (distance star-distance)
  (spectral-class star-spectral-class))
```

After the define-record-type keyword, the first subform must be a symbol, giving the name of the type. The second must be a non-empty list of symbols; the first symbol in the list becomes the name of the constructor, and all the subsequent ones become the parameters of the constructor. The third subform must be a symbol giving the name of the classification predicate. All of the remaining subforms are lists—two-element lists, in our record type definitions— in which the first symbol gives the name of a field of the record and the second gives the name of the selector for that field.

The record type definition shown above effectively defines six procedures: `make-star`, `proto-star?`, `star-name`, `star-magnitude`, `star-distance`, and `star-spectral-class`. Scheme's record type definitions do not automatically define disaggregators or equality predicates, so we'll have to define those separately.

The tuples that `define-record-type` introduces place no constraints on the kinds of values that are stored in the various fields. This is why there's no equality predicate; Scheme extends `equal?` to handle record types along with all the others, and assumes that this will be sufficient. Similarly, the classification predicate `proto-star?` determines whether the value it receives is indeed a record and has the correct number of fields, but otherwise imposes no constraint. That's why I've given it a different name. The *real* classification predicate `star?` just takes `proto-star?` as a starting point.

For our purposes, the classification and equality predicates really should take the types of the fields into account. Fortunately, this is straightforward. A full definition of `star` as a tuple type using records looks like this:

```
(define-record-type star
  (make-star name magnitude distance spectral-class)
  proto-star?
  (name star-name)
  (magnitude star-magnitude)
  (distance star-distance)
  (spectral-class star-spectral-class))

(define destar
  (dispatch star-name star-magnitude star-distance star-spectral-class))

(define star? (^and proto-star?
                    (pipe star-name string?)
                    (pipe star-magnitude number?)
                    (pipe star-distance number?)
                    (pipe star-spectral-class symbol?)))

(define star=? (^and (compare-by star-name string=?)
                     (compare-by star-magnitude =)
                     (compare-by star-distance =)
                     (compare-by star-spectral-class symbol=?)))
```

Exercises

3.9–1 Using `define-record-type`, implement a tuple type *song*, representing a digital recording of a musical performance. The components of the tuple should include the name of the song, the name of the performing artist or group, the year in which it was released, the playing time in seconds, the file format of the recording, and the file size in bytes.

3.9–2 Using the implementation you provided in the previous exercise, define a procedure `total-ogg-playing-time` that receives a list of *song* values and returns the sum of the playing times of all of the songs in the list that are stored in the Ogg file format.

3.9–3 With the same implementation, define a procedure `how-many-by` that receives the name of a performer or group and a list of songs and returns a count of the number of songs on the list by that performer or group.

3.10 Trees

The recursive definition of a *linear* data structure indicates that a non-empty instance of the structure directly contains one and only one substructure of the same type. For instance, the *list* data structure is linear: A non-empty list contains a list as its `rest`. Recursion managers for linear structures reflect this definition, in that they construct singly recursive procedures.

We can sometimes design a more efficient algorithm for a particular problem if we arrange the values that we need to process in a data container that has a *non-linear* structure, directly containing two or more substructures of the same type, or even a variable number of such substructures. The components of a non-linear structure often implicitly carry information about other components and substructures, and this information can be used to simplify the processing of those other components or to eliminate superfluous computations. Often this implicit information takes the form of an invariant that every instance of the structure satisfies *by construction*. We write the primitives for the data structure in such a way that every value of the data type that can be returned by any of the primitives satisfies the invariant.

A natural way to start branching out from linear structures is to consider a possible extension of the idea of a list. Recall that the equation that specifies the *list* type is

$$list \quad = \quad null \,|\, (any \times list)$$

That is, either a list is empty, or it comprises a value and another list. Thus it is natural to advance to a structure called a *binary tree* or, in this book, simply a *tree*, with the following specification:

$$tree \quad = \quad null \,|\, (any \times tree \times tree)$$

That is, either a tree is empty, or it comprises a value and *two* other trees, which we'll call its *left subtree* and *right subtree*.

There are several good ways to model trees in Scheme. The one that we'll develop here uses two kinds of tuples, one for the empty tree and another for non-empty trees. (An alternative model is suggested in the exercises at the end of this section.)

```
(define-record-type empty-tree
  (make-empty-tree)
  empty-tree?)
(define de-empty-tree black-hole)
(define empty-tree=? (constant #t))
```

This odd-looking record type definition defines a tuple type with no components. Since there are no type constraints to enforce on the fields, we don't need to use the "proto-" technique to get a classification predicate in this case; the one that `define-record-type` generates is fine. So we get a constructor, `make-empty-tree`, that receives no arguments and always returns an empty tree; a rather pointless disaggregator `de-empty-tree` that receives an empty tree and returns no value, a classification predicate `empty-tree?`, and an equality predicate `empty-tree=?`—also rather pointless, since it always returns #t.

The definition of the *non-empty-tree* type is more interesting:

```
(define-record-type non-empty-tree
  (make-non-empty-tree root left right)
  proto-non-empty-tree?
  (root non-empty-tree-root)
  (left non-empty-tree-left)
  (right non-empty-tree-right))

(define de-non-empty-tree (dispatch non-empty-tree-root
                                    non-empty-tree-left
                                    non-empty-tree-right))
(define (non-empty-tree? something)
  (and (proto-non-empty-tree? something)
       (tree? (non-empty-tree-left something))
       (tree? (non-empty-tree-right something))))
(define (non-empty-tree=? tr-0 tr-1)
  (and (equal? (non-empty-tree-root tr-0) (non-empty-tree-root tr-1))
       (tree=? (non-empty-tree-left tr-0) (non-empty-tree-left tr-1))
       (tree=? (non-empty-tree-right tr-0)
               (non-empty-tree-right tr-1))))
```

The omission of a test for the root component in the classification predicate indicates that any value whatever can appear at that position. Like *pair* and *list*, the `tree` type is a generic structure.

The definition of `non-empty-tree?` uses a classification predicate `tree?` that we haven't defined yet. Similarly, `non-empty-tree=?` relies on a general equality predicate for trees, `tree=?`. However, since *tree* is the sum type of the types *empty-tree* and *non-empty-tree*, which do not overlap, the needed definitions are straightforward:

```
(define tree? (^vel empty-tree? non-empty-tree?))
```

```
(define tree=? (^vel (every empty-tree?)
                     (^et (every non-empty-tree?)
                          non-empty-tree=?)))
```

It's handy to have a name for the frequently occurring special case of `make-non-empty-tree` in which both subtrees are empty:

```
(define singleton-tree
  (sect make-non-empty-tree <> (make-empty-tree) (make-empty-tree)))
```

A singleton tree that constitutes a part of a tree T is a *leaf* of T, whereas a tree that is part of T but has a non-empty subtree of its own is an *internal node* of T.

As with lists, we'll sometimes want to specify that a tree contain only values of a particular type. Classification and equality predicates for such homogeneous tree types are easy variations on `tree?` and `tree=?`:

```
(define (tree-of-numbers? something)
  (or (empty-tree? something)
      (and (non-empty-tree? something)
           (number? (non-empty-tree-root something))
           (tree-of-numbers? (non-empty-tree-left something))
           (tree-of-numbers? (non-empty-tree-right something)))))
(define (tree-of-numbers=? left right)
  (or (and (empty-tree? left)
           (empty-tree? right))
      (and (non-empty-tree? left)
           (non-empty-tree? right)
           (= (non-empty-tree-root left)
              (non-empty-tree-root right))
           (tree-of-numbers=? (non-empty-tree-left left)
                              (non-empty-tree-left right))
           (tree-of-numbers=? (non-empty-tree-right left)
                              (non-empty-tree-right right)))))
```

Again, we can abstract the common elements of the pattern into higher-order tools: `tree-of`, which constructs a classification predicate for a homogeneous tree type from a classification predicate for the type of values it contains, and `tree-of=`, which similarly derives an equality predicate for the homogeneous tree type from the equality predicate for the element type:

```
(define (tree-of right-type-of-element?)
  (rec (ok? something)
    (or (empty-tree? something)
        (and (non-empty-tree? something)
             (right-type-of-element? (non-empty-tree-root something))
             (ok? (non-empty-tree-left something))
             (ok? (non-empty-tree-right something))))))
```

```
(define (tree-of= element=?)
  (rec (equivalent? left right)
    (or (and (empty-tree? left)
             (empty-tree? right))
        (and (non-empty-tree? left)
             (non-empty-tree? right)
             (element=? (non-empty-tree-root left)
                        (non-empty-tree-root right))
             (equivalent? (non-empty-tree-left left)
                          (non-empty-tree-left right))
             (equivalent? (non-empty-tree-right left)
                          (non-empty-tree-right right))))))
```

The Principle of Tree Induction

The class of trees can be defined recursively as the least inclusive class C that meets these requirements:

- The empty tree is a member of C.

- A non-empty tree in which the left and right subtrees are both members of C is also a member of C.

This definition leads immediately to a *principle of tree induction*: If the empty tree is a member of some class C', and every non-empty tree in which the left and right subtrees are members of C' is also a member of C', then every tree is a member of C'.

To illustrate the principle of tree induction, let's use it to prove the correctness of the `tree-size` procedure, which computes the total number of values stored in a tree (counting duplicates as distinct):

```
(define (tree-size tr)
  (if (empty-tree? tr)
      0
      (add1 (+ (tree-size (non-empty-tree-left tr))
               (tree-size (non-empty-tree-right tr))))))
```

Let C' be the class of trees of which `tree-size` correctly counts and returns the number of elements.

- *Base case.* Given the empty tree, `tree-size` immediately returns 0, which is the correct result.

- *Induction step.* Suppose that `tree-size` returns the correct result when given the left subtree of some non-empty tree `tree`, and also when given the right subtree of `tree`, so that both of those subtrees belong to C'. Given `tree` itself, then, `tree-size` adds the numbers of elements in the subtrees and then adds 1 to the sum. This yields the correct answer, since `tree` contains all the elements in its subtrees and in addition contains its root element. So `tree` is also a member of C'.

From these two steps, it follows by the principle of tree induction that every tree is a member of C'—in other words, that `tree-size` always returns the correct count.

Managing Recursion with Trees

We arrived at the notion of a tree by extending the notion of a list. In designing tools for managing recursion using trees, then, it is natural to consider the analogue of our basic tool for managing list recursion, `fold-list`.

Recall that the `fold-list` procedure receives two arguments, of which the first is a procedure that is invoked when the list being folded is empty and the second is a procedure that is invoked when that list is not empty. The first procedure is nullary and returns the base-case results. The second procedure synthesizes its result from the first element of the list and the results of a recursive call, which folds over the rest of the list.

The `fold-tree` procedure has a similar interface. Again, it receives a nullary procedure that generates the base-case results (for an empty tree) and a synthesizing procedure that returns the results for a non-empty tree. This time, however, the synthesizing procedure will have to collect and operate on the results of *two* recursive calls, one for each subtree:

```
(define (fold-tree base combiner)
  (rec (folder tr)
    (if (empty-tree? tr)
        (base)
        (apply combiner
               (non-empty-tree-root tr)
               (collect-map folder
                            (list (non-empty-tree-left tr)
                                  (non-empty-tree-right tr)))))))
```

It is not difficult to see the similarity of this code to the definition of `tree-size`, and indeed it is quite easy to define `tree-size` using `fold-tree`. (I have left this as an end-of-section exercise.)

There is another way to measure trees, one that takes account of their shape as well as the quantity of their components: The *height* of a tree is the largest number of nodes one might encounter in descending a tree through successive subtrees until an empty tree is reached. It can be defined recursively as follows:

1. The height of an empty tree is 0.

2. The height a non-empty tree is one greater than the greater of the heights of its left and right subtrees.

This recursive definition translates directly into an algorithm that uses folding:

```
(define tree-height
  (fold-tree (create 0) (run >all-but-initial max add1)))
```

Yet another example is `detree`, which returns all of the values in a given tree, in preorder (root first, then the values from the left subtree, then those from the right subtree):

```
(define detree (fold-tree (create) values))
```

There are many cases in which one or both of the recursive calls contribute nothing to the results of the procedure, so they can be omitted. We'll use `fold-tree` only when the results of both calls are needed in the subsequent computation.

Then again, we sometimes don't know in advance whether the recursive calls will be needed or not. Here, for instance, is a predicate that determines whether every element of a given tree satisfies a given unary predicate:

```
(define (for-all-in-tree? condition-met? tr)
  ((rec (ok? subtree)
     (or (empty-tree? subtree)
         (and (condition-met? (non-empty-tree-root subtree))
              (ok? (non-empty-tree-left subtree))
              (ok? (non-empty-tree-right subtree)))))
   tr))
```

The `for-all-in-tree?` procedure descends recursively into the tree as long as the root of each subtree that it reaches satisfies `condition-met?`. However, each of the recursive invocations is terminated at once when a non-satisfying value is encountered, no matter where in the tree it is.

Like lists, trees can be unfolded as well as folded. In other words, we can write "output-directed" recursive procedures that build trees as their results, provided that we can explain what to do at each stage.

Let's start with a useful example: a procedure `list->ordered-tree` that receives a list of numbers and returns a tree containing those numbers, with the additional constraint that, unless the tree is empty, all of the numbers in its left subtree are less than or equal to the number at its root, which in turn is less than all of the numbers in its right subtree:

```
(define (list->ordered-tree ls)
  (if (empty-list? ls)
      (make-empty-tree)
      (make-non-empty-tree (first ls)
        (list->ordered-tree (filter (sect <= <> (first ls))
                                    (rest ls)))
        (list->ordered-tree (filter (sect < (first ls) <>)
                                    (rest ls))))))
```

The use of recursion incidentally guarantees that the constraint holds not only for the entire tree that results from this construction, but also for every subtree nested within it.

More generally, unfolding a tree involves determining, from whatever arguments we're given, (1) whether to return an empty tree; (2) if we aren't going to return an empty tree, how to construct the root of the result tree; and (3 and 4) how to simplify the given arguments so as to provide suitable arguments for the recursive calls that will generate the left and right subtrees of the result tree. The `unfold-tree` procedure receives the four procedures that carry out these parts of the computation and returns a procedure that applies them at the right points:

```
(define (unfold-tree final? producer left-step right-step)
  (rec (unfolder . arguments)
    (if (apply final? arguments)
        (make-empty-tree)
        (make-non-empty-tree (apply producer arguments)
                             (apply (pipe left-step unfolder) arguments)
                             (apply (pipe right-step unfolder)
                                    arguments)))))
```

For instance, the `list->ordered-tree` procedure can be defined as follows, using some of the adapters from §2.5 to define the procedures that filter out the sublists of a given non-empty list:

```
(define list->ordered-tree
  (unfold-tree empty-list?
               first
               (run deprepend (~initial (curry (converse <=))) filter)
               (run deprepend (~initial (curry <)) filter)))
```

`make-empty-tree` (afp trees)
$\rightarrow$ *tree(any)*
Return an empty tree.

`de-empty-tree` (afp trees)
tree(any) $\rightarrow$
tr
Return no values (the components of an empty tree).

`empty-tree?` (afp trees)
any $\rightarrow$ *Boolean*
something
Determine whether something is an empty tree.

`empty-tree=?` (afp trees)
tree(any), tree(any) $\rightarrow$ *Boolean*
left   right
Determine whether left and right are the same empty tree (i.e., always return #t).
Precondition: left is an empty tree.
Precondition: right is an empty tree.

make-non-empty-tree   (afp trees)
α, $tree(\alpha)$, $tree(\alpha)$ $\rightarrow tree(\alpha)$
root left   right
Construct a non-empty tree with root as its root, left as its left subtree, and right as its
right subtree.

non-empty-tree-root   (afp trees)
$tree(\alpha)\ \rightarrow \alpha$
tr
Return the root of tr.
Precondition: tr is a non-empty tree.

non-empty-tree-left   (afp trees)
$tree(\alpha)\ \rightarrow tree(\alpha)$
tr
Return the left subtree of tr.
Precondition: tr is a non-empty tree.

non-empty-tree-right   (afp trees)
$tree(\alpha)\ \rightarrow tree(\alpha)$
tr
Return the right subtree of tr.
Precondition: tr is a non-empty tree.

de-non-empty-tree   (afp trees)
$tree(\alpha)\ \rightarrow \alpha, tree(\alpha), tree(\alpha)$
tr
Return the root, left subtree, and right subtree of tr.
Precondition: tr is a non-empty tree.

non-empty-tree?   (afp trees)
$any\qquad \rightarrow Boolean$
something
Determine whether something is a non-empty tree.

non-empty-tree=?   (afp trees)
$tree(any),\ tree(any)\ \rightarrow Boolean$
left   right
Determine whether left and right have the same structure and the same elements in corre-
sponding positions.
Precondition: left is a non-empty tree.
Precondition: right is a non-empty tree.

tree?   (afp trees)
$any\qquad \rightarrow Boolean$
something
Determine whether something is a tree.

tree=?   (afp trees)
$tree(any),\ tree(any)\ \rightarrow Boolean$
left   right
Determine whether left and right have the same structure and the same elements in corresponding positions.

singleton-tree   (afp trees)
$\alpha\qquad \rightarrow tree(\alpha)$
element
Construct a tree with element as its root and only element.

tree-of   (afp trees)
$(any\ \rightarrow Boolean)\qquad \rightarrow (any\qquad \rightarrow Boolean)$
right-type-of-element?   something
Construct a predicate that determines whether something is a tree containing only values that
satisfy right-type-of-element?.
Precondition: right-type-of-element? can receive any value.

tree-of=   (afp trees)
(α, β → Boolean) → (tree(α), tree(β) → Boolean)
element=?   left   right
Construct a predicate that determines whether `left` and `right` have the same structure and
contain elements that satisfy `element=?` in corresponding positions.
Precondition: `element=?` can receive any elements of `left` and `right` respectively.

tree-size   (afp trees)
tree(any) → natural-number
tr
Compute the number of elements in `tr`.

fold-tree   (afp trees)
(→ α ...), (β, α ... → α ...) → (tree(β) → α ...)
base   combiner   tr
Construct a procedure that returns the results of invoking `base` if `tr` is empty. If `tr` is non-
empty, the constructed procedure applies itself recursively to the left and right subtrees of `tr`
and returns the results of applying `combiner` to the root of `tr` and the results of the recursive
invocations.
Precondition: `combiner` can receive the root of any leaf of `tr` and the results of two invocations
of `base`.
Precondition: `combiner` can receive the root of any internal node of `tr` and either the results of
two invocations of `combiner`, or the results of an invocation of `base` followed by the results of
an invocation of `combiner`, or the results of an invocation of `combiner` followed by the results
of an invocation of `base`.

tree-height   (afp trees)
tree(any) → natural-number
tr
Compute the height of `tr`.

detree   (afp trees)
tree(α) → α ...
tr
Return all of the values contained in `tr`.

for-all-in-tree?   (afp trees)
(α → Boolean), tree(α) → Boolean
condition-met?   tr
Determine whether all of the values contained in `tr` satisfy `condition-met?`.
Precondition: `condition-met?` can receive any element of `tr`.

unfold-tree   (afp trees)
(α ... → Boolean?), (α ... → β), (α ... → α ...), (α ... → α ...) →
final?   producer   left-step   right-step
                                                          (α ...   → tree(β))
                                                          arguments
Construct a procedure that first determines whether the elements of `arguments` satisfy `final?`.
If so, the constructed procedure returns an empty tree. Otherwise, it returns a non-empty
tree in which the root element is the result of applying `producer` to the elements of `arguments`,
the left subtree is the result of first applying `left-step` to the elements of `arguments` and
then applying the constructed procedure recursively to the results, and the right subtree is
the result of first applying `right-step` to the elements of `arguments` and then applying the
constructed procedure recursively to the results.
Precondition: `final?` can receive the elements of `arguments`.
Precondition: `final?` can receive the results of any invocation of `left-step`.
Precondition: `final?` can receive the results of any invocation of `right-step`.
Precondition: If the elements of `arguments` do not satisfy `final?`, then `producer` can receive
them.
Precondition: If the results of an invocation of `left-step` do not satisfy `final?`, then `producer`
can receive them.
Precondition: If the results of an invocation of `right-step` do not satisfy `final?`, then `producer`

can receive them.

Precondition: If the elements of arguments do not satisfy final?, then left-step can receive them.

Precondition: If the results of an invocation of left-step do not satisfy final?, then left-step can receive them.

Precondition: If the results of an invocation of right-step do not satisfy final?, then left-step can receive them.

Precondition: If the elements of arguments do not satisfy final?, then right-step can receive them.

Precondition: If the results of an invocation of left-step do not satisfy final?, then right-step can receive them.

Precondition: If the results of an invocation of right-step do not satisfy final?, then right-step can receive them.

Exercises

3.10–1 Define tree-size, using fold-tree to manage the recursion.

3.10–2 Define a procedure mirror-tree that receives a tree and returns a tree containing the same values, with left and right reversed. For instance, the value of the call

```
(mirror-tree (make-non-empty-tree 2
                (make-non-empty-tree 0
                  (make-empty-tree)
                  (make-non-empty-tree 1
                    (make-empty-tree)
                    (make-empty-tree)))
                (make-non-empty-tree 3
                  (make-non-empty-tree 4
                    (make-empty-tree)
                    (make-empty-tree))
                  (make-non-empty-tree 5
                    (make-empty-tree)
                    (make-empty-tree)))))
```

should be

```
(make-non-empty-tree 2
  (make-non-empty-tree 3
    (make-non-empty-tree 5
      (make-empty-tree)
      (make-empty-tree))
    (make-non-empty-tree 4
      (make-empty-tree)
      (make-empty-tree)))
  (make-non-empty-tree 0
    (make-non-empty-tree 1
      (make-empty-tree)
      (make-empty-tree))
    (make-empty-tree)))
```

3.10–3 Define a procedure `leaf-count` that determines how many leaves a given tree contains.

3.10–4 Define a procedure `tree-map` that is analogous to the `map` procedure for lists: It receives two or more arguments, of which the first is a single-valued procedure and all the others are trees of the same size and shape, and returns another tree of the same size and shape. Each value in the result tree should be the result of applying the given procedure to corresponding elements of the given trees.

For instance, the value of the call

```
(tree-map *
          (make-non-empty-tree 2
            (make-non-empty-tree 0
              (make-empty-tree)
              (make-non-empty-tree 1
                (make-empty-tree)
                (make-empty-tree)))
            (make-non-empty-tree 3
              (make-non-empty-tree 4
                (make-empty-tree)
                (make-empty-tree))
              (make-non-empty-tree 5
                (make-empty-tree)
                (make-empty-tree))))
          (make-non-empty-tree 8
            (make-non-empty-tree 6
              (make-empty-tree)
              (make-non-empty-tree 7
                (make-empty-tree)
                (make-empty-tree)))
            (make-non-empty-tree 9
              (make-non-empty-tree 10
                (make-empty-tree)
                (make-empty-tree))
              (make-non-empty-tree 11
                (make-empty-tree)
                (make-empty-tree)))))
```

should be

```
(make-non-empty-tree 16
  (make-non-empty-tree 0
    (make-empty-tree)
    (make-non-empty-tree 7
      (make-empty-tree)
      (make-empty-tree)))
  (make-non-empty-tree 27
    (make-non-empty-tree 40
```

```
        (make-empty-tree)
        (make-empty-tree))
    (make-non-empty-tree 55
        (make-empty-tree)
        (make-empty-tree))))
```

3.10–5 Define an extended version of the `for-all-in-tree?` predicate that receives an n-ary procedure and n trees that have the same size and shape, for any positive integer n, and returns #t if the predicate is satisfied by every group of values in corresponding positions in the given trees.

3.10–6 A *foo-tree* of depth 0 is empty. For any positive integer n, a foo-tree of depth n has the symbol `foo` as its root and foo-trees of depth $n - 1$ as its subtrees. Using `unfold-list`, define a procedure `foo-tree` that receives a natural number and returns a foo-tree of the specified depth.

3.11   Bushes

The next step away from linearity in our data structures would be to combine an element with *three* substructures, to form a *ternary tree*. We could then continue with quaternary, quinary, and senary trees, and so on indefinitely. Reflecting that such structures are likely to be increasingly specialized in their use, however, we arrive at the idea of a *bush*: a data structure like a list or a tree, but with no fixed degree of branching. Either a bush is empty, or it consists of one element (its *root*) and zero or more bushes (its *children*). Saying the same thing more formally, the equation

$$bush \;\; = \;\; null \,|\, (any \times bush^*)$$

specifies the *bush* type.

Lists provide an excellent model for bushes: An empty bush is represented by an empty list, and a larger bush by a list in which the first element is the root of the bush and the remaining elements are the children.

It is convenient to define a single constructor, `bush`, for empty and non-empty bushes alike. Given no arguments, it returns an empty bush; given one or more arguments, of which all but the first are bushes, it returns the non-empty bush with the first argument as the root and the other arguments as the children. This gives us a particularly elegant definition of the constructor:

```
(define bush list)
```

The selectors are also easy. Each of them has the precondition that its argument, which must be a bush, is not empty. It turns out that it is almost always more convenient to have the children of a bush stored in a list than split into separate values, so we'll implement the `bush-children` selector to return that list:

```
(define bush-root first)
(define bush-children rest)
```

Sometimes we'll want both the root and the children:

```
(define debush deprepend)
```

The discriminator predicates `empty-bush?` and `non-empty-bush?` distinguish the two components of the sum type:

```
(define empty-bush? empty-list?)
(define non-empty-bush? non-empty-list?)
```

The classification predicate `bush?` follows the description of the model: To represent a bush, a value must be either an empty list or a non-empty list in which each element after the first is a bush:

```
(define (bush? something)
  (and (list? something)
       (or (empty-list? something)
           (and (non-empty-list? something)
                (for-all? bush? (rest something))))))
```

Similarly, two bushes are equal if both are empty, or if neither is empty and they have the same root and equal children:

```
(define (bush=? left right)
  (or (and (empty-bush? left) (empty-bush? right))
      (and (non-empty-bush? left)
           (non-empty-bush? right)
           (equal? (bush-root left) (bush-root right))
           (let ((lefts (bush-children left))
                 (rights (bush-children right)))
             (and (= (length lefts) (length rights))
                  (for-all? (pipe delist bush=?)
                            (zip lefts rights)))))))
```

The `bush-of` and `bush-of=` procedures build customized classification and equality predicates for homogeneous bushes:

```
(define (bush-of right-type-of-element?)
  (rec (ok? something)
    (or (empty-list? something)
        (and (non-empty-list? something)
             (right-type-of-element? (first something))
             (for-all? ok? (rest something))))))
```

```
(define (bush-of= element=?)
  (rec (equivalent? left right)
    (or (and (empty-bush? left)
             (empty-bush? right))
        (and (non-empty-bush? left)
             (non-empty-bush? right)
             (element=? (bush-root left) (bush-root right))
             (let ((lefts (bush-children left))
                   (rights (bush-children right)))
               (and (= (length lefts) (length rights))
                    (for-all? (pipe delist equivalent?)
                              (zip lefts rights)))))))))
```

The Principle of Bush Induction

By now, it should not be surprising to find that proofs about bush-related procedures often use the *principle of bush induction*, which is based on the recursive definition of bushes as the least inclusive class C that meets these requirements:

- The empty bush is a member of C.

- A non-empty bush in which every child is a member of C is also a member of C.

The principle of bush induction says that if the empty bush is a member of some class C', and every non-empty bush in which every child is a member of C' is also a member of C', then every bush is a member of C'.

Managing Recursion with Bushes

A recursive procedure that follows the structure of a bush and folds over it begins by testing whether the bush is empty; if so, it returns the results of a given base procedure. Otherwise, the procedure is applied recursively to *each* child in the bush, and the combiner procedure is applied to the root element of the bush and all of the results of the recursive calls. The results returned by the combiner are the values of the original call to the recursive procedure.

The fold-bush procedure receives the base and combiner procedures and returns the recursive procedure that folds over a given bush:

```
(define (fold-bush base combiner)
  (rec (folder arbusto)
    (if (empty-bush? arbusto)
        (base)
        (apply combiner (bush-root arbusto)
                        (collect-map folder (bush-children arbusto))))))
```

As an example of its use, let's work up a procedure `bush->list` that receives any bush and returns a list of its values.

If the bush is empty, the procedure should return an empty list, so our base procedure generates that value: `(create (list))`.

For all other cases, we'll need a combiner procedure, which will receive the root of the bush and the results of applying `bush->list` recursively to all of the children of the bush. Each of those results will be a list of the values that one child contains. We can combine those elements with `append`, and then add the root to the beginning of the result list with `prepend` to get the list of all of the values in the whole bush.

Assembling the pieces, we get this definition:

```
(define bush->list
  (fold-bush (create (list))
             (lambda (root . recursive-results)
               (cons root (apply append recursive-results)))))
```

The `for-all-in-bush?` procedure, which determines whether each of the values that a given bush contains satisfies a given predicate, has a different structure, so that it can back out of the recursion as soon as it finds a non-satisfying element:

```
(define (for-all-in-bush? condition-met? arbusto)
  ((rec (ok? subbush)
     (or (empty-bush? subbush)
         (and (condition-met? (bush-root subbush))
              (for-all? ok? (bush-children subbush)))))
   arbusto))
```

We can also define an unfolder for bushes, though superficially it's a little less flexible than its analogues for lists and trees, because the procedure it returns is always unary:

```
(define (unfold-bush final? producer step)
  (rec (unfolder guide)
    (if (final? guide)
        (bush)
        (receive step-results (step guide)
          (apply bush (producer guide) (map unfolder step-results))))))
```

Given the guide argument, the `final?` predicate determines whether to terminate the recursion, returning an empty bush. If `final?` is not satisfied, `producer` is applied to the guide argument to obtain the root of the result bush, and the `step` argument is applied to adjust the guide for the recursive calls; it may return any number of results. Finally, `unfolder` is applied recursively to each of the results of the invocation of `step`, returning in each case a bush that becomes one of the children of the result.

The restriction that bush unfolders are unary is, in practice, not very confining, since we can use `list` and `delist` as adapters in situations that seem initially to call for multi-argument bush unfolders.

Here's an example of the use of `unfold-bush`. For any natural number n, an *iota-bush* of magnitude n is a bush that has n as its root and has n children, each of which is itself an iota-bush. The magnitudes of the children of an iota-bush of magnitude n are $n-1, n-2, \ldots, 1, 0$. The `iota-bush` procedure constructs and returns an iota-bush of the magnitude specified by its argument, which must be a natural number:

```
(define iota-bush
  (unfold-bush (constant #f)
               identity
               (lower-ply-natural black-hole values)))
```

---

bush   (afp bushes)
$\rightarrow bush(\alpha)$
Return an empty bush.

bush   (afp bushes)
$any, \ bush(\alpha) \ \ldots \ \rightarrow bush(\alpha)$
root   children
Return a bush with root as its root and children as its children.

bush-root   (afp bushes)
$bush(\alpha) \ \rightarrow \alpha$
arbusto
Return the root of arbusto.
Precondition: arbusto is not empty.

bush-children   (afp bushes)
$bush(\alpha) \ \rightarrow bush(\alpha)$
arbusto
Return the children of arbusto.
Precondition: arbusto is not empty.

debush   (afp bushes)
$bush(\alpha) \ \rightarrow \ | \ \alpha, \ bush(\alpha) \ \ldots$
arbusto
Return all of the components of arbusto.

empty-bush?   (afp bushes)
$bush(any) \ \rightarrow Boolean$
arbusto
Determine whether arbusto is empty.

non-empty-bush?   (afp bushes)
$bush(any) \ \rightarrow Boolean$
arbusto
Determine whether arbusto is non-empty.

bush?   (afp bushes)
$any \qquad \rightarrow Boolean$
something
Determine whether something is a bush.

bush=?   (afp bushes)
$bush(\alpha), \ bush(\beta) \ \rightarrow Boolean$
left   right

Determine whether left and right are the same bush, that is, whether they have the same structure and contain the same values at corresponding positions.

bush-of (afp bushes)
(any → Boolean) → *(any → Boolean)*
right-type-of-element? something
Construct a predicate that determines whether something is a bush containing only values that satisfy right-type-of-element?.
Precondition: right-type-of-element? can receive any value.

bush-of= (afp bushes)
(α, β → Boolean) → *(bush(α), bush(β) → Boolean)*
element=? left right
Construct a predicate that determines whether left and right are the same bush, that is, whether they have the same structure and contain values that satisfy element=? in corresponding positions.
Precondition: element=? can receive any element of left as its first argument and any element of right as its second.

fold-bush (afp bushes)
(→ α ...), (β, α ... → α ...) → *(bush(β) → α ...)*
base combiner arbusto
Construct a procedure that returns the results of invoking base if arbusto is empty. If arbusto is non-empty, the constructed procedure applies itself recursively to each child of arbusto and returns the results of applying combiner to the root of arbusto and the results of the recursive invocations.
Precondition: combiner can receive the root of any leaf of arbusto and the results of an invocation of base.
Precondition: combiner can receive the root of any internal node of arbusto and the results of any number of invocations of either base or combiner.

bush->list (afp bushes)
bush(α) → list(α)
arbusto
Construct a list of the values in arbusto.

for-all-in-bush? (afp bushes)
(α → Boolean), bush(α) → Boolean
condition-met? arbusto
Determine whether each of the values in arbusto satisfies condition-met?.
Precondition: condition-met? can receive any value in arbusto.

unfold-bush (afp bushes)
(α → Boolean), (α → β), (α → α ...) → *(α → bush(β))*
final? producer step guide
Construct a procedure that first determines whether guide satisfies final?. If so, the constructed procedure returns the empty bush. Otherwise, it returns a non-empty bush in which the root element is the result of applying producer to guide, and the children are the results of first applying step to guide and then applying the constructed procedure recursively to each of the results.
Precondition: final? can receive guide.
Precondition: final? can receive the result of any invocation of step.
Precondition: If guide does not satisfy final?, then producer can receive it.
Precondition: If any of the results of an invocation of step does not satisfy final?, then producer can receive it.
Precondition: If guide does not satisfy final?, then step can receive it.
Precondition: If any of the results of an invocation of step does not satisfy final?, then step can receive it.

Exercises

3.11–1 Define a procedure bush-sum that determines the sum of the values that a given bush contains.

3.11–2 Define a procedure bush-size that determines how many values a given bush contains (counting duplicates as distinct).

3.11–3 Define a procedure bush-map that can receive two or more arguments, of which the first is a single-valued procedure and the others are bushes of the same size and shape, and returns another bush of the same size and shape. Each value in the result bush should be the result of applying the given procedure to corresponding elements of the given bushes.

3.11–4 Let's say that a bush is a *counter bush* if it is empty (in which case its *depth* is 0) or if, for some natural number n, it has n as its root (in which case its depth is n) and has $n - 1$ children, each of which is a counter bush of depth $n - 1$. So, for instance, a counter bush of depth 4 looks like this:

```
(bush 4 (bush 3 (bush 2 (bush 1))
                (bush 2 (bush 1)))
        (bush 3 (bush 2 (bush 1))
                (bush 2 (bush 1)))
        (bush 3 (bush 2 (bush 1))
                (bush 2 (bush 1))))
```

Using unfold-bush, define a procedure counter-bush that receives a natural number as argument and returns a counter bush of the depth it specifies.

3.12   Bags

A *bag* is a data structure that can contain any number of values, but does not impose an order on them as a list does. Think of a cloth bag with its contents rattling around freely inside, with no fixed arrangement. We can put things in and take things out, but we can't take out the "first" thing or use natural numbers as positional indices.

Scheme does not support bags explicitly, but it is customary to model bags as lists, by ignoring the order of the elements. We can make the data abstraction more explicit by providing new names and, in some cases, new definitions for the bag operations that we choose as primitives.

In this model, the representation is not one-to-one, since one and the same bag will be represented by lists with the same elements, differently arranged. For instance, a bag containing just the symbol alpha, the symbol beta, and the symbol alpha again is equally well represented by any of the three values (list 'alpha 'alpha 'beta), (list 'alpha 'beta 'alpha), and (list 'beta 'alpha 'alpha). We shall say that these values are "equal as bags" and arrange not to distinguish them when we want to treat them as bags. (Since the `equal?` predicate does distinguish them, we won't use `equal?` as a criterion of sameness for bags.)

Basic Bag Procedures

Our roster of bag primitives begins with a classification predicate that determines whether a given value is or is not a bag. In our model, every bag is a list and every list represents some bag, so the `bag?` predicate can be `list?` under a new name:

```
(define bag? list?)
```

Similarly, we can obtain a classification predicate for any homogeneous bag type from `bag-of`, which will be simply an alias for `list-of`:

```
(define bag-of list-of)
```

Secondly, we need to be able to construct bags. Here, again, our choice of model makes this trivial: The `bag` procedure, which can receive any number of arguments and returns a bag containing them, is an alias for `list`:

```
(define bag list)
```

The corresponding disaggregator is `debag`. It is correct to implement this as `delist`, but in this case it's particularly important to use a different name, since the postconditions of `debag` are different from those of `delist`: The `delist` procedure guarantees that the order of its results corresponds to the order of the elements in a given list. The `debag` procedure can't make any such guarantee, since it is given a bag, and the values that a bag contains aren't in any particular order:

```
(define debag delist)
```

Like lists, bags are often built up incrementally, rather than all at once, as the `bag` procedure does it. So it would be useful to have a procedure analogous to `prepend`, to add one new value to the contents of a bag. We could define such a procedure using `bag` and `debag`:

```
(define (put-into-bag new aro)
  (receive aro-contents (debag aro)
    (apply bag new aro-contents)))
```

In practice, however, we'll take the shortcut that our choice of model provides, which is much more efficient:

```
(define put-into-bag prepend)
```

Similarly, we'll sometimes need the converse procedure, which receives a non-empty bag, extracts a value from it, and returns that value and a bag containing the rest of the contents of the given bag. This is the bag analogue of deprepend, except that its postcondition doesn't make any guarantees about which value we get from the bag—since bags aren't ordered, there is no "first" element. Again, we could define this as

```
(define take-from-bag
  (pipe debag (dispatch >initial (pipe >all-but-initial bag))))
```

but we'll take the shortcut instead:

```
(define take-from-bag deprepend)
```

A predicate, empty-bag?, distinguishes the bag that has no values in it from other bags:

```
(define empty-bag? empty-list?)
```

Finally, we'll need an equality predicate, bag=?, and a procedure bag-of= for constructing equality predicates for homogeneous bags. The strategy is to walk through one of the two given bags (that is, lists) in order, using extract to remove each of its elements from the other one. If extract ever signals a failure, the two bags cannot be equal. When we reach the end of the first bag, we check whether the other one is completely empty. If it is, the two bags are equal. Here's the implementation of bag=?:

```
(define (bag=? left right)
  (if (empty-list? left)
      (empty-list? right)
      (receive (first-of-left rest-of-left) (deprepend left)
        (receive (sought rest-of-right)
                 (extract (equal-to first-of-left) right)
          (and (box? sought)
               (bag=? rest-of-left rest-of-right))))))
```

The predicates that bag-of= constructs use the same logic, but invoke specific predicates (rather than the generic equal?) to compare elements:

```
(define (bag-of= element=?)
  (rec (equivalent? left right)
    (if (empty-list? left)
        (empty-list? right)
        (receive (first-of-left rest-of-left) (deprepend left)
          (receive (sought rest-of-right)
                   (extract (sect element=? first-of-left <>) right)
            (and (box? sought)
                 (equivalent? rest-of-left rest-of-right)))))))
```

The `bag-of=` procedure has a subtle precondition. Because we have no control over the order in which values are taken from `left` and matching values from `right`, the `element=?` predicate must be such that the order makes no difference. Some binary predicates correlate values in the two bags in subtle ways, and we may get incorrect results unless `element=?` meets the following condition:

> For any values `left-0`, `left-1`, `right-0`, and `right-1`, if `left-0` and `right-0` satisfy `element=?`, and `left-1` and `right-0` satisfy `element=?`, and `left-0` and `right-1` satisfy `element=?`, then `left-1` and `right-1` satisfy `element=?`.

The caller should ensure that `element=?` meets this precondition. For equality predicates, fortunately, it is easy to guarantee this.

Instead of adding to the procedures so far introduced by similarly aliasing other list procedures, we'll treat them as the primitives in terms of which all other bag operations are defined, abstracting from the dependence of bags on the list model. Let's look now at methods for constructing these other operations.

Bag Operations

The `take-from-bag` procedure gives us no control over the nature or identity of the value that it pulls from a bag. A more powerful procedure, `extract-from-bag`, can be used to choose a value that has some distinguishing characteristic, which is supplied in the form of a unary predicate. In effect, a call to `extract-from-bag` says: Find, in this bag, the value that satisfies this condition and return it, along with a bag containing all the unselected values.

One difficulty with this design is that it seems to require us to supply a predicate that exactly one of the values in the bag satisfies. Often we won't know enough about the contents of the bag to guarantee such a precondition. We'll cope with this difficulty by lowering our expectations. If we supply `extract-from-bag` with a predicate that several values in the bag satisfy, we'll allow it to give us *any* of those values as the result.

It is now apparent that `extract-from-bag` is closely analogous to the `extract` procedure for lists—so closely that we can use the same strategy, substituting bag primitives for list primitives. We can also recycle the idea of boxing the result of a successful search, while returning #f as the first result if the search fails:

```
(define (extract-from-bag condition-met? aro)
  ((rec (extracter areto)
     (if (empty-bag? areto)
         (values #f areto)
         (receive (chosen others) (take-from-bag areto)
           (if (condition-met? chosen)
               (values (box chosen) others)
               (receive (sought relicts) (extracter others)
```

```
                  (values sought (put-into-bag chosen relicts)))))))
    aro))
```

Of course, in our model, `extract-from-bag` is not merely *analogous* to `extract`, but *identical* to it: We've defined the same procedure twice, just using different names for some of the procedures it invokes. However, this definition of `extract-from-bag` would work without change under *any* model of bags that supports the `put-into-bag`, `take-from-bag`, and `empty-bag?` procedures. This modularity is the point of the implementation.

The *cardinality* of a bag is the number of values that it contains (counting duplicates as distinct). It's analogous to the length of a list, and we could compute it by adapting one of our definitions of `length`, but instead let's illustrate another strategy: We'll use `tally` to unfold the result as a natural number, counting the number of times we can take a value from the bag before it is empty:

```
(define bag-cardinality (tally empty-bag? (pipe take-from-bag >next)))
```

There are bag analogues of `for-all?` and `exists?`:

```
(define (for-all-in-bag? condition-met? aro)
  ((rec (ok? areto)
     (or (empty-bag? areto)
         (receive (chosen others) (take-from-bag areto)
           (and (condition-met? chosen) (ok? others)))))
   aro))
(define exists-in-bag? (run (~initial ^not) for-all-in-bag? not))
```

Managing Recursion with Bags

We'll often want to accumulate a result by starting with some base value and progressively merging in the values extracted from the bag, one at a time. The `fold-bag` procedure is a recursion manager that abstracts the pattern of folding over the members of a bag, just as `fold-list` abstracts folding over the elements of a list:

```
(define (fold-bag base combiner)
  (recur empty-bag? (pipe black-hole base) take-from-bag combiner))
```

We'll need to be rather careful about the use of `fold-bag`, however, because we don't want our results to depend on the order in which we happen to take the contents of the bag out for processing. The procedure that we use as the combiner should meet an *order-independence condition*, requiring that

```
(receive results (apply combiner alpha starters)
  (apply combiner beta results))
```

and

```
(receive results (apply combiner beta starters)
  (apply combiner alpha results))
```

return the same results, no matter what the values of `alpha` and `beta` and the elements of `starters` are.

For instance, we can construct a bag with the combined contents of two given bags by taking one of the bags as a starting point and folding over the other, putting each of its members into the result:

```
(define (bag-union left right)
  ((fold-bag (create right) put-into-bag) left))
```

Note that `put-into-bag` meets the order-independence condition described above (provided that we regard its result as a bag, not a list!).

To take another example, we can use `fold-bag` to construct an analogue of `map` that applies a procedure to every member of a bag and collects the results in a new bag:

```
(define (map-bag procedure aro)
  ((fold-bag (create (bag)) (pipe (~initial procedure) put-into-bag))
   aro))
```

Whereas the `map` procedure for lists has variable arity, it is not useful to generalize `map-bag` in that way, because there is no way to identify "corresponding elements" in two or more bags.

Now that we have `fold-bag` as an analogue of `fold-list`, we can define the bag equivalents of the `filter`, `remp`, and `partition` procedures by replacing calls to the list procedures with calls to the corresponding procedures for bags:

```
(define (filter-bag keep? aro)
  ((fold-bag bag (conditionally-combine keep? put-into-bag)) aro))
(define remp-bag (pipe (~initial ^not) filter-bag))
(define (partition-bag condition-met? aro)
  ((fold-bag (create (bag) (bag))
             (lambda (candidate ins outs)
               (if (condition-met? candidate)
                   (values (put-into-bag candidate ins) outs)
                   (values ins (put-into-bag candidate outs)))))
   aro))
```

Bags can also be constructed recursively, using an `unfold-bag` procedure analogous to `unfold-list`:

```
(define (unfold-bag final? producer step)
  (build final? (constant (bag)) producer step put-into-bag))
```

---

bag?   (afp bags)
any   → *Boolean*
something
Determine whether something is a bag.

bag-of   (afp bags)
(any → Boolean)   → *(any   → Boolean)*
right-type-of-value?   something
Construct a predicate that determines whether something is a bag in which every value satisfies
right-type-of-value?.
Precondition: right-type-of-value? can receive any value.

bag   (afp bags)
α ...   → *bag(α)*
arguments
Construct a bag containing the elements of arguments.

debag   (afp bags)
bag(α) → *α ...*
aro
Return the values that aro contains (in any order).

put-into-bag   (afp bags)
α, bag(α) → *bag(α)*
new aro
Construct a bag containing new, in addition to all of the values in aro.

take-from-bag   (afp bags)
bag(α) → *α, bag(α)*
aro
Return one of the values in aro and a bag containing all of the other values in aro.
Precondition: aro is not empty.

empty-bag?   (afp bags)
bag(any) → *Boolean*
aro
Determines whether aro is empty.

bag=?   (afp bags)
bag(any), bag(any) → *Boolean*
left   right
Determine whether left and right are the same bag, that is, whether the same values are in
both (regardless of order, but counting duplicates as distinct within each bag).

bag-of=   (afp bags)
(α, β → Boolean) → *(bag(α), bag(β) → Boolean)*
element=?   left   right
Construct a procedure that determines whether, for each value in left, there is a corresponding
value in right such that those values satisfy element=?, and vice versa.
Precondition: element=? can receive any value in left as its first argument and any value in
right as its second.
Precondition: For any values left-0, left-1, right-0, and right-1, if left-0 and right-0
satisfy element=?, and left-1 and right-0 satisfy element=?, and left-0 and right-1 satisfy
element=?, then left-1 and right-1 satisfy element=?.

extract-from-bag   (afp bags)
(α → Boolean), bag(α) → *(box(α) | Boolean), bag(α)*
condition-met? aro
Search aro for a value that satisfies condition-met?. If and when such an element is found,
return a box containing that value and a bag containing the other values in aro; otherwise,
return #f and aro.
Precondition: condition-met? can receive any element of aro.

bag-cardinality   (afp bags)

bag(any) $\rightarrow$ *natural-number*
aro
Compute the number of values aro contains.

for-all-in-bag?   (afp bags)
(α $\rightarrow$ Boolean), bag(α) $\rightarrow$ *Boolean*
condition-met? aro
Determine whether all of the values in aro satisfy condition-met?.
Precondition: condition-met? can receive any value in aro.

exists-in-bag?   (afp bags)
(α $\rightarrow$ Boolean), bag(α) $\rightarrow$ *Boolean*
condition-met? aro
Determine whether at least one of the values in aro satisfies condition-met?.
Precondition: condition-met? can receive any value in aro.

fold-bag   (afp bags)
($\rightarrow$ α ...), (β, α ... $\rightarrow$ α ...) $\rightarrow$ *(bag(β) $\rightarrow$ α ...)*
base   combiner   aro
Construct a procedure that returns the results of invoking base if aro is empty. If aro is not
empty, the constructed procedure takes a value out of aro, applies itself recursively to a bag
containing the other values in aro, and returns the results of applying combiner to the taken
value and the results of the recursive invocation.
Precondition: combiner can receive any value in aro and the results of an invocation of base.
Precondition: combiner can receive any value in aro and the results of an invocation of
combiner.
Precondition: combiner satisfies the order-independence condition.

bag-union   (afp bags)
bag(α), bag(α) $\rightarrow$ *bag(α)*
left   right
Construct a bag containing all of the values that left and right contain.

map-bag   (afp bags)
(α $\rightarrow$ β), bag(α) $\rightarrow$ *bag(β)*
procedure aro
Construct a bag containing each of the results of applying procedure to a value in aro.
Precondition: procedure can receive any value in aro.

filter-bag   (afp bags)
(α $\rightarrow$ Boolean), bag(α) $\rightarrow$ *bag(α)*
keep?   aro
Construct a bag containing the values in aro that satisfy keep?.
Precondition: keep? can receive any value in aro.

remp-bag   (afp bags)
(α $\rightarrow$ Boolean), bag(α) $\rightarrow$ *bag(α)*
exclude?   .   aro
Construct a bag containing the values in aro that do not satisfy exclude?.
Precondition: exclude? can receive any value in aro.

partition-bag   (afp bags)
(α $\rightarrow$ Boolean), bag(α) $\rightarrow$ *bag(α), bag(α)*
condition-met? aro
Construct two bags, one containing the values in aro that satisfy condition-met?, the other
those that do not.
Precondition: condition-met? can receive any value in aro.

unfold-bag   (afp bags)
(α ... $\rightarrow$ Boolean), (α ... $\rightarrow$ β), (α ... $\rightarrow$ α ...) $\rightarrow$ *(α ... $\rightarrow$ bag(β))*
final?   producer   step   arguments
Construct a procedure that first determines whether the elements of arguments satisfy final?.
If so, the constructed procedure returns the empty bag. Otherwise, it returns a bag containing
the result of applying producer to the elements of arguments, in addition to the values in the
bag obtained by first applying step to the elements of arguments and then applying the

constructed procedure recursively to the results.
Precondition: `final?` can receive the elements of `arguments`.
Precondition: `final?` can receive the results of any invocation of `step`.
Precondition: If the elements of `arguments` do not satisfy `final?`, then `producer` can receive them.
Precondition: If the results of an invocation of `step` do not satisfy `final?`, then `producer` can receive them.
Precondition: If the elements of `arguments` do not satisfy `final?`, then `step` can receive them.
Precondition: If the results of an invocation of `step` do not satisfy `final?`, then `step` can receive them.

Exercises

3.12–1   Define a procedure `bag-sum` that computes the sum of the values in a given bag of numbers.

3.12–2   The *multiplicity* of a value v in a bag b is the number of values that b contains that are the same as v. (We'll use `equal?` to test whether two values are "the same," in this sense.) Define a procedure `multiplicity` that computes the multiplicity of a given value in a given bag. For instance, the value of the call '(multiplicity 'foo (bag 'bar 'foo 'quux 'foo 'bar 'wombat 'foo))' is 3, because three of the values in the bag are the symbol `foo`. (Hint: Use `conditionally-tally`.)

3.12–3   Design and implement an analogue for bags of the `filtermap` procedure for lists, which is described in Exercise 3.7–6.

3.12–4   Define a procedure `iota-bag` that receives any natural number as argument and returns a bag containing all of the natural numbers less than the one given.

3.12–5   The *prime factorization* of a positive integer n is a bag of prime natural numbers whose product is n. For instance, the prime factorization of 120 is (bag 2 2 2 3 5), and the prime factorization of 1 is an empty bag. Define a procedure `prime-factorization` that computes and returns the prime factorization of a given positive integer.

3.12–6   Using `unfold-bag`, define a procedure `make-bag` that receives two arguments, of which the first is a natural number, and returns a bag containing the specified number of values, each of which is the second argument. For instance, the value of the call '(make-bag 5 'foo)' is (bag 'foo 'foo 'foo 'foo 'foo).

3.12–7   Define a `bag-of-ratios` procedure that receives two bags of numbers, the second of which does not contain 0, and returns a bag of the ratios that can be obtained by dividing a value from the first bag by a value from the second bag. For instance, the value of the call '(bag-of-ratios (bag 4 -7 -12 9) (bag -5 15 8))' is (bag -4/5 4/15 1/2 7/5 -7/15 -7/8 12/5 -4/5 -3/2 -9/5

3/5 9/8). (Note that the value −4/5 has multiplicity 2 in the result bag—it appears once as the ratio of 4 to −5, and again as the ratio of −12 to 15.)

3.12–8 Define a procedure, without-duplicates, that receives any bag and returns a similar bag containing the same values, but with no duplicate values. (In other words, every value in a bag returned by without-duplicates has multiplicity 1 in that bag.)

3.13 Equivalence Relations

In many algorithms, we are called upon to test whether a value v is equal to a value w, or is the same as w, or simply *is* w. The exact meanings of such phrases are not always apparent, and the same values may, in different contexts, be considered equal or unequal, the same or different. We have already seen, for example, that (list 0 1) and (list 1 0) are different when considered as lists, but the same when considered as representations of bags. Whether to count v and w as the same value is often a *decision* that the algorithm designer makes by considering which alternative would be more useful or more convenient in a particular context.

In general, a well-designed algorithm reckons v and w to be the same when they are indistinguishable at the desired level of abstraction or in the intended context. For example, a programmer dealing with alphanumeric strings might use a predicate that performs a case-insensitive comparison to test whether two strings are the same when designing an interface for some environment in which users will observe no distinction between an upper-case letter and its lower-case equivalent. In a different application, intended for an environment in which users are likely to distinguish A from a, the same programmer might instead use a case-sensitive criterion of string equality.

To accommodate such decisions, many of the algorithms that we'll encounter require the caller to supply a binary *equivalence predicate* that the algorithm can invoke whenever it needs a decision about whether two values are the same. In practice, there is often an obvious choice, so we'll try to make the specification of the equivalence predicate unobtrusive. On the other hand, using a coarser-than-usual equivalence predicate—one that treats values as "the same" even when the programmer, at least, can distinguish them—is sometimes a powerful and concise technique, and it's often a good idea to stop and reflect before making a decision.

We shall assume throughout, as a precondition, that any binary predicate supplied to play this role expresses an *equivalence relation*. The domain of this relation (the class of values that it relates) must include all the values to which the binary predicate will be applied. A relation R with domain D is an equivalence relation if and only if it has all three of the following characteristics:

1. R is *reflexive*: For any element a of D, a bears the relation R to itself.

2. R is *symmetric*: For any elements a and b of D, a bears R to b if and only if b bears R to a.

3. R is *transitive*: For any elements a, b, and c of D, if a bears R to b and b bears R to c, then a bears R to c.

For instance, the predicate `same-in-parity?` (from §2.5) expresses an equivalence relation on the domain of integers, according to which two integers are "the same" if they have the same parity (that is, if they are both even or both odd) and "different" if one is even and one is odd. This relation is reflexive, since every integer has the same parity as itself. It is symmetric, since if a has the same parity as b, then b has the same parity as a. And it is transitive, since if a has the same parity as b and b the same parity as c, then a has the same parity as c.

All of the equality predicates that we have introduced (such as `symbol=?`, `tree=?`, and the results of calls to equality-predicate constructors such as `list-of=`) express equivalence relations, and Scheme provides several others as primitives. For instance, one that is related to our discussion of case sensitivity above is `char-ci=?`, which receives two characters and determines whether they are alike when their case is ignored.

Let's take this opportunity to define procedures that construct specialized equality and classification predicates for pairs and boxes, which we didn't pause to provide in §3.4 and §3.5.

When we want to work with pairs of a special type, we'll often want to specialize the car and cdr components in different ways. The meta-procedures that generate classification and equality predicates for such specialized pairs will have two arguments, one for the car position and one for the cdr. For the procedure that constructs specialized classification predicates, these should be classification predicates for the components of the pairs:

```
(define (pair-of car-tester? cdr-tester?)
  (^et pair? (^et (pipe car car-tester?) (pipe cdr cdr-tester?))))
```

For the procedure that constructs specialized equality predicates, the arguments should be equivalence predicates that compare the respective components:

```
(define (pair-of= same-car? same-cdr?)
  (^et (compare-by car same-car?) (compare-by cdr same-cdr?)))
```

In retrospect, we could use `pair-of=` to construct the generic `pair=?` procedure, as `(pair-of= equal? equal?)`.

Note, however, that the predicates `same-car?` and `same-cdr?` need not be the "natural" equality predicates for the data types involved. For instance, if we're designing a new type that is implemented by pairs in which the car is always an integer and the cdr is always a list, we might decide to define the equality predicate for our type as `(pair-of= same-in-parity? (pipe (compare-by length`

=))) rather than as (pair-of= = list=?). We choose different predicates depending on what our algorithms should treat as "the same."

Similarly, a specialized classification predicate for boxes applies a given classification predicate to its contents:

```
(define (box-of contents-tester?)
  (^et box? (pipe debox contents-tester?)))
```

An equality predicate for boxes applies an equivalence predicate to their contents:

```
(define box-of= (sect compare-by debox <>))
```

and again box=? could be defined as (box-of= equal?).

Extending Equivalence Relations

To test whether more than two values are alike with respect to a particular equivalence relation, we can extend the arity of that relation. The all-alike procedure constructs the extended-arity version of a given equivalence relation:

```
(define (all-alike equivalent?)
  (lambda arguments
    (or (empty-list? arguments)
        (receive (initial remaining) (deprepend arguments)
          (for-all? (sect equivalent? initial <>) remaining)))))
```

If there are no values to be compared, the assertion that they are all alike is "vacuously true"—that is, true because no counterexamples are possible. If there is at least one value, we check whether they are all alike by determining whether the first one is equivalent to each of the others. If so, then, by symmetry, each of the others is also equivalent to the first one; then, by transitivity, it follows that all the others are also equivalent to one another.

The all-different procedure, which constructs predicates that determine whether all of their arguments *differ* with respect to a given equivalence relation, is not as simple. Since the complement of an equivalence relation need not be transitive, we have to compare every argument against every other to be sure that no two are equivalent:

```
(define (all-different equivalent?)
  (pipe list
        (check empty-list?
               (run deprepend (~initial (curry equivalent?)) exists? not)
               rest)))
```

For instance, the predicate returned by the call

```
(all-different (compare-by (sect mod <> 10) =))
```

determines whether all of its arguments have different remainders on division by 10.

---

char-ci=?   (scheme char)
character, character, character ...   → *Boolean*
left   right   others
Determine whether the "case-folded" versions of left, right, and the elements of others are the same (that is, whether left, right, and the elements of others are the same if differences of case are ignored).

pair-of   (afp pairs)
(any → Boolean), (any → Boolean) → (any   → Boolean)
car-tester?   cdr-tester?   something
Construct a predicate that determines whether something is a pair in which the car satisfies car-tester? and the cdr satisfies cdr-tester?.
Precondition: car-tester? can receive any value.
Precondition: cdr-tester? can receive any value.

pair-of=   (afp pairs)
(α, α → Boolean), (β, β → Boolean) → (pair(α, β), pair(α, β) → Boolean)
same-car?   same-cdr?   left   right
Construct a predicate that determines whether left and right are the same by checking whether their cars satisfy same-car? and their cdrs satisfy same-cdr?.
Precondition: same-car? is an equivalence relation.
Precondition: same-car? can receive the car of left and the car of right.
Precondition: same-cdr? is an equivalence relation.
Precondition: same-cdr? can receive the cdr of left and the cdr of right.

box-of   (afp boxes)
(any → Boolean) → (any   → Boolean)
contents-tester?   something
Construct a predicate that determines whether something is a box containing a value that satisfies contents-tester?.
Precondition: contents-tester? can receive any value.

box-of=   (afp boxes)
(α, α → Boolean) → (box(α), box(α) → Boolean)
same-contents?   left   right
Construct a predicate that determines whether left and right are the same, by checking whether their contents satisfy same-contents?.
Precondition: same-contents? is an equivalence relation.
Precondition: same-contents? can receive the contents of left and the contents of right.

all-alike   (afp lists)
(α, α → Boolean) → (α ...   → Boolean)
equivalent?   arguments
Construct a predicate that the elements of arguments satisfy if and only if every two of them satisfy equivalent?.
Precondition: equivalent? is an equivalence relation.
Precondition: equivalent? can receive any elements of arguments.

all-different   (afp lists)
(α, α → Boolean) → (α ...   → Boolean)
equivalent?   arguments
Construct a predicate that the elements of arguments satisfy if and only if no two of them satisfy equivalent?.
Precondition: equivalent? is symmetric.
Precondition: equivalent? can receive any elements of arguments.

Exercises

3.13–1   Is the predicate <= an equivalence relation on the domain of integers? Justify your answer.

3.13–2   Is the predicate (pipe (~each (sect div <> 10)) =) an equivalence relation on the domain of integers? Justify your answer.

3.13–3   Is the predicate (constant #f) an equivalence relation on the domain of symbols? Justify your answer.

3.13–4   Define a predicate `disjoint-bags` that receives two bags and returns #t if there is no value that they both contain and #f if there is at least one such value.   Give a counterexample to show that `disjoint-bags?` is not an equivalence relation.

3.13–5   Define a variable-arity extension of `disjoint-bags` that can receive any number of bags as arguments and returns #t if there is no value that two or more of them contain and #f if there is at least one value that is common to at least two of the bags.

3.14   Sets

A *set* is a data structure that can contain any number of values. The values in a set are unordered, as in a bag. Unlike bags, however, sets cannot contain values "more than once." Any two members of a set are distinct and different values, and so there is no notion of multiplicity (see Exercise 3.12–2) for sets—a value either is or is not a member of a given set, and that's the end of the story.

It is natural, then, to model values of the *set* type as bags that meet the constraint that no two of their values are the same. However, this once more raises the question of what should count as "the same." Since the answer to this question is dependent on the context of use and, for practical purposes, on the nature of the application that one is developing, no one equivalence relation is suitably universal.

Whenever we construct a set, therefore, we'll supply a binary predicate, expressing the criterion of sameness that we want to use as an equivalence relation. For generic sets, we can use `equal?` for this purpose. Note, however, that the same value may count as a set under one criterion of sameness and not under another. For instance, the values (bag 0 1) and (bag 1 0) satisfy the predicate `bag=?`, and so a single set using `bag=?` as its criterion of sameness could not contain both of them. However, under the implementation of bags that we developed in §3.12, a predicate like `list=?` or `equal?` can distinguish (bag 0 1) from (bag 1 0), so they might appear in the same set if it used one of these predicates as its criterion of sameness.

Instead of a single classification predicate for sets, therefore, we'll have one for each possible criterion of sameness. The `set-classification` procedure receives a binary predicate and constructs an appropriate classification predicate:

```
(define (set-classification equivalent?)
  (^et bag? (pipe debag (all-different equivalent?)))))
```

We'll use the name 'set?' for the classification predicate for generic sets:

```
(define set? (set-classification equal?))
```

Similarly, the `set-of` procedure needs a criterion-of-sameness argument as well as the classification predicate for the type of the members of a set:

```
(define (set-of right-type-of-member? equivalent?)
  (^et bag? (pipe debag (^et (every right-type-of-member?)
                             (all-different equivalent?)))))))
```

The analogues for sets of the `put-into-bag` procedure also have different criteria of sameness. They pose another question in design as well: What should happen when the caller tries to add a value to a set that already has it as a member? Would that violate a precondition, resulting in an error? Should it be handled as a failure, with a result interface like that of `extract-from-bag`? It turns out that a third approach is more useful: We'll just discard the duplicate value and return the given set unchanged.

The `set-adjoiner` procedure receives an equivalence relation and returns a procedure that adds a value to a set, using this strategy of discarding duplicates:

```
(define (set-adjoiner equivalent?)
  (^if (pipe (~initial (curry equivalent?)) exists-in-bag?)
       >next
       put-into-bag))
```

Again, we'll give a separate name to the generic version:

```
(define put-into-set (set-adjoiner equal?))
```

The running time of the procedures that `set-adjoiner` constructs increases with the number of members in the set argument, since each new candidate for membership has to be compared to all of the previous ones. In some cases, though, we can establish as a precondition that the value that we want to add to a set is not equivalent to any of its members. For such cases, we'll use the `fast-put-into-set` procedure instead:

```
(define fast-put-into-set put-into-bag)
```

The `set-maker` procedure receives an equivalence relation and returns a variable-arity constructor for sets, applying the given equivalence relation as its criterion of sameness for members:

```
(define (set-maker equivalent?)
  (extend-to-variable-arity (bag) (set-adjoiner equivalent?)))
```

We'll call the variable-arity constructor for generic sets set:

```
(define set (set-maker equal?))
```

The rest of the set primitives don't need to know what the set's criterion of sameness is, so they can be identical to their analogues for bags:

```
(define deset debag)
```

```
(define take-from-set take-from-bag)
```

```
(define empty-set? empty-bag?)
```

```
(define set=? bag=?)
```

```
(define set-of= bag-of=)
```

Managing Recursion with Sets

The tools for managing recursion with sets are analogues of the corresponding tools for bags. The fold-set procedure is the most common of them. It constructs and returns a procedure that receives a set. If the set is empty, the returned procedure invokes a base procedure to generate its results; if not, the returned procedure takes one member out of the set, invokes itself recursively on the rest of the set, and applies a combiner procedure to the extracted member of the original set and the results of the recursive call.

```
(define (fold-set base combiner)
  (recur empty-set? (pipe black-hole base) take-from-set combiner))
```

Under our implementation of sets, in fact, fold-set is the same procedure as fold-bag (since empty-set? is just an alias for empty-bag? and take-from-set for take-from-bag).

Since the mapping and unfolding procedures return newly constructed sets, we'll define higher-order procedures that return mappers and unfolders that use specified equivalence relations in the construction:

```
(define (set-mapper equivalent?)
  (lambda (procedure aro)
    ((fold-set (set-maker equivalent?)
               (pipe (~initial procedure) (set-adjoiner equivalent?)))
     aro)))
```

```
(define (set-unfolder equivalent?)
  (lambda (final? producer step)
    (build final?
           (constant ((set-maker equivalent?)))
           producer
           step
           (set-adjoiner equivalent?))))
```

If we need only generic sets, we can use the simpler `map-set` and `unfold-set` procedures:

```
(define map-set (set-mapper equal?))

(define unfold-set (set-unfolder equal?))
```

We'll also find it useful to have a fast version of `map-set` for cases in which we can guarantee as a precondition that all of the values that we generate and put into the result set are distinct, so that comparisons aren't needed:

```
(define (fast-map-set procedure aro)
  ((fold-set set (pipe (~initial procedure) fast-put-into-set)) aro))
```

Filtering and Partitioning Sets

The filtering and partitioning procedures do not need explicit equivalence-relation arguments, even though they also construct sets, because their results are all subsets of given sets. When the given sets were constructed, explicit testing excluded duplicates. Consequently, a subset of such a set cannot contain any two values that would satisfy that equivalence relation. For the same reason, we can use `fast-put-into-set` to add a value to the result set. (It would be pointless to check whether it is already a member of the set, since we can prove that it is not.)

```
(define (filter-set keep? aro)
  ((fold-set set (conditionally-combine keep? fast-put-into-set)) aro))

(define remp-set (pipe (~initial ^not) filter-set))

(define (partition-set condition-met? aro)
  ((fold-set (create (set) (set))
             (lambda (candidate ins outs)
               (if (condition-met? candidate)
                   (values (fast-put-into-set candidate ins) outs)
                   (values ins (fast-put-into-set candidate outs)))))
   aro))
```

Additional Set Operations

We can now provide algorithms for a number of common operations on sets.

The cardinality of a set is the number of members it has. We could compute the cardinality of a given set by tallying, as we did with bags in §3.12, but this time let's use fold-set to describe essentially the same recursive method. If the given set is empty, we generate 0 and return it. Otherwise, we take out a member, discard it, and add 1 to the cardinality of the rest of the set:

```
(define cardinality (fold-set (create 0) (pipe >next add1)))
```

The extract-from-set selector, which extracts a member of a given set satisfying a given predicate, is analogous to extract-from-bag. Like extract-from-bag, extract-from-set returns a box containing the sought item if it succeeds, or #f (unboxed) if it fails:

```
(define (extract-from-set condition-met? aro)
  ((rec (extracter areto)
     (if (empty-set? areto)
         (values #f areto)
         (receive (chosen others) (take-from-set areto)
           (if (condition-met? chosen)
               (values (box chosen) others)
               (receive (sought relicts) (extracter others)
                 (values sought (fast-put-into-set chosen relicts)))))))
   aro))
```

In many cases, the value that we want to extract from the set is one of its members, and the only point of the extraction is to get a set from which that value has been removed. The remove-from-set procedure carries out this operation, returning only the post-extraction set:

```
(define (remove-from-set delend aro)
  ((rec (remover areto)
     (receive (chosen others) (take-from-set areto)
       (if (equal? delend chosen)
           others
           (fast-put-into-set chosen (remover others)))))
   aro))
```

The for-all-in-set? predicate tests whether each member of a given set satisfies a given unary predicate, and is defined like for-all-in-bag?:

```
(define (for-all-in-set? condition-met? aro)
  ((rec (ok? areto)
     (or (empty-set? areto)
         (receive (chosen others) (take-from-set areto)
           (and (condition-met? chosen) (ok? others)))))
   aro))
```

Similarly, `exists-in-set?` tests whether at least one member of a given set satisfies a given unary predicate:

```
(define exists-in-set? (run (~initial ^not) for-all-in-set? not))
```

One easy application of `exists-in-set?` is `member?`, which determines whether a given value is a member of a given set:

```
(define member? (pipe (~initial (curry equal?)) exists-in-set?))
```

Actually, the `member?` predicate is only for use with generic sets. The `set-membership` procedure receives an equivalence relation as its argument and returns a membership predicate that is appropriate for sets that use that equivalence relation as their criterion of sameness:

```
(define (set-membership equivalent?)
  (pipe (~initial (curry equivalent?)) exists-in-set?))
```

The `subset?` predicate determines whether one given set is a subset of another, that is, whether each of its members is also a member of the other:

```
(define (subset? left right)
  (for-all-in-set? (sect member? <> right) left))
```

Again, `subset?` is for generic sets. If we need a different criterion of sameness, we'll generate a customized version by applying `set-subsethood` to it:

```
(define (set-subsethood equivalent?)
  (let ((mem? (set-membership equivalent?)))
    (lambda (left right)
      (for-all-in-set? (sect mem? <> right) left))))
```

Since two sets have the same members if each is a subset of the other, we could have defined `set=?` as `(^et subset? (converse subset?))`, but the strategy we actually adopted is more efficient.

Union, Intersection, and Difference

The *union* of two sets has as its members all values that are members of either or both of those sets. We can form it by starting with either of the sets as a base and folding over the other, adjoining its members one by one. Since the adjoiner depends on the criterion of sameness, we'll start with a `set-unioner` meta-procedure:

```
(define (set-unioner equivalent?)
  (lambda (left right)
    ((fold-set (create right) (set-adjoiner equivalent?)) left)))
```

The union procedure, then, is the unioner for generic sets:

```
(define (union left right)
  ((fold-set (create right) put-into-set) left))
```

We can use a faster version of union when the two sets are known to have no common members:

```
(define (fast-union left right)
  ((fold-set (create right) fast-put-into-set) left))
```

The *intersection* of two sets has as its members the values that are members of both of them. To construct the intersection, we can start with either set and filter it by membership in the other:

```
(define (intersection left right)
  (filter-set (sect member? <> right) left))

(define (set-intersectioner equivalent?)
  (let ((mem? (set-membership equivalent?)))
    (lambda (left right)
      (filter-set (sect mem? <> right) left))))
```

Two sets are *disjoint* if their intersection is empty:

```
(define disjoint? (pipe intersection empty-set?))

(define (set-disjointness equivalent?)
  (pipe (set-intersectioner equivalent?) empty-set?))
```

The *set difference* of two sets is the set of all members of the first that are *not* members of the second:

```
(define (set-difference left right)
  (remp-set (sect member? <> right) left))

(define (set-differencer equivalent?)
  (let ((mem? (set-membership equivalent?)))
    (lambda (left right)
      (remp-set (sect mem? <> right) left))))
```

---

set-classification   (afp sets)
$(\alpha, \alpha \rightarrow Boolean) \rightarrow (any \rightarrow Boolean)$
equivalent?   something
Construct a predicate that determines whether something is a set, using equivalent? as the criterion of sameness among the members of the putative set.
Precondition: equivalent? is symmetric.
Precondition: equivalent? can receive any values.

set?   (afp sets)
$any \rightarrow Boolean$
something

Determine whether something is a set, using equal? as the criterion of sameness among the members of the putative set.

set-of   (afp sets)
(any → Boolean),   (α, α → Boolean) → (any   → Boolean)
right-type-of-member? equivalent?   something
Construct a predicate that determines whether something is a set of which all the members satisfy right-type-of-member?, using equivalent? as the criterion of sameness among the members of the putative set.
Precondition: right-type-of-member? can receive any value.
Precondition: equivalent? can receive any values that satisfy right-type-of-member?.
Precondition: equivalent? is symmetric.

set-adjoiner   (afp sets)
(α, α → Boolean) → (α, set(α) → set(α))
equivalent?   new aro
Construct a procedure that, in turn, constructs a set containing the members of aro and, in addition, new, provided that no member of aro and new satisfy equivalent?.
Precondition: equivalent? is an equivalence relation.
Precondition: equivalent? can receive new and any member of aro.

put-into-set   (afp sets)
α, set(α) → set(α)
new aro
Construct a set containing the members of aro and, in addition, new, provided that new is not a member of aro.

fast-put-into-set   (afp sets)
α, set(α) → set(α)
new aro
Construct a set containing new and the members of aro.
Precondition: new is not a member of aro.

set-maker   (afp sets)
(α, α → Boolean) → (α ...   → set(α))
equivalent?   arguments
Construct a procedure that, in turn, constructs a set with the elements of arguments as its members, excluding duplicates (as determined by equivalent?).
Precondition: equivalent? is an equivalence relation.
Precondition: equivalent? can receive any elements of arguments.

set   (afp sets)
α ...   → set(α)
arguments
Construct a set with the elements of arguments as its members, excluding duplicates.

deset   (afp sets)
set(α) → α ...
aro
Return the members of aro.

take-from-set   (afp sets)
set(α) → α, set(α)
aro
Return a member of aro and a set with the other members of aro as its members.
Precondition: aro is not empty.

empty-set?   (afp sets)
set(any) → Boolean
aro
Determine whether aro is empty.

set=?   (afp sets)
set(any), set(any) → Boolean
left   right

Determine whether left and right have the same members.

set-of=   (afp sets)
$(\alpha, \beta \rightarrow Boolean)\ \rightarrow\ (set(\alpha),\ set(\beta)\ \rightarrow\ Boolean)$
member=?   left   right
Construct a predicate that determines whether left and right have the same members, using
member=? as the criterion of sameness.
Precondition: member=? can receive any member of left as its first argument and any member
of right as its second.
Precondition: For any values left-0, left-1, right-0, and right-1, if left-0 and right-0
satisfy member=?, and left-1 and right-0 satisfy member=?, and left-0 and right-1 satisfy
member=?, then left-1 and right-1 satisfy member=?.

fold-set   (afp sets)
$(\rightarrow \alpha \dots),\ (\beta, \alpha \dots \rightarrow \alpha \dots)\ \rightarrow\ (set(\beta)\ \rightarrow \alpha \dots)$
base   combiner   aro
Construct a procedure that returns the results of invoking base if aro is empty. If aro is not
empty, the constructed procedure takes a member out of aro, applies itself recursively to the
set of the other members of aro, and returns the results of applying combiner to the taken
value and the results of the recursive invocation.
Precondition: combiner can receive any member of aro and the results of any invocation of
base.
Precondition: combiner can receive any member of aro and the results of any invocation of
combiner.

set-mapper   (afp sets)
$(\alpha, \alpha \rightarrow Boolean)\ \rightarrow\ ((\beta \rightarrow \alpha),\ set(\beta)\ \rightarrow set(\alpha))$
equivalent?   procedure aro
Construct a procedure that, in turn, constructs a set, the members of which are the results
of applying procedure to members of aro. The criterion of sameness for members of the
constructed set is equivalent?.
Precondition: equivalent? can receive any results of invocations of procedure.
Precondition: equivalent? is an equivalence relation.
Precondition: procedure can receive any member of aro.

set-unfolder   (afp sets)
$(\alpha, \alpha \rightarrow Boolean)\ \rightarrow\ ((\beta \dots \rightarrow Boolean),\ (\beta \dots \rightarrow \alpha),\ (\beta \dots \rightarrow \beta \dots)\ \rightarrow$
equivalent?   final?   producer   step
$$(\beta \dots \qquad \rightarrow set(\alpha)))$$
                                          arguments
Construct a procedure that, in turn, constructs a procedure that first determines whether the
elements of arguments satisfy final?. If so, the inner constructed procedure returns the empty
set. Otherwise, it returns a set containing the result of applying producer to the elements
of arguments, in addition to the members of the set obtained by first applying step to the
elements of arguments and then applying the inner constructed procedure recursively to the
results, excluding duplicates. The criterion of sameness for members of the constructed set is
equivalent?.
Precondition: equivalent? can receive any results of invocations of producer.
Precondition: equivalent? is an equivalence relation.
Precondition: final? can receive the elements of arguments.
Precondition: final? can receive the results of any invocation of step.
Precondition: If the elements of arguments do not satisfy final?, then producer can receive
them.
Precondition: If the results of an invocation of step do not satisfy final?, then producer can
receive them.
Precondition: If the elements of arguments do not satisfy final?, then step can receive them.
Precondition: If the results of an invocation of step do not satisfy final?, then step can
receive them.

map-set   (afp sets)
$(\alpha \rightarrow \beta),\ set(\alpha)\ \rightarrow set(\beta)$
procedure aro

Construct a set containing each of the results of applying procedure to a value in aro, excluding duplicates.

Precondition: procedure can receive any member of aro.

unfold-set   (afp sets)

$(\alpha \ldots \rightarrow Boolean), \ (\alpha \ldots \rightarrow \beta), \ (\alpha \ldots \rightarrow \alpha \ldots) \ \rightarrow (\alpha \ldots \ \rightarrow set(\beta))$
final?   producer   step   arguments

Construct a procedure that first determines whether the elements of arguments satisfy final?. If so, the constructed procedure returns the empty set. Otherwise, it returns a set containing the result of applying producer to the elements of arguments, in addition to the members of the set obtained by first applying step to the elements of arguments and then applying the constructed procedure recursively to the results, excluding duplicates.

Precondition: final? can receive the elements of arguments.

Precondition: final? can receive the results of any invocation of step.

Precondition: If the elements of arguments do not satisfy final?, then producer can receive them.

Precondition: If the results of an invocation of step do not satisfy final?, then producer can receive them.

Precondition: If the elements of arguments do not satisfy final?, then step can receive them.

Precondition: If the results of an invocation of step do not satisfy final?, then step can receive them.

fast-map-set   (afp sets)

$(\alpha \rightarrow \beta), \ set(\alpha) \ \rightarrow set(\beta)$
procedure aro

Construct a set containing each of the results of applying procedure to a value in aro.

Precondition: procedure can receive any member of aro.

Precondition: The results of applying procedure to different members of aro are different.

filter-set   (afp sets)

$(\alpha \rightarrow Boolean), \ set(\alpha) \ \rightarrow set(\alpha)$
keep?   aro

Construct a set containing the values in aro that satisfy keep?.

Precondition: keep? can receive any value in aro.

remp-set   (afp sets)

$(\alpha \rightarrow Boolean), \ set(\alpha) \ \rightarrow set(\alpha)$
exclude?   aro

Construct a set containing the values in aro that do not satisfy exclude?.

Precondition: exclude? can receive any value in aro.

partition-set   (afp sets)

$(\alpha \rightarrow Boolean), \ set(\alpha) \ \rightarrow set(\alpha), set(\alpha)$
condition-met?   aro

Construct two sets, one containing the values in aro that satisfy condition-met?, the other those that do not.

Precondition: condition-met? can receive any value in aro.

cardinality   (afp sets)

$set(any) \ \rightarrow natural\text{-}number$
aro

Compute the number of members of aro.

extract-from-set   (afp sets)

$(\alpha \rightarrow Boolean), \ set(alpha) \ \rightarrow (box(\alpha) \mid Boolean), set(\alpha)$
condition-met?   aro

Search aro for a value that satisfies condition-met?. If and when such an element is found, return a box containing that value and a set containing the other values in aro; otherwise, return #f and aro.

Precondition: condition-met? can receive any element of aro.

remove-from-set   (afp sets)

$\alpha, \quad set(\alpha) \ \rightarrow set(\alpha)$
delend aro

Construct a set containing all of the members of aro except for delend.
Precondition: delend is a member of aro.

for-all-in-set? (afp sets)
$(\alpha \rightarrow Boolean),\ set(\alpha)\ \rightarrow Boolean$
condition-met? aro
Determine whether all of the values in aro satisfy condition-met?.
Precondition: condition-met? can receive any value in aro.

exists-in-set? (afp sets)
$(\alpha \rightarrow Boolean),\ set(\alpha)\ \rightarrow Boolean$
condition-met? aro
Determine whether at least one of the values in aro satisfies condition-met?.
Precondition: condition-met? can receive any value in aro.

member? (afp sets)
$\alpha,\quad set(\alpha)\ \rightarrow Boolean$
item aro
Determine whether item is a member of aro.

set-membership (afp sets)
$(\alpha, \alpha \rightarrow Boolean)\ \rightarrow (\alpha,\quad set(\alpha)\ \rightarrow Boolean)$
equivalent?   item aro
Construct a predicate that determines whether item is a member of aro using equivalent? as
its criterion of sameness.
Precondition: equivalent? can receive any members of aro.
Precondition: equivalent? is an equivalence relation.

subset? (afp sets)
$set(\alpha),\ set(\alpha)\ \rightarrow Boolean$
left   right
Determine whether left is a subset of right.

set-subsethood (afp sets)
$(\alpha, \alpha \rightarrow Boolean)\ \rightarrow (set(\alpha),\ set(\alpha)\ \rightarrow Boolean)$
equivalent?   left   right
Construct a predicate that determines, using equivalent? as its criterion of sameness, whether
left is a subset of right.
Precondition: equivalent? can receive any member of left and any member of right.
Precondition: equivalent? is an equivalence relation.

set-unioner (afp sets)
$(\alpha, \alpha \rightarrow Boolean)\ \rightarrow (set(\alpha),\ set(\alpha)\ \rightarrow set(\alpha))$
equivalent?   left   right
Construct a procedure that constructs a set containing every member of left and every
member of right, using equivalent? as its criterion of sameness.
Precondition: equivalent? can receive any member of left or of right.
Precondition: equivalent? is an equivalence relation.

union (afp sets)
$set(\alpha),\ set(\alpha)\ \rightarrow set(\alpha)$
left   right
Construct a set containing every member of left and every member of right.

fast-union (afp sets)
$set(\alpha),\ set(\alpha)\ \rightarrow set(\alpha)$
left   right
Construct a set containing every member of left and every member of right.
Precondition: No member of left is a member of right.

intersection (afp sets)
$set(\alpha),\ set(\alpha)\ \rightarrow set(\alpha)$
left   right
Construct a set containing the common members of left and right.

set-intersectioner (afp sets)

$(\alpha,\ \alpha \rightarrow Boolean)\ \rightarrow (set(\alpha),\ set(\alpha)\ \rightarrow set(\alpha))$
equivalent?   left   right
Construct a procedure that constructs a set containing the common members of left and
right, using equivalent? as its criterion of sameness.
Precondition: equivalent? can receive any member of left and any member of right.
Precondition: equivalent? is an equivalence relation.

disjoint?   (afp sets)
$set(\alpha),\ set(\alpha)\ \rightarrow Boolean$
left   right
Determine whether left and right are disjoint.

set-disjointness   (afp sets)
$(\alpha,\ \alpha \rightarrow Boolean)\ \rightarrow (set(\alpha),\ set(\alpha)\ \rightarrow Boolean)$
equivalent?   left   right
Construct a predicate that determines, using equivalent? as its criterion of sameness, whether
left and right are disjoint.
Precondition: equivalent? can receive any member of left and any member of right.
Precondition: equivalent? is an equivalence relation.

set-difference   (afp sets)
$set(\alpha),\ set(\alpha)\ \rightarrow set(\alpha)$
left   right
Construct the set of members of left that are not members of right.

set-differencer   (afp sets)
$(\alpha,\ \alpha \rightarrow Boolean)\ \rightarrow (set(\alpha),\ set(\alpha)\ \rightarrow set(\alpha))$
equivalent?   left   right
Construct a procedure that constructs the set of members of left that are not members of
right, using equivalent? as its criterion of sameness.
Precondition: equivalent? can receive any member of left and any member of right.
Precondition: equivalent? is an equivalence relation.

Exercises

3.14–1   Define a procedure set-disparity that receives two generic sets and
returns a set containing the values that belong to one of the given sets but not
to both. For instance, the value of the call '(set-disparity (set 0 1 2 3)
(set 0 2 4 6))' is (set 1 3 4 6).

3.14–2   Extend the arity of the union procedure to obtain a grand-union
procedure that can receive any number of generic sets as arguments and returns
a single set that comprises all of the members of the given sets.

3.14–3   Extend the arity of the intersection procedure to obtain a
grand-intersection procedure that can receive one or more generic sets as
arguments and returns the set of their common members (i.e., the values that
belong to all of the given sets). Explain the rationale for excluding the case of
zero arguments.

3.14–4   Define a predicate all-disjoint? that can receive any number of arguments, all of which are generic sets, and returns #f if any two of its arguments
have one or more common members, and #t if every pair of them is disjoint.

3.14–5   In the *von Neumann model* of the natural numbers, each natural
number is the set of all natural numbers less than itself. So 0 is the empty

set, (set), since there are no natural numbers less than 0; 1 is (set (set)), the set in which 0 is the only element; 2 is (set (set) (set (set))), the set containing only 0 and 1; and so on. Reimplement the primitive procedures for natural numbers using the von Neumann model.

3.15 Tables

A *table* is a data structure in which some values (the *keys*) are individually associated with other values (the *entries*), subject to the constraint that a given key is associated with at most one entry in a given table. In practice, a table is often used like a unary procedure that requires its argument to be a key and returns the entry associated with that key. In this role, tables are sometimes called *finite functions*, and indeed it is sometimes convenient to use Scheme procedures to model tables. However, the model that we'll develop here implements tables as bags of pairs, with each pair containing a key and the entry with which it is associated.

The classification predicate for generic tables first determines whether its argument is a bag of pairs, then makes sure that no two of those pairs have the same key:

```
(define table?
  (^et (bag-of pair?)
       (run (sect map-bag car <>) debag (all-different equal?))))
```

When we prefer to specialize the types of the keys and entries, the procedure that constructs our specialized classification predicate receives the classification predicates for those types and the equality predicate for the key type as arguments:

```
(define (table-of key? entry? key=?)
  (^et (bag-of (pair-of key? entry?))
       (run (sect map-bag car <>) debag (all-different key=?))))
```

Tables are sometimes constructed one association at a time, sometimes all at once. For incremental construction, the options are analogous to those for sets: If we know that the key is not already in the table, we can use a fast adjoiner to put the new association into the table. Otherwise, we'll need to test the key against all the keys that are already in the table, so as to avoid duplication. If the table is generic, we'll use the equal? procedure to compare the keys; for specialized tables, we'll invoke a higher-order procedure to obtain a specialized adjoiner.

The fast adjoiner, fast-put-into-table, constructs the key-entry pair and puts it into the bag that implements the table:

```
(define (fast-put-into-table key entry tab)
  (put-into-bag (cons key entry) tab))
```

The generic adjoiner, `put-into-table`, first tries to extract an association for the given key from the bag. Regardless of whether this attempt succeeds or fails, it then adds the new association to the second value returned by `extract-from-bag`. The effect is that, if the key was already associated with some entry, the new association replaces the old one (and the entry formerly associated with the key is discarded); otherwise, the new association is added to the table, exactly as in `fast-put-into-table`:

```
(define (put-into-table key entry tab)
  (receive (discarded tab-without-key)
           (extract-from-bag (pipe car (equal-to key)) tab)
    (put-into-bag (cons key entry) tab-without-key)))
```

The `table-adjoiner` procedure receives the equality relation for keys and returns a custom adjoiner that uses that relation in place of `equal?`:

```
(define (table-adjoiner key=?)
  (lambda (key entry tab)
    (receive (discarded tab-without-key)
             (extract-from-bag (pipe car (sect key=? <> key)) tab)
      (put-into-bag (cons key entry) tab-without-key))))
```

Theoretically, we have the same three possibilities for the all-at-once table constructors. However, when all of the key-entry associations are available at once, it is easier to check the fast constructor's precondition. This approach also leaves us with more options when the precondition fails. So we'll implement only the fast all-at-once constructor. It can receive any number of arguments, each of which must be a key-entry pair, and assembles them into a table, relying on the precondition that all of the keys are distinct:

```
(define table bag)
```

Our repertoire of basic procedures for tables includes three selectors: `lookup` to recover the entry associated with a given key, `table-keys` to recover all the keys in a table, and `table-entries` to recover all the entries.

In the implementation of `lookup`, there is a significant design decision to make: What should happen when `lookup` receives a key that is not associated with any entry in the given table? One alternative is to make the key's presence in the table a precondition of `lookup`. However, testing that condition in advance will often be slow and awkward. Another possibility is to have `lookup` return `null` or some other special value when the lookup fails. As with the `extract-from-bag` procedure in §3.12, however, any such designated value could be mistaken for the result of a successful lookup. A third option is for `lookup` to box the result of a successful search and return `#f`, unboxed, if the search is unsuccessful.

For `lookup`, however, still another alternative is available: We can allow the caller to provide, in addition to the table and the key, a "default value" to be

returned if there is no association for the key in the table. This third argument
is optional, and if it is absent lookup uses #f to signal a failed search. However,
we'll see that allowing the caller to supply a default value makes it easy to
express some common programming patterns elegantly and concisely.

Here, then, is the implementation of lookup:

```
(define (lookup key tab . extras)
  (let ((default (if (empty-list? extras) #f (first extras))))
    ((rec (searcher aro)
       (if (empty-bag? aro)
           default
           (receive (chosen others) (take-from-bag aro)
             (if (equal? key (car chosen))
                 (cdr chosen)
                 (searcher others)))))
     tab)))
```

The table-searcher procedure constructs an analogue of lookup that uses
a specified equivalence relation (in place of equal?) to compare keys:

```
(define (table-searcher key=?)
  (lambda (key tab . extras)
    (let ((default (if (empty-list? extras) #f (first extras))))
      ((rec (searcher aro)
         (if (empty-bag? aro)
             default
             (receive (chosen others) (take-from-bag aro)
               (if (key=? key (car chosen))
                   (cdr chosen)
                   (searcher others)))))
       tab))))
```

To recover the keys from a table, we can use fold-bag, selecting the appropriate component of each association. The keys are known to be distinct, so it
is appropriate for the table-keys procedure to return them in a set, and we can
use fast-put-into-set to build it up:

```
(define table-keys
  (fold-bag set (pipe (~initial car) fast-put-into-set)))
```

The table-entries procedure, on the other hand, returns a bag, since we
want to keep all of the entries, even if they are duplicated:

```
(define table-entries (sect map-bag cdr <>))
```

The delete-from-table procedure removes the association for a given key
from a given table and discards it, returning the revised table. (If no such
association exists, it returns the given table unchanged.) We'll implement it by
applying extract-from-bag and discarding the association that is recovered:

```
(define (delete-from-table key tab)
  ((pipe extract-from-bag >next) (pipe car (equal-to key)) tab))
```

Here the predicate (pipe car (equal-to key)) checks whether a particular association within the table has a car that matches the key we're looking for (with equal? as the criterion of sameness). The procedure computed as (pipe extract-from-bag >next) receives this predicate and the table as arguments, invokes extract-from-bag to pull out the association (if there is one), and then invokes >next as a postprocessor to discard the deleted association, returning the rest of the bag.

When the table uses a specialized equality predicate for keys, we'll use the table-deleter procedure to construct a customized deletion procedure:

```
(define (table-deleter key=?)
  (lambda (key tab)
    ((pipe extract-from-bag >next) (pipe car (sect key=? <> key)) tab)))
```

We can determine the number of associations in a table (its *size*) by computing the cardinality of the bag that implements it:

```
(define table-size bag-cardinality)
```

To complete the basic table operations, we should supply generic and specialized equality procedures. The generic one is easy: Two tables are equal if they contain associations (that is, pairs) that are equal:

```
(define table=? (bag-of= pair=?))
```

The table-of= procedure receives two equivalence relations and constructs a customized equality predicate that determines whether two tables are the same, using the first equivalence relation as the criterion of sameness for keys and the second as the criterion of sameness for values:

```
(define table-of= (pipe pair-of= bag-of=))
```

Updating Tables

As an example of the use of tables, let's write a procedure to compute the *spectrum* of a given generic bag: a table in which the keys are the values in the bag and the corresponding entries are the multiplicities of those members.

The spectrum of an empty bag is obviously an empty table, with no keys and no entries. To compute the spectrum of a non-empty bag, we can take any value out of it, compute the spectrum of the rest of the bag, and use lookup to find out the multiplicity of the extracted value in the rest of the bag (supplying 0 as the default value in case the extracted value is not in the rest of the bag at all). We then increment that multiplicity and put the association of the extracted value with the new multiplicity into the spectrum for the rest of the bag. Remember that `put-into-table` removes from the table any association with the same key as the new one, so this operation either extends the table to accommodate a new key or updates it to replace any previous association for that key:

```
(define spectrum
  (fold-bag table (lambda (chosen subspectrum)
                    (put-into-table chosen
                                    (add1 (lookup chosen subspectrum 0))
                                    subspectrum))))
```

The `spectrum` procedure uses `lookup` and `put-into-table` in a pattern that occurs quite frequently: `lookup` extracts a value from a table, the value is operated on in some way (in this case, by `add1`), and then `put-into-table` stores the result of the operation back into the table. The `table-update` procedure abstracts this pattern. It can receive an optional argument, specifying the default value for the lookup:

```
(define (table-update key updater tab . extras)
  (put-into-table key (updater (apply lookup key tab extras)) tab))
```

We could then replace the `lambda`-expression in the definition of `spectrum` with '`(sect table-update <> add1 <> 0)`'.

Given an equivalence relation, the `table-updater` procedure constructs a specialized variant of `table-update` that uses that equivalence relation as its criterion of sameness when comparing keys:

```
(define (table-updater key=?)
  (let ((adjoiner (table-adjoiner key=?))
        (searcher (table-searcher key=?)))
    (lambda (key updater tab . extras)
      (adjoiner key (updater (apply searcher key tab extras)) tab))))
```

---

table?   (afp tables)
any   → *Boolean*
something
Determine whether something is a table.

table-of   (afp tables)
(any → Boolean), (any → Boolean), (α, α → Boolean) → (any   → Boolean)
key?   entry?   key=?   something
Construct a predicate that determines whether something is a table, using key? to determine whether some value is a key, entry? to determine whether some value is an entry, and key=? to determine whether two values are the same key.
Precondition: key? can receive any value.
Precondition: entry? can receive any value.
Precondition: key=? is an equivalence relation.
Precondition: key=? can receive any values that satisfy key?.

fast-put-into-table   (afp tables)
$\alpha,\ \ \beta,\ \ \ \ \ table(\alpha,\ \beta)\ \ \rightarrow\ table(\alpha,\ \beta)$
key entry tab
Construct a table similar to tab, except that key is associated with entry.
Precondition: key is not associated with any entry in tab.

put-into-table   (afp tables)
$\alpha,\ \ \beta,\ \ \ \ \ table(\alpha,\ \beta)\ \ \rightarrow\ table(\alpha,\ \beta)$
key entry tab
Construct a table similar to tab, except that key is associated with entry. (If tab already
associates key with some value, the new association displaces the old one.)

table-adjoiner   (afp tables)
$(\alpha,\ \alpha \rightarrow Boolean)\ \ \rightarrow\ (\alpha,\ \ \beta,\ \ \ \ table(\alpha,\ \beta)\ \ \rightarrow\ table(\alpha,\ \beta))$
key=?   key entry tab
Construct a procedure that, in turn, constructs a table similar to tab, except that key is
associated with entry, using key=? as its criterion of sameness of keys. (If tab already associates
key with some value, the new association displaces the old one.)
Precondition: key=? is an equivalence relation.
Precondition: key=? can receive key and any key in tab.

table   (afp tables)
$pair(\alpha,\ \beta)\ ... \ \ \rightarrow\ table(\alpha,\ \beta)$
associations
Construct a table in which the car of each element of associations is associated (as a key)
with the cdr of that element of associations (as an entry).
Precondition: No two elements of associations have the same car.

lookup   (afp tables)
$\alpha,\ \ table(\alpha,\ \beta),\ \beta\ ...\ \ \rightarrow\ \beta\ |\ Boolean$
key tab   extras
Search in tab for an association with key as its key. When and if one is found, return the entry
with which key is associated; otherwise, return the initial element of extras, or #f if extras is
empty.

table-searcher   (afp tables)
$(\alpha,\ \alpha \rightarrow Boolean)\ \ \rightarrow\ (\alpha,\ \ table(\alpha,\ \beta),\ \beta\ ...\ \ \rightarrow\ \beta\ |\ Boolean)$
key=?   key tab   extras
Construct a procedure that searches in tab for an association with key as its key, using key=?
as its criterion of sameness of keys. If the constructed procedure finds such an association,
it returns the entry with which key is associated; otherwise, it returns the initial element of
extras, or #f if extras is empty.
Precondition: key=? is an equivalence relation.
Precondition: key=? can receive key and any key in tab.

table-keys   (afp tables)
$table(\alpha,\ any)\ \ \rightarrow\ set(\alpha)$
tab
Return a set comprising the keys for which tab contains associations.

table-entries   (afp tables)
$table(any,\ \alpha)\ \ \rightarrow\ bag(\alpha)$
tab
Return a bag comprising the entries with which tab associates keys.

delete-from-table   (afp tables)
$\alpha,\ \ table(\alpha,\ \beta)\ \ \rightarrow\ table(\alpha,\ \beta)$
key tab
Construct a table similar to tab, but containing no association for key. (If tab contains no
association for key to begin with, return tab.)

table-deleter   (afp tables)
$(\alpha,\ \alpha \rightarrow Boolean)\ \ \rightarrow\ (\alpha,\ \ table(\alpha,\ \beta)\ \ \rightarrow\ table(\alpha,\ \beta))$
key=?   key tab

Construct a procedure that, in turn, constructs a table similar to tab, but containing no association for any value that, with key, satisfies key=?.
Precondition: key=? is an equivalence relation.
Precondition: key=? can receive key and any key in tab.

table-size   (afp tables)
table(any, any) → *natural-number*
tab
Compute the number of associations in tab.

table=?   (afp tables)
table(any, any), table(any, any) → *Boolean*
left   right
Determine whether left and right are the same table—that is, whether they contain the same keys, associated with the same entries.

table-of=   (afp tables)
(α, α → Boolean), (β, β → Boolean) → *(table(α, β), table(α, β)* → *Boolean)*
same-key?   same-entry?   left   right
Construct a predicate that determines whether left and right are the same table, using same-key? as the criterion of sameness for keys and same-entry? as the criterion of sameness for entries.
Precondition: same-key? is an equivalence relation.
Precondition: same-key? can receive any key in left and any key in right.
Precondition: same-entry? is an equivalence relation.
Precondition: same-entry? can receive any entry in left and any entry in right.

table-update   (afp tables)
α,   (β → β), table(α, β), β ... → *table(α, β)*
key updater   tab   extras
Look up key in tab, apply updater to the entry with which tab associates key, associate key with the result returned by updater, and construct a table similar to tab, except that the new association displaces the previous association for key. If tab does not associate key with any value, apply updater instead to the initial element of extras, or to #f if extras is empty.
Precondition: updater can receive any entry in tab.
Precondition: If tab contains no association for key and extras is empty, then updater can receive #f.
Precondition: If tab contains no association for key and extras is not empty, then updater can receive the initial element of extras.

table-updater   (afp tables)
(α, α → Boolean) → *(α,   (β → β), table(α, β), β ...* → *table(α, β))*
key=?   key updater   tab   extras
Construct a procedure that looks up key in tab (using key=? as its criterion of sameness), applies updater to the entry with which tab associates key, associates key with the result returned by updater, and constructs a table similar to tab, except that the new association displaces the previous association for key. If tab does not associate key with any value, the constructed procedure applies updater instead to the initial element of extras, or to #f if extras is empty.
Precondition: key=? is an equivalence relation.
Precondition: key=? can receive any keys in tab.
Precondition: updater can receive any entry in tab.
Precondition: If tab contains no association for key and extras is empty, then updater can receive #f.
Precondition: If tab contains no association for key and extras is not empty, then updater can receive the initial element of extras.

Exercises

3.15–1 Write an expression of which the value is a table that associates each of the integers from 0 to 999 with its square.

3.15–2 A generic table is *invertible* if no two of its entries are the same (as determined by `equal?`). Define a unary predicate `invertible?` that determines whether a given generic table is invertible.

3.15–3 If T is an invertible generic table, then the *inverse* of T is a table that contains the same associations, but with keys and entries swapped: If T associates a key k with an entry e, then the inverse of T associates e (as key) with k (as entry). Define a unary predicate `inverse` that constructs and returns the inverse of a given invertible generic table. (Hint: Fold over the keys of T.)

3.15–4 Design and implement appropriate "fold" and "unfold" procedures for tables.

3.16   Buffers

A computation that produces values that are needed in another computation often collects them in a data structure that the other computation accesses. If the order of the values is irrelevant, the data structure is typically a bag or a set. A list is the appropriate data structure when the order of access is the reverse of the order of construction: The item that the producing computation places at the beginning of the list, where the computation that receives it can access it immediately, is (in the order of construction) the last item to have been prepended, and conversely the item that was prepended to the list before any of the others is the last one that the receiving computation will reach.

In some cases, we prefer to impose the opposite order on the data structure: We want the receiving computation to have immediate access to the item that was added to the data structure before any of the others, and in general we want the receiving computation to work its way through the items in the order in which they were produced. A *buffer* is a data structure that supports this ordering. When we take an item out of a buffer, we remove it from the front of the structure, as with a list; but when we put an item into a buffer, it is added at the far end.

Although it is possible to use a list to represent a buffer, replacing `prepend` with `postpend` and renaming the other basic operations, this approach is not satisfactory when the buffer is large, so that the far end can be reached only by traversing the entire list. Ideally, we'd like to be able either to add a value to a buffer or to take away its initial value without examining any of the other values. In other words, we want *both* ends of the buffer to be directly accessible.

If we use only one list, it is not possible to make both ends of the buffer accessible. A better idea is to use two lists—a "fore" list for the values at or near the front of the buffer, and an "aft" list for those at or near the end of the buffer. The aft list is arranged in reverse order, so that the last item to have been put into the buffer is at the beginning of the aft list. That way, we can apply prepend to the *aft* list to put another item into the buffer, and deprepend to the *fore* list to take a value out.

The difficulty with this scheme, of course, is that if we add values only to the aft list and take them only from the fore list, we run out of values in the fore list before the buffer is empty, because all of its components are piled up in the aft list. From time to time, therefore, we'll need to shift values from the aft list to the fore list, reversing their order in the process.

Even though the running time of the reverse procedure is a linear function of the length of the list it is given (as we saw in §3.6), we wouldn't want to invoke reverse every time we put an item into a buffer or take one out. Fortunately, in applications that work with buffers, relatively few of the calls to the buffer procedures need to use reverse at all. It's never needed when we add an item to the buffer, since we can prepend to the aft list unconditionally. When we take an item from the buffer by deprepending the fore list, however, we have to ensure that the precondition for deprepend is satisfied, that is, that the fore list is not empty. Usually this precondition is met. The reverse procedure is invoked only when it is not.

In most applications of buffers, the new buffer returned by a call to the put-into-buffer or take-from-buffer procedure effectively takes the place of the one submitted to it as an argument. The algorithm needs only one buffer at any given stage, and never uses the same buffer in two separate computations.

In such applications, the longer the list we reverse when we are obliged to perform a reversal, the less likely it is that another reversal will be needed soon. If we *amortize* the cost of the reversal over a long sequence of operations, including both adding values and taking them away, by averaging the case in which the reversal is required with the many cases in which it is not, we find that the average is independent of the size of the buffer: No value goes through the reversal more than once in such a sequence of operations, so the total time required for reversals is bounded by a linear function of the number of operations performed.

We lose this running-time guarantee, however, if we use the same buffer more than once, and in particular if we apply take-from-buffer to it more than once. The time-consuming reversal of the aft list may be required each time. So, as with sources, we'll try to arrange our computations so that we never run take-from-buffer twice on the same buffer.

We can define a buffer, then, as a pair of lists—the fore list in the car of the pair and the aft list in the cdr. We get the classification predicate buffer? immediately:

```
(define buffer? (pair-of list? list?))
```

If the computation that puts items into a new buffer happens to have them available all at once, it can invoke the variable-arity procedure `buffer` just to drop them into the `fore` list, in the order specified in the call:

```
(define buffer (pipe list (sect cons <> (list))))
```

Most often, however, we'll give `buffer` no arguments, invoking it simply to get an empty buffer, as the starting point for later additions.

When a computation is ready to put a value into a buffer, it invokes the `put-into-buffer` procedure, which prepends the value to the aft list:

```
(define (put-into-buffer item buf)
  (cons (car buf) (prepend item (cdr buf))))
```

To take a value from a buffer, returning both the value and the new buffer, is a little more complicated. We first check whether the fore list is empty by applying the predicate

```
(pipe car empty-list?)
```

If the fore list is empty, we take the aft list, reverse it, deprepend the reversed list to obtain the value to be removed and the new fore list, and pair the new fore list with a new empty aft list. Here's the procedure that runs through these steps in order:

```
(run cdr reverse deprepend (~next (sect cons <> (list))))
```

If the fore list is not empty, on the other hand, we separate the fore and aft lists (using `decons`) and obtain the value to be removed by applying `first` to the fore list, and the remainder of the buffer by pairing the rest of the fore list with the entire aft list:

```
(pipe decons (dispatch (pipe >initial first)
                       (pipe (~initial rest) cons)))
```

Assembling these snippets gives us the definition of `take-from-buffer`:

```
(define take-from-buffer
  (^if (pipe car empty-list?)
       (run cdr reverse deprepend (~next (sect cons <> (list))))
       (pipe decons (dispatch (pipe >initial first)
                              (pipe (~initial rest) cons)))))
```

It is a precondition of the `take-from-buffer` procedure that the buffer is not empty (if the fore list is empty, the aft list must have at least one item in it, and vice versa). The `empty-buffer?` predicate can be used to test this precondition:

```
(define empty-buffer? (pipe decons (every empty-list?)))
```

To define the equality predicate `buffer=?` as `(pair-of= list=? list=?)` would be a blunder, since that procedure incorrectly distinguishes buffers that split their fore and aft lists in different places, even if they contain the same items in the same order. We'll instead start by defining a higher-order procedure that receives an equivalence relation and constructs a procedure taking items out of the buffers being compared until one or both of them is empty, comparing corresponding items along the way:

```
(define (buffer-of= element=?)
  (rec (equivalent? left right)
    (or (and (empty-buffer? left)
             (empty-buffer? right))
        (and (not (empty-buffer? left))
             (not (empty-buffer? right))
             (receive (left-item new-left) (take-from-buffer left)
               (receive (right-item new-right) (take-from-buffer right)
                 (and (element=? left-item right-item)
                      (equivalent? new-left new-right))))))))
```

The generic `buffer=?` procedure is the special case in which we use `equal?` to compare items:

```
(define buffer=? (buffer-of= equal?))
```

Note that these equality predicates, although they may entail many calls to `take-from-buffer`, never apply that procedure to the same buffer twice. At each level of recursion, we get a different buffer to operate on. The equality predicates, therefore, have linear running times.

Managing Recursion with Buffers

The procedure for unfolding a buffer is analogous to the procedures for unfolding lists and bags:

```
(define (unfold-buffer final? producer step)
  (build final? (constant (buffer)) producer step put-into-buffer))
```

One could also define a `fold-buffer` procedure that would be closely analogous to `fold-list`. In practice, however, the analogue of `process-list` fits more naturally with the "first in, first out" arrangement that buffers provide:

```
(define (process-buffer base combiner)
  (run (lambda (buf)
         (receive starters (base)
           (apply values buf starters)))
```

```
(iterate (pipe >initial empty-buffer?)
         (lambda (subbuf . results-so-far)
            (receive (item new-subbuf) (take-from-buffer subbuf)
               (receive new-results
                           (apply combiner item results-so-far)
                  (apply values new-subbuf new-results)))))
   >all-but-initial))
```

---

buffer?   (afp buffers)
any   → *Boolean*
something
Determine whether something is a buffer.

buffer   (afp buffers)
$\alpha \ldots$ → *buffer(α)*
arguments
Construct a buffer containing the elements of arguments.

put-into-buffer   (afp buffers)
α,   *buffer(α)* → *buffer(α)*
item buf
Construct a buffer containing the values in buf and, in addition, item.

take-from-buffer   (afp buffers)
buffer(α) → α, *buffer(α)*
buf
Return a value from buf and a buffer similar to buf, but without the returned value.
Precondition: buf is not empty.

empty-buffer?   (afp buffers)
buffer(any) → *Boolean*
buf
Determine whether buf is empty.

buffer-of=   (afp buffers)
$(\alpha, \beta \rightarrow Boolean)$ → *(buffer(α), buffer(β)* → *Boolean)*
element=?   left   right
Construct a predicate that determines whether left and right are the same, that is, whether
they contain the same values in the same order, using element=? as the criterion of sameness.
Precondition: element=? can receive any value in left as its first argument and any value in
right as its second.

buffer=?   (afp buffers)
buffer(any), *buffer(any)* → *Boolean*
left   right
Determine whether left and right contain the same values in the same order.

unfold-buffer   (afp buffers)
$(\alpha \ldots \rightarrow Boolean)$, $(\alpha \ldots \rightarrow \beta)$, $(\alpha \ldots \rightarrow \alpha \ldots)$ → $(\alpha \ldots$ → *buffer(β))*
final?   producer   step   arguments
Construct a procedure that first determines whether the elements of arguments satisfy final?.
If so, the constructed procedure returns the empty buffer. Otherwise, it returns a non-
empty buffer in which the foremost value is the result of applying producer to the elements of
arguments, and the rest of the values are stored in a buffer that is the result of first applying
step to the elements of arguments and then applying the constructed procedure recursively to
the results.
Precondition: final? can receive the elements of arguments.
Precondition: final? can receive the results of any invocation of step.
Precondition: If the elements of arguments do not satisfy final?, then producer can receive
them.
Precondition: If the results of an invocation of step do not satisfy final?, then producer can

receive them.

Precondition: If the elements of arguments do not satisfy final?, then step can receive them.

Precondition: If the results of an invocation of step do not satisfy final?, then step can receive them.

process-buffer   (afp buffers)
$(\rightarrow \alpha \ldots), \ (\beta, \alpha \ldots \rightarrow \alpha \ldots) \ \rightarrow \ (\mathit{buffer}(\beta) \ \rightarrow \alpha \ldots)$
base   combiner   buf

Construct a procedure that iteratively applies combiner to a value from buf and the results of the previous iteration (or to the results of invoking base, if there was no previous iteration). The constructed procedure returns the results of the last application of combiner.

Precondition: combiner can receive the foremost value in buf and the results of an invocation of base.

Precondition: combiner can receive any but the foremost value in buf and the results of any invocation of combiner.

Exercises

3.16–1   Define a procedure buffer-size that computes the number of items in a buffer (counting duplicates as distinct). Do not rely on the structure of our model of buffers!

3.16–2   Define a procedure shuffle-buffers that receives two buffers of equal size and returns a buffer in which items from those two buffers alternate. For instance, the value of the call '(shuffle-buffers (buffer 'a 'b 'c) (buffer 'd 'e 'f))' should be a buffer containing the symbols a, d, b, e, c, and f, in that order.

3.16–3   Define a procedure split-by-parity that receives a buffer of integers and returns two buffers, one containing all of the even items from the given buffer and the other containing all of the odd items. Within each result buffer, items should have the same relative order as in the given buffer.

Chapter 4

Sorting

Many algorithms either take advantage of some principle of arrangement among the values on which they operate, or apply some such principle to those values. In the commonest case, we think of values of the same type as having a linear order, and we consider algorithms for imposing that order on the members of a bag or set, yielding a list in which the arrangement of the elements exemplifies the ordering principle.

4.1   Ordering Relations

In computations, we express a principle of arrangement as a binary predicate that receives two arguments, `left` and `right`, and determines whether `left` may precede `right`. However, not every binary predicate expresses a linear order. The kind of predicate we want expresses a relation R, defined on a domain D, that meets the following conditions:

1. R is *connected*: For any elements a and b of D, either a bears R to b or b bears R to a.

2. R is *transitive* (as in §3.13).

Connexity ensures that we can arrange any values in the domain by following the principle. If R were not connected, then there would be values a and b such that neither bore R to the other. In that case, neither could correctly precede the other in an arrangement.

Transitivity ensures that the arrangement is internally consistent. If R is not transitive, then there are values a, b, and c such that a bears R to b and b bears R to c, but a does not bear R to c. If we try to arrange such values in a linear order, we would place a before b and b before c, but then find that a should not precede c. Worse yet, if R is connected, then the fact that a does not bear R to

c would imply that c bears R to a, so we'd have a cyclic arrangement—a before b before c before a—instead of a linear one.

An *ordering relation*, then, is one that is connected and transitive. There is no general algorithm for determining whether a given binary predicate expresses an ordering relation. However, it is usually easy to prove this property in real cases.

Some primitive Scheme predicates express ordering relations on certain classes of values: We have already seen <= for numbers; analogously, Scheme supports string<=? for strings and char<=? for characters, but provides no ordering relations for Booleans, symbols, procedures, pairs, or lists.

For any values a and b in the domain of an ordering relation R, one of them bears R to the other, and so the other bears the converse relation R' to it; so R' is also connected. Similarly, the converse R' is transitive: For any values a, b, and c in the domain, if a bears R' to b and b bears R' to c, then by the definition of "converse" c bears R to b and b bears R to a. Since R is transitive, it follows that c bears R to a, and hence, again by the definition of "converse," a bears R' to c. Thus the converse of any ordering relation is also an ordering relation. In particular, >=, string>=?, and char>=? are all ordering relations. The converse of an ordering relation specifies a linear order that is the reverse of the one that the relation itself specifies (e.g., descending instead of ascending).

Implicitly Defined Equivalence Relations

An ordering relation R implicitly defines an equivalence relation $\stackrel{R}{=}$. Two elements of D count as "equal under the ordering" if each of them bears the ordering relation to the other. This induced equivalence relation is sometimes much coarser than identity, since values are treated as equivalent whenever the ordering cannot distinguish them. Fortunately, in the most common cases the implicitly defined equivalence relations are also the "natural" ones. For instance, <= implicitly defines =, string<=? implicitly defines string=?, and char<=? implicitly defines char=?.

Testing Whether a List Is Ordered

A list is said to be *ordered* with respect to a given ordering relation if each of its elements bears the ordering relation to every element that it precedes in the list. The transitivity of ordering relations makes it possible to determine whether a list is ordered without comparing every possible pair of elements; we need only look at pairs of elements that occupy adjacent positions in the list. If all such pairs are correctly arranged, the list is ordered.

It is straightforward to define a procedure that receives an ordering relation and a list and determines whether the list is ordered with respect to the specified ordering relation:

```
(define (ordered? may-precede? ls)
  ((^vel empty-list?
        (rec (first-ordered? sublist)
          (receive (initial others) (deprepend sublist)
            (or (empty-list? others)
                (and (may-precede? initial (first others))
                     (first-ordered? others)))))))
   ls))
```

The empty list is treated as a special case. If a list has no elements, then it is vacuously true that any two of its elements are correctly arranged, no matter what the ordering relation is.

Given a non-empty list, `ordered?` separates its first element from the rest and supplies the pieces to the recursive internal predicate `first-ordered?`. This predicate stops, returning #t, if the rest of the list is empty (a one-element list is also, trivially, ordered); it stops, returning #f, if the first element fails to bear the ordering relation to the first element of the rest of the list; and otherwise it calls itself recursively to confirm that the rest of the list is ordered.

Searching for an Extreme Value

If we have a non-empty bag of values for which some ordering relation can be defined, we often want to find an *extreme* member of the bag, that is, one that bears the ordering relation to every member of the bag. For instance, in a bag of natural numbers, an extreme member with respect to the >= relation is one that is greater than or equal to all the others. (The connexity of the ordering relation guarantees that the extreme member also bears that relation to itself; ordering relations, as defined above, are always reflexive.)

As one step in finding an extreme member, it will be helpful to have a procedure that receives two values and returns whichever one of them bears the ordering relation to the other. The `prior-by` procedure converts the predicate that expresses a given ordering relation into such a procedure. (For instance, the `lesser` procedure from §1.9 is `(prior-by <=)`.)

```
(define prior-by (sect ^if <> >initial >next))
```

In other cases, we'll want our comparison procedure to return both of the given values, in the order specified by the ordering relation. (In other words, it returns its arguments either unchanged or swapped.) The `arrange-by` procedure converts the predicate that expresses the ordering relation into such a procedure:

```
(define arrange-by (sect ^if <> values >exch))
```

Once an ordering relation is specified, finding the extreme is a simple application of `fold-bag`. We start the process by taking any value from the bag. If this leaves the bag empty, we're done. Otherwise, in the recursive call, we find

the extreme value from the rest of the bag. By connexity, either our starter
member bears the ordering relation to this recursive extreme value, or vice
versa; we return whichever of the two bears the ordering relation to the other.
The extreme procedure receives an ordering relation and returns a customized
procedure for extracting the extreme value from a bag:

```
(define (extreme may-precede?)
  (let ((prior (prior-by may-precede?)))
    (lambda (aro)
      (receive (starter others) (take-from-bag aro)
        ((fold-bag (create starter) prior) others)))))
```

The extreme-and-others procedure is a variant of this idea, returning not
only the extreme value in the bag but also a bag comprising all of the other
values, as in take-from-bag and extract-from-bag. In the base case, where the
given bag contains only one value, we need to return an empty bag along with
that value:

```
(create starter (bag))
```

The combiner for the non-base case receives three arguments: a value from the
given bag and the results of a recursive call, which are the extreme value from
the rest of the given bag and a bag containing all the non-extreme values. The
combiner will compare the new value with the extreme value from the rest of
the bag, keeping whichever one of them the ordering places ahead of the other
and putting the other one into the bag with the other non-extreme values:

```
(lambda (new so-far unchosen)
  (receive (leader trailer) (arrange new so-far)
    (values leader (put-into-bag trailer unchosen))))
```

Dropping these pieces into the correct slots in the call to fold-bag gives us
the definition for extreme-and-others:

```
(define (extreme-and-others may-precede?)
  (let ((arrange (arrange-by may-precede?)))
    (lambda (aro)
      (receive (starter others) (take-from-bag aro)
        ((fold-bag (create starter (bag))
                   (lambda (new so-far unchosen)
                     (receive (leader trailer) (arrange new so-far)
                       (values leader (put-into-bag trailer unchosen)))))
         others)))))
```

Finding the extreme element in a set or a list is exactly like finding it in a
bag:

```
(define (extreme-in-set may-precede?)
  (let ((prior (prior-by may-precede?)))
    (lambda (aro)
      (receive (starter others) (take-from-set aro)
        ((fold-set (create starter) prior) others)))))
(define (extreme-in-list may-precede?)
  (let ((prior (prior-by may-precede?)))
    (lambda (ls)
      (receive (starter others) (deprepend ls)
        ((fold-list (create starter) prior) others)))))
```

However, if we also want to recover the rest of the list from which the extreme element has been extracted, we have to proceed a little more carefully in order to preserve the original order of the remaining elements. Applying `fold-list` as we applied `fold-bag` doesn't work: When `fold-list` deprepends the list, it sends the "rest" part into a recursive call, but doesn't make it available directly to the combiner. In this case, the combiner would be something like

```
(lambda (initial so-far unchosen)
  (if (may-precede? initial so-far)
      (values initial others)
      (values so-far (prepend new unchosen))))
```

where `initial` and `others` are the results of deprepending the given list. The recursive pattern that `fold-list` abstracts makes `initial` available to the combiner, but not `others`.

The solution is to write out the recursive procedure in full:

```
(define (extreme-and-others-in-list may-precede?)
  (rec (extracter ls)
    (receive (initial others) (deprepend ls)
      (if (empty-list? others)
          (values initial (list))
          (receive (so-far unchosen) (extracter others)
            (if (may-precede? initial so-far)
                (values initial others)
                (values so-far (prepend initial unchosen))))))))
```

Compound Ordering Relations

When two values in the domain of an ordering relation R bear that relation to each other, we'll sometimes adduce a second ordering S on the same domain to "break the tie." In effect, S is the backup algorithm that fixes the relative positions of the values in an ordered list when R fails to determine which of them should precede the other. The *compound ordering relation* that uses R as its primary means of ordering values and S as the backup algorithm is

```
(^vel (^not (converse R)) (^et R S))
```

A value u bears this relation to v whenever v does not bear R to u (in which case, since R is connected, u must bear R to v, and so u may precede v). When v *does* bear R to u and u also bears R to v, then S breaks the tie: u also bears the compound relation to v when they are equal under R and u bears S to v.

Of course, there may be situations in which u and v are equal under both R and S, while yet another ordering relation T might be able to distinguish them. Let's therefore define compound-ordering as a procedure of variable arity that receives any number of ordering relations and returns an ordering relation that applies those ordering relations successively until it finds one that can distinguish the values (or runs out of tie-breakers):

```
(define compound-ordering
  (extend-to-variable-arity values?
                            (lambda (primary tie-breaker)
                              (^vel (^not (converse primary))
                                    (^et primary tie-breaker)))))
```

The values? predicate is provided as the base-case value to ensure that, if none of the given ordering relations breaks the tie, each of the given values bears the compound ordering relation to the other (thus ensuring its connexity). Note that, technically, values? *is* an ordering relation, being both connected and transitive. For most purposes, however, it is too permissive to be useful, since it says that any value may precede any other, so that every list is "ordered" by values?.

Lexicographic Ordering

When the components of pairs or lists belong to types that are themselves thought of as ordered, it is possible to define ordering relations for the pairs or lists in terms of those underlying orderings. One common approach is a generalization of the way the entries for words are arranged in a dictionary. The alphabet specifies the underlying ordering, determining which of two individual letters comes first (for instance, M comes before R, but after J). The entry for a word w_0 precedes the entry for another word w_1 in the dictionary if the leftmost letter in w_0 that differs from the corresponding letter in w_1 precedes it in the alphabet, or if w_0 is a prefix of w_1. In effect, the *alphabetical order* of the letters determines the *lexicographic order* of the words.

For instance, the Scheme predicates char<=? and string<=? are related in this way. The char<=? predicate expresses the alphabetical order of values of the *character* type, and string<=? is the lexicographic extension of that order to sequences of characters.

We can implement the algorithms for performing such extensions in higher-order procedures. Let's consider pairs first. The cars of some pairs that we're interested in might belong to the domain of an ordering relation R, and their cdrs to the domain of an ordering relation S. If we consider the car of a pair to be "earlier" or "to the left of" its cdr, then the analogue of dictionary ordering would be a compound ordering in which the primary algorithm is to apply R to the cars of the pairs and the secondary, tie-breaking algorithm is to apply S to their cdrs. The procedure `pair-lex` implements this idea:

```
(define (pair-lex car-may-precede? cdr-may-precede?)
  (compound-ordering (compare-by car car-may-precede?)
                     (compare-by cdr cdr-may-precede?)))
```

There are actually two ways of generalizing this idea to lists. If the lists to be compared are equal in length, but might require the use of different ordering relations at different positions, the appropriate extension is

```
(define fixed-list-lex
  (extend-to-variable-arity values?
                            (lambda (initial-may-precede? for-rest)
                              (compound-ordering
                               (compare-by first initial-may-precede?)
                               (compare-by rest for-rest)))))
```

For instance, if we had adopted the list model for stars (as described in §3.9), we might define an ordering relation `star<=?` on the domain of stars as

```
(fixed-list-lex string<=? <= values? values?)
```

to compare stars first by name, then (as between stars with the same name) by magnitude (the brighter star first). It is unlikely that two stars will have the same name and the same magnitude, so we accept any arrangement if such a case arises. Actually, the `fixed-list-lex` procedure is flexible enough to fill in the "don't care" relation `values?` after a certain point in the list. For instance, the predicate

```
(fixed-list-lex string<=? <=)
```

returns exactly the same results as the preceding definition of `star<=?`.

The other way of generalizing lexicographic ordering to lists allows lists of different lengths to be compared, but presupposes that the same ordering relation is to be applied at each position, as alphabetical order is used at each position in a word to arrange the entries in a dictionary. The only additional assumption that we need is that an empty list bears the lexicographic ordering relation to *every* list:

```
(define (list-lex may-precede?)
  (rec (ok? left right)
    (or (empty-list? left)
```

```
(and (non-empty-list? right)
    (or (not (may-precede? (first right) (first left)))
        (and (may-precede? (first left) (first right))
            (ok? (rest left) (rest right)))))))))
```

---

string<=   (scheme base)
string,   string,   string ... $\rightarrow$ *Boolean*
initial next   others
Determine whether initial, next, and the elements of others are in non-decreasing dictionary order.

char<=   (scheme base)
character, character, character ... $\rightarrow$ *Boolean*
initial   next   others
Determine whether initial, next, and the elements of others are in non-decreasing order (according to their Unicode scalar values).

string>=   (scheme base)
string,   string,   string ... $\rightarrow$ *Boolean*
initial next   others
Determine whether initial, next, and the elements of others are in non-increasing (reverse) dictionary order.

char>=   (scheme base)
character, character, character ... $\rightarrow$ *Boolean*
initial   next   others
Determine whether initial, next, and the elements of others are in non-increasing order (according to their Unicode scalar values).

ordered?   (afp ordering-relations)
$(\alpha, \alpha \rightarrow Boolean), \; list(\alpha) \; \rightarrow Boolean$
may-precede?   ls
Determine whether ls is ordered with respect to may-precede?.
Precondition: may-precede? is an ordering relation.
Precondition: may-precede? can receive any elements of ls.

prior-by   (afp ordering-relations)
$(\alpha, \alpha \rightarrow Boolean) \; \rightarrow (\alpha, \quad \alpha \qquad \rightarrow \alpha)$
may-precede?   left right
Construct a procedure that returns whichever of left and right bears may-precede? to the other.
Precondition: may-precede? is an ordering relation.
Precondition: may-precede? can receive left and right.

arrange-by   (afp ordering-relations)
$(\alpha, \alpha \rightarrow Boolean) \; \rightarrow (\alpha, \quad \alpha \qquad \rightarrow \alpha, \alpha)$
may-precede?   left right
Construct a procedure that returns left and right, placing first whichever of them bears may-precede? to the other.
Precondition: may-precede? is an ordering relation.
Precondition: may-precede? can receive left and right.

extreme   (afp ordering-relations)
$(\alpha, \alpha \rightarrow Boolean) \; \rightarrow (bag(\alpha) \; \rightarrow \alpha)$
may-precede?   aro
Construct a procedure that returns a value in aro that bears may-precede? to every value in aro.
Precondition: may-precede? is an ordering relation.
Precondition: may-precede? can receive any values in aro.
Precondition: aro is not empty.

extreme-and-others   (afp ordering-relations)

$(\alpha, \alpha \rightarrow Boolean) \rightarrow (bag(\alpha) \rightarrow \alpha, bag(\alpha))$
may-precede?   aro
Construct a procedure that returns a value in aro that bears may-precede? to every value in aro and a bag containing all of the other values in aro.
Precondition: may-precede? is an ordering relation.
Precondition: may-precede? can receive any values in aro.
Precondition: aro is not empty.

extreme-in-set   (afp ordering-relations)
$(\alpha, \alpha \rightarrow Boolean) \rightarrow (set(\alpha) \rightarrow \alpha)$
may-precede?   aro
Construct a procedure that returns a value in aro that bears may-precede? to every value in aro.
Precondition: may-precede? is an ordering relation.
Precondition: may-precede? can receive any values in aro.
Precondition: aro is not empty.

extreme-in-list   (afp ordering-relations)
$(\alpha, \alpha \rightarrow Boolean) \rightarrow (list(\alpha) \rightarrow \alpha)$
may-precede?   ls
Construct a procedure that returns an element of ls that bears may-precede? to every value in ls.
Precondition: may-precede? is an ordering relation.
Precondition: may-precede? can receive any elements of ls.
Precondition: ls is not empty.

extreme-and-others-in-list   (afp ordering-relations)
$(\alpha, \alpha \rightarrow Boolean) \rightarrow (list(\alpha) \rightarrow \alpha, list(\alpha))$
may-precede?   ls
Construct a procedure that returns an element of ls that bears may-precede? to every element of ls and a list containing all of the other elements of ls, in the same relative order.
Precondition: may-precede? is an ordering relation.
Precondition: may-precede? can receive any elements of ls.
Precondition: ls is not empty.

compound-ordering   (afp ordering-relations)
$(\alpha, \alpha \rightarrow Boolean) \ldots \rightarrow (\alpha, \quad \alpha \quad \rightarrow Boolean)$
orderings   left right
Construct an ordering relation that applies the elements of orderings, one by one, to left and right until one of them determines which takes precedence.
Precondition: Every element of orderings is an ordering relation.
Precondition: Every element of orderings can receive left and right.

pair-lex   (afp ordering-relations)
$(\alpha, \alpha \rightarrow Boolean), (\beta, \beta \rightarrow Boolean) \rightarrow (pair(\alpha, \beta), pair(\alpha, \beta) \rightarrow Boolean)$
car-may-precede? cdr-may-precede?   left   right
Construct a lexicographic ordering relation for pairs, applying car-may-precede? to their cars as a primary ordering and cdr-may-precede? to their cdrs as a tie-breaker.
Precondition: car-may-precede? is an ordering relation.
Precondition: car-may-precede? can receive the car of left and the car of right.
Precondition: cdr-may-precede? is an ordering relation.
Precondition: cdr-may-precede? can receive the cdr of left and the cdr of right.

fixed-list-lex   (afp ordering-relations)
$(\alpha, \alpha \rightarrow Boolean) \ldots \rightarrow (list(\alpha), list(\alpha) \rightarrow Boolean)$
orderings   left   right
Construct a lexicographic ordering of lists, applying the first of the ordering relations to the initial elements of the lists, then (if necessary) the second ordering relation to their next elements, and so on.
Precondition: Every element of orderings is an ordering relation.
Precondition: The length of orderings is less than or equal to the length of left.
Precondition: The length of orderings is less than or equal to the length of right.

Precondition: Every element of orderings can receive the element at the corresponding position in left and the element at the corresponding position in right.

```
list-lex                                            (afp ordering-relations)
(α, α → Boolean)  →  (list(α), list(α)  →  Boolean)
may-precede?              left      right
```
Construct a lexicographic ordering for lists, using may-precede? to compare corresponding elements.
Precondition: may-precede? is an ordering relation.
Precondition: may-precede? can receive any element of left and any element of right.

Exercises

4.1–1   Define an ordering relation new-<= for values of the "reimplemented" natural-number type in §3.4.

4.1–2   Prove that every ordering relation is reflexive.

4.1–3   Show that

```
(lambda (left right)
  (>= (sum left) (sum right)))
```

is an ordering relation on the domain of all lists of numbers. What equivalence relation does this ordering relation induce?

4.1–4   Prove that if R is an ordering relation, then $\overset{R}{=}$ is an equivalence relation.

4.1–5   Prove that, for any ordering relation R defined on a domain D, the relation R^* is also an ordering relation, where, for any elements a and b of D, a bears R^* to b if and only if either b bears R to a or a does not bear R to b.

4.2   Sorting Algorithms

Because the arrangement of the elements of a list is significant, and we can determine and operate on that arrangement computationally, a list contains more information than a bag or a set with the same components. We can *store* information in the arrangement of the elements—sometimes information over and above the information contained in the elements themselves, but more often redundant information about those elements, which can be used to simplify some operations on the list and to make them more efficient. The operation of imposing a useful arrangement on an unordered collection of values is called *sorting*. A canonical sorting procedure receives a bag and returns a list that is ordered with respect to some useful ordering relation.

Under our implementation of sets, in which a set is actually identical with a bag that has the same members, which in turn is identical with some list, we could apply any such sorting procedure directly to a set or a list. However, we'll instead keep our procedures independent of the implementation by inserting an appropriate preprocessing adapter when we want to sort a set or a list:

```
(define set->bag (fold-set bag put-into-bag))

(define list->bag (fold-list bag put-into-bag))
```

There are many techniques for sorting, and it is instructive to identify their strengths and to consider the circumstances that make one algorithm more appropriate than another to a particular case.

Sorting by Insertion

The basic idea of the *insertion sort* algorithm is to take any value from the unordered bag, sort the remaining values in the bag, and insert the chosen value into the resulting ordered list at its correct position—following all of the values to which it does not bear the ordering relation, and preceding only those to which it *does* bear that relation. The list that results from such an insertion is also ordered, provided that we preserve the relative positions of the elements among which the new value is being inserted.

Since an empty list is (trivially) ordered, and an insertion that receives an ordered list also returns an ordered list, the principle of bag induction guarantees that the result of applying the insertion sort algorithm to any bag is an ordered list. Since each value from the bag is inserted once and only once, it is also easy to see that the elements of the completed list are exactly the values in the given bag.

Given an ordering relation, the `inserter` procedure constructs a customized insertion procedure that works its way down a given list, passing by all the elements to which the new value does not bear the ordering relation (and which therefore, by connexity, bear the ordering relation to the new value). Eventually we either reach the end of the list or encounter an element to which the new value bears the ordering relation. At that point, we prepend the new value and back out of the list, restoring the bypassed elements in front of the new one:

```
(define (inserter may-precede?)
  (lambda (new ls)
    ((rec (ins sublist)
       (if (empty-list? sublist)
           (list new)
           (if (may-precede? new (first sublist))
               (prepend new sublist)
               (prepend (first sublist) (ins (rest sublist))))))
     ls)))
```

To sort a bag, we fold the insertion procedure over it, starting from an empty list:

```
(define (sort may-precede? aro)
  ((fold-bag list (inserter may-precede?)) aro))
```

Sorting by Selection

Conversely, in the *selection sort* algorithm, we select the extreme value from
the given bag, using (extreme-and-others may-precede?) to obtain the rest
of the given bag as well. Then we sort the rest of the bag and prepend the
extreme value to the result. Prepending the extreme to an ordered list of values
to which it bears the ordering relation obviously yields an ordered list, so again
the principle of bag recursion guarantees the correctness of the result:

```
(define (sort may-precede? aro)
  (let ((selector (extreme-and-others may-precede?)))
    ((rec (sorter areto)
       (if (empty-bag? areto)
           (list)
           (receive (chosen others) (selector areto)
             (prepend chosen (sorter others)))))
     aro)))
```

The insertion sort and selection sort algorithms work very slowly on large
bags. The reason is that none of the information about may-precede? that is
obtained during the selection or insertion of one value from the bag is kept and
reused at any later stage. When it is time to select or insert another value from
the bag, a completely new sequence of comparisons is made, even if the outcome
of some of those comparisons could be inferred from earlier results.

Quicksort

One way to obtain a more efficient algorithm, therefore, is to store the information that we collect during one pass over the values in the bag, and subsequently
use it to shorten the subsequent computations.

In the *quicksort* algorithm, we take any value from a non-empty bag and
compare each of the other values in the bag to it, separating those that bear the
relation expressed by the ordering to the chosen value from those that do not.
Let's call the chosen value the *pivot*. In the ordered list that we are trying to
construct, any value that bears the ordering relation to the pivot can precede
it, and the pivot can precede any value that does not bear the ordering relation
to it (since by connexity the pivot bears the ordering relation to such a value).
Also, by transitivity, any value that bears the ordering relation to the pivot can
precede any value that does not.

So if we proceed to arrange just the values that bear the ordering relation
to the pivot into an ordered list, and separately arrange just the values that
do not bear the ordering relation to the pivot into another ordered list, we can
obtain the entire ordered list by catenating these two lists, with the pivot placed
between them. The partitioning operation divides the problem into two smaller
and *independent* subproblems of the same kind. If both problems are considerably smaller than the original, as they are when about half of the other values

in the bag bear the ordering relation to the pivot, many of the comparisons that
insertion sort or selection sort would have to make repeatedly can be avoided
completely, because they concern values that are placed in separate subbags
during partitioning:

```
(define (sort may-precede? aro)
  ((rec (sorter areto)
    (if (empty-bag? areto)
        (list)
        (receive (pivot others) (take-from-bag areto)
          (receive (fore aft)
                   (partition-bag (sect may-precede? <> pivot) others)
            (catenate (sorter fore) (prepend pivot (sorter aft)))))))))
  aro))
```

The quicksort algorithm sorts a large bag very quickly when most of the
pivots it chooses result in nearly equal partitions. On the other hand, it is
no faster than insertion or selection sort when it (unluckily) always chooses an
extreme value from the bag as its pivot.

Sorting by Merging

The principle of dividing a bag into two subbags of equal or nearly equal size,
sorting each subbag separately, and quickly combining the resulting ordered lists
is the basis for another algorithm, *merge sort*. Instead of splitting the bag on
the basis of ordering relative to a pivot value, merge sort begins by ignoring the
ordering relation and splitting the bag into equal parts, regardless of contents.
Each of the parts is then sorted recursively, yielding an ordered list. Finally, the
ordered lists are merged into one long ordered list; at this point, it is necessary
to compare some of the elements, but the connexity and transitivity of the
ordering make many of the possible comparisons unnecessary.

Let's begin with the procedure for splitting a bag into two bags of equal or
nearly equal size. In the base case, splitting an empty bag yields two empty
bags. In any other case, we take a value from the bag, split the rest of the bag
into two equal or nearly equal parts, and add the chosen value back into one of
them, being careful to choose the smaller one if we receive bags of unequal size
from the recursive call. To ensure that this choice is always made correctly, we'll
make it an invariant of the recursive procedure that, of the two bags it returns,
the cardinality of the first is either equal to or one greater than the cardinality
of the second. By adding the chosen value to the second bag and then swapping
their positions, we reestablish the invariant at each level of recursion:

```
(define split-bag-evenly
  (fold-bag (create (bag) (bag))
            (dispatch (pipe (adapter 0 2) put-into-bag) >next)))
```

To merge two ordered lists, we perform a kind of simultaneous list recursion over both. There are two base cases: If either list is empty, return the other. If neither is empty, compare their first elements; whichever one bears the ordering relation to the other can precede the other in the merged list, so we prepend it to the result of a recursive call that merges the rest of the elements in the list we chose from with the whole of the other list:

```
(define (merge-lists may-precede? left right)
  ((rec (merger subleft subright)
     (if (empty-list? subleft)
         subright
         (if (empty-list? subright)
             subleft
             (if (may-precede? (first subleft) (first subright))
                 (prepend (first subleft)
                          (merger (rest subleft) subright))
                 (prepend (first subright)
                          (merger subleft (rest subright)))))))
   left right))
```

Now we can fit these pieces into the overall structure of merge sort. The base case of the divide-and-conquer recursion is the case in which the bag contains only one value; in that case, no splitting and merging is needed, since the ordered list is just the one-element list containing that value. The empty bag can be handled as a special case even before we invoke the divide-and-conquer recursion. It won't arise as the result of splitting, because we'll split only when our bag contains two or more values. Since the subbags resulting from the split are of equal or nearly equal cardinality, each of them will contain at least one value.

When the bag contains two or more values, then, we split it, sort each subbag with a recursive call, and invoke merge-lists to combine the resulting ordered lists into one long ordered list:

```
(define (sort may-precede? aro)
  (if (empty-bag? aro)
      (list)
      ((rec (sorter areto)
         (receive (chosen others) (take-from-bag areto)
           (if (empty-bag? others)
               (list chosen)
               (receive (left right) (split-bag-evenly areto)
                 (merge-lists may-precede?
                              (sorter left)
                              (sorter right))))))
       aro)))
```

set->bag   (afp sets)
$set(\alpha) \rightarrow bag(\alpha)$
aro
Construct a bag containing the members of aro.

list->bag   (afp bags)
$list(\alpha) \rightarrow bag(\alpha)$
ls
Construct a bag containing the elements of ls.

inserter   (afp ordering-relations)
$(\alpha, \alpha \rightarrow Boolean) \rightarrow (\alpha, list(\alpha) \rightarrow list(\alpha))$
may-precede?   new ls
Construct a procedure that constructs a list, ordered by may-precede?, containing new and the elements of ls.
Precondition: may-precede? is an ordering relation.
Precondition: may-precede? can receive new and any element of ls.
Precondition: ls is ordered (by may-precede?).

sort   (afp sorting insertion-sort)
$(\alpha, \alpha \rightarrow Boolean), bag(\alpha) \rightarrow list(\alpha)$
may-precede?   aro
Construct a list that has the values in aro as its elements and is ordered by may-precede?.
Precondition: may-precede? is an ordering relation.
Precondition: may-precede? can receive any values in aro.

sort   (afp sorting selection-sort)
$(\alpha, \alpha \rightarrow Boolean), bag(\alpha) \rightarrow list(\alpha)$
may-precede?   aro
Construct a list that has the values in aro as its elements and is ordered by may-precede?.
Precondition: may-precede? is an ordering relation.
Precondition: may-precede? can receive any values in aro.

sort   (afp sorting quicksort)
$(\alpha, \alpha \rightarrow Boolean), bag(\alpha) \rightarrow list(\alpha)$
may-precede?   aro
Construct a list that has the values in aro as its elements and is ordered by may-precede?.
Precondition: may-precede? is an ordering relation.
Precondition: may-precede? can receive any values in aro.

split-bag-evenly   (afp sorting mergesort)
$bag(\alpha) \rightarrow bag(\alpha), bag(\alpha)$
aro
Construct two bags, differing in cardinality by at most one, the bag-union of which is aro.

merge-lists   (afp sorting mergesort)
$(\alpha, \alpha \rightarrow Boolean), list(\alpha), list(\alpha) \rightarrow list(\alpha)$
may-precede?   left   right
Construct a list, ordered with respect to may-precede?, that contains all of the elements of left and all of the elements of right.
Precondition: may-precede? is an ordering relation.
Precondition: may-precede? can receive any element of left and any element of right.
Precondition: left is ordered with respect to may-precede?.
Precondition: right is ordered with respect to may-precede?.

sort   (afp sorting mergesort)
$(\alpha, \alpha \rightarrow Boolean), bag(\alpha) \rightarrow list(\alpha)$
may-precede?   aro
Construct a list that has the values in aro as its elements and is ordered by may-precede?.
Precondition: may-precede? is an ordering relation.
Precondition: may-precede? can receive any values in aro.

Exercises

4.2–1 What changes would one make in the procedure that implements insertion sort to enable it to accept a list instead of a bag as its second argument? What changes would one make in the procedure that implements merge sort?

4.2–2 Define a procedure `sorted-associations` that receives a table and an ordering relation for the keys in that table and returns a list of the key-entry pairs in that table, ordered by their keys.

4.2–3 Modify the `unfold-list` procedure so that it receives an additional argument, `may-precede?`, which must be an ordering relation, and returns a procedure that always returns a list that is ordered with respect to that relation.

4.3   Binary-Search Trees

Most applications that use tree structures impose additional requirements on their structure or the arrangement of data within them. These additional requirements are called *tree invariants*, and they are enforced by adding preconditions to the `make-non-empty-tree` constructor and to any procedures that use it to construct results.

For example, the *binary-search-tree invariant*, with respect to a particular ordering relation, requires that in a non-empty tree, every value in the left subtree bears the ordering relation to the root value, which in turn bears the ordering relation to every value in the right subtree, and moreover that the left and right subtrees meet the same requirement.

As we saw in §4.1, the ordering relation induces an equivalence relation. In many applications that use binary-search trees, one of the most frequent and time-consuming operations is *searching* the binary-search tree, that is, determining whether any of the values in it bears the induced equivalence relation to a given value. The advantage of imposing the binary-search-tree invariant is that we can use it to speed up the process of searching the tree.

It is always possible to add a new value to a binary-search tree while preserving its invariant, as the following procedure definition shows:

```
(define (put-into-binary-search-tree may-precede?)
  (lambda (new bst)
    ((rec (putter subtree)
       (if (empty-tree? subtree)
           (singleton-tree new)
           (receive (root left right) (de-non-empty-tree subtree)
             (if (may-precede? new root)
                 (make-non-empty-tree root (putter left) right)
                 (make-non-empty-tree root left (putter right))))))
     bst)))
```

In the base case of the recursion, putting a new value into an empty tree yields a tree that (vacuously) satisfies the binary tree invariant. In any other case, we compare the new value to the one at the root of the given tree. If the new value bears the ordering relation to the one at the root, we put it into the left subtree, thus preserving the invariant that all of the values of the left subtree bear the ordering relation to the root. Otherwise, by connexity, the root bears the ordering to the new value, so we put the new value into the right subtree, preserving the invariant that the root bears the ordering relation to all of the values of its right subtree. The number of values in the subtree into which we descend is less than the number of values in the current tree, so after a finite number of recursive calls we must reach the base case—an empty subtree. The conclusion that `put-into-binary-search-tree` *always* succeeds in preserving the invariant now follows by the principle of tree induction.

We search for a value by making a similar descent along one branch of a tree until we either find the value we're looking for at the root of a subtree or reach an empty tree. We'll return the sought value, boxed, when the search succeeds, and #f, unboxed, when it fails.

This time, we descend into the left subtree only when we have confirmed that the root does *not* bear the ordering relation to the value we're looking for, and into the right subtree only when the value we're looking for does *not* bear the ordering relation to the root. This leaves open the possibility of stopping at the root of the current tree if neither of these conditions is satisfied—that is, if the value sought is equivalent to the root of the current subtree, in the sense that each bears the ordering relation to the other:

```
(define (search-binary-search-tree may-precede?)
  (lambda (sought bst)
    ((rec (searcher subtree)
       (if (empty-tree? subtree)
           #f
           (receive (root left right) (de-non-empty-tree subtree)
             (if (not (may-precede? root sought))
                 (searcher left)
                 (if (not (may-precede? sought root))
                     (searcher right)
                     (box root))))))
     bst)))
```

Testing the Binary-Search-Tree Invariant

To determine whether a given tree satisfies the binary-search-tree invariant with respect to a given ordering relation, we might simply translate the statement of the invariant into Scheme, thus:

```
(define (binary-search-tree-invariant? may-precede? tr)
  ((rec (ok? subtree)
```

```
    (or (empty-tree? subtree)
        (receive (root left right) (de-non-empty-tree subtree)
          (and (for-all-in-tree? (sect may-precede? <> root) left)
               (for-all-in-tree? (sect may-precede? root <>) right)
               (ok? left)
               (ok? right)))))
  tr))
```

However, this approach is unnecessarily inefficient. If we first determine that the left and right subtrees of the given tree satisfy the binary-search-tree invariant, it is not necessary to compare *all* of their components to the root. The left subtree, if it is not empty, contains one value to which every value in that subtree bears the ordering relation; if this value bears the ordering relation to the root, then (by transitivity) so does every other element in the left subtree. Similarly, if the right subtree is not empty, one of the values in it bears the ordering relation to every value in it, so that it is sufficient to compare the root to that one value from the right subtree.

We can find these special values in the left and right subtrees efficiently by taking advantage of the binary-search-tree invariant. Suppose first that we're looking, in a subtree T, for the value to which every value in T bears the ordering relation. There is no reason to consider any of the values in the subtree of T, since they all bear the ordering relation to the root and, hence, to all of the values in the right subtree of T. If the right subtree of T is empty, therefore, the root is the value that we're looking for. Otherwise, the value that we're looking for is in the right subtree T' of T, and the same logic applies there: Forget about the left subtree of T', settle for the root if the right subtree of T' is empty, and otherwise descend into that right subtree and repeat the process.

In short, the value to which every value in a non-empty binary-search tree bears the ordering relation is the *rightmost* value in that tree, and the following procedure finds it. No comparisons are necessary. We locate the rightmost value just by following the structure of the tree:

```
(define (rightmost tr)
  (let ((right (non-empty-tree-right tr)))
    (if (empty-tree? right)
        (non-empty-tree-root tr)
        (rightmost right))))
```

Similarly, the *leftmost* value in a binary-search tree bears the ordering relation to every value in that tree:

```
(define (leftmost tr)
  (let ((left (non-empty-tree-left tr)))
    (if (empty-tree? left)
        (non-empty-tree-root tr)
        (leftmost left))))
```

   In the following `binary-search-tree-invariant?` procedure, the recursion manager applies four conditions to a non-empty tree, confirming (1) that the left subtree is a binary-search tree; (2) that the right subtree is a binary-search tree; (3) that the rightmost value of the left subtree, if there is one, bears the ordering relation to the root; and (4) that the root bears the ordering relation to the leftmost value of the right subtree, if there is one:

```
(define (binary-search-tree-invariant? may-precede? tr)
  ((rec (ok? subtree)
     (or (empty-tree? subtree)
         (receive (root left right) (de-non-empty-tree subtree)
           (and (ok? left)
                (ok? right)
                (or (empty-tree? left)
                    (may-precede? (rightmost left) root))
                (or (empty-tree? right)
                    (may-precede? root (leftmost right)))))))
   tr))
```

Extracting a Value from a Binary-Search Tree

If we want not merely to find a value in a binary-search tree but to *extract* it, returning it and a reduced binary-search tree from which it has been deleted, some care is needed to ensure that the reduced tree still satisfies the binary-search-tree invariant. Notice, in the `search-binary-search-tree` procedure above, that whenever we find a value, we find it at the root of a subtree. Removing the value at the root disconnects the two child subtrees from the main tree. We'll have to join the child subtrees together somehow, without changing the ordering of the values they contain.

   However, if we postpone that difficulty by positing a `join-trees` procedure that can achieve the desired result, the rest of the job of extraction isn't too difficult: We descend along one branch as in `search-binary-search-tree`, moving left or right at each step as specified by the relative ordering of the root and the value sought, until we either reach an empty tree or find the value to be extracted. In the former case, the value for which we're searching isn't in the tree, so we return #f and an empty tree. In the latter case, we box the root and return it, along with the result of joining its children:

```
(define (extract-from-binary-search-tree may-precede?)
  (lambda (sought bst)
    ((rec (extracter subtree)
       (if (empty-tree? subtree)
           (values #f (make-empty-tree))
           (receive (root left right) (de-non-empty-tree subtree)
             (if (not (may-precede? root sought))
                 (receive (extracted others) (extracter left)
```

```
                    (values extracted
                          (make-non-empty-tree root others right)))
              (if (not (may-precede? sought root))
                  (receive (extracted others) (extracter right)
                    (values extracted
                          (make-non-empty-tree root left others)))
                  (values (box root) (join-trees left right)))))))))
      bst)))
```

Note that we must rebuild the tree we return at *every* level of the recursion, not just the last one, since every subtree along the entire branch that we follow to reach the extracted value is now different, at least to the extent of no longer containing that value.

Now let's turn to the `join-trees` procedure, which receives two binary-search trees and combines them into one binary-search tree. When `join-trees` is invoked by `extract-from-binary-search-tree`, all of the values of the first binary-search tree bear the ordering relation to all of the values of the second binary-search tree. Our implementation will rely on this precondition.

If either of the trees to be joined is empty, we can simply return the other one. Otherwise, we'll make the two trees into children of a common root, to which every value of the first tree bears the ordering relation, and which bears the ordering relation to every value of the second tree. It makes no difference whether we choose the rightmost value of the first tree or the leftmost of the second tree to be the new root. (The code below arbitrarily implements the former alternative.)

When we promote the rightmost value of the first tree to be the new root, we have to extract it from its current position within the left child. However, this is one of the easy cases of extraction, since the right child of the rightmost value in a tree is always empty, so that we can always lift the left child of that value into its place.

The `extract-rightmost` procedure deals with this special case. It is a precondition of this procedure that the tree it is given is not empty, so we'll ensure that this is so when we invoke `extract-rightmost`. The extraction always succeeds, so no boxing or unboxing is necessary:

```
(define (extract-rightmost tr)
  (receive (root left right) (de-non-empty-tree tr)
    (if (empty-tree? right)
        (values root left)
        (receive (extracted new-right) (extract-rightmost right)
          (values extracted
                (make-non-empty-tree root left new-right))))))
```

As in the `rightmost` procedure, left subtrees need not be explored at all, and no comparisons are necessary. The structure of the tree tells us everything we need to know.

Now the `join-trees` procedure is simple:

```
(define (join-trees fore aft)
  (if (empty-tree? fore)
      aft
      (if (empty-tree? aft)
          fore
          (receive (new-root new-fore) (extract-rightmost fore)
            (make-non-empty-tree new-root new-fore aft)))))
```

Binary-Search-Tree Sort

To use binary-search trees to sort a bag, fold over the bag to construct a binary-search tree with the same values, then flatten it into a list, preserving the leftmost-to-rightmost order of the values in the tree.

The tree->list procedure performs this order-preserving flattening operation:

```
(define tree->list
  (fold-tree list (lambda (root from-left from-right)
                    (catenate from-left (prepend root from-right)))))
```

The binary-search-tree invariant ensures that this leftmost-to-rightmost arrangement is the one imposed by the ordering relation:

```
(define (sort may-precede? aro)
  (tree->list ((fold-bag make-empty-tree
                         (put-into-binary-search-tree may-precede?))
               aro)))
```

---

put-into-binary-search-tree   (afp binary-search-trees)
$(\alpha, \alpha \to Boolean) \to (\alpha, \ tree(\alpha) \ \to tree(\alpha))$
may-precede?   new bst
Construct a procedure that, in turn, constructs a tree that satisfies the binary-search-tree invariant with respect to may-precede? and is similar to bst except that it contains new along with all of the values in bst.
Precondition: may-precede? is an ordering relation.
Precondition: may-precede? can receive new and any value in bst.
Precondition: bst satisfies the binary-search-tree invariant with respect to may-precede?.

search-binary-search-tree   (afp binary-search-trees)
$(\alpha, \alpha \to Boolean) \to (\alpha, \ \ \ \ tree(\alpha) \ \to box(\alpha) \mid Boolean)$
may-precede?   sought bst
Construct a procedure that searches within bst for a value equivalent to sought, using as its criterion of sameness the equivalence relation induced by may-precede?. If the search is successful, the constructed procedure returns a box containing the matching value from bst; if not, it returns #f, unboxed.
Precondition: may-precede? is an ordering relation.
Precondition: may-precede? can receive sought and any value in bst, in either order.
Precondition: bst satisfies the binary-search-tree invariant with respect to may-precede?.

rightmost   (afp trees)
$tree(\alpha) \ \to \alpha$
tr

Return the rightmost value in tr.
Precondition: tr is not empty.

leftmost   (afp trees)
tree(α) → α
tr
Return the leftmost value in tr.
Precondition: tr is not empty.

binary-search-tree-invariant?   (afp binary-search-trees)
(α, α → Boolean), tree(α) → *Boolean*
may-precede?   tr
Determine whether tr satisfies the binary-search-tree invariant with respect to may-precede?.
Precondition: may-precede? is an ordering relation.
Precondition: may-precede? can receive any values in tr.

extract-from-binary-search-tree   (afp binary-search-trees)
(α, α → Boolean) → *(α,   tree(α)* → *box(α) | Boolean, tree(α))*
may-precede?   sought bst
Construct a procedure that searches within bst for a value equivalent to sought, using as
its criterion of sameness the equivalence relation induced by may-precede?. If the search is
successful, the constructed procedure returns a box containing the matching value from bst
and a tree that satisfies the binary-search-tree invariant with respect to may-precede? and
contains all of the other values in bst; if not, the constructed procedure returns #f, unboxed,
and bst.
Precondition: may-precede? is an ordering relation.
Precondition: may-precede? can receive sought and any value in bst, in either order.
Precondition: bst satisfies the binary-search-tree invariant with respect to may-precede?.

extract-rightmost   (afp trees)
tree(α) → α, *tree(α)*
tr
Return the rightmost value in tr and a tree, similar to tr, containing all of the other values
in tr.
Precondition: tr is not empty.

join-trees   (afp binary-search-trees)
tree(α), tree(α) → *tree(α)*
fore   aft
Construct a tree containing all of the values in fore and all of the values in aft. If fore and
aft satisfy the binary-search-tree invariant with respect to some ordering relation, and every
value in fore bears that relation to every value in aft, then the constructed tree also satisfies
that invariant.

tree->list   (afp trees)
tree(α) → *list(α)*
tr
Construct a list of the values in tr, in order from leftmost to rightmost.

sort   (afp sorting binary-search-tree-sort)
(α, α → Boolean), bag(α) → *list(α)*
may-precede?   aro
Construct a list that has the values in aro as its elements and is ordered by may-precede?.
Precondition: may-precede? is an ordering relation.
Precondition: may-precede? can receive any values in aro.

Exercises

4.3–1 Define a procedure tree->finite-source that constructs a finite source
containing the values in a given tree, from leftmost to rightmost.

4.3–2   Define a procedure `leaf-list` that returns a list of the values stored in the leaf nodes of a tree, observing the condition that, if the tree satisfies the binary-search-tree invariant with respect to some ordering relation, then the list returned by `leaf-list` is ordered by that relation.

4.3–3   Define a procedure `combine-trees` that receives an ordering relation as its argument and returns another procedure, which in turn receives two binary-search trees, each of which satisfies the binary-search-tree invariant with respect to that ordering relation, and constructs a single binary-search tree, also satisfying that invariant, containing all of the values in both of the given trees.

4.3–4   Define a procedure `in-range` that receives two numbers, `lower` and `upper`, and a tree of numbers, `tr`, that satisfies the binary-search-tree invariant with respect to `<=`, and returns a list, ordered by `<=`, of the values stored in `tr` that are greater than or equal to `lower` and less than `upper`.

4.4   Red-Black Trees

In a curious way, the utility of binary-search trees is limited by their generality. They can speed up searching and sorting considerably, but only when, at most of the internal nodes, values are more or less evenly distributed between the left and right subtrees. To see why, let's consider how the shape of a binary-search tree affects the performance of the algorithms that operate on it.

During an unsuccessful search in a binary-search tree, and during the insertion of a new value, we descend from the root of the tree to one of its subtrees, from there to one of the subtrees of that subtree, and so on, until we reach an empty tree. Let's call the sequence of subtrees that we encounter in this way a *descent sequence*. When the binary-search tree is "stringy" and unbalanced, with most of its internal nodes having subtrees of very different sizes, descent sequences can be very long. In the worst case, where each internal node has a subtree that is completely empty, the height of the tree is equal to its size, so that there is a descent sequence that goes through *every* internal node before reaching an empty tree. A search operation in such a tree is no more efficient than an element-by-element search through a list; the extra structure of the binary-search tree only slows things down in such a case.

We'd prefer to work with binary-search trees in which the height is much less than the size. In a tree of height n, no descent sequence contains more than $n + 1$ subtrees, counting the empty tree that terminates it. Thus the height of a tree expresses a limit on the worst-case performance of search and insertion operations on it. It is easy to prove by mathematical induction that the maximum size of a tree of height n is $2^n - 1$, so there is room for considerable improvement in the worst-case performance of procedures like `put-into-binary-search-tree` and `search-binary-search-tree`.

Fortunately, the generality of the tree structure also provides a solution to this problem. For any of the shapes that a tree of n nodes can take on, it is possible to store any n values in a tree of that shape without violating the binary-search-tree invariant. As we construct a binary-search tree, therefore, we can keep track of how stringy it is, and reshape it if its subtrees become too severely unbalanced, without losing that invariant. Doing this, in effect, adds a shape invariant to the ordering invariant, so that any tree that our procedures return is well-shaped and suitable for *fast* searching.

Choosing the shape invariant entails a tradeoff. If we make it extremely restrictive, say by requiring that the height be as small as theoretically possible, searches are guaranteed to be as fast as possible, but the process of reshaping the tree after an insertion or a deletion becomes extremely slow. For many applications, it is more efficient to employ a shape invariant that blocks only extreme imbalances, but can be reestablished quickly after an insertion or deletion. We'll look at one such invariant, the *red-black invariant*, and the data structure that supports it, which is called a *red-black tree*.

In a red-black tree, each subtree is thought of as having a color, either red or black. An empty red-black tree is always black, while a non-empty red-black tree can be of either color. The goal of the shape invariant is to constrain descent sequences in the tree, so that they do not vary too much in length. The red-black invariant, which we'll state formally a little later on, accomplishes this goal by ensuring (1) that every descent sequence within a tree contains exactly the same number of black subtrees, and (2) that the number of red subtrees in a descent sequence is less than or equal to the number of black ones. The variability in the number of red subtrees gives us the flexibility we need to reestablish the invariant easily after an insertion or a deletion, and the constancy of the number of black subtrees implies that no descent sequence is more than twice as long as any other, thus setting a reasonable limit on the worst-case performance of the algorithms for search and insertion.

The first step towards achieving this goal is to require that a red-black tree can be colored red only if both of its subtrees are black. This ensures that any red subtree in a descent sequence is followed immediately by a black one, thus guaranteeing that the number of black subtrees in the sequence equals or exceeds the number of red ones, which is part (1) of the statement of our goal.

To see how we get to part (2) of the goal, let's define a function m that determines the maximum number of non-empty black subtrees in any of the descent sequences in a given tree. We can define this function recursively, as follows:

- If T is the empty red-black tree, then $m(T) = 0$: The only descent sequence is the one-element sequence comprising T itself, and in this case T doesn't count (because it is empty).

- If T is a non-empty red-black tree, and T is red, then $m(T) = \max(m(T_L), m(T_R))$, where T_L and T_R are the left and right subtrees of T: Any descent sequence for T begins with T itself and continues with a descent sequence for one or the other of its subtrees. Since T is red, then, the largest possible number of black subtrees in a descent sequence for T is equal to the largest possible number of black subtrees for one of the subtrees.

- If T is a non-empty red-black tree, and T is black, then $m(T) = \max(m(T_L), m(T_R)) + 1$, by similar reasoning.

The shape constraint imposed on red-black trees is that $m(T_L) = m(T_R)$ at *every* node. No matter where we are in the tree, no matter which of the subtrees comes next in a descent sequence, we are going to encounter exactly the same number of non-empty black subtrees.

The red-black invariant on a tree T is the conjunction of the color constraint, the shape constraint, and the recursive constraint on the subtrees of T:

- If T is red, then T_L and T_R are both black.

- If T is not empty, then $m(T_L) = m(T_R)$.

- If T is not empty, then both T_L and T_R satisfy the red-black invariant.

The recursivity of the last constraint ensures that the subtree headed by any node within T also satisfies the invariant.

Implementing Red-Black Trees

In the implementation of red-black trees, it is convenient to store the color of any non-empty tree as part of its root. We can pair a symbol denoting the color with the actual content of the root. Structurally, then, a red-black tree is a tree of pairs in which the car of each pair is one of the symbols red or black. We can express this structure in type equations:

$$color \;=\; red \mid black$$
$$red\text{-}black\text{-}tree(\alpha) \;=\; tree(pair(color,\ \alpha))$$

Here *color* is an enumeration type and *red* and *black* are the one-value types in the sum. It's easy to write the classification and equivalence predicates for these types:

```
(define color?
  (^et symbol?
       (^vel (sect symbol=? <> 'red)
             (sect symbol=? <> 'black))))

(define color=? symbol=?)

(define red-black-tree? (tree-of (pair-of color? values?)))

(define red-black-tree=? (tree-of= (pair-of= color=? equal?)))
```

To determine the color of a red-black tree, we can use the predicate red?, which extracts the root of a non-empty tree and inspects the car of that root pair, where the color is stored:

```
(define red?
  (^et non-empty-tree?
      (run non-empty-tree-root car (sect color=? <> 'red))))
```

It will also be useful to have a procedure that extracts and returns the element stored in the root, apart from the accompanying color:

```
(define red-black-tree-element (pipe non-empty-tree-root cdr))
```

Now let's develop the predicate that tests whether a structure of this sort satisfies the red-black invariant. To avoid computing the values of the function m for small subtrees over and over again (and to avoid computing them at all when they don't affect the outcome), we can integrate the calculation of m into the recursive testing procedure at the heart of the algorithm. Instead of returning #t when it discovers that some subtree S satisfies the red-black invariant, as a plain predicate would do, this recursive procedure can return the more useful value $m(S)$. The caller can then use not to distinguish the negative result #f from a natural number indicating success.

Note that the empty tree vacuously satisfies the red-black invariant, so that the recursive procedure returns 0 immediately when it encounters the empty tree.

```
(define satisfies-red-black-invariant?
  (pipe (rec (m-or-failure tr)
          (if (empty-tree? tr)
              0
              (let ((tr-left (non-empty-tree-left tr))
                    (tr-right (non-empty-tree-right tr)))
                (if (and (red? tr)
                         (or (red? tr-left) (red? tr-right)))
                    #f
                    (let ((left-m (m-or-failure tr-left)))
                      (if (not left-m)
                          #f
                          (let ((right-m (m-or-failure tr-right)))
                            (if (not right-m)
                                #f
                                (if (not (= left-m right-m))
                                    #f
                                    (if (red? tr)
                                        left-m
                                        (add1 left-m)))))))))))
        natural-number?))
```

The red-black trees that we'll use in searching and sorting have the appro-priate structure, satisfy the red-black invariant, and also satisfy the binary-search-tree invariant with respect to some ordering on the tree's elements. If `may-precede?` is the ordering, then in a red-black tree we'll need to use (`compare-by cdr may-precede?`) to arrange the roots:

```
(define (red-black-search-tree? may-precede? something)
  (and (red-black-tree? something)
       (satisfies-red-black-invariant? something)
       (binary-search-tree-invariant? (compare-by cdr may-precede?)
                                      something)))
```

Color Flips and Rotations

The insertion and deletion algorithms for red-black trees rearrange and recolor the components of the trees on which they operate in order to ensure that the results satisfy the red-black invariant. Although these modifications are in some cases rather intricate, they are constructed from three simple procedures: `color-flip`, `rotate-left`, and `rotate-right`.

The `color-flip` procedure can be applied to a non-empty tree when neither of its subtrees is empty and neither of them has the same color as the tree itself. It consists simply of changing all three colors: that of the tree, and that of its subtrees. A color flip on T leaves $m(T)$ unchanged (although both $m(T_L)$ and $m(T_R)$ are reduced or increased by 1), and so preserves the shape constraint in the red-black invariant. We'll use color flips to deal with some of the cases in which an insertion or a deletion would otherwise cause a violation of the color constraint:

```
(define color-flip
  (let ((opposite (lambda (col)
                    (if (color=? col 'red) 'black 'red))))
    (let ((flip-root (run decons (~initial opposite) cons)))
      (let ((flip (run de-non-empty-tree
                       (~initial flip-root)
                       make-non-empty-tree)))
        (run de-non-empty-tree
          (cross flip-root flip flip)
          make-non-empty-tree)))))
```

The `rotate-left` procedure modifies the structure of a non-empty tree that has a red right subtree. The component at the root of the right subtree is promoted to become the root component in the modified tree, while the former root becomes the root of its left subtree. Other subtrees are reattached so as to preserve the binary-search-tree invariant. This operation also preserves $m(T)$:

```
(define (rotate-left tr)
  (let ((right (non-empty-tree-right tr)))
    (make-non-empty-tree
      (cons (if (red? tr) 'red 'black) (red-black-tree-element right))
      (make-non-empty-tree (cons 'red (red-black-tree-element tr))
                           (non-empty-tree-left tr)
                           (non-empty-tree-left right))
      (non-empty-tree-right right)))))
```

The `rotate-right` procedure is the inverse of `rotate-left`, moving the component at the root of a red left subtree up to the root and the root component down into the right subtree:

```
(define (rotate-right tr)
  (let ((left (non-empty-tree-left tr)))
    (make-non-empty-tree
      (cons (if (red? tr) 'red 'black) (red-black-tree-element left))
      (non-empty-tree-left left)
      (make-non-empty-tree (cons 'red (red-black-tree-element tr))
                           (non-empty-tree-right left)
                           (non-empty-tree-right tr)))))
```

Insertion

During the insertion procedure, the new component is always added as a leaf, a singleton tree, replacing an empty tree at the end of the appropriate branch. Just as in `put-into-binary-search-tree`, we descend the tree, one level on each recursive call, comparing the value to be inserted with each root that we encounter, in order to identify the point at which to attach the leaf.

We'll follow the practice of making each new leaf red. Since its subtrees are both empty, and hence black, this ensures that it satisfies the first constraint of the red-black invariant, at least internally. Also, attaching a red leaf to a red-black tree that already satisfies the shape constraint of the red-black invariant results in a tree that also satisfies that constraint: Neither a red leaf nor the empty tree it replaces has any descent sequences containing non-empty black nodes, so the m function maps both to 0.

The only problem that could arise, then, is that we might be attaching the red leaf as the left or right subtree of a tree T that is itself red, thus violating the color constraint at T. In most cases, as we'll see below, we can restore the invariant by performing a rotation or two at the level just above T, but a particularly intractable situation occurs when T is itself a subtree of a tree T' and the other subtree of T' is also red. The best way to deal with this case is to ensure that it never arises in the first place.

We can accomplish this by invoking `color-flip` pre-emptively as we descend the branch. Every time we find a black tree with two red subtrees, we'll substitute the corresponding red tree with black subtrees for it before invoking the

descent procedure recursively. When we reach the end of the branch and attach
the red leaf, this preliminary color-flipping ensures that either the node to which
we attach the leaf is itself black or else it has a black sibling.

The `lift-red` procedure detects the situation just described (a non-empty
tree, presumed to be black, with two red subtrees) and performs the color flip:

```
(define lift-red
  (^if (^et (pipe non-empty-tree-left red?)
            (pipe non-empty-tree-right red?))
       color-flip
       identity))
```

After the insertion, as we return from the invocations of the recursive procedure that took us down the branch, we may encounter situations in which a
red tree has a red subtree, either as a direct result of the insertion of the new
red leaf or as the result of some previous color flip or rotation. We're now in
a position to deal with all such cases by performing rotations. To simplify and
speed up the tests by which the rotations are selected, we'll add yet another
invariant to the collection that our trees satisfy: In red-black trees that our
`put-into-red-black-tree` procedure returns, every subtree (at any level) that
has one red subtree and one black subtree will have the red one as its *left* subtree and the black one as its *right* subtree. A tree that satisfies the red-black
invariant and this new invariant as well is called a *left-leaning red-black tree*.

The `left-leaning?` predicate determines whether a given red-black tree satisfies this invariant:

```
(define (left-leaning? tr)
  (or (empty-tree? tr)
      (receive (ignored left right) (de-non-empty-tree tr)
        (and (or (red? left) (not (red? right)))
             (left-leaning? left)
             (left-leaning? right)))))
```

The advantage of working with left-leaning red-black trees is that it's much
easier to determine which rotations are needed to correct the situation in which
a red tree T with a black sibling has one red subtree and one black subtree. In
general red-black trees, T itself can be either a left subtree or a right subtree
within a larger tree, and T's red subtree can be either on the left or on the right.
Each of the four cases requires a different sequence of rotations. In left-leaning
red-black trees, on the other hand, this situation can arise only when T is a
left subtree and its red subtree is its left subtree, so the sequence of rotations is
always the same.

To establish the left-leaning invariant obliges us to perform a few more rotations (beyond those required to establish the red-black invariant), but the
simplification of the process of selecting the rotations compensates for this extra work.

The `lean-left` procedure detects a situation in which the left-leaning invariant is violated and performs a left rotation to bring the tree back into conformance:

```
(define lean-left
  (^if (^et (pipe non-empty-tree-left (^not red?))
            (pipe non-empty-tree-right red?))
       rotate-left
       identity))
```

The `rebalance-reds` procedure detects the situation in which a red left subtree has a red left subtree of its own (either as the result of the rotation performed by `lean-left`, or as the result of an insertion, or as the result of a color flip) and performs a right rotation. The resulting tree remains black, but the colors are rearranged so that both of its subtrees are red (and the subtrees of those subtrees are all black), thus reestablishing the color constraint in the red-black invariant:

```
(define rebalance-reds
  (^if (pipe non-empty-tree-left
             (^et red? (pipe non-empty-tree-left red?)))
       rotate-right
       identity))
```

There's one remaining possible violation of the red-black invariant that `rebalance-reds` doesn't address: If the entire red-black tree is red, or becomes red as the result of a color flip, and if its left subtree becomes red as a consequence of an insertion or a rotation, the tree violates the color constraint. We can address this by piling on yet another invariant: The insertion and deletion procedures will return only black trees. To accomplish this, we'll simply wait until the recursion has built up the entire result, and then force the color stored at the root to be black! Changing the color of the root node of the tree from red to black raises $m(T)$ by 1, but has no effect on the value of the m function at any other node, so that the shape constraint is still met.

The `force-color` procedure imposes a color on any non-empty red-black tree, while preserving the colors of its subtrees:

```
(define (force-color new-color tr)
  (receive (root left right) (de-non-empty-tree tr)
    (receive (ignored element) (decons root)
      (make-non-empty-tree (cons new-color element) left right))))
```

Adding a call to `lift-red` as a preprocessing adapter, adding calls to `lean-left` and `rebalance-reds` as postprocessing adapters to the central recursion in `put-into-binary-search-tree`, and postprocessing the final tree to make sure that it is black gives us the definition of `put-into-red-black-tree`:

```
(define (put-into-red-black-tree may-precede?)
  (lambda (new tr)
    ((pipe (rec (putter subtree)
              (if (empty-tree? subtree)
                  (singleton-tree (cons 'red new))
                  (receive (root left right)
                           (de-non-empty-tree (lift-red subtree))
                    (rebalance-reds
                      (lean-left
                        (if (may-precede? new (cdr root))
                            (make-non-empty-tree
                              root (putter left) right)
                            (make-non-empty-tree
                              root left (putter right)))))))))
           (sect force-color 'black <>))
     tr)))
```

Search

The search procedure is the same as for any other binary-search trees, except
that the root of each subtree contains a color, which we discard when performing
comparisons during the search:

```
(define (search-red-black-tree may-precede?)
  (lambda (sought tr)
    ((rec (searcher subtree)
        (if (empty-tree? subtree)
            #f
            (receive (root left right) (de-non-empty-tree subtree)
              (if (not (may-precede? (cdr root) sought))
                  (searcher left)
                  (if (not (may-precede? sought (cdr root)))
                      (searcher right)
                      (box (cdr root)))))))
     tr)))
```

Deletion

The deletion procedure, extract-from-red-black-tree, requires even more care
to ensure that the red-black, left-leaning, and binary-search-tree invariants are
all restored after the deletion. As with other binary-search trees, we'll descend
through the tree recursively, looking for the element to delete (let's call it d).
If we reach an empty tree, indicating that d is not in the tree, we'll return #f
and the empty tree. If we reach a tree whose root element matches d, though,
we'll extract it from the tree, box it, and return the box, along with a black,
left-leaning red-black tree that satisfies the red-black invariant, contains all of

the elements of the given tree other than d, and satisfies the binary-search-tree invariant.

In this process, we'll have to do some preparatory work to ensure that deleting the element at the root of some proper subtree T does not change the value of $m(T)$. If T and its subtrees T_L and T_R are all black, it may be impossible to accomplish this. Consider, for instance, the case in which T is a black leaf, so that $m(T) = 1$. There is only one element to delete, and deleting it leaves the empty tree, for which the value of m is 0. There is just no way to satisfy the desired postcondition in this case. Color flips and rotations at higher levels of the tree won't solve the problem. (They preserve the shape invariant when it is satisfied to begin with, but they also preserve violations of the shape invariant.)

In designing the insertion procedure, we avoided a similarly intractable situation by performing pre-emptive color flips during the descent along a branch, to make sure that that situation could never arise. We can use the same strategy here: As we descend a branch of the tree, we'll just have to reconfigure the tree somehow, to make sure that our search never takes us to a black subtree T with two black subtrees!

Let's call such subtrees *unsafe*. The `safe-red-black-tree?` predicate determines whether a given tree T is safe:

```
(define safe-red-black-tree?
  (^or empty-tree? red? (pipe non-empty-tree-left red?)))
```

Provided that T satisfies the left-leaning invariant, it would be redundant to add a test at the end to see whether the right subtree is red. The only case in which that test would be reached is one in which the left subtree is already known to be black, and in that case the left-leaning invariant implies that the right subtree must also be black.

Before we try to call the recursive procedure to extract d from T, then, we'll perform some pre-emptive operations to ensure that T is safe, so that we'll never be confronted with the intractable situation described above. In particular, if we delete a leaf, it will always be a red one, since black leaves are unsafe. Deleting a red leaf leaves the value of the m function at every remaining node unchanged and so preserves the shape constraint of the red-black invariant.

We may have to address this problem at the outset, because the entire tree from which d is to be extracted may be unsafe (and indeed we may find d immediately, at the root of the entire tree). In this case, however, there is an easy solution: We can change the color stored in the root node from black to red! Here is a preprocessing adapter that tests T and repaints it if needed:

```
(^if safe-red-black-tree? identity (sect force-color 'red <>))
```

Changing the color of the root node from black to red decreases the value of the m function of the entire tree by 1, but again has no effect on the value of the m function at any proper subtree, so that the shape constraint in the red-black invariant remains true. The color constraint and the left-leaning invariant also remain true, since both subtrees are known to be black. Having made the tree red and therefore safe, we can proceed with the call to the recursive extraction procedure.

In that procedure, we first check whether the given tree T is empty, indicating that d wasn't in the tree to begin with. In this case, as specified above, the procedure returns #f and T.

If T is not empty, we determine whether the element stored in its root bears the ordering relation to d. If so, we know that the deletion, if there is going to be one, won't occur inside the left subtree T_L; it will either be at the root or in the right subtree T_R. Before proceeding any further, therefore, we'll pre-emptively reconfigure T to ensure that T_R is safe. The avoid-unsafe-right procedure defined below performs any color flips and rotations that are needed to ensure this. We invoke avoid-unsafe-right even before we test to see whether d is at the root of T, because avoid-safe-right may have to perform a right rotation that puts a different element at the root, pushing the value that was formerly at the root into the right subtree.

An unsafe T_R is black and has two black subtrees. If T_L is red, then the color constraint in the red-black invariant ensures that T itself is black. In this case, the solution is to perform a right rotation on T. The right subtree of the rotated tree will be red and therefore safe.

On the other hand, if T_L is black, then both subtrees of T are black. Since T itself is safe (otherwise, the caller would not have applied the recursive procedure to it in the first place), T must be red. Moreover, T_L cannot be empty, since then $m(T_L)$ would be less than $m(T_R)$. (The value of m for the empty tree would be 0, while $m(T_R)$ is positive, since T_R is black and has a black left subtree.) So we can do a color flip on T, making T black and T_L and T_R both red.

This makes T_R safe, but breaks the color constraint at T_L if T_L has at least one red subtree. To eliminate this problem, we can perform a right rotation at T, followed by another color flip on the tree resulting from the rotation. The resulting tree T' is red, and both T'_L and T'_R are now black, but T'_R has at least one red subtree.

At this point, it is possible that T'_R is not left-leaning, but one last rotation can remedy that—a left rotation of T'_R, required only if T'_R has a black left subtree and a red right subtree. Applying lean-left to T'_R gives us a right subtree that is guaranteed to be left-leaning, to satisfy the red-black invariant, and (at last!) to be safe.

Collecting all these steps, we get the following definition for the avoid-unsafe-right procedure:

```
(define avoid-unsafe-right
  (^if (pipe non-empty-tree-right safe-red-black-tree?)
       identity
       (^if (pipe non-empty-tree-left red?)
            rotate-right
```

```
(pipe color-flip
      (^if (run non-empty-tree-left non-empty-tree-left red?)
          (run rotate-right
               color-flip
               de-non-empty-tree
               (cross identity identity lean-left)
               make-non-empty-tree)
          identity)))))
```

If d was at the root or in the right subtree of the given tree to begin with, then it is also at the root or in the right subtree of the tree that `avoid-unsafe-right` returns, since none of the transformations that `avoid-unsafe-right` performs can move any elements into the left subtree (although it can move elements *out* of the left subtree, as the result of the right rotation).

We can now proceed to determine whether d bears the ordering relation to the root element of the possibly rearranged tree. If it does, we've found our match, and can go on to extract the root element (and we'll see how to do this later on). If d does not bear the ordering relation to the root element of the possibly rearranged tree, we can invoke the extraction procedure recursively on the right subtree, which is known to be safe.

This recursive invocation brings back the extracted element (or #f, if d turns out not to have been in the tree to begin with) and a left-leaning red-black tree containing the remaining elements from the right subtree. Moreover, the recursive procedure preserves the value of the m function, so that replacing the old right subtree with the new one restores the shape invariant. However, the color of the new subtree may be different from the color of the old one. In particular, it may be red even if the old one was black. As a result, replacing the old right subtree with the new one may result in a tree that doesn't satisfy the left-leaning invariant. We'll address this problem by invoking `lean-left` as a postprocessing adapter.

The `avoid-unsafe-right` procedure rearranges a tree to make sure that we'll never descend into an unsafe right subtree. Predictably, we'll also need an `avoid-unsafe-left` procedure, for cases in which we discover that the root element of T does *not* bear the ordering relation to d, so that we must look for d in the left subtree T_L. How can we ensure that T_L is safe?

An unsafe T_L is black and has a black left subtree. This implies that T_R is also black (otherwise T would not satisfy the left-leaning invariant) and non-empty (otherwise $m(T_L)$ would be greater than $m(T_R)$, violating the shape constraint in the red-black invariant). Moreover, T is red (otherwise T would be unsafe, and the caller would never have given it to the deletion procedure to begin with). So we can perform a color flip, making T black and its children red.

This makes T_L safe, but could violate the color constraint in T_R, since T_R may have at least one red subtree. If it does, we can fix that problem by performing a right rotation on T_R, a left rotation on T, and another color flip.

This tricky maneuver effectively pushes the excess redness to the top of the tree. In the resulting tree, the left subtree is once again safe (it is black, but its left subtree is red). The new right subtree, however, sometimes fails to satisfy the left-leaning invariant, so as the final step we apply `lean-left` to the right subtree to restore it. Here's the code:

```
(define avoid-unsafe-left
  (^if (pipe non-empty-tree-left safe-red-black-tree?)
       identity
       (pipe color-flip
             (^if (run non-empty-tree-right non-empty-tree-left red?)
                  (run de-non-empty-tree
                       (cross identity identity rotate-right)
                       make-non-empty-tree
                       rotate-left
                       color-flip
                       de-non-empty-tree
                       (cross identity identity lean-left)
                       make-non-empty-tree)
                  identity)))))
```

The `avoid-unsafe-left` procedure can move elements into the left subtree of T (during the call to `rotate-left`), but cannot move any elements out, so we know that d, if it is present in the tree at all, will still be found in the left subtree, which is now safe. So we can invoke the recursive procedure on the left subtree in order to extract d. We'll again have to apply `lean-left` when reassembling the tree after the extraction, this time because the new left subtree returned by the recursive invocation may be black even if the one we gave it was red.

So we now know how to descend into either a left or a right subtree if we need to. It's now time to go back and work out what we do when the element at the root of the current tree T is the one we want to delete. We'll need a red-black analogue of the `join-trees` procedure to combine the left and right subtrees after the deletion. However, it's more complicated in this case, because we have to ensure that the resulting tree satisfies the red-black and left-leaning invariants as well as the binary-search-tree invariant.

The `join-trees` procedure in §4.3 extracted the rightmost element of the left subtree and promoted it to be the new root. With left-leaning red-black trees, however, it turns out that the leftmost element of the right subtree is more easily extracted than the rightmost element of the left subtree. Either one would be a satisfactory new root, preserving the binary-search-tree invariant, so we'll choose the one that is easier to code.

The idea of the `extract-leftmost-from-red-black-tree` procedure is to descend through the tree, always moving to a safe left subtree, until we reach a node in which the left subtree is empty. We'll run `avoid-unsafe-left` at each step to make sure that every node we encounter is a safe one.

When we reach a node that has an empty left subtree, we'll find that its right subtree is also empty. (A red right subtree would violate the left-leaning invari-

ant, and a non-empty black right subtree would violate the shape constraint in
the red-black invariant, since the m function maps an empty subtree to 0 and
a non-empty subtree to some greater number.) So the leftmost node must be a
leaf. Black leaves are unsafe, but we have ensured that every node we descend
to is safe, so this leaf must be red. Therefore, we can just lop it off, returning
the empty tree in its place, preserving the shape constraint for the entire tree.

Replacing a red leaf with an empty tree changes what was formerly a red node
to a black one, so as we back out of the recursion we must invoke `lean-left`
at each step to make sure that our reconstructed trees once more satisfy the
left-leaning invariant.

```
(define (extract-leftmost-from-red-black-tree tr)
  (if (empty-tree? (non-empty-tree-left tr))
      (values (red-black-tree-element tr) (make-empty-tree))
      (receive (root left right)
               (de-non-empty-tree (avoid-unsafe-left tr))
        (receive (chosen others)
                 (extract-leftmost-from-red-black-tree left)
          (values chosen (lean-left
                           (make-non-empty-tree root others right)))))))
```

One important feature of `extract-leftmost-from-red-black-tree` is that the
tree it returns as its second result is the same color as `tr`, unless `tr` is a red leaf
(in which case the second result is the empty tree, which is necessarily black).

Now let's look at the `join-red-black-trees` procedure. If neither `left` nor
`right` is empty, the procedure needs to know what color the new root should
be, so there is a third parameter—the color of the deleted root—that was not
needed in `join-trees`. (The `join-red-black-trees` procedure has to match the
color of the tree from which d was extracted, so that the m function will assign
the same value to the tree that `join-red-black-trees` constructs.)

The two special cases are easy. If `left` is empty, then so is `right` (since they
were the subtrees of a left-leaning tree before the extraction of d), so we just
return an empty tree. An empty tree is black, which doesn't match `root-color`
(since the tree from which d was extracted was a safe leaf, therefore red), but
the m function assigns the same value, 0, to an empty tree and a red leaf, so
the shape constraint in the red-black invariant will be preserved.

If `left` is not empty but `right` is, then `left` can only be a red leaf (since otherwise m would assign a greater value to `left` than to `right`), so that `root-color`
is black. To satisfy all the invariants, we can force the color of `left` to be black
and return the result.

Finally, if neither subtree is empty, we recover the leftmost element of the
right subtree, paint it to match `root-color`, and put it at the root of the original
left subtree and the revised right subtree. The color constraint is preserved,
since the newly constructed tree has the same color as the one from which d was
extracted, its left subtree is unchanged and so has the same color, and its right
subtree is either the same color or has changed from red to black (in which case

the root color must have been black to begin with). As noted above, m always assigns to the tree returned by `join-red-black-tree` the same value as the tree from which d was extracted:

```
(define (join-red-black-trees root-color left right)
  (if (empty-tree? left)
      (make-empty-tree)
      (if (empty-tree? right)
          (force-color 'black left)
          (receive (leftmost new-right)
                   (extract-leftmost-from-red-black-tree right)
            (make-non-empty-tree (cons root-color leftmost)
                                 left
                                 new-right)))))
```

By the time we finish all of the recursive invocations of the recursive deletion procedure and emerge from the initial invocation, color flipping may result in a final tree that is red. As in `put-into-red-black-tree`, we'll want to ensure that every tree that is returned by `extract-from-red-black-tree` is black. The postprocessing adapter that achieves this is

```
(~next (^if empty-tree? identity (sect force-color 'black <>)))
```

In other words: Tweak the second result (the tree), leaving it alone if it's empty, but otherwise forcing its color to black.

Here's the full definition of `extract-from-red-black-tree`:

```
(define (extract-from-red-black-tree may-precede?)
  (lambda (sought tr)
    ((run
      (^if safe-red-black-tree? identity (sect force-color 'red <>))
      (rec (extracter subtree)
        (if (empty-tree? subtree)
            (values #f subtree)
            (if (may-precede? (red-black-tree-element subtree) sought)
                (receive (root left right)
                         (de-non-empty-tree (avoid-unsafe-right subtree))
                  (if (may-precede? sought (cdr root))
                      (values (box (cdr root))
                              (join-red-black-trees
                                (car root) left right))
                      (receive (result new-right) (extracter right)
                        (values result
                                (lean-left (make-non-empty-tree
                                             root left new-right))))))
                (receive (root left right)
                         (de-non-empty-tree (avoid-unsafe-left subtree))
                  (receive (result new-left) (extracter left)
```

```
            (values result
                    (lean-left (make-non-empty-tree
                                root new-left right))))))))
     (~next (^if empty-tree? identity (sect force-color 'black <>))))
     tr)))
```

Implementing Tables with Red-Black Trees

One reason for the interest in red-black trees is that an implementation of the *table* type using red-black trees can be much more efficient than the bag implementation we used in §3.15, particularly when the tables are large. Such an implementation is possible whenever there is an easily computed ordering relation R with a domain that includes all possible keys for the table, and the criterion of sameness for keys is the equivalence relation that R induces. For instance, if the keys are strings, it is natural to take `string<=?` as the ordering relation and `string=?` as the criterion of sameness.

The big advantage of the red-black-tree implementation of tables is that searches and deletions can take advantage of the binary-search-tree invariants to find key-entry pairs quickly. The bag implementation pulls one pair after another out of the bag until it finds the right one, which is a slow and uneven approach when there are a lot of pairs. Because red-black tables maintain both the binary-search-tree invariant with respect to the ordering of their keys and the shape constraint in the red-black invariant, the number of steps required in a search or in a deletion is proportional to the logarithm of the number of entries in the table, rather than to the number of entries itself.

The interface to red-black tables is similar to the interface given for tables in §3.15, except that only the analogues of `table-keys`, `table-entries`, and `table-size` can be generic. All of the other procedures depend on the ordering relation on the keys, and so are implemented only through higher-order procedures that can receive that relation as an argument.

We'll begin with a higher-order procedure that produces classification predicates, `rbtable-of`. A red-black table is a red-black tree in which the elements are pairs. (In the type definition, α is the type of the keys and β is the type of the entries.)

$$rbtable(\alpha, \beta) \;\; = \;\; red\text{-}black\text{-}tree(pair(\alpha, \beta))$$

Each pair should contain a key (in the car position) associated with an entry (in the cdr position). The tree should be black. It should satisfy the binary-search-tree invariant with respect to the ordering operation on its keys. It should satisfy the left-leaning invariant. Finally, it should contain no duplicate keys.

The definition of `rbtable-of` formulates each these characteristics and combines them with `^and`. The `rbtable-of` procedure receives as arguments the classification predicates for keys and entries and the ordering relation for keys in the table:

```
(define (rbtable-of key? entry? key<=?)
  (^and (tree-of (pair-of color? (pair-of key? entry?)))
        (^not red?)
        (sect red-black-search-tree? (compare-by car key<=?) <>)
        (^vel empty-tree? left-leaning?)
        (run tree->list
             (let ((cadr (pipe cdr car)))
               (sect map cadr <>))
             delist
             (all-different (^et key<=? (converse key<=?))))))
```

There are fast and slow adjoiners, so that we can bypass the search for
duplicate keys if the caller can establish that duplication is impossible. The
simpler version is `fast-rbtable-adjoiner`, which builds each key-entry association and invokes a procedure constructed by `put-into-red-black-tree` to add
the association to the table:

```
(define (fast-rbtable-adjoiner key<=?)
  (let ((putter (put-into-red-black-tree (pipe (~each car) key<=?))))
    (lambda (key entry tab)
      (putter (cons key entry) tab))))
```

The slow adjoiner begins by deleting the old association from the tree, so we'll
postpone its definition until after we've defined the deletion procedure.

Similarly, we can repeatedly invoke the procedure constructed by `put-into-`
`red-black-tree` to build a table from any number of key-entry pairs, provided
that all the keys are distinct. The `rbtable-builder` procedure receives the
ordering relation on the keys and returns a specialized table-building procedure
of this kind:

```
(define (rbtable-builder key<=?)
  (pipe list
        (fold-list make-empty-tree
                   (put-into-red-black-tree (pipe (~each car) key<=?)))))
```

The `rbtable-searcher` procedure receives the ordering relation on the keys
and returns an appropriately specialized lookup procedure, which invokes a tree-
search procedure (constructed by `search-red-black-tree`) and postprocesses
the result to put it in the form we expect from a table lookup: the entry with
which the key is associated, if there is one; otherwise, the optionally specified
default value, or #f if no default value is specified:

```
(define (rbtable-searcher key<=?)
  (let ((key-entry<=? (pipe (~each car) key<=?)))
    (let ((searcher (pipe (~initial (sect cons <> null))
                          (search-red-black-tree key-entry<=?))))
      (lambda (key tab . extras)
        (let ((search-result (searcher key tab)))
```

```
         (if (box? search-result)
             (cdr (debox search-result))
             (if (empty-list? extras) #f (first extras))))))))
```

To recover the keys or the entries from a red-black table, we fold over the tree that implements it, collecting the results in a set (for the keys) or a bag (for the entries):

```
(define rbtable-keys
  (fold-tree set
             (lambda (root left-keys right-keys)
               (fast-put-into-set (car (cdr root))
                                  (fast-union left-keys right-keys)))))
(define rbtable-entries
  (fold-tree bag
             (lambda (root left-entries right-entries)
               (put-into-bag (cdr (cdr root))
                             (bag-union left-entries right-entries)))))
```

The `rbtable-deleter` procedure constructs specialized deletion procedures that invoke the appropriate extraction procedures constructed by `extract-from-red-black-tree`. After a successful extraction, the specialized deletion procedure discards the extracted result and returns just the tree containing the other values; after an unsuccessful extraction, the specialized deletion procedure returns the original tree, without complaining:

```
(define (rbtable-deleter key<=?)
  (let ((extracter (pipe (~initial (sect cons <> null))
                         (extract-from-red-black-tree
                           (pipe (~each car) key<=?)))))
    (lambda (key tab)
      (receive (result tab-without-key) (extracter key tab)
        (if (box? result) tab-without-key tab)))))
```

It is now trivial to implement the slow adjoiner as a (possible) deletion followed by a fast adjunction:

```
(define (rbtable-adjoiner key<=?)
  (let ((adjoiner (fast-rbtable-adjoiner key<=?))
        (deleter (rbtable-deleter key<=?)))
    (lambda (key entry tab)
      (adjoiner key entry (deleter key tab)))))
```

The size of a red-black table is simply the size of the red-black tree that implements it:

```
(define rbtable-size tree-size)
```

The equality predicate for tables should be satisfied whenever two tables contain the same keys, associated with the same entries. This means that we want to abstract from the shapes, structures, and colors of the underlying red-black trees and consider only the associations they contain. We can use `tree->list` to flatten the trees into lists, and perform a map to eliminate the colors, leaving two lists of key-entry pairs. If `equal?` is an adequate criterion of sameness for both keys and entries, we can define our equality predicate for tables thus:

```
(define rbtable=? (compare-by (pipe tree->list (sect map cdr <>))
                              (list-of= pair=?)))
```

If we want to produce more specialized equality predicates that explicitly recognize different criteria of sameness for keys, for entries, or for both, we can use `rbtable-of=` to generate them:

```
(define (rbtable-of= same-key? same-entry?)
  (compare-by (pipe tree->list (sect map cdr <>))
              (list-of= (pair-of= same-key? same-entry?))))
```

Lastly, the `rbtable-updater` procedure receives the ordering relation on keys and constructs a specialized updating procedure. Such a procedure, in turn, receives a key, a procedure for modifying an entry, a table, and an optional default value, and constructs a table similar to the given table, except that the entry for the key has been updated by applying the modification procedure to it. If there was no association of the key in the table to begin with, a new association is added; the entry is obtained by applying the modification procedure to the default value, or to `#f` if no default is specified.

We could do this by performing a search followed by a slow adjunction, but that would mean traversing a branch of the underlying tree three times: once for the search, once for the deletion (if the search was successful, at least), and once for the addition of the revised entry. We can save some effort by extracting the old association immediately and using both results to figure out how to proceed. If we get a box back as the result, we can debox it, extract the entry from the association pair, and apply the modification procedure; if not, we can apply the updater to the default value (or `#f`) instead. In either case, we can then use the fast adjoiner to put the new association into the table, since extraction got rid of the old one:

```
(define (rbtable-updater key<=?)
  (let ((adjoiner (fast-rbtable-adjoiner key<=?))
        (extracter (pipe (~initial (sect cons <> null))
                         (extract-from-red-black-tree
                           (pipe (~each car) key<=?)))))
    (lambda (key updater tab . extras)
      (receive (result tab-without-key) (extracter key tab)
        (adjoiner key
                  (updater (if (box? result)
```

```
                              (cdr (debox result))
                              (if (empty-list? extras)
                                  #f
                                  (first extras))))
                tab-without-key)))))
```

---

color?   (afp red-black-trees)
any   → *Boolean*
something
Determine whether something is a color (specifically, red or black).

color=?   (afp red-black-trees)
color color → *Boolean*
left, right
Determine whether left and right are the same color.

red-black-tree?   (afp red-black-trees)
any   → *Boolean*
something
Determine whether something has the structure of a red-black tree.

red-black-tree=?   (afp red-black-trees)
red-black-tree(any), red-black-tree(any) → *Boolean*
left   right
Determine whether left and right have the same shape and contain the same values and
colors at corresponding positions.

red?   (afp red-black-trees)
red-black-tree(any) → *Boolean*
tr
Determine whether tr is red.

red-black-tree-element   (afp red-black-trees)
red-black-tree(α) → *α*
tr
Return the value stored at the root of tr.
Precondition: tr is not empty.

satisfies-red-black-invariant?   (afp red-black-trees)
red-black-tree(any) → *Boolean*
tr
Determine whether tr satisfies the red-black invariant.

red-black-search-tree?   (afp red-black-trees)
(α, α → Boolean) any   → *Boolean*
may-precede?   something
Determine whether something is a red-black tree, satisfying both the red-black invariant and
the binary-search-tree invariant (with respect to may-precede?).
Precondition: may-precede? is an ordering relation.
Precondition: If something is a tree of pairs, then may-precede? can receive the cdrs of any of
those pairs.

color-flip   (afp red-black-trees)
red-black-tree(α) → *red-black-tree(α)*
tr
Change the color of tr and the colors of both of its immediate subtrees.
Precondition: tr is not empty.
Precondition: Neither subtree of tr is empty.
Precondition: The color of tr is different from the color of both of its subtrees.

rotate-left   (afp red-black-trees)
red-black-tree(α) → *red-black-tree(α)*
tr

Construct a red-black tree containing the same elements as tr, but with the element at the root of its right subtree raised into the root position, the former root becoming the root of its left subtree.

Precondition: tr is not empty.
Precondition: The right subtree of tr is not empty.
Precondition: The right subtree of tr is red.

rotate-right   (afp red-black-trees)
red-black-tree(α) → *red-black-tree(α)*
tr

Constructs a red-black tree containing the same elements as tr, but with the element at the root of its left subtree raised into the root position, the former root becoming the root of its right subtree.

Precondition: tr is not empty.
Precondition: The left subtree of tr is not empty.
Precondition: The left subtree of tr is red.

lift-red   (afp red-black-trees)
red-black-tree(α) → *red-black-tree(α)*
tr

If both subtrees of tr are red, construct a color-flipped version of tr; otherwise, return tr unchanged.

Precondition: tr is black.
Precondition: tr is not empty.

left-leaning?   (afp red-black-trees)
red-black-tree(any) → *Boolean*
tr

Determine whether tr satisfies the left-leaning invariant.

lean-left   (afp red-black-trees)
red-black-tree(α) → *red-black-tree(α)*
tr

If tr has a black left subtree and a red right subtree, construct a left-rotated version of tr; otherwise, return tr unchanged.

Precondition: tr is not empty.

rebalance-reds   (afp red-black-trees)
red-black-tree(α) → *red-black-tree(α)*
tr

If tr has a red left subtree that also has a red left subtree, construct a right-rotated version of tr; otherwise, return tr unchanged.

Precondition: tr is not empty.

force-color   (afp red-black-trees)
color,   *red-black-tree(α)* → *red-black-tree(α)*
new-color tr

Constructs a red-black tree similar to tr, but with new-color as its color.

Precondition: tr is not empty.

put-into-red-black-tree   (afp red-black-trees)
(α, α → Boolean) → *(α, red-black-tree(α)* → *red-black-tree(α))*
may-precede?   new tr

Construct a procedure that, in turn, constructs a black, left-leaning red-black tree that satisfies the red-black invariant, is ordered with respect to may-precede?, and contains all of the values in tr as well as new.

Precondition: may-precede? is an ordering relation.
Precondition: may-precede? can receive new and any value in tr.
Precondition: tr satisfies the red-black invariant.
Precondition: tr satisfies the left-leaning invariant.
Precondition: tr satisfies the binary-search-tree invariant with respect to may-precede?.

search-red-black-tree   (afp red-black-trees)

$(\alpha, \alpha \rightarrow Boolean) \rightarrow (\alpha, \qquad red\text{-}black\text{-}tree(\alpha) \rightarrow box(\alpha) \mid Boolean)$
may-precede?   sought tr

Construct a procedure that searches within tr for a value equivalent to sought, using as its criterion of sameness the equivalence relation induced by may-precede?. If the search is successful, the constructed procedure returns a box containing the matching value from tr; if not, it returns #f, unboxed.

Precondition: may-precede? is an ordering relation.

Precondition: may-precede? can receive sought and any value in tr, in either order.

Precondition: tr satisfies the binary-search-tree invariant with respect to may-precede?.

safe-red-black-tree?   (afp red-black-trees)
red-black-tree(any) $\rightarrow$ *Boolean*
tr

Determine whether tr is "safe," that is, whether it can be guaranteed that an attempt to extract from tr will either fail (because tr contains no matching element) or result in the deletion of a red leaf.

Precondition: tr satisfies the left-leaning invariant.

avoid-unsafe-right   (afp red-black-trees)
red-black-tree(α) $\rightarrow$ *red-black-tree(α)*
tr

If the right subtree of tr is safe, return tr; otherwise, construct a red-black tree that contains the same elements as tr, satisfies the red-black invariant, and has a safe right subtree that satisfies the left-leaning invariant.

Precondition: tr is not empty.

Precondition: tr is safe.

Precondition: tr satisfies the red-black invariant.

Precondition: tr satisfies the left-leaning invariant.

avoid-unsafe-left   (afp red-black-trees)
red-black-tree(α) $\rightarrow$ *red-black-tree(α)*
tr

If the left subtree of tr is safe, return tr; otherwise, construct a red-black tree that contains the same elements as tr, satisfies the red-black and left-leaning invariants, and has a safe left subtree.

Precondition: tr is not empty.

Precondition: tr is safe.

Precondition: tr satisfies the red-black invariant.

Precondition: tr satisfies the left-leaning invariant.

extract-leftmost-from-red-black-tree   (afp red-black-trees)
red-black-tree(α) $\rightarrow$ *red-black-tree(α)*
tr

Extract the leftmost element of tr and return it, along with a black, left-leaning red-black tree containing the rest of the elements of tr and satisfying the red-black invariant.

Precondition: tr is not empty.

Precondition: tr is safe.

Precondition: tr satisfies the red-black invariant.

Precondition: tr satisfies the left-leaning invariant.

join-red-black-trees   (afp red-black-trees)
color,   red-black-tree(α), red-black-tree(α) $\rightarrow$ *red-black-tree(α)*
root-color left   right

Construct a left-leaning red-black tree that contains all of the elements of left and right, satisfies the red-black invariant, and has root-color as its color (unless left or right is empty, in which case the result is black regardless of the value of root-color).

Precondition: If left is empty, then right is empty.

Precondition: left satisfies the red-black invariant.

Precondition: left satisfies the left-leaning invariant.

Precondition: right is safe.

Precondition: right satisfies the red-black invariant.

Precondition: right satisfies the left-leaning invariant.
Precondition: The m function maps left and right to the same number.

extract-from-red-black-tree   (afp red-black-trees)
$(\alpha, \alpha \rightarrow Boolean) \rightarrow (\alpha, \rightarrow box(\alpha) \mid Boolean, red\text{-}black\text{-}tree(\alpha))$
may-precede?   sought
Construct a procedure that searches within tr for a value equivalent to sought, using as
its criterion of sameness the equivalence relation induced by may-precede?. If the search is
successful, the constructed procedure returns a box containing the matching value from tr
as its first result; if not, it returns #f, unboxed. In either case, the second result is a black,
left-leaning red-black tree that satisfies the red-black invariant and the binary-search-tree
invariant with respect to may-precede? and contains all of the other values in tr.
Precondition: may-precede? is an ordering relation.
Precondition: may-precede? can receive sought and any value in tr, in either order.
Precondition: tr satisfies the red-black invariant.
Precondition: tr satisfies the left-leaning invariant.
Precondition: tr satisfies the binary-search-tree invariant with respect to may-precede?.

rbtable-of   (afp red-black-tables)
$(any \rightarrow Boolean), (any \rightarrow Boolean), (\alpha, \alpha \rightarrow Boolean) \rightarrow (any \rightarrow Boolean)$
key?   entry?   key<=?   something
Construct a predicate that determines whether something is a red-black table ordered by
key<=?, using key? to determine whether some value is a key, entry? to determine whether
some value is an entry, and the equivalence relation induced by key<=? as the criterion of
sameness for keys.
Precondition: key? can receive any value.
Precondition: entry? can receive any value.
Precondition: key<=? is an ordering relation.
Precondition: key<=? can receive any values that satisfy key?.

fast-rbtable-adjoiner   (afp red-black-tables)
$(\alpha, \alpha \rightarrow Boolean) \rightarrow (\alpha, \beta, rbtable(\alpha, \beta) \rightarrow rbtable(\alpha, \beta))$
key<=?   key entry tab
Construct a procedure that, in turn, constructs a table similar to tab, except that key is
associated with entry, using key<=? as the ordering relation for keys.
Precondition: key<=? is an ordering relation.
Precondition: key<=? can receive key and any key in tab.
Precondition: key is not a key in tab.
Precondition: tab is ordered by key<=?.

rbtable-builder   (afp red-black-tables)
$(\alpha, \alpha \rightarrow Boolean) \rightarrow (pair(\alpha, \alpha) \ldots \rightarrow rbtable(\alpha, \beta))$
key<=?   associations
Construct a procedure that, in turn, constructs a table, using key<=? as its ordering relation,
in which the car of each element of associations is associated (as a key) with the cdr of that
element of associations (as an entry).
Precondition: key<=? is an ordering relation.
Precondition: key<=? can receive the cars of any elements of associations.
Precondition: No two elements of associations have the same car.

rbtable-searcher   (afp red-black-tables)
$(\alpha, \alpha \rightarrow Boolean) \rightarrow (\alpha, rbtable(\alpha, \beta), \beta \ldots \rightarrow \beta \mid Boolean)$
key<=?   key tab   extras
Construct a procedure that searches in tab for an association with key as its key, using key<=?
as the ordering relation for keys. If the constructed procedure finds such an association, it
returns the entry with which key is associated; otherwise, it returns the initial element of
extras, or #f if extras is empty.
Precondition: key<=? is an ordering relation.
Precondition: key<=? can receive key and any key in tab.
Precondition: tab is ordered by key<=?.

rbtable-keys   (afp red-black-tables)

rbtable(α, any) → *set(α)*
tab
Construct a set comprising the keys for which tab contains associations.

rbtable-entries   (afp red-black-tables)
rbtable(any, α) → *bag(α)*
tab
Construct a bag comprising the entries with which tab associates keys.

rbtable-deleter   (afp red-black-tables)
(α, α → Boolean) → *(α, rbtable(α, β)* → *rbtable(α, β))*
key<=?   key tab
Construct a procedure that, in turn, constructs a table similar to tab, with key<=? as its
ordering relation, but containing no association for key. (If no such association exists to begin
with, the constructed procedure returns tab.)
Precondition: key<=? is an ordering relation.
Precondition: key<=? can receive key and any key in tab.
Precondition: tab is ordered by key<=?.

rbtable-adjoiner   (afp red-black-tables)
(α, α → Boolean) → *(α, β, rbtable(α, β)* → *rbtable(α, β))*
key<=?   key entry tab
Construct a procedure that, in turn, constructs a table similar to tab, except that key is
associated with entry, using key<=? as the ordering relation for keys. (If tab already associates
key with some value, the new association displaces the old one.)
Precondition: key<=? is an ordering relation.
Precondition: key<=? can receive key and any key in tab.
Precondition: tab is ordered by key<=?.

rbtable-size   (afp red-black-tables)
rbtable(any, any) → *natural-number*
tab
Compute the number of associations in tab.

rbtable=?   (afp red-black-tables)
rbtable(any, any), rbtable(any, any) → *Boolean*
left   right
Determine whether left and right contain the same keys, associated with the same entries.

rbtable-of=   (afp red-black-tables)
(α, β → Boolean), (γ, δ → Boolean) → *(rbtable(α, γ), rbtable(β, δ)* → *Boolean)*
same-key?   same-entry?   left   right
Construct a procedure that determines whether left and right are the same table, using
same-key? as the criterion of sameness for keys and same-entry? as the criterion of sameness
for entries.
Precondition: same-key? can receive any key in left and any key in right.
Precondition: same-entry? can receive any entry in left and any entry in right.

rbtable-updater   (afp red-black-tables)
(α, α → Boolean) → *(α, (β → β), rbtable(α, β), β ...* → *rbtable(α, β))*
key<=?   key updater tab   extras
Construct a procedure that looks up key in tab (using key<=? as the ordering relation on keys),
applies updater to the entry with which tab associates key, associates key with the result
returned by updater, and constructs a table similar to tab, except that the new association
replaces the previous association for key. If tab does not associate key with any value, the
constructed procedure instead applies updater to the initial element of extras, or to #f if
extras is empty.
Precondition: key<=? is an ordering relation.
Precondition: key<=? can receive any keys in tab.
Precondition: updater can receive any entry in tab.
Precondition: tab is ordered by key<=?.
Precondition: If tab contains no association for key and extras is empty, then updater can
receive #f.

Precondition: If tab contains no association for key and extras is not empty, then updater can receive the first element of extras.

Exercises

4.4-1 List all of the possible shape and color patterns for red-black trees that satisfy both the red-black invariant and the left-leaning invariant and have six or fewer elements. Identify those that are not safe.

4.4-2 Prove, by mathematical induction, that the maximum size of a tree of height n is $2^n - 1$, for any natural number n.

4.4-3 Prove that extracter, the central recursive procedure in the definition of extract-from-red-black-tree, preserves the value of the m function: If T' is the second result of applying extracter to T, then $m(T') = m(T)$.

4.4-4 Modify rbtable-keys so that it returns the keys of the given table as a list rather than a set. Prove that the list is ordered by the ordering relation for the underlying red-black tree.

4.5 Heaps

A heap is a data structure that is arranged so as to provide immediate access to an *extreme* element—one that bears some ordering relation to every other element of the heap. For instance, in a heap of numbers respecting the ordering relation expressed by <=, the least of the numbers in the heap is immediately accessible. Our interface to a heap comprises the following operations:

- A classification predicate that determines whether a given value is or is not a heap.

- Two constructors: empty-heap to construct a heap containing no elements, and a procedure that adds a new element to a heap, respecting the ordering relation.

- A predicate empty-heap? that distinguishes heaps with no elements (for which it returns #t) from heaps with one or more (for which it returns #f).

- A selector that receives a non-empty heap and returns two results: the extreme element of the heap and a new heap comprising all of the other elements of the original heap.

- An equality predicate that determines whether two heaps respecting the same ordering relation have the same elements.

In addition, an implementation of heaps may support a merging procedure, which receives two heaps respecting the same ordering relation and returns one large heap containing all of the elements of both. It is possible to define the merging procedure using the constructors and selector, but in many implementations of heaps it is more convenient and more efficient to define the merging procedure first, relying on special properties of the selected model, and to use it to define the second constructor and the selector. Since the merging procedure is also useful to application programmers, it is often included as a heap primitive as well.

One particularly efficient implementation of heaps uses bushes to model them. Let's begin by representing an empty heap as an empty bush:

```
(define (empty-heap)
  (bush))

(define empty-heap? empty-bush?)
```

For non-empty heaps, we'll use bushes that satisfy the following invariants:

1. The *nesting invariant*: Every child in a non-empty heap is itself a non-empty heap. (In other words, a bush that has an empty bush as one of its descendants does not qualify as a heap.)

2. The *heap-ordering invariant*: The extreme element of a non-empty heap is the root element of the non-empty bush that represents it, and each child in the bush has the same property—that is, the root element of each child bears the ordering relation to all of the elements of that child.

Given an ordering relation, the `satisfies-heap-invariants?` procedure constructs a custom procedure that tests whether a non-empty bush satisfies these invariants, with respect to that ordering relation:

```
(define (satisfies-heap-invariants? may-precede?)
  (rec (ok? arbusto)
    (let ((root (bush-root arbusto)))
      (for-all? (^and (^not empty-bush?)
                      (pipe bush-root (sect may-precede? root <>)))
                ok?)
                (bush-children arbusto)))))
```

We must ensure that every bush that any of our heap primitives returns satisfies these invariants. One advantage of defining a `merge-heaps` procedure first is that we can assign to this procedure the responsibility for maintaining the invariants, provided that we then use it systematically to construct all non-empty heaps.

There is an obvious way to merge two non-empty heaps into one, preserving heap ordering: Determine whether the root of the first bears the ordering relation to the root of the second. If so, make the second heap into one of the children of the first heap. Otherwise, since the ordering relation is connected, the root of the second heap bears the ordering relation to the root of the first heap, so make the first heap into one of the children of the second. That is,

```
(define (merge-heaps may-precede?)
  (lambda (left right)
    (if (empty-bush? left)
        right
        (if (empty-bush? right)
            left
            (let ((lroot (bush-root left))
                  (lchildren (bush-children left))
                  (rroot (bush-root right))
                  (rchildren (bush-children right)))
              (if (may-precede? lroot rroot)
                  (apply bush lroot right lchildren)
                  (apply bush rroot left rchildren)))))))
```

Now we're ready to implement the heap interface. There is no such thing as a "generic heap," since there is no natural ordering relation that includes all values in its domain,[1] so we'll proceed directly to heap-of, the higher-level procedure that constructs classification predicates for specific kinds of heaps.

A classification predicate for heaps conjoins the classification predicate for bushes with the test of the invariants. We must supply the ordering relation so that our classification predicate can check the heap-ordering invariant, and we must supply a predicate that distinguishes values that are in the domain of may-precede? from values that are not, so that our classification predicate can check the preconditions for the applicability of the ordering relation to the components of a bush that it receives:

```
(define (heap-of may-precede? in-domain?)
  (^and (bush-of in-domain?)
        (sect for-all-in-bush? in-domain? <>)
        (^vel empty-bush? (satisfies-heap-invariants? may-precede?))))
```

To put an element into a heap, we make it into a one-element bush with no children, which trivially meets both heap invariants, and merge it with the existing heap. Given the ordering relation for the heap, the heap-adjoiner procedure constructs the appropriate procedure for adding an element to a heap in this way:

```
(define (heap-adjoiner may-precede?)
  (pipe (~initial bush) (merge-heaps may-precede?)))
```

---

[1] Well, there's values?. But it's pointless to use values? to arrange a heap.

The selector easily recovers the extreme element of a heap by taking its root, but then faces the difficulty of making a single heap out of all the children of the given heap, while preserving the heap invariants. There are several possible strategies:

- Fold over a list of the children, merging at each step:

```
(define (heap-list-folder may-precede?)
  (fold-list empty-heap (merge-heaps may-precede?)))
```

- If there are any children, find the one with the root that bears the ordering relation to all the other roots; make all the other children into additional children of this one. (Note that, because of the nesting invariant, none of the children are empty heaps, so each can provide a root.)

```
(define (heap-list-catenator may-precede?)
  (let ((extract-from-list (extreme-and-others-in-list
                              (compare-by bush-root may-precede?))))
    (lambda (ls)
      (if (empty-list? ls)
          (empty-heap)
          (receive (leader others) (extract-from-list ls)
            (receive (new-root . new-children) (debush leader)
              (apply bush new-root
                     (catenate new-children others)))))))))
```

- Merge pairs of children using merge-heaps, then fold over a list of the results:

```
(define (heap-list-merger may-precede?)
  (let ((merge (merge-heaps may-precede?)))
    (rec (pairwise ls)
      (if (empty-list? ls)
          (empty-heap)
          (if (empty-list? (rest ls))
              (first ls)
              (merge (merge (first ls) (first (rest ls)))
                     (pairwise (rest (rest ls)))))))))
```

There is some empirical evidence that subsequent operations on heaps constructed in the third way, which are called *pairing heaps*, are more efficient in practice, so that's the approach that we'll use in constructing selectors for heaps:

```
(define (heap-extractor may-precede?)
  (dispatch bush-root
            (pipe bush-children (heap-list-merger may-precede?))))
```

   The constructor for heap-equality predicates follows a pattern that is now
familiar, except that the criterion of sameness for corresponding elements is that
each bears the ordering relation that the heap respects to the other:

```
(define (heap-of= may-precede?)
  (let ((extract-from-heap (heap-extractor may-precede?)))
    (rec (equivalent? left right)
      (or (and (empty-heap? left)
               (empty-heap? right))
          (and (not (empty-heap? left))
               (not (empty-heap? right))
               (receive (lchosen lothers) (extract-from-heap left)
                 (receive (rchosen rothers) (extract-from-heap right)
                   (and (may-precede? lchosen rchosen)
                        (may-precede? rchosen lchosen)
                        (equivalent? lothers rothers)))))))))
```

Folding and Unfolding Heaps

We can construct heap folders and heap unfolders in the usual ways, supplying
the ordering relation as an additional argument:

```
(define (fold-heap may-precede? base combiner)
  (let ((extract-from-heap (heap-extractor may-precede?)))
    (rec (folder amaso)
      (if (empty-heap? amaso)
          (base)
          (receive (chosen others) (extract-from-heap amaso)
            (receive recursive-results (folder others)
              (apply combiner chosen recursive-results)))))))

(define (unfold-heap may-precede? final? producer step)
  (build final?
         (constant (empty-heap))
         producer
         step
         (heap-adjoiner may-precede?)))
```

   For heap processors, let's take the opportunity to cast the implementation
in a more fluid style than we used for `process-list`:

```
(define (process-heap may-precede? base combiner)
  (let ((extract-from-heap (heap-extractor may-precede?)))
    (let ((processor
           (rec (processor amaso . intermediates)
             (if (empty-heap? amaso)
                 (delist intermediates)
                 (receive (chosen others) (extract-from-heap amaso)
```

```
                 (receive new-results
                       (apply combiner chosen intermediates)
                    (apply processor others new-results)))))))
        (receive base-values (base)
           (sect apply processor <> base-values)))))
```

Heap Sort

Heaps have many uses. One that we can appreciate immediately is sorting. If
we have a bag of values and want to put them into a list, ordered with respect
to the relation may-precede?, we can first transfer the values from a bag to a
heap, then extract the values, in order, from the heap to construct the sorted
list. For the first half of the process, we can use a procedure constructed by
fold-bag, and for the second half, a procedure constructed by fold-heap, thus:

```
(define (heap-sort may-precede? aro)
   ((fold-heap may-precede? list prepend)
     ((fold-bag empty-heap (heap-adjoiner may-precede?)) aro)))
```

---

empty-heap   (afp heaps)
$\rightarrow bush(any)$
Construct a heap with no elements.

empty-heap?   (afp heaps)
$bush(any) \rightarrow Boolean$
amaso
Determine whether the heap amaso is empty.

satisfies-heap-invariants?   (afp heaps)
$(\alpha, \alpha \rightarrow Boolean) \rightarrow (bush(\alpha) \rightarrow Boolean)$
may-precede?   arbusto
Construct a predicate that determines whether arbusto satisfies the heap invariants with
respect to may-precede?.
Precondition: may-precede? is an ordering relation.
Precondition: may-precede? can receive any elements of arbusto.

merge-heaps   (afp heaps)
$(\alpha, \alpha \rightarrow Boolean) \rightarrow (bush(\alpha), bush(\alpha) \rightarrow bush(\alpha))$
may-precede?   left   right
Construct a procedure that, in turn, constructs a bush that satisfies the heap invariants with
respect to may-precede? and contains every element of left and every element of right.
Precondition: may-precede? is an ordering relation.
Precondition: may-precede? can receive any element of left and any element of right.
Precondition: left satisfies the heap invariants with respect to may-precede?.
Precondition: right satisfies the heap invariants with respect to may-precede?.

heap-of   (afp heaps)
$(\alpha, \alpha \rightarrow Boolean), (any \rightarrow Boolean) \rightarrow (any \rightarrow Boolean)$
may-precede?   in-domain?   something
Construct a predicate that determines whether something is a bush in which every element sat-
isfies in-domain? and the entire bush satisfies the heap invariants with respect to may-precede?.
Precondition: may-precede? is an ordering relation.
Precondition: may-precede? can receive any values that satisfy in-domain?.

heap-adjoiner   (afp heaps)
$(\alpha, \alpha \to Boolean) \to (\alpha, \ bush(\alpha) \to bush(\alpha))$
may-precede?   new amaso
Construct a procedure that, in turn, constructs a bush similar to amaso, containing new and
all of the elements of amaso and satisfying the heap invariants with respect to may-precede?.
Precondition: may-precede? is an ordering relation.
Precondition: may-precede? can receive new and any element of amaso.
Precondition: amaso satisfies the heap invariants with respect to may-precede?.

heap-list-merger   (afp heaps)
$(\alpha, \alpha \to Boolean) \to (list(bush(\alpha)) \to bush(\alpha))$
may-precede?   heap-list
Construct a procedure that, in turn, constructs a bush that contains all of the elements of
elements of heap-list and satisfies the heap invariants with respect to may-precede?.
Precondition: may-precede? is an ordering relation.
Precondition: may-precede? can receive any elements of elements of heap-list.
Precondition: Every element of heap-list satisfies the heap invariants with respect to
may-precede?.

heap-extractor   (afp heaps)
$(\alpha, \alpha \to Boolean) \to (bush(\alpha) \to \alpha, bush(\alpha))$
may-precede?   amaso
Construct a procedure that returns an element of amaso that bears may-precede? to every
element of amaso, along with a bush that contains all of the other elements of amaso and
satisfies the heap invariants with respect to may-precede?.
Precondition: may-precede? is an ordering relation.
Precondition: may-precede? accepts any elements of amaso.
Precondition: amaso is not empty.
Precondition: amaso satisfies the heap invariants with respect to may-precede?.

heap-of=   (afp heaps)
$(\alpha, \alpha \to Boolean) \to (bush(\alpha), bush(\alpha) \to Boolean)$
may-precede?   left   right
Construct a predicate that determines whether left and right are equivalent as heaps, that
is, whether they are equal in size and contain elements that correspond, in the sense that each
bears may-precede? to the other.
Precondition: may-precede? is an ordering relation.
Precondition: may-precede? can receive any element of left and any element of right, in
either order.
Precondition: left satisfies the heap invariants with respect to may-precede?.
Precondition: right satisfies the heap invariants with respect to may-precede?.

fold-heap   (afp heaps)
$(\alpha, \alpha \to Boolean), (\to \beta \ldots), (\alpha, \beta \ldots \to \beta \ldots) \to (bush(\alpha) \to \beta \ldots)$
may-precede?   base   combiner   amaso
Construct a procedure that returns the results of invoking base if amaso is empty. If amaso is
not empty, the constructed procedure extracts an element of amaso that bears may-precede?
to every element of amaso and applies itself recursively to a bush that contains the remaining
elements of amaso and satisfies the heap invariants with respect to may-precede?, returning the
results of applying combiner to the extracted value and the results of the recursive invocation.
Precondition: may-precede? is an ordering relation.
Precondition: may-precede? can receive any elements of amaso.
Precondition: combiner can receive any element of amaso and the results of an invocation of
base.
Precondition: combiner can receive any element of amaso and the results of any invocation of
combiner.
Precondition: amaso satisfies the heap invariants with respect to may-precede?.

unfold-heap   (afp heaps)
$(\alpha, \alpha \to Boolean), (\beta \ldots \to Boolean), (\beta \ldots \to \alpha), (\beta \ldots \to \beta \ldots) \to$
may-precede?   final?   producer   step

$$(\beta \; ... \qquad\qquad \rightarrow \; bush(\alpha))$$
                arguments

Construct a procedure that first determines whether the elements of arguments satisfy final?. If so, the constructed procedure returns an empty bush. Otherwise, it returns a bush that satisfies the heap invariants with respect to may-precede? and contains the result of applying producer to the elements of arguments, as well as the elements of the result of first applying step to the elements of arguments and then applying the constructed procedure recursively to the results.

Precondition: may-precede? is an ordering relation.

Precondition: may-precede? can receive any results of producer.

Precondition: final? can receive the elements of arguments.

Precondition: final? can receive the results of any invocation of step.

Precondition: If the elements of arguments do not satisfy final?, then producer can receive them.

Precondition: If the results of an invocation of step do not satisfy final?, then producer can receive them.

Precondition: If the elements of arguments do not satisfy final?, then step can receive them.

Precondition: If the results of an invocation of step do not satisfy final?, then step can receive them.

process-heap   (afp heaps)
$(\alpha, \alpha \rightarrow Boolean), \; (\rightarrow \beta \; ...), \; (\alpha, \beta \; ... \rightarrow \beta \; ...) \; \rightarrow \; (bush(\alpha) \; \rightarrow \beta \; ...)$
may-precede?   base   combiner   amaso

Construct a procedure that iteratively applies combiner to an element of amaso and the results of the previous iteration (or to the results of invoking base, if there was no previous iteration). The iteration takes up the elements of amaso in the order specified by may-precede?. The constructed procedure returns the results of the last application of combiner.

Precondition: may-precede? is an ordering relation.

Precondition: may-precede? can receive any elements of amaso.

Precondition: combiner can receive an element of amaso that bears may-precede? to every element of amaso and the results of an invocation of base.

Precondition: combiner can receive any element of amaso and the results of any invocation of combiner.

Precondition: amaso satisfies the heap invariants with respect to may-precede?.

sort   (afp sorting heapsort)
$(\alpha, \alpha \rightarrow Boolean), \; bag(\alpha) \; \rightarrow \; list(\alpha)$
may-precede?   aro

Construct a list that has the values in aro as its elements and is ordered by may-precede?.

Precondition: may-precede? is an ordering relation.

Precondition: may-precede? can receive any values in aro.

Exercises

4.5–1 Define a procedure heap that can receive one or more arguments, of which the first is an ordering relation and the others are values in the domain of that relation, and returns a heap containing those values.

4.5–2 Define a procedure heap-size that determines the number of elements in a heap.

4.5–3 Reimplement the heap primitives using trees rather than bushes.

4.6 Order Statistics

For any bag of cardinality n and any natural number k less than n, a *kth order statistic* of the bag, relative to an ordering relation R, is a value m in the bag such that at least $k + 1$ values in the bag, including m itself, bear R to m, and m bears R to at least $n - k$ values in the bag, including itself. For instance:

- The 0th order statistic of the bag bears R to every value in the bag.

- Every value in the bag bears R to the $(n - 1)$th order statistic.

- If n is odd, then the median value in the bag is its $\lfloor n/2 \rfloor$th order statistic.

Suppose that there is a list of the values in the bag, ordered with respect to R, in which m is at position k. Then m is a kth order statistic of the bag, since the k members that precede m in the list, as well as m itself (making $k + 1$ in all), bear R to m, and m bears R to itself and to each of the $n - k - 1$ members that follow it in the list (making $n - k$ in all).

We can therefore compute the kth order statistic of a bag by sorting the bag and indexing into the resulting list:

```
(define (order-statistic-by-sorting may-precede? aro index)
  (list-ref (sort may-precede? aro) index))
```

This method, however, is inefficient. Much of the computation that the sorting procedure carries out is irrelevant, consisting of comparisons between values that both precede or both follow the order statistic in the ordered list. A better algorithm would use information derived from early comparisons to narrow the scope of the problem, discarding without further examination values that are known not to be the desired order statistic.

We might begin our search for a kth order statistic of a bag by selecting a pivot value and partitioning the rest of the bag around it, as in one step of the quicksort algorithm. Let n be the cardinality of the original bag and j the cardinality of the first of the subbags resulting from the partition (the one containing values that bear R to the pivot), leaving $n - j - 1$ values (none of which bear R to the pivot) for the second subbag. There are now three possibilities, depending on the relation between j and k:

- $j < k$. In this case, none of the values in the first subbag, nor the pivot itself, can be a kth order statistic, because k or fewer values in the original bag bear R to them. So we can continue the search in the second subbag, looking for its $(k-j-1)$th order statistic. Because $k-j$ values in the second subbag, all j members of the first subbag, and the pivot bear R to it—$k+1$ members altogether—and because it bears R to $(n - j - 1) - (k - j - 1)$, or $n - k$, values in the second subbag, a $(k - j - 1)$th order statistic of the second bag is a kth order statistic of the original bag.

- $j = k$. In this case, the pivot is the desired order statistic, since the j values in the first bag, as well as the pivot itself, bear R to the pivot, making $k+1$ altogether, and the pivot bears R to itself and to each of the $n - j - 1$ values in the second bag, making $n - k$ altogether.

- $j > k$. In this case, no value in the second subbag can be a kth order statistic. For suppose that x, a value in the second subbag, were a kth order statistic of the original bag. Then it would bear R to $n - k$ values in the original bag. Since the second subbag has only $n - j$ members, x would have to bear R to the pivot, or to some member of the first subbag and hence again, by transitivity, to the pivot. But the partitioning step placed x in the second subbag because it does *not* bear R to the pivot. So the supposition that x is a *kth* order statistic is untenable.

  Moreover, if the pivot is a kth order statistic of the original bag, then it bears R to at least $n - k$ values in the original bag, and hence to at least $j - k$ values in the first subbag (since there are only $n - j$ other values in the original bag). Since $j > k$, therefore, there is at least one value in the first subbag to which the pivot bears R. Let x be any value in the first subbag to which the pivot bears R. Then, by transitivity, every value in the original bag that bears R to the pivot also bears R to x, and x bears R to every value in the original bag to which the pivot bears R. So x is also a kth order statistic of the original bag.

  Regardless of whether the pivot is a kth order statistic of the original bag, therefore, we can continue the search in the first subbag, looking for its kth order statistic, since a kth order statistic of that first subbag is a kth order statistic of the original bag.

In order to decide efficiently which of these three cases applies, we use a variant of the `partition-bag` procedure that returns j, the cardinality of the first subbag, as an additional result:

```
(define (partition-bag-with-count condition-met? aro)
  ((fold-bag (create 0 (bag) (bag))
             (lambda (item count ins outs)
               (if (condition-met? item)
                   (values (add1 count) (put-into-bag item ins) outs)
                   (values count ins (put-into-bag item outs)))))
   aro))
```

The `order-statistic` procedure now partitions repeatedly, discarding at each stage the bag that is known not to contain the kth order statistic, until it encounters a pivot that is just right:

```
(define (order-statistic may-precede? aro index)
  ((rec (partitioner areto index)
     (receive (pivot others) (take-from-bag areto)
```

```
      (receive (count ins outs)
              (partition-bag-with-count (sect may-precede? <> pivot)
                                        others)
          (if (< index count)
              (partitioner ins index)
              (if (< count index)
                  (partitioner outs (- index (add1 count)))
                  pivot)))))
    aro index))
```

---

partition-bag-with-count   (afp bags)
$(\alpha \rightarrow Boolean),\ bag(\alpha)\ \rightarrow natural\text{-}number,\ bag(\alpha),\ bag(\alpha)$
condition-met?   aro
Return the number of values in aro that satisfy condition-met?, a bag containing those values,
and a bag containing the values in aro that do not satisfy condition-met?.
Precondition: condition-met? can receive any values in aro.

order-statistic   (afp order-statistics)
$(\alpha, \alpha \rightarrow Boolean),\ bag(\alpha),\ natural\text{-}number\ \rightarrow \alpha$
may-precede?   aro   index
Return a value such that more than index values in aro bear may-precede? to it, and it bears
may-precede? to at least as many values in aro as the amount by which the cardinality of aro
exceeds index.
Precondition: may-precede? is an ordering relation.
Precondition: may-precede? can receive any values in aro.
Precondition: index is less than the cardinality of aro.

Exercises

4.6–1   Define a procedure median that returns the median value in a given
bag, with respect to a given ordering relation, provided that every value in the
bag is in the domain of that relation. (If the cardinality of the bag is even, your
procedure may return either of the middle values.)

4.6–2   Define a procedure quantile that receives an ordering relation, a bag
of values in the domain of that ordering relation, and a positive integer q, and
returns a list of $q - 1$ elements: the $\lceil nk/q \rceil$th order statistics, where n is the
cardinality of the bag, k is a positive integer in the range from 1 to $q - 1$, and
$\lceil nk/q \rceil$ is the least integer not less than nk/q. (For instance, when $q = 2$, the list
returned has one value, the median. When $q = 100$, it contains 99 values—the
percentile values, to which respectively at least 1%, 2%, . . . , 99% of the values
in the bag bear the ordering relation.)

4.6–3   Show that if a value v is simultaneously the jth and kth order statistic
in a bag, with respect to an ordering relation R, then the bag contains at least
$|k - j| + 1$ values that are equivalent to v, under the equivalence relation $\stackrel{R}{=}$
induced by R.

Chapter 5

Combinatorial Constructions

Because of the generality and flexibility of the data structures that we developed in Chapter 3, many common computational procedures can be implemented as operations on such structures, either to build additional structures meeting some interesting constraint, or to enumerate such additional structures. The branch of mathematics that deals with these operations is called combinatorics. In this chapter, we'll see the algorithms that our tool kit provides for expressing such operations.

5.1   Cartesian Products

The *Cartesian product* $A \times B$ of two bags A and B is the bag containing every pair in which the car is a member of A and the cdr is a member of B. It is not immediately obvious how to use a recursion manager such as `fold-bag` to define a procedure that constructs the Cartesian product of two bags: We have to choose one or the other as the guide for the recursion, yet it seems as if we have to fold over both. On the other hand, resorting to some more basic recursion manager such as `build` and using both of the given bags as guide values doesn't capture the basic logic either. We don't want to run through A and B in parallel; instead, we want to run through all of the values in B once for *each* of the values in A, applying `cons` at each step and collecting all of the results in a big bag.

The solution is to divide the problem into two recursive operations, one of which can be nested inside the other. Let's consider the operation on B first. In our ultimate `Cartesian-product` procedure, we'll use this operation to pair some fixed value from A with each of the values from B. From the point of view of the operation on B, the fixed value from A is just a constant. We can bind it to a name, such as `car-value`, and take it as a given for this operation.

Since we're starting with a bag B, and the result of the operation is a bag in which each value in B is paired with `car-value`, it's natural to use `map-bag` as the recursion manager, with

```
(sect cons car-value <>)
```

as the procedure that converts a value in B into the corresponding value in the result bag. Let's give a name, cons-with-each, to this mapping operation on B:

```
(define (cons-with-each car-value bag-of-cdrs)
  (map-bag (sect cons car-value <>) bag-of-cdrs))
```

Now for the recursion on A. Every time we apply the procedure

```
(sect cons-with-each <> B)
```

to a value in A, we get back a bag containing some of the pairs that we want. To repeat this operation for every value of A, map-bag doesn't quite do the job, since we would wind up with a bag of bags of pairs. Instead, we want to dump all of the pairs into one big bag as we go. But we can use fold-bag as the recursion manager for the recursion guided by A, with bag-union as the procedure that collects the pairs:

```
(define (Cartesian-product left right)
  ((fold-bag bag (pipe (~initial (sect cons-with-each <> right))
                       bag-union))
   left))
```

The cardinality of a Cartesian product is the product of the cardinalities of the bags from which it is derived. As in many of the combinatorial constructions to follow, the constructed value can take up an inconveniently large amount of memory. For this reason, we'll also consider a version that returns a finite source rather than a bag, so that we can compute the pairs one by one, as needed, instead of having to build them all explicitly into the data structure. This version of the procedure also features nested recursion, but uses source-expressions at key points in the process so that most of the computation is deferred until the source is tapped. To make these points visible, we'll write out the mapping and folding mechanisms as rec-expressions:

```
(define (cons-with-each-source car-value bag-of-cdrs)
  ((rec (mapper subbag)
     (if (empty-bag? subbag)
         (finite-source)
         (source (receive (cdr-value others) (take-from-bag subbag)
                   (values (cons car-value cdr-value)
                           (mapper others))))))
   bag-of-cdrs))
```

```
(define (Cartesian-product-source left right)
  ((rec (folder subbag)
     (if (empty-bag? subbag)
         (finite-source)
         (source (receive (car-value others) (take-from-bag subbag)
                   (tap (catenate-sources
                          (cons-with-each-source car-value right)
                          (folder others)))))))
   left))
```

At first glance, it might seem that the definitions of Cartesian-product and Cartesian-product-source would not lend themselves to arity extension, since a pair always has exactly two components. The most straightforward way to generalize the basic idea to more than two operands is to have the results be bags of lists rather than bags of pairs, with the length of each list equal to the number of operands. So, for instance, the values belonging to the generalized Cartesian product of bags A, B, C, and D are four-element lists, each list having a value from A as its initial element, then a value from B, then a value from C, and finally a value from D.

We can define this generalized Cartesian product procedure as an arity extension of a binary operation that receives a bag of new initial elements and a bag of lists of length n, and prepends each initial element to each of the lists to obtain a list of length $n + 1$, collecting the results in a bag. Notice that this binary operation exemplifies the same each-to-each pattern as the Cartesian-product operation. Indeed, the implementation of this procedure is almost identical to Cartesian-product! The only difference is that we use prepend, rather than cons, to build each component of the result. (Of course, even this difference vanishes when we consider that Scheme implements lists as pair structures. Recall that we defined prepend as an alias for cons.)

Again, the logic of the operation is easier to follow if we put each level of recursion in a different procedure. There are now three of them, counting the one that performs the arity extension. Here are the first two steps:

```
(define (prepend-to-each new-initial aro)
  (map-bag (sect prepend new-initial <>) aro))

(define (prepend-each-to-each initials aro)
  ((fold-bag bag (pipe (~initial (sect prepend-to-each <> aro))
                       bag-union))
   initials))
```

In extending the arity of prepend-each-to-each to obtain a procedure that computes generalized Cartesian products, we'll also need a starter value, to deal with the zero-argument case, in which the procedure receives zero bags as arguments and returns a bag of zero-length lists. It would be a mistake to return an empty bag in this situation. The goal of the procedure is to produce a bag containing *every* possible list of length n, with its elements taken from the

n bags supplied as arguments; when $n = 0$, we want to return a bag containing every possible list of length 0—a bag with the empty list as its only element.

Here, then, is the definition of `generalized-Cartesian-product`:

```
(define generalized-Cartesian-product
  (extend-to-variable-arity (bag (list)) prepend-each-to-each))
```

We can generalize the `Cartesian-product-source` procedure in a similar way, with `prepend` again replacing `cons` and `(finite-source (list))` as the value to be returned when no arguments are received.

When all of the arguments in a call to `generalized-Cartesian-product` are the same bag, the result is a *Cartesian power* of that bag, with the "exponent" being the number of arguments. For instance, if A is a bag containing just the integers 0 and 1, then its third Cartesian power A^3 is a bag containing `(list 0 0 0)`, `(list 0 0 1)`, `(list 0 1 0)`, `(list 0 1 1)`, `(list 1 0 0)`, `(list 1 0 1)`, `(list 1 1 0)`, and `(list 1 1 1)`.

The `Cartesian-power` procedure receives a bag and a natural-number exponent and computes Cartesian powers directly:

```
(define (Cartesian-power aro len)
  ((fold-natural (create (bag (list)))
                 (sect prepend-each-to-each aro <>))
   len))
```

The call to `fold-natural` manages the recursion over the lengths of the list, so that the list-extension operation is performed the correct number of times (starting from the empty list).

Ordering Cartesian Products

When the values from which we want to produce the pairs or lists in a Cartesian product are ordered in some way, we often want the resulting Cartesian product to reflect that ordering. In such cases, our procedures for computing Cartesian products should start with lists or finite sources rather than bags, and should also return lists or finite sources.

If we simply adapt the definitions given above, substituting list or source operations for bag operations, the ordering of the lists in the resulting Cartesian product or power is the lexicographic ordering obtained by applying `list-lex` (§4.1) to the ordering relation for the given list or source. For instance, applying the `ordered-Cartesian-power-source` procedure defined below to a list of numbers ordered by `<=` yields a source that produces the elements of the specified Cartesian power in lexicographic order (that is, ordered by `(list-lex <=)`). As usual, it will be best to work up to the definition of `ordered-Cartesian-power-source` in stages, considering each of the three recursions separately. However, there is no difficulty in adapting the procedures defined above to the new goal:

```
(define (ordered-prepend-to-each-source new-initial src)
  (map-finite-source (sect prepend new-initial <>) src))

(define (ordered-prepend-each-to-each-source initials src)
  ((rec (folder sublist)
     (if (empty-list? sublist)
         (finite-source)
         (source
           (receive (new-initial others) (deprepend sublist)
             (tap (catenate-sources
                    (ordered-prepend-to-each-source new-initial src)
                    (folder others)))))))))
   initials))

(define (ordered-Cartesian-power-source ls len)
  ((rec (recurrer remaining)
     (if (zero? remaining)
         (finite-source (list))
         (ordered-prepend-each-to-each-source
           ls (recurrer (sub1 remaining)))))
   len))
```

Ranking and Unranking

When we need some, but not all, of the values in a combinatorial construction
such as an ordered Cartesian product or power, an alternative to using sources
is to compute each such value directly from its *rank*, that is, its position in the
ordering. For instance, in the ordered Cartesian product of (list 'a 'b 'c)
and (list 'w 'x 'y 'z), the pair (cons 'b 'y) occupies position 6 in the list
(using zero-based indexing, as in a call to list-ref), following four pairs with a
as their cars and then two other pairs, (cons 'b 'w) and (cons 'b 'x). Given
the rank, we can compute the pair that occupies that rank directly, without
going through the rest of the construction of the Cartesian product. It is also
possible to reverse the process, computing the rank of a given pair. These
computations are respectively called *unranking* and *ranking*.

As an introduction to algorithms for ranking and unranking, let's write a
procedure that determines the position of a given value within a given list—a
kind of inverse of the list-ref procedure. If the value occurs more than once in
the list, our procedure can return the least of the positions; if it does not occur
at all, we'll signal the failure by returning #f rather than a natural number.

To compute the position, we work our way down the list, comparing each
element to the one we're looking for, and carrying along a count of the elements
that don't match. When we find the one we're looking for, we return the current
count; if we reach the end of the list without finding it, we return #f. Here's
the implementation:

```
(define (position-in val ls)
  ((rec (searcher sublist count)
     (if (empty-list? sublist)
         #f
         (if (equal? (first sublist) val)
             count
             (searcher (rest sublist) (add1 count)))))
   ls 0))
```

This version of position-in presupposes that equal? is a suitable criterion of sameness.

Note that, if the list ls contains duplicate values, then the unranking procedure (list-ref) and the ranking procedure (position-in) are not exact inverses: (list-ref (position-in v ls) ls) is always v (or at least a value that is the same as v, as determined by equal?), but (position-in (list-ref n ls) ls) is not always n—it could be the position of some duplicate of the value at position n. In general, ranking and unranking algorithms are inverses only when there can be no duplication among the items being ranked.

With position-in as a building block, we can now proceed to some more ambitious ranking and unranking procedures. Let's start with (ungeneralized) Cartesian products, as in the example discussed above.

The Cartesian-product-ranker procedure receives two lists and returns a procedure that determine the rank of a pair in the Cartesian product of those lists. The algorithm determines the position of the car and the cdr in their respective lists, then multiplies the car's position by the length of the second list to compute how many pairs with lesser cars precede the given pair in the ordered Cartesian product. Adding the result of this multiplication to the cdr's position (which indicates how many pairs with the *same* car precede the given one) yields the desired rank:

```
(define (Cartesian-product-ranker left right)
  (let ((right-length (length right)))
    (run decons
         (cross (sect position-in <> left) (sect position-in <> right))
         (~initial (sect * <> right-length))
         +)))
```

The procedure uses position-in to determine the positions of values in the given lists, so equal? is its criterion of sameness both for cars and for cdrs.

The corresponding unranking algorithm performs the reverse computations, using div-and-mod to recover the appropriate list indices, list-ref to select the appropriate elements, and cons to put them into the desired pair:

```
(define (Cartesian-product-unranker left right)
  (let ((right-length (length right)))
    (run (sect div-and-mod <> right-length)
         (cross (sect list-ref left <>) (sect list-ref right <>))
```

```
      cons)))
```

The call to `div-and-mod` presupposes that the length of `right` is non-zero. This is consistent with the preconditions of ranking and unranking operations: If the length of `right` is 0, then `right` is empty, so that the Cartesian product is also empty, and there are no pairs and no ranks in it!

For generalized Cartesian products of n lists, it's useful to think of each position in the length-n lists in the result as having a "positional weight," analogous to the positional weights of digits in a numeral—the powers of ten in a decimal numeral, for instance. The rightmost position in the list has a positional weight of 1; the next-to-rightmost has a positional weight equal to the length of the last of the given lists; the one just to the left of that has a positional weight equal to the product of the lengths of the last two given lists; and so on. The idea is that "advancing" from one element of the kth given list to the next moves you forward a number of positions in the lexicographic ordering equal to the positional weight associated with the kth position.

It is easiest to compute the positional weights from the lengths of all but the first of the given lists. Given any list of natural numbers, we can derive a set of positional weights from it, basically by taking, at each position, the product of all the natural numbers from that position to the end of the list:

```
(define positional-weights
  (fold-list (create (list 1))
             (lambda (element weights)
               (cons (* element (first weights)) weights))))
```

The ranking and unranking procedures for generalized Cartesian products use the positional weights derived from the lengths of the given lists as multipliers and divisors, as `right-length` was used in the corresponding procedures for plain Cartesian products. In the ranking algorithm, we can use `map` to work in parallel on all the positions in the list we're trying to rank:

```
(define (generalized-Cartesian-product-ranker . lists)
  (let ((weights (positional-weights (map length (rest lists)))))
    (run (sect map position-in <> lists)
         (sect map * <> weights)
         sum)))
```

To do the arithmetic in the matching unranker, we'll need a procedure that receives a number and a list of positional weights and uses `div-and-mod` to break out the separate indices for the given lists, one by one:

```
(define (separate-indices number weights)
  (if (empty-list? weights)
      (list)
      (receive (quot rem) (div-and-mod number (first weights))
        (cons quot (separate-indices rem (rest weights))))))
```

The unranker, then, uses `separate-indices` to recover the indices and
`list-ref` to extract the elements:

```
(define (generalized-Cartesian-product-unranker . lists)
  (let ((weights (positional-weights (map length (rest lists)))))
    (pipe (sect separate-indices <> weights)
          (sect map list-ref lists <>))))
```

Procedures for ranking and unranking in ordered Cartesian powers are left
as exercises. They use the same basic algorithms as the procedures for ordered
generalized Cartesian products, but the positional weights are computed as
descending powers of the length of the given list.

---

cons-with-each   (afp bags)
α, $bag(\beta)$ $\rightarrow$ $bag(pair(\alpha, \beta))$
car-value bag-of-cdrs
Construct a bag containing every pair that has `car-value` as its car and a value from
`bag-of-cdrs` as its cdr.

Cartesian-product   (afp products-and-selections)
$bag(\alpha)$, $bag(\beta)$ $\rightarrow$ $bag(pair(\alpha, \beta))$
left   right
Construct a bag containing all the pairs in which the car is a value in `left` and the cdr a value
in `right`.

cons-with-each-source   (afp bags)
α, $bag(\beta)$ $\rightarrow$ $source(pair(\alpha, \beta))$
car-value bag-of-cdrs
Construct a finite source containing every pair that has `car-value` as its car and a value from
`bag-of-cdrs` as its cdr.

Cartesian-product-source   (afp products-and-selections)
$bag(\alpha)$, $bag(\beta)$ $\rightarrow$ $source(pair(\alpha, \beta))$
left   right
Construct a finite source containing all the pairs in which the car is a value in `left` and the
cdr a value in `right`.

prepend-to-each   (afp bags)
α, $bag(list(\alpha))$ $\rightarrow$ $bag(list(\alpha))$
new-initial aro
Construct a bag of lists containing every list formed by prepending `new-initial` to a list in
`aro`.

prepend-each-to-each   (afp bags)
$bag(\alpha)$, $bag(list(\alpha))$ $\rightarrow$ $bag(list(\alpha))$
initials aro
Construct a bag containing every list formed by prepending a value in `initials` to a list in
`aro`.

generalized-Cartesian-product   (afp products-and-selections)
$bag(\alpha)$ ... $\rightarrow$ $bag(list(\alpha))$
factors
Construct a bag of lists such that the length of each list is equal to the number of elements of
`factors` and each element of each list is a value in the corresponding element of `factors`.

Cartesian-power   (afp products-and-selections)
$bag(\alpha)$, $natural$-$number$ $\rightarrow$ $bag(list(\alpha))$
aro   len
Construct a bag containing every list of length `len` in which the elements are all values in `aro`
(possibly including duplicates).

`ordered-prepend-to-each-source` (afp sources)

α, $\qquad$ $source(list(\alpha))$ $\rightarrow$ $source(list(\alpha))$
new-initial src

Construct a finite source containing the results of prepending new-initial to each of the lists from src, in order.

Precondition: src is a finite source.

`ordered-prepend-each-to-each-source` (afp sources)

$list(\alpha)$, $\quad$ $source(list(\alpha))$ $\rightarrow$ $source(list(\alpha))$
initials src

Construct a finite source containing the results of prepending each element of initials to each of the lists in src, in lexicographic order.

Precondition: src is a finite source.

`ordered-Cartesian-power-source` (afp products-and-selections)

$list(\alpha)$, $natural\text{-}number$ $\rightarrow$ $source(list(\alpha))$
ls $\qquad$ len

Construct a finite source containing every list of length len containing values taken from ls (allowing duplicates). The finite source produces these lists in the lexicographic order induced by the order of ls.

Precondition: ls is ordered.

`position-in` (afp lists)

any, $list(any)$ $\rightarrow$ $natural\text{-}number$ | $Boolean$
val ls

Determine the least position at which val occurs in ls, returning #f if there is no such position.

`Cartesian-product-ranker` (afp products-and-selections)

$list(\alpha)$, $list(\beta)$ $\rightarrow$ $(pair(\alpha, \beta)$ $\rightarrow$ $natural\text{-}number)$
left $\quad$ right $\qquad$ pr

Construct a procedure that computes the rank of pr in the ordered Cartesian product of left and right.

Precondition: left is ordered.

Precondition: right is ordered.

Precondition: The car of pr is an element of left.

Precondition: The cdr of pr is an element of right.

`Cartesian-product-unranker` (afp products-and-selections)

$list(\alpha)$, $list(\beta)$ $\rightarrow$ $(natural\text{-}number$ $\rightarrow$ $pair(\alpha, \beta))$
left $\quad$ right $\qquad$ rank

Construct a procedure that, in turn, constructs the pair in position rank in the ordered Cartesian product of left and right.

Precondition: left is ordered.

Precondition: right is ordered.

Precondition: rank is less than the product of the lengths of left and right.

`positional-weights` (afp lists)

$list(natural\text{-}number)$ $\rightarrow$ $list(natural\text{-}number)$
numlist

Compute a list of the positional weights of the digits in a mixed-base numeral, given a list, numlist, of the bases.

Precondition: Every element of numlist is positive.

`generalized-Cartesian-product-ranker` (afp products-and-selections)

$list(\alpha)$ ... $\rightarrow$ $(list(\alpha)$ $\rightarrow$ $natural\text{-}number)$
lists $\qquad$ ls

Construct a procedure that computes the rank of ls in the ordered generalized Cartesian product of the elements of lists.

Precondition: Every element of lists is ordered.

Precondition: Every element of ls is an element of the corresponding element of lists.

`separate-indices` (afp lists)

$natural\text{-}number$, $list(natural\text{-}number)$ $\rightarrow$ $list(natural\text{-}number)$
number $\qquad$ weights

Construct a list of values of the digits for the numeral for number in a mixed-base system of numeration, using weights as the positional weights.
Precondition: Every element of weights is positive.

generalized-Cartesian-product-unranker   (afp products-and-selections)
$list(\alpha) \ldots \rightarrow (natural\text{-}number \rightarrow list(\alpha))$
lists   rank

Construct a procedure that, in turn, constructs the list in position rank in the generalized Cartesian product of the elements of lists.
Precondition: Every element of lists is ordered.
Precondition: rank is less than the product of the lengths of the elements of lists.

Exercises

5.1–1   Adapt the Cartesian-power procedure so that it returns a source of lists rather than a bag of lists.

5.1–2   Adapt the generalized-Cartesian-product procedure so that it operates on ordered lists rather than bags and returns a lexicographically ordered list of lists rather than a bag of lists.

5.1–3   Design and implement ranking and unranking procedures for ordered Cartesian powers.

5.2   List Selections

Sublists

A *sublist* of a given list aro is a list of adjacent elements of aro that preserves their original order relative to one another. For instance, (list 'gamma 'delta 'epsilon) is a sublist of (list 'alpha 'beta 'gamma 'delta 'epsilon 'zeta).

A *suffix*, or *tail*, of a given list aro is a sublist that comprises all of the elements of aro at or after some position. Equivalently, we could say that a suffix is formed by dropping some number of elements (possibly zero) from the beginning of aro.

A *prefix* of a given list aro is a sublist that comprises all of the elements of aro at or *before* some position—one formed by *taking away* some number of elements (possibly zero) from the beginning of aro.

Having seen the take and drop procedures, we already know how to construct individual prefixes and suffixes of a given list, and by combining take and drop we can obtain any particular sublist in which we're interested (§3.7). For the corresponding combinatorial constructions, however, we want to obtain *every* possible prefix of a given list, every possible suffix, every possible sublist.

Let's begin with suffixes. The suffixes procedure receives a list and constructs and returns a bag containing all of the suffixes of the list. For instance, (suffixes (list 'alpha 'beta 'gamma 'delta 'epsilon)) is

```
(bag (list 'alpha 'beta 'gamma 'delta 'epsilon)
     (list 'beta 'gamma 'delta 'epsilon)
     (list 'gamma 'delta 'epsilon)
     (list 'delta 'epsilon)
     (list 'epsilon)
     (list))
```

We can use recursion to construct this bag. In the base case, where the given list is empty, the bag contains just one value: The empty list is the only suffix of itself. In any other case, we construct the bag of all suffixes of the rest of the list, then put in one more suffix—the entire list.

This recursion is not of the form that `fold-list` supports, since the combiner needs the entire list and not just its first element. The more general recursion manager `build` handles it, though, if we take the list as the guide value: `empty-list?` detects the base case, `bag` constructs the terminal result, `rest` receives a non-empty list and "steps down" to the next simpler case, and `put-into-bag` adds the top-level list (unchanged, so the `derive` parameter in this case is simply `identity`) to the result of the recursive call:

```
(define suffixes (build empty-list? bag identity rest put-into-bag))
```

Replacing `bag` with `list` and `put-into-bag` with `prepend` gives us a version of `suffixes` that constructs a list of suffixes that is *almost* lexicographically ordered, with `drop` as its ranking procedure and `(pipe (~each length) -)` as its unranking procedure. (Either can be curried to produce higher-order procedures analogous to those in §5.1.) The only glitch is that, in the list delivered by the revised procedure, the empty suffix comes last, whereas in a lexicographic order it would precede all of the other suffixes. But we can exclude the empty suffix from the result, if we like, by changing `bag` to `(constant (list))` rather than to `list`:

```
(define ordered-non-empty-suffixes
  (build empty-list? (constant (list)) identity rest prepend))
```

The `prefixes` procedure receives a list and constructs a bag containing all of the prefixes of the list. For example, `(prefixes (list 'alpha 'beta 'gamma 'delta 'epsilon))` is

```
(bag (list)
     (list 'alpha)
     (list 'alpha 'beta)
     (list 'alpha 'beta 'gamma)
     (list 'alpha 'beta 'gamma 'delta)
     (list 'alpha 'beta 'gamma 'delta 'epsilon))
```

Once again, list recursion is the key to the algorithm. In the base case, we find again that the empty list is the only prefix of itself. In any other case, we separate the first element from the rest of the given list, construct the bag of prefixes of the rest of the list, and somehow combine the first element with that bag to obtain a bag of prefixes for the entire list. The prepend-to-each procedure does most of the job. Prepending the first element to each prefix of the rest of the list gives us all but one of the prefixes of the entire list—all of them except the empty prefix, which we have to add as a separate element. So a definition using fold-list looks like this:

```
(define prefixes
  (fold-list (create (bag (list)))
             (pipe prepend-to-each (sect put-into-bag (list) <>))))
```

This time, changing bag to list and put-into-bag to prepend gives us a result list that is lexicographically ordered, with take as its unranking procedure; in the other direction, we can compute the rank of a given prefix simply by taking its length.

If we want all of the sublists of a given list, including the "interior" ones, we can regard each sublist as a prefix of some suffix. This implies that if we first construct all the suffixes of the given list, and then take all the prefixes of each of those suffixes and collect them in one big bag, we'll have all of the sublists.

As a first cut at this procedure, we can invoke suffixes to give us a bag of the suffixes, and fold over that bag, applying prefixes to each suffix and collecting the results with bag-union:

```
(define sublists
  (pipe suffixes (fold-bag bag (pipe (~initial prefixes) bag-union))))
```

This definition, however, produces an empty sublist before and after each element of the list (as the empty prefix of the suffix beginning at that point). For instance, under the preceding definition, (sublists (list 'a 'b 'c 'd 'e)) is

```
(bag (list)
     (list 'a)
     (list 'a 'b)
     (list 'a 'b 'c)
     (list 'a 'b 'c 'd)
     (list 'a 'b 'c 'd 'e)
     (list)
     (list 'b)
     (list 'b 'c)
     (list 'b 'c 'd)
     (list 'b 'c 'd 'e)
     (list)
     (list 'c)
```

```
        (list 'c 'd)
        (list 'c 'd 'e)
        (list)
        (list 'd)
        (list 'd 'e)
        (list)
        (list 'e)
        (list))
```

For some purposes, this may be exactly what we want. In most applications, however, the empty sublists just get in the way and slow things down. They also mess up the lexicographic ordering of the result of the ordered version of this procedure.

We could postprocess the result of `sublists` by piping it into (`sect remp empty-list? <>`), but it would be more elegant to avoid generating the empty lists to begin with, by replacing `prefixes` with a procedure that leaves it out:

```
(define non-empty-prefixes
  (fold-list bag (pipe (~next (sect put-into-bag (list) <>))
                       prepend-to-each))))
```

Here the idea is to start with no lists at all in the base case, and then use the combiner to add an empty list to the bag of sublists received as the result of the recursive call, before prepending the new initial element to every list in that bag.

So our official definition of `sublists` will be:

```
(define sublists
  (pipe suffixes
        (fold-bag bag (pipe (~initial non-empty-prefixes) bag-union))))
```

Arguably this procedure should be called `non-empty-sublists`, but it is convenient to have this shorter name for the procedure that is much more commonly invoked in practice.

The definition of the ordered version of `sublists` (and of the procedures on which it depends) is left an exercise, but we can deal fairly quickly with the algorithms for ranking and unranking. For instance, in lexicographic order, the (non-empty) sublists of the list of characters (#\W #\X #\Y #\Z) (which is ordered by char<=?) is

```
(#\W)
(#\W #\X)
(#\W #\X #\Y)
(#\W #\X #\Y #\Z)
(#\X)
(#\X #\Y)
(#\X #\Y #\Z)
```

```
(#\Y)
(#\Y #\Z)
(#\Z)
```

To compute the rank of a sublist, then, we can use its first element to figure out the range of positions in this ordering at which the sublists beginning with that element occur, and then use the length of the sublist to figure out where in this range the sublist itself lies. The first half of this computation uses the `termial` procedure, which computes the sum of the natural numbers less than or equal to a given natural number. One of the exercises in §1.9 asked you to provide a definition of `termial`, and with the resources of Chapter 2 we could give its recursive definition concisely as '(ply-natural (create 0) +)'. However, it is more efficient to compute it directly from the closed-form expression for the sum: The termial of a natural number n is $\frac{n(n+1)}{2}$:

```
(define (termial number)
  (halve (* number (add1 number))))
```

Let L be our original list, let n be the length of L, let e be the initial element of the sublist that we're trying to rank, and let j be the position of e in L. The range of the ranks of sublists beginning with e starts at `(- (termial n)` `(termial (- n j)))`. To see why, note that there are `(termial n)` non-empty sublists altogether, and `(termial (- n j))` of them are also sublists of the suffix beginning with e. These last cannot precede any sublist beginning with e in the lexicographic ordering.

The curried version of our ranking procedure for lexicographically ordered non-empty sublists, therefore, is

```
(define (sublist-ranker ls)
  (let ((len (length ls)))
    (let ((number-of-sublists (termial len)))
      (pipe (dispatch (run first
                           (sect position-in <> ls)
                           (sect - len <>)
                           termial
                           (sect - number-of-sublists <>))
                      (pipe length sub1))
            +))))
```

For the unranking procedure, we can pack most of the arithmetic into an inverse of the `termial` procedure. The `antitermial` procedure receives a natural number t and returns two values, rather like the results of `div-and-mod`: the greatest natural number n whose termial does not exceed t, and the remainder r when that termial is subtracted from t. (The definition of "termial" guarantees that the second result is always a natural number less than or equal to the first result.)

The approach that we'll use to compute this inverse is called "binary search" or "bisection." We start with two natural numbers, a lower bound l and an upper bound u, chosen so as to guarantee that the value n that we are seeking is strictly less than u but not less than l. In the `antitermial` procedure, we can choose $l = 0$ and $u = t + 1$; no matter what t is, its antitermial n must be less than $t + 1$ and cannot be less than 0.

This establishes a range in which the value must lie. We then bisect that range, computing a value m that lies halfway between l and u. If the termial of m is less than or equal to t, then we can use m as an improved lower bound, since the number that we are seeking cannot be less than m. If, on the other hand, the terminal of m is greater than n, then we can use m as an improved exclusive upper bound; the number we are seeking must be less than m. Thus in either case we reduce the range of possible values.

We can then repeat this process of narrowing the range containing the sought value, stopping when our revised upper bound is the successor of our revised lower bound, so that the range of possible values contains only one natural number, which is therefore the value we are looking for.

In Scheme,

```
(define (antitermial number)
  ((rec (converge lower upper)
     (if (= (add1 lower) upper)
         (values lower (- number (termial lower)))
         (let ((mid (halve (+ lower upper))))
           (if (< number (termial mid))
               (converge lower mid)
               (converge mid upper)))))
   0 (add1 number)))
```

A procedure constructed by `sublist-unranker`, then, uses `antitermial` to walk back the computation performed in `sublist-ranker`:

```
(define (sublist-unranker ls)
  (let ((len (length ls)))
    (let ((number-of-sublists (termial len)))
      (lambda (rank)
        (receive (position-from-end delends)
                 (antitermial (- (sub1 number-of-sublists) rank))
          (take (drop ls (- (sub1 len) position-from-end))
                (- (add1 position-from-end) delends)))))))
```

Sections

Sometimes we need just the sublists of a specified length (assumed to be positive and less than or equal to the length of the given list). The `sections` procedure constructs a bag of equal-length sublists. For instance, `(sections (list 'alpha 'beta 'gamma 'delta 'epsilon) 3)` is

```
(bag (list 'alpha 'beta 'gamma)
     (list 'beta 'gamma 'delta)
     (list 'gamma 'delta 'epsilon))
```

We can picture the algorithm as sliding a window of fixed size along the list, with one of the sublists of the specified length showing through at each stage. When we shift the window one position to the right, an element drops out at the left and a new element becomes visible at the right, so we get a new sublist.

One's first thought is again to use list recursion, using `take` to get a prefix of the given list and adding that prefix to the bag of sections of the rest of the list. The problem is to identify the base case efficiently. It's not the case where the list is empty, but rather the one in which the length of the list is equal to the length specified for the sublists. (The precondition for the `take` procedure won't be met if we proceed to lists that are shorter than the length of the desired sublists.)

On the other hand, it's inconvenient to compute the length of the list in each recursive call. A better idea is to compute the difference between the length of the given list and the length of the desired sublists, just once, at the beginning of the computation. This tells us how many recursive calls will be needed, and we can just count them down, stopping when we reach 0. (That's the easier way to identify the base case.)

So in this recursion, we need two guide values: the list from which we want to take sections, and the count of recursive calls remaining. When the count is 0, we need the whole of the list, since the length of the given list and the length of the desired sublists are equal; so in this case we'll just put the list in a bag by itself. When the count is positive, we take a prefix and put it in a bag returned by a recursive call; in that recursive call, the list is one element shorter (that is, we shift the window one position rightwards) and the count of recursive calls is one less.

Here's the translation of this idea into Scheme:

```
(define (sections ls len)
  ((rec (sectioner subls count)
     (if (zero? count)
         (bag subls)
         (put-into-bag (take subls len)
                       (sectioner (rest subls) (sub1 count)))))
   ls (- (length ls) len)))
```

To rank a section in the lexicographic ordering, find the position of its first element in the original list; to unrank a natural number r, drop r elements from `ls` and take the first `len` elements of the result.

Subsequences and Selections

In all of the preceding cases, we have constructed our results from groups of *adjacent* elements of a given list. Let's now abandon this restriction and consider how to find all the ways of selecting any elements, adjacent or not, from a given list (while preserving their relative order)—what we'll call the *subsequences* of the list and implement in a subsequences procedure. For instance, (subsequences (list 'alpha 'beta 'gamma 'delta)) is

```
(bag (list)
     (list 'delta)
     (list 'gamma)
     (list 'gamma 'delta)
     (list 'beta)
     (list 'beta 'delta)
     (list 'beta 'gamma)
     (list 'beta 'gamma 'delta)
     (list 'alpha)
     (list 'alpha 'delta)
     (list 'alpha 'gamma)
     (list 'alpha 'gamma 'delta)
     (list 'alpha 'beta)
     (list 'alpha 'beta 'delta)
     (list 'alpha 'beta 'gamma)
     (list 'alpha 'beta 'gamma 'delta))
```

A list recursion again appears to be the natural approach for this procedure to take, and the base case, as usual, is easy: The only subsequence of the empty list is the empty list itself. For any non-empty list, we can split off the first element, again as usual, and issue a recursive call to get a bag of the subsequences of the rest of the list. What then?

We begin by noticing that every subsequence of the rest of the list counts as a subsequence of the entire list, one that happens not to include the first element. We need to combine that bag with the bag of all the subsequences that *do* include the first element. How can we construct those? As we see from the example, they are in one-to-one correspondence with the subsequences of the rest of the list. Prepending the first element to each of the first-element-lacking subsequences yields a first-element-having subsequence. So we can invoke prepend-to-each to prepend the first element to each member of the recursive result, then bag-union to bring together the first-element-lacking subsequences and the first-element-having ones:

```
(define subsequences (fold-list (create (bag (list)))
                                (pipe (dispatch >next prepend-to-each)
                                      bag-union)))
```

The ordered version of subsequences (in which list replaces bag and append replaces bag-union) returns a list of subsequences that is not ordered by the lexicographic ordering induced by the ordering of the list's original elements. The ordering that it produces is a more interesting and useful one, however: If we think of the subsequences algorithm as recording at each step whether or not it prepends the current element of the given list to a subsequence, then each subsequence corresponds to a different sequence of such decisions, one for each element of the list. If we represent each such decision as a Boolean (#t if the element is prepended to the subsequence, #f if it is not prepended), then for each subsequence (such as (list 'alpha 'gamma)) there is a corresponding list of Boolean values (in this case, (list #t #f #t #f)—that is: "Prepend alpha, don't prepend beta, prepend gamma, don't prepend delta"). The list that the ordered version of subsequences returns gives the subsequences in the lexicographic order of the corresponding lists of Booleans (assuming that #f precedes #t at each position).

This correspondence between subsequences of ls and lists of Boolean values is interesting in its own right. We can write procedures to compute it easily, in either direction:

```
(define subsequence->list-of-Booleans
  (curry (rec (constructor ls subseq)
          (if (empty-list? ls)
              (list)
              (if (and (non-empty-list? subseq)
                       (equal? (first ls) (first subseq)))
                  (prepend #t (constructor (rest ls) (rest subseq)))
                  (prepend #f (constructor (rest ls) subseq)))))))

(define list-of-Booleans->subsequence
  (curry (rec (constructor ls bools)
          (if (empty-list? ls)
              (list)
              (let ((recursive-result (constructor (rest ls)
                                                   (rest bools))))
                (if (first bools)
                    (prepend (first ls) recursive-result)
                    recursive-result))))))
```

This gives us another way to obtain the subsequences of ls:

```
(define (subsequences ls)
  (map-bag (list-of-Booleans->subsequence ls)
           (Cartesian-power (bag #f #t) (length ls))))
```

We can also rank or unrank with respect to the order described above by composing the ranking and unranking operations for Cartesian powers of (list #f #t) with the transfer procedures just shown.

If we want only subsequences of a specified length, which we'll call *selections*, a different algorithm is called for. To get an idea of how it might work, let's look at the value of a sample call: (selections (list 'alpha 'beta 'gamma 'delta 'epsilon) 3) is

```
(bag (list 'alpha 'beta 'gamma)
     (list 'alpha 'beta 'delta)
     (list 'alpha 'beta 'epsilon)
     (list 'alpha 'gamma 'delta)
     (list 'alpha 'gamma 'epsilon)
     (list 'alpha 'delta 'epsilon)
     (list 'beta 'gamma 'delta)
     (list 'beta 'gamma 'epsilon)
     (list 'beta 'delta 'epsilon)
     (list 'gamma 'delta 'epsilon))
```

We can keep the idea of invoking bag-union to bring together selections that exclude the first element of the given list and selections that include it. The difference in this case is that the two bags must be constructed by separate recursive calls, since the first-element-including selections are formed by prepending the first element to *shorter* selections, while the first-element-excluding selections must already be of the desired size.

Keeping track of the desired length of the selection also means that there are two base cases for the recursion—one in which the given list is empty, and another in which the length of the selection is 0. The test for a zero-length selection comes first, since a zero-length selection can be made from any list, whether or not it is empty (the empty list is a zero-length selection from itself), while no selection of a positive length can be made from an empty list at all:

```
(define (selections ls len)
  (if (zero? len)
      (bag (list))
      (if (empty-list? ls)
          (bag)
          (bag-union (prepend-to-each (first ls)
                                      (selections (rest ls) (sub1 len)))
                     (selections (rest ls) len)))))
```

The ordered version of this algorithm returns a lexicographically ordered list of selections.

The number of selections of length k from a list of length n is the binomial coefficient $\binom{n}{k}$, which can be computed as

$$\frac{n \cdot (n-1) \cdot \cdots \cdot (n-k+1)}{k \cdot (k-1) \cdot \cdots \cdot 1}.$$

Since $\binom{n}{k} = \binom{n}{n-k}$ regardless of the values of n and k (selecting k values to keep from a list of n is exactly the same operation as selecting $n-k$ values to exclude from the same list), it's advantageous to choose the computation that entails fewer multiplications. The following definition incorporates this optimization:

```
(define (binomial n k)
  (let ((short (lesser k (- n k))))
    (div ((recur (sect < n <>) (constant 1) (dispatch identity add1) *)
          (add1 (- n short)))
         (factorial short))))
```

The procedure that recur constructs computes the numerator by generating and multiplying by each factor.

To establish the correctness of this count, look back at our definition of selections. The first base case, in which $k = 0$, yields exactly one selection, and both the numerator and the denominator of the binomial-coefficient expression in this case are "vacuous" products that evaluate to 1, so that $\binom{n}{0} = 1$ regardless of the value of n. The second base case, in which $n = 0$ and $k > 0$, yields no selections, and indeed the numerator of the binomial-coefficient expression in this case is a product in which the first factor is 0, so that $\binom{0}{k} = 0$ when $k > 0$. For the induction step, when n and k are both positive, the hypothesis of induction guarantees that the procedure constructs $\binom{n-1}{k-1}$ selections beginning with the first element of the given list, and $\binom{n-1}{k}$ selections not beginning with that element. By the definition of the binomial coefficient, then,

$$
\binom{n-1}{k-1} + \binom{n-1}{k}
$$

$$
= \frac{(n-1) \cdot (n-2) \cdots (n-1-(k-1)+1)}{(k-1) \cdot (k-2) \cdots 1}
$$

$$
+ \frac{(n-1) \cdot (n-2) \cdots (n-1-k+1)}{k \cdot (k-1) \cdots 1}
$$

$$
= \frac{(n-1) \cdot (n-2) \cdots (n-k+1)}{(k-1) \cdot (k-2) \cdots 1}
$$

$$
+ \frac{(n-1) \cdot (n-2) \cdots (n-k)}{k \cdot (k-1) \cdots 1}
$$

$$
= \frac{((n-1) \cdot (n-2) \cdots (n-k+1)) \cdot k}{k \cdot (k-1) \cdots 1}
$$

$$
+ \frac{((n-1) \cdot (n-2) \cdots (n-k+1)) \cdot (n-k)}{k \cdot (k-1) \cdots 1}
$$

$$
= \frac{((n-1) \cdot (n-2) \cdots (n-k+1)) \cdot (k+n-k)}{k \cdot (k-1) \cdots 1}
$$

$$
= \frac{n \cdot (n-1) \cdots (n-k+1)}{k \cdot (k-1) \cdots 1}
$$

$$
= \binom{n}{k}.
$$

Thus the binomial coefficient gives the correct count in every case.

We can use binomial coefficients to rank and unrank selections. In this case, it is best *not* to curry the procedures, since the recursive algorithms call for many different choices of `ls` and `len`.

The rank of a selection of length 0 is always 0. Otherwise, we compare the first element of the selection with the first element of the list from which it was selected. If they match, then the rank is the same as the rank of the rest of the selection among the one-shorter selections from the rest of the list. Otherwise, the selection must follow all of the selections beginning with the first element of the list, and we can use `binomial` to figure out how many of those there are. Adding to that count the rank of the selection among the same-length selections from the rest of the list gives us the rank of the selection in the entire list:

```
(define (selection-rank ls len selection)
  (if (zero? len)
      0
      (if (equal? (first selection) (first ls))
          (selection-rank (rest ls) (sub1 len) (rest selection))
          (+ (binomial (length (rest ls)) (sub1 len))
             (selection-rank (rest ls) len selection)))))
```

The logic of unranking is similar. If `len` is 0, the only possible selection is the empty list. Otherwise, we invoke `binomial` to figure out how many selections include the first element of `ls`. If the given rank is less than that number, then we commit to the first element of `ls` as the first element of the selection, and pass the rank along to the appropriate recursive call in order to pick up the rest of the elements; otherwise, we subtract the binomial coefficient from the rank and pass the difference along to the recursive call, ignoring the first element of `ls`.

```
(define (selection-unrank ls len rank)
  (if (zero? len)
      (list)
      (let ((count (binomial (length (rest ls)) (sub1 len))))
        (if (< rank count)
            (prepend (first ls)
                     (selection-unrank (rest ls) (sub1 len) rank))
            (selection-unrank (rest ls) len (- rank count))))))
```

---

suffixes   (afp products-and-selections)
$list(\alpha) \rightarrow bag(list(\alpha))$
ls
Construct a bag containing all of the suffixes of ls.

ordered-non-empty-suffixes   (afp products-and-selections)
$list(\alpha) \rightarrow list(list(\alpha))$
ls
Construct a lexicographically ordered list of all of the non-empty suffixes of ls.
Precondition: ls is ordered.

prefixes   (afp products-and-selections)
$list(\alpha)\ \to\ bag(list(\alpha))$
ls
Construct a bag containing all of the prefixes of ls.

non-empty-prefixes   (afp products-and-selections)
$list(\alpha)\ \to\ bag(list(\alpha))$
ls
Construct a bag containing all of the non-empty prefixes of ls.

sublists   (afp products-and-selections)
$list(\alpha)\ \to\ bag(list(\alpha))$
ls
Construct a bag containing all of the non-empty sublists of ls.

termial   (afp arithmetic)
$natural\text{-}number\ \to\ natural\text{-}number$
number
Compute the sum of the natural numbers up to and including number.

sublist-ranker   (afp products-and-selections)
$list(\alpha)\ \to\ (list(\alpha)\ \to\ natural\text{-}number)$
ls   subls
Construct the rank of subls in the lexicographically ordered list of non-empty sublists of ls.
Precondition: ls is ordered.
Precondition: subls is a sublist of ls.

antitermial   (afp arithmetic)
$natural\text{-}number\ \to\ natural\text{-}number,\ natural\text{-}number$
number
Compute the greatest natural number whose termial does not exceed number and the amount
by which number exceeds that termial.

sublist-unranker   (afp products-and-selections)
$list(\alpha)\ \to\ (natural\text{-}number\ \to\ list(\alpha))$
ls   rank
Construct a procedure that determines which of the sublists of ls is in position rank in the
lexicographic ordering of those sublists.
Precondition: ls is ordered.
Precondition: rank is less than the termial of the length of ls.

sections   (afp products-and-selections)
$list(\alpha),\ natural\text{-}number\ \to\ bag(list(\alpha))$
ls   len
Construct a bag containing the sections of ls of length len.
Precondition: len is less than or equal to the length of ls.

subsequences   (afp products-and-selections)
$list(\alpha)\ \to\ bag(list(\alpha))$
ls
Construct a bag containing the subsequences of ls, that is, the lists whose elements are drawn
from ls, appearing in the same relative order as in ls.

subsequence->list-of-Booleans   (afp products-and-selections)
$list(\alpha)\ \to\ (list(\alpha)\ \to\ list(Boolean))$
ls   subseq
Construct a procedure that, in turn, constructs the list of Boolean values that corresponds to
subseq, indicating at each position whether the element at that position in ls is included in
subseq.
Precondition: subseq is a subsequence of ls.

list-of-Booleans->subsequence   (afp products-and-selections)
$list(\alpha)\ \to\ (list(Boolean)\ \to\ list(\alpha))$
ls   bools
Construct a procedure that, in turn, constructs the subsequence of ls to which bools corre-

sponds, each element of bools indicating whether the element at the corresponding position in ls is included in the subsequence.
Precondition: The length of ls is equal to the length of bools.

selections   (afp products-and-selections)
$list(\alpha)$, *natural-number* $\rightarrow bag(list(\alpha))$
ls   len
Construct a bag containing all of the subsequences of ls of length len.
Precondition: len is less than or equal to the length of ls.

binomial   (afp arithmetic)
natural-number, natural-number $\rightarrow$ *natural-number*
n   k
Compute the binomial coefficient of n and k, that is, the number of distinct ways of choosing k objects from a collection of n distinguishable objects.
Precondition: k is less than or equal to n.

selection-rank   (afp products-and-selections)
$list(\alpha)$, *natural-number, $list(\alpha)$* $\rightarrow$ *natural-number*
ls   len   selection
Compute the rank of selection in the lexicographic ordering of all selections of length len from ls.
Precondition: ls is ordered.
Precondition: len is less than or equal to the length of ls.
Precondition: selection is a selection from ls, and its length is len.

selection-unrank   (afp products-and-selections)
$list(\alpha)$, *natural-number, natural-number* $\rightarrow list(\alpha)$
ls   len   rank
Construct the selection that is in position rank in the lexicographic ordering of all selections of ls of length len.
Precondition: ls is ordered.
Precondition: len is less than or equal to the length of ls.
Precondition: rank is less than or equal to the binomial coefficient of the length of ls and len.

Exercises

5.2–1   Prove that, for every natural number n, the termial of n is equal to $\binom{n}{2}$.

5.2–2   Define a procedure ordered-sublists that receives an ordered list and returns a list of its sublists, in lexicographic order.

5.2–3   Define a procedure with-trues that receives two natural numbers, n and t, and constructs a bag containing all the length-n lists of Boolean values in which exactly t of the elements are #t (and therefore exactly $n - t$ are #f). (It is a precondition of this procedure that $t \leq n$.)

5.2–4   Define a procedure lexrank-subsequence that computes the rank of a given subsequence in the *lexicographic* ordering of the subsequences of a given (ordered) list, and a procedure lexunrank-subsequence that constructs the subsequence of a given (ordered) list that has the given rank in the lexicographic ordering of its subsequences.

5.2–5   Define a procedure selection-source that receives an ordered list and a natural number less than or equal to the length of that list and returns a

finite source containing the selections of the specified length from that list, in
lexicographic order.

5.3   Bag Selections

Next, let's consider the possibilities for constructing combinatorial objects from
values extracted from a bag rather than a list, so that there is no initial order
to take into account. Just as the prepend-to-each procedure is a useful step in
many of the list constructions, the corresponding put-into-each-bag procedure
figures in several of the bag constructions that we'll consider below. It receives
a value and a bag of bags as arguments and returns a similar bag of bags, but
with the new value added to each one:

```
(define (put-into-each-bag new araro)
  (map-bag (sect put-into-bag new <>) araro))
```

The analogue of subsequences is the subbags procedure, which chooses values from a given bag in every possible way, returning a bag of the bags that
contain the choices. The algorithm that we used in defining subsequences also
underlies the definition of subbags: Given a non-empty bag, we use recursive
calls to form all the subbags that exclude a selected member, then add the selected member to each of those bags, and finally collect all the bags of both
kinds:

```
(define subbags
  (fold-bag (create (bag (bag)))
            (pipe (dispatch >next put-into-each-bag) bag-union)))
```

We may want to specify the size of each of the subbags that we're interested
in (just as we specified the sizes of sections and selections in §5.2). In this
case, the subbag is a *combination*, in the mathematical sense. The definition
of the combinations procedure is again analogous to that of the selections
procedure:

```
(define (combinations aro size)
  (if (zero? size)
      (bag (bag))
      (if (empty-bag? aro)
          (bag)
          (receive (chosen others) (take-from-bag aro)
            (bag-union (put-into-each-bag chosen
                                          (combinations others
                                                        (sub1 size)))
                       (combinations others size))))))
```

As with other combinatorial constructions, it is often useful to return a source that generates the combinations of a given size, drawn from a given bag, rather than a bag in which they are all explicitly constructed:

```
(define (combinations-source aro size)
  (if (zero? size)
      (finite-source (bag))
      (if (empty-bag? aro)
          (finite-source)
          (source (receive (chosen others) (take-from-bag aro)
                    (tap (catenate-sources
                           (map-finite-source
                             (sect put-into-bag chosen <>)
                             (combinations-source others (sub1 size)))
                           (combinations-source others size)))))))))
```

---

put-into-each-bag   (afp bags)
α, $bag(bag(\alpha))$ $\rightarrow$ $bag(bag(\alpha))$
new araro
Construct a bag of bags, similar to araro except that new has been added to each of the bags in it.

subbags   (afp products-and-selections)
$bag(\alpha)$ $\rightarrow$ $bag(bag(\alpha))$
aro
Construct a bag containing all of the bags that can be formed from values in aro.

combinations   (afp products-and-selections)
$bag(\alpha)$, natural-number $\rightarrow$ $bag(bag(\alpha))$
aro   size
Construct a bag containing all of the bags of cardinality size that can be formed from values in aro.
Precondition: size is less than or equal to the cardinality of aro.

combinations-source   (afp products-and-selections)
$bag(\alpha)$, natural-number $\rightarrow$ $source(bag(\alpha))$
aro   size
Construct a source containing all of the bags of cardinality size that can be formed from values in aro.
Precondition: size is less than or equal to the cardinality of aro.

Exercises

5.3–1   Define a procedure subsets that constructs a bag containing all of the subsets of a given set.

5.3–2   Define a procedure subbags-source that constructs a finite source containing all of the subbags of a given bag.

5.3–3   If a bag contains numbers, its *weight* is the sum of those numbers. Define a procedure weight-limited-subbags that receives as arguments a bag B of natural numbers and a natural number n and returns a bag containing all of the subbags of B whose weight is less than or equal to n.

5.4 Permutations

Another common task is to construct all the *permutations* of the members of a bag, that is, the lists that can be constructed by arranging those members in various orders. (The number of occurrences of a value in such a list must be equal to its multiplicity in the bag.) For example, (permutations (bag 'alpha 'beta 'gamma 'delta)) is

```
(bag (list 'alpha 'beta 'gamma 'delta)
     (list 'alpha 'beta 'delta 'gamma)
     (list 'alpha 'gamma 'beta 'delta)
     (list 'alpha 'gamma 'delta 'beta)
     (list 'alpha 'delta 'beta 'gamma)
     (list 'alpha 'delta 'gamma 'beta)
     (list 'beta 'alpha 'gamma 'delta)
     (list 'beta 'alpha 'delta 'gamma)
     (list 'beta 'gamma 'alpha 'delta)
     (list 'beta 'gamma 'delta 'alpha)
     (list 'beta 'delta 'alpha 'gamma)
     (list 'beta 'delta 'gamma 'alpha)
     (list 'gamma 'alpha 'beta 'delta)
     (list 'gamma 'alpha 'delta 'beta)
     (list 'gamma 'beta 'alpha 'delta)
     (list 'gamma 'beta 'delta 'alpha)
     (list 'gamma 'delta 'alpha 'beta)
     (list 'gamma 'delta 'beta 'alpha)
     (list 'delta 'alpha 'beta 'gamma)
     (list 'delta 'alpha 'gamma 'beta)
     (list 'delta 'beta 'alpha 'gamma)
     (list 'delta 'beta 'gamma 'alpha)
     (list 'delta 'gamma 'alpha 'beta)
     (list 'delta 'gamma 'beta 'alpha))
```

The empty list is the only permutation of the empty bag. To construct the permutations of a non-empty bag, we take out each of its members in turn and prepend it to each permutation of the rest of the members, collecting all of the results in a bag. Apart from the special case in which the bag that it is given is empty, then, the permutations procedure works by folding over that bag, so that each of its members has a turn to be taken out and prepended to each of the permutations of the others.

```
(define (permutations aro)
  (if (empty-bag? aro)
      (bag (list))
      ((fold-bag bag
                 (lambda (chosen recursive-result)
                   (receive (ignored others)
                            (extract-from-bag (equal-to chosen) aro)
                     (bag-union (prepend-to-each chosen
                                                 (permutations others))
                                recursive-result))))
       aro)))
```

In the ordered version of this procedure, which receives an ordered list rather than a bag and produces the permutations in lexicographic order, we'll extract an element from the list by position rather than by testing it with equal?. If a bag contains duplicate values, it makes no difference which one of the duplicates is removed by any invocation of extract-from-bag. But if a list contains duplicate values, it may make a difference in the result which of them we extract, depending on the nature of the ordering. (Actually, this can't happen inside the afp libraries, because no equality predicate available within afp distinguishes values more finely than equal? does. But the *Revised*[7] *Report on the Algorithmic Language Scheme* supports some other equality predicates, such as eq?, that examine the locations in memory that values occupy, and hence can distinguish values that are located in different places, even if equal? counts them as the same.)

Our extraction procedure, then, will be all-but-position, which constructs a list comprising all of the elements of a given list except the one at a given position:

```
(define (all-but-position ls position)
  (if (zero? position)
      (rest ls)
      (prepend (first ls)
               (all-but-position (rest ls) (sub1 position)))))
```

Thus the ordered version of permutations is

```
(define (ordered-permutations ls)
  (let ((len (length ls)))
    (if (zero? len)
        (list (list))
        ((rec (recurrer position)
           (if (= position len)
               (list)
               (catenate
                (prepend-to-each (list-ref ls position)
                                 (ordered-permutations
                                  (all-but-position ls position)))
```

```
                        (recurrer (add1 position)))))
          0))))
```

Given the recursive structure of the natural numbers (§2.9), it is more usual to start a recursion at some natural number and run it down to 0. Here we proceed in the opposite direction, starting at 0 and running up to len, in order to place the permutations that begin with the initial element of the given list at the beginning of the result list.

We can also write a version that produces a source to provide the permutations in lexicographic order, constructing each one only when and if it is needed:

```
(define (ordered-permutations-source ls)
  (let ((len (length ls)))
    (if (zero? len)
        (finite-source (list))
        ((rec (recurrer position)
           (if (= position len)
               (finite-source)
               (source
                 (let ((prepender
                         (ordered-prepend-to-each-source
                           (list-ref ls position)
                           (ordered-permutations-source
                             (all-but-position ls position)))))
                   (tap (catenate-sources
                          prepender
                          (recurrer (add1 position))))))))))
       0))))
```

Ranking and Unranking

To compute the rank of a permutation p in the lexicographic ordering of all of the permutations of an ordered list, we use the position k of its first element e in the original ordered list to calculate how many permutations begin with elements that precede e. If n is the length of the original ordered list, then there are (factorial n) permutations in all, and (factorial (sub1 n)) that begin with a specific element. Hence there are (* k (factorial (sub1 n))) permutations that begin with elements that precede e in the original list, and so that number is the lower bound for the rank of a permutation that begins with e.

To this lower bound, we should add the number of permutations that precede p within the block of permutations that begin with e. But this number is equal to the rank of (rest p) among the permutations of (all-but-position p k). This suggests a recursive strategy, implemented in the following definition. (In the base case, both the permutation and the ordered list are empty, so the rank of the permutation is obviously 0.)

```
(define (permutation-rank ls perm)
  (if (empty-list? ls)
      0
      (let ((position (position-in (first perm) ls)))
        (+ (* position (factorial (sub1 (length ls))))
           (permutation-rank (all-but-position ls position)
                             (rest perm))))))
```

The unranking algorithm uses the same arithmetical idea: Identify the first element, e, of the sought permutation by figuring out how many blocks of (`factorial (sub1 n)`) permutations precede it and using the result as an index into the original list. The remainder is the rank of the rest of the permutation within the block beginning with e, so use a recursive call to construct it:

```
(define (permutation-unrank ls rank)
  (if (empty-list? ls)
      (list)
      (receive (position subrank)
               (div-and-mod rank (factorial (sub1 (length ls))))
        (prepend (list-ref ls position)
                 (permutation-unrank (all-but-position ls position)
                                     subrank)))))
```

---

permutations   (afp permutations)
$bag(\alpha) \rightarrow bag(list(\alpha))$
aro
Construct a bag containing every list that can be formed from the values in aro, using each value exactly once.

all-but-position   (afp lists)
$list(\alpha),\ natural\text{-}number \rightarrow list(\alpha)$
ls   position
Construct a list comprising all of the elements of ls except the one at position position.
Precondition: ls is not empty.
Precondition: position is less than the length of ls.

ordered-permutations   (afp permutations)
$list(\alpha) \rightarrow list(list(\alpha))$
ls
Construct a list containing all the permutations of ls, in lexicographic order.
Precondition: ls is ordered.

ordered-permutations-source   (afp permutations)
$list(\alpha) \rightarrow source(list(\alpha))$
ls
Construct a finite source containing all the permutations of ls, in lexicographic order.
Precondition: ls is ordered.

permutation-rank   (afp permutations)
$list(\alpha),\ list(\alpha) \rightarrow natural\text{-}number$
ls   perm
Compute the rank of perm in the lexicographic ordering of the permutations of ls.
Precondition: ls is ordered.
Precondition: perm is a permutation of ls.

permutation-unrank   (afp permutations)
list(α), natural-number $\rightarrow$ *list(α)*
ls   rank
Construct the permutation that is in position rank in the lexicographic ordering of the permutations of ls.
Precondition: ls is ordered.
Precondition: rank is less than the factorial of the length of ls.

Exercises

5.4–1   An *inversion* in a permutation p of an ordered list is a pair of distinct elements that are "out of order," so that the element that has a lesser position in p does not bear the ordering relation to the other element. Define a procedure inversions that receives a list and an ordering relation and computes the number of inversions in that list with respect to that ordering relation.

5.4–2   An *even permutation* of an ordered list is one in which the number of inversions is even. Define a procedure even-permutations that receives an ordered list and returns a list of its even permutations, in lexicographic order. (One could generate all permutations and then use filter to extract the even ones, but it is better to generate just the even ones to begin with.)

5.4–3   Here is an alternative strategy for constructing the permutations of the values in a given bag of cardinality n:

- If the bag is empty ($n = 0$), return (bag (list)).

- Otherwise, invoke take-from-bag to obtain a value, chosen, and a bag, others, containing the rest of the values.

- Call this procedure recursively to obtain a bag, other-perms, containing the permutations of others.

- For each of the $(n - 1)$-element lists in other-perms, insert chosen into that list at each possible position, to obtain n different lists of n elements: one in which chosen is at the beginning, another in which it is at position 1, and so on down to one in which chosen is at the end.

- Collect all of these n-element lists in a bag and return it.

Define an alternative-permutations procedure implementing this strategy.

5.4–4   We can obtain a version of the alternative-permutations procedure that returns an ordered list of permutations by substituting list operations for bag operations. However, the ordering of the permutations in the result-list is not lexicographic. Describe the ordering relation that the ordered version of alternative-permutations imposes and define ranking and unranking procedures for it.

5.5 Partitions

Bag Partitions

To *partition* a bag is to distribute the values it contains into non-empty subbags, so that taking the bag union of those subbags would reconstitute the original bag. For instance, if the given bag contains the symbols alpha, beta, gamma, and delta, one way to partition it is to distribute these symbols into three subbags, one containing only beta, one containing only gamma, and one containing alpha and delta. The order of the subbags is not significant. We'll also use the term "partition" to refer to a bag containing the subbags resulting from the distribution.

The rationale for requiring the subbags making up a partition to be non-empty is to avoid an unbounded proliferation of essentially similar partitions, differing only in how many copies of the empty bag they contain.

The goal of the combinatorial construction that we'll implement in the partitions procedure is to construct a bag containing all of the partitions of a given bag. Thus the value of (partitions aro) is (take a deep breath) a bag of bags of bags of values in aro. For instance, (partitions (bag 'alpha 'beta 'gamma 'delta)) is

```
(bag (bag (bag 'alpha) (bag 'beta) (bag 'gamma) (bag 'delta))
     (bag (bag 'alpha 'beta) (bag 'gamma) (bag 'delta))
     (bag (bag 'alpha 'gamma) (bag 'beta) (bag 'delta))
     (bag (bag 'alpha 'delta) (bag 'beta) (bag 'gamma))
     (bag (bag 'alpha) (bag 'beta 'gamma) (bag 'delta))
     (bag (bag 'alpha 'beta 'gamma) (bag 'delta))
     (bag (bag 'alpha 'delta) (bag 'beta 'gamma))
     (bag (bag 'alpha) (bag 'beta 'delta) (bag 'gamma))
     (bag (bag 'alpha 'beta 'delta) (bag 'gamma))
     (bag (bag 'alpha 'gamma) (bag 'beta 'delta))
     (bag (bag 'alpha) (bag 'beta) (bag 'gamma 'delta))
     (bag (bag 'alpha 'beta) (bag 'gamma 'delta))
     (bag (bag 'alpha 'gamma 'delta) (bag 'beta))
     (bag (bag 'alpha) (bag 'beta 'gamma 'delta))
     (bag (bag 'alpha 'beta 'gamma 'delta)))
```

To avoid confusion, not to mention vertigo, let's orient ourselves by numbering the levels here. Let's say that the particular values that we're shuffling around from aro into these subbags are "level-0" values. They could be values of any type (although we'll assume that equal? is an appropriate sameness criterion for them), but the partitions procedure is not even going to look at their type and will ignore any internal structure that they may have. In the example above, the level-0 values are the symbols alpha, beta, gamma, and delta.

Bags of level-0 values, such as aro itself and its subbags, are "level-1" values. Bags of level-1 values, such as a single partition of aro, are "level-2" values. Bags of level-2 values, such as the value of a call to partitions, are "level-3"

values: bags of bags of bags of level-0 values. The level number thus indicates
the number of layers of enclosure in bags.

When aro is the empty bag, it might seem at first that it is impossible to
form any partitions of it, but that turns out not to be correct: The empty bag
(considered as a level-2 value) is a partition of the empty bag (considered as a
level-1 value), because it is vacuously true that every level-0 value in the level-
1 empty bag can be distributed to a non-empty level-1 bag within the level-2
empty bag. The fact that the level-2 empty bag doesn't *have* any non-empty
level-1 bags in it is not an obstacle, since we never actually need to accommodate
a level-0 value from the level-1 empty bag (because there are none).

Since the level-2 empty bag is a valid partition of the level-1 empty bag, the
partitions procedure returns, in the base case, a level-3 bag containing only
the level-2 empty bag. That is: (partitions (bag)) is (bag (bag)).

Given a non-empty level-1 bag, the partitions procedure can pull out one
level-0 value and invoke itself recursively to obtain a level-3 bag containing all
of the partitions of the rest of the bag. Each of these partitions is a level-2
bag. Putting the extracted level-0 value into any level-1 bag in any of these
partitions yields a partition of aro as a whole, and adding a singleton level-1
bag containing only the extracted level-0 value to any of the partitions of the
rest of the bag also yields a partition of aro.

Let's build up gradually to the implementation of this operation. One of the
small steps involves removing a level-1 bag from a level-2 partition, so that we
can subsequently put the result of adding a level-0 value to that level-1 bag into
a new level-2 partition. We can use extract-from-bag to locate the level-1 bag,
keeping only the second result:

```
(define remove-bag-from-bag
  (run (~initial (curry bag=?)) extract-from-bag >next))
```

The ~initial adapter at the beginning of the pipeline replaces the level-1 bag
with a unary procedure that can be satisfied only by something that bears bag=?
to it. This is the procedure that extract-from-bag applies to each of the values
in the level-2 bag, in order to find and extract the matching level-1 bag. The
postprocessing adapter >next discards the level-1 bag and returns the level-2
bag resulting from the extraction.

The extend-partition procedure receives a level-0 value and one of the
level-2 partitions of the rest of aro and returns a level-3 bag containing all the
partitions of aro that can be formed from them in either of the ways described
above. The call to map-bag carries out the extensions that involve putting new
into one of the level-1 bags inside the level-2 partition araro. The other calls
to put-into-bag take care of the other kind of extension, the one that adds the
singleton bag containing new as a new component of the partition:

```
(define (extend-partition new araro)
  (put-into-bag (put-into-bag (bag new) araro)
```

```
            (map-bag (pipe (dispatch
                              (sect put-into-bag new <>)
                              (sect remove-bag-from-bag <> araro))
                       put-into-bag)
                araro)))
```

Every partition of a bag can be formed in one and only one of these ways from some partition of the rest of the bag, so it is now straightforward to code partitions:

```
(define partitions
  (fold-bag (create (bag (bag)))
            (run (~initial (curry extend-partition))
                 map-bag
                 (fold-bag bag bag-union))))
```

The outer call to fold-bag runs through the level-0 values in the given bag, supplying each as the new argument in a call to extend-partitions. In the base case, where the given bag is empty, a level-3 bag containing an empty level-2 bag is returned, as described above. In the recursive case, the preprocessing adapter (~initial (curry extend-partition)) constructs the appropriate mapping procedure, which map-bag applies to each partition in the result of the recursive call. The postprocessing adapter applies bag-union along the bag that map-bag returns (which is a level-4 bag!) to collect the extended partitions into one big level-3 bag.

Note that, if the original level-1 bag contains duplicate values, there will be duplicates among the partitions as well.

Partitioning Natural Numbers

The term "partition" is also applied to a related (but simpler) operation on natural numbers: A partition of n is a bag of positive integers whose sum is n. For instance, the partitions of 5 are

```
(bag 1 1 1 1 1)
(bag 2 1 1 1)
(bag 2 2 1)
(bag 3 1 1)
(bag 3 2)
(bag 4 1)
(bag 5)
```

The connection to bag partitions is that the partitions of n give the possible cardinalities of the subbags in a partition of a bag of cardinality n.

It's easiest to define a procedure that constructs the partitions of a given natural number in two stages, beginning with a procedure that constructs partitions under a constraint on the greatest values in those partitions. The `bounded-number-partitions` receives the number that we want to partition and an upper bound on the values that the partitions may contain, and returns a bag containing just those partitions:

```
(define (bounded-number-partitions number bound)
  (if (zero? number)
      (bag (bag))
      (if (zero? bound)
          (bag)
          (if (< number bound)
              (bounded-number-partitions number (sub1 bound))
              (bag-union (bounded-number-partitions number (sub1 bound))
                  (map-bag (sect put-into-bag bound <>)
                      (bounded-number-partitions
                          (- number bound) bound)))))))
```

The advantage of defining `bounded-number-partitions` first is that we can use bound as a guide to the recursion. There are two base cases. If number is 0, then the only partition is the empty bag, no matter what bound is; so we return a bag containing just that partition. If number is positive but bound is 0, then no partition respecting the bound is possible, so we return an empty bag. In the recursive case, we first look to see whether number is strictly less than bound. If it is, then there are no partitions that include bound, so we can reduce the upper bound to (`sub1 bound`) without losing any—the recursive invocation will compute them all. In the remaining case, where number is not less than bound, there will be two kinds of partitions: those that do not include bound at all, which we can get from a recursive call in which we reduce the upper bound to (`sub1 bound`), and those that include at least one copy of bound, which we can get by adding bound to every partition of (`- number bound`) with the same upper bound.

The `number-partitions` procedure itself is the special case of `bounded-number-partitions` in which the upper bound is the number to be partitioned, so that initially the constraint is completely unrestrictive (no partition of n will contain values greater than n in any case):

```
(define (number-partitions number)
  (bounded-number-partitions number number))
```

---

remove-bag-from-bag   (afp bags)
$bag(\alpha),\ bag(bag(\alpha))\ \rightarrow\ bag(bag(\alpha))$
aro   araro
Construct a bag of bags, similar to araro except that aro (if present in araro) has been removed.

extend-partition   (afp partitions)
$\alpha,\ bag(bag(\alpha))\ \rightarrow\ bag(bag(bag(\alpha)))$
new araro
Construct a bag containing variations of araro. In each variation, new has either been put

into one of the elements of araro or (in one case) put into a bag by itself, and this bag put into a bag with the elements of araro.

partitions   (afp partitions)
bag(α) → *bag(bag(bag(α)))*
aro
Construct a bag containing all of the partitions of aro, each partition being a bag containing the subbags of aro into which the values in aro have been distributed.

bounded-number-partitions   (afp partitions)
natural-number, natural-number → *bag(bag(natural-number))*
number   bound
Construct a bag containing all of the partitions of number in which each value is less than or equal to bound.

number-partitions   (afp partitions)
natural-number → *bag(bag(natural-number))*
number
Construct a bag containing the partitions of number: bags of positive integers that add up to number.

Exercises

5.5–1 Compute by hand the partitions of (bag 0 1 2 3 4). (Hint: There are fifty-two of them.)

5.5–2 There is a correspondence between the partitions of a given bag and the equivalence relations with that bag as their domain: Two values are in the same subbag if and only if they bear the equivalence relation to each other. Write a procedure induced-partition that receives a bag and an equivalence relation and returns the partition of the bag that corresponds to that equivalence relation, restricted to the domain of values in the bag. (For instance, the value of '(induced-partition (bag 0 1 2 3) same-by-parity?)' is (bag (bag 0 2) (bag 1 3)).)

5.5–3 Compute by hand the partitions of 8.

5.5–4 Define a procedure number-partition-count that computes the number of partitions of a given number. (One could do this by generating a bag of those partitions and then taking its cardinality. Use recursion and arithmetic instead.)

5.5–5 Define a procedure fixed-size-number-partitions that receives two natural numbers m and n as arguments and returns a bag containing all of the partitions of n of cardinality m. (One could do this by generating all the partitions of n and filtering to get the partitions of the correct cardinality, but that would be inelegant and inefficient. Use recursion over m to construct only partitions of the specified cardinality.)

Chapter 6

Graphs

A *graph* is a data structure that expresses a relation between values that are members of some finite domain. Graphs are more elaborate structures than most of those that we've seen, and there are many procedures even for common operations such as construction and selection. As usual, we'll implement a model of graphs by choosing a small number of these as elementary, relying on the internal structure of our model. We can then define all of the other graph procedures in terms of these, abstracting from the implementation.

6.1   Implementing Graphs

The values in the domain of a graph are called the *vertices* of the graph. When a vertex u bears the relation to a vertex v within a graph, we say that there is an *arc* from u to v. In some graphs, an additional value is associated with each arc. This associated value is the arc's *label* (or, when the value is a number, its *weight* or *cost*).

We'll represent graphs as a product type:

$$graph(\alpha, \beta) \;=\; set(\alpha) \times set(arc(\alpha, \beta)).$$

A graph is a pair in which the car is a set of values (the vertices) and the cdr a set of arcs connecting those vertices. Here α is the type of the vertices and β is the type of the arc labels, if any.

The Scheme implementation is trivial:

```
(define make-graph cons)

(define vertices car)

(define arcs cdr)
```

© Springer-Verlag GmbH Germany, part of Springer Nature 2018
J. D. Stone, *Algorithms for Functional Programming*,
https://doi.org/10.1007/978-3-662-57970-1_6

There is no need to specify or constrain the nature of vertices—any value can be a vertex—but we'll need an explicit implementation of arcs. We'll model each arc as a tuple comprising the *tail* and *head* of the arc, which are the vertices at which the arc begins and ends (that is, the vertex that bears the relation, and the vertex to which it bears that relation, respectively), and its label:

$$arc(\alpha,\ \beta)\ =\ \alpha \times \alpha \times \beta.$$

By convention, we'll put the null value in the label field of an arc that has no label. The constructor `make-arc`, the selectors `arc-tail`, `arc-head`, `arc-label`, and `dearc`, the type predicate `arc?`, and the equality predicate `arc=?` are defined by the technique described in §3.9. We'll assume that `equal?` is a satisfactory criterion of sameness for vertices and labels:

```
(define-record-type arc
  (make-arc tail head label)
  arc?
  (tail arc-tail)
  (head arc-head)
  (label arc-label))

(define dearc (dispatch arc-tail arc-head arc-label))

(define arc=? (^and (compare-by arc-tail equal?)
                    (compare-by arc-head equal?)
                    (compare-by arc-label equal?)))
```

As an illustration of some of the arc procedures, consider the predicate `same-endpoints?`, which determines whether two arcs have the same head and the same tail (regardless of their labels):

```
(define same-endpoints? (^et (compare-by arc-head equal?)
                             (compare-by arc-tail equal?)))
```

This predicate will be useful in building graphs, since ordinarily we wouldn't want two arcs in the same graph with the same tail and head even if they are differently labeled.

Another simple operation on arcs is `reverse-arc`, which swaps the head and tail of a given arc, constructing one that goes in the opposite direction:

```
(define reverse-arc (run dearc >exch make-arc))
```

The reverse of an arc is said to be *antiparallel* to it. More generally, two arcs are antiparallel if the head of each is the tail of the other (even if their labels are different).

The type predicate for graphs is satisfied only when its argument is a pair, the car of the pair is a set, and the cdr of the pair is a set of arcs. It also requires that the tail and head of each arc be members of the set of vertices and that no two members of the set of arcs have the same tail and head:

```
(define (graph? something)
  (and (pair? something)
       (let ((vertices-candidate (car something))
             (arcs-candidate (cdr something)))
         (and (set? vertices-candidate)
              ((set-of arc? same-endpoints?) arcs-candidate)
              (subset? (map-set arc-tail arcs-candidate)
                       vertices-candidate)
              (subset? (map-set arc-head arcs-candidate)
                       vertices-candidate)))))
```

The generic equality predicate for graphs tests whether its arguments have the same vertices (that is, whether their sets of vertices are equal as sets) and the same arcs (that is, whether their respective sets of arcs satisfy (set-of= arc=?)):

```
(define graph=? (^et (compare-by vertices set=?)
                     (compare-by arcs (set-of= arc=?))))
```

Note that in comparing arcs between graphs, our criterion of sameness is arc=?, so that graphs that differ only in the labels on their arcs still count as distinct. In the definition of graph?, on the other hand, we used a different criterion of sameness, same-endpoints?, to ensure that no graph contains two arcs with the same tail and the same head, regardless of whether their labels match.

Graph Construction

We can construct graphs by building them up one component at a time, as we have built up other data structures in previous sections.

An empty graph is, naturally, represented by a pair of empty sets. Invoking the empty-graph procedure generates one:

```
(define (empty-graph)
  (make-graph (set) ((set-maker same-endpoints?))))
```

We can extend a given graph either by adding a new vertex or by adding an arc from one existing vertex to another (or even to the same one—an arc can have the same vertex as its tail and its head).

When we add a vertex, we'll assume that initially it is unrelated to any other vertex in the graph, so that no arcs are added with it. Then the constructor needs only the new vertex and the graph to which it is to be added:

```
(define (add-vertex new-vertex graph)
  (make-graph (fast-put-into-set new-vertex (vertices graph))
              (arcs graph)))
```

It is a precondition of this procedure that `new-vertex` is not already a vertex of
`graph`; otherwise, we would have to use the slow version of `put-into-set`.

Sometimes we know all of the vertices for the graph we want to build before
we know the arcs. In that case, we might as well take the *arcless graph* on those
vertices as our starting point, instead of building it up one vertex at a time:

```
(define arcless-graph (sect make-graph <> ((set-maker same-endpoints?))))
```

When adding a new arc, we must specify both the tail and the head of the
arc, as well as its label:

```
(define (add-labeled-arc tail head label graph)
  (make-graph (vertices graph)
              (fast-put-into-set (make-arc tail head label)
                                 (arcs graph))))
```

It is a precondition of this procedure that `graph` does not already include an arc
from `tail` to `head` (even one that carries a different label). We also presuppose
that `tail` and `head` are vertices of the graph.

Adding an arc without a label is a special case of `add-labeled-arc`:

```
(define add-arc (sect add-labeled-arc <> <> null <>))
```

On occasion, we'll also need the operations of deleting a vertex or an arc
from a given graph. Arc deletion is easier, since we can simply filter out the
unwanted arc, identifying it by its endpoints:

```
(define (delete-arc tail head graph)
  (make-graph (vertices graph)
              (rem-set (^et (pipe arc-tail (equal-to tail))
                            (pipe arc-head (equal-to head)))
                       (arcs graph))))
```

The `delete-arc` procedure does not complain if asked to delete a non-existent
arc. It returns the given graph, unchanged, in such a case.

There will also be situations in which we want to replace some arc in a graph
with a new arc connecting the same vertices, but having a different label. This
operation consists of a deletion followed by an addition:

```
(define (replace-arc tail head label graph)
  (add-labeled-arc tail head label (delete-arc tail head graph)))
```

To delete a vertex, it is not sufficient to delete it from the graph's vertex
set. We must also go through the arcs and remove the ones in which the vertex
occurs as tail or head:

```
(define (delete-vertex delend graph)
  (let ((is-delend? (equal-to delend)))
    (make-graph (remp-set is-delend? (vertices graph))
                (remp-set (^vel (pipe arc-tail is-delend?)
                                (pipe arc-head is-delend?))
                          (arcs graph)))))
```

Again, deleting a vertex that is not present to begin with has no effect.

On occasion, we'll want to *restrict* a graph to a subset of its vertices, discarding all the vertices that are not in that subset and all of the arcs that begin or end at those vertices. The `restriction` procedure receives the subset and the graph to be restricted and returns the restricted graph. The idea is to fold over the set of vertices to be excluded, deleting each one:

```
(define (restriction keepers graph)
  ((fold-set (create graph) delete-vertex)
   (set-difference (vertices graph) keepers)))
```

Graphs and Relations

Since most of the relations that we've discussed in previous chapters have infinite domains, we've implemented them as binary predicates. When a relation has a finite domain, however, we can also use a graph to model it, and indeed we'll often want to switch back and forth between representing it as a predicate and as a graph. The `relation-graph` procedure receives the domain of a relation and a predicate expressing it and constructs the corresponding unlabeled graph, testing every possible pair of vertices to determine whether they should be connected by an arc:

```
(define (relation-graph domain relation)
  (let ((maybe-add-arc (lambda (tail head aro)
                         (if (relation tail head)
                             (fast-put-into-set (make-arc tail head null)
                                                aro)
                             aro))))
    (make-graph domain
                ((fold-set set
                           (lambda (tail arcs-so-far)
                             ((fold-set (create arcs-so-far)
                                        (sect maybe-add-arc tail <> <>))
                              domain)))
                 domain))))
```

Conversely, we can derive the predicate representation of a relation from its graph by having the predicate search through the graph's arcs:

```
(define (related-by graph)
  (lambda (tail head)
    (exists-in-set? (^et (pipe arc-tail (equal-to tail))
                         (pipe arc-head (equal-to head)))
                    (arcs graph))))
```

However, if we are doing many such searches, we can make the constructed predicate more efficient by preprocessing the arcs into an *adjacency representation*—a table in which the keys are the vertices of the graph and the entry with which a vertex is associated is a set of the heads of the arcs with that vertex as their tail:

```
(define (adjacency-representation graph)
  ((fold-set (create ((fold-set table
                                (sect fast-put-into-table <> (set) <>))
                      (vertices graph)))
             (lambda (arc tab)
               (table-update (arc-tail arc)
                             (sect fast-put-into-set (arc-head arc) <>)
                             tab)))
   (arcs graph)))
```

The related-by procedure can look up a tail vertex in this table, then search the associated list for the head vertex. (It is safe to use the result of the call to lookup without supplying a default value, since an adjacency representation has an entry for every vertex, even if it's an empty list.)

```
(define (related-by graph)
  (let ((adjacency (adjacency-representation graph)))
    (lambda (tail head)
      (member? head (lookup tail adjacency)))))
```

To illustrate the use of these procedures, let's implement a few common operations involving the construction of graphs.

The *complete graph* on a given set is the graph that has an (unlabeled) arc from each member to each member. It is simply the relation graph for the values? predicate, taking the given set as the domain:

```
(define complete-graph (sect relation-graph <> values?))
```

The *graph converse* of a graph G has the same vertices as G, but its arcs are the reverses of the arcs of G. With our low-level representation, we could define the procedure for computing the graph converse as

```
(define (graph-converse graph)
  (make-graph (vertices graph) (fast-map-set reverse-arc (arcs graph))))
```

In the case of an unlabeled graph, however, we could get the same result by applying the `converse` adapter to the predicate representing the relation:

```
(define (graph-converse graph)
  (relation-graph (vertices graph) (converse (related-by graph))))
```

Either version of the procedure could be applied to a labeled graph as well. The low-level construction preserves the labels, whereas the one using `relation-graph` replaces them with `null`.

The *complement* of a graph G is a graph that has the same vertices as G, but has an arc connecting vertices if and only if G does *not* have such an arc. Shifting representations makes it easy to define the procedure that computes the complement of a graph: We need only apply `^not` to the predicate representation:

```
(define (graph-complement graph)
  (relation-graph (vertices graph) (^not (related-by graph))))
```

If R and S are relations with the same domain, then the relational product of R and S is the relation that holds between values a and c in that domain when a bears R to some value b that, in turn, bears S to c. When the domain is finite, so that R and S are represented by graphs, the `graph-product` procedure computes the graph of their relational product:

```
(define (graph-product left right)
  (let ((left? (related-by left))
        (right? (related-by right))
        (domain (vertices left)))
    (relation-graph domain
                    (lambda (tail head)
                      (exists-in-set? (^et (sect left? tail <>)
                                           (sect right? <> head))
                                      domain)))))
```

Properties of Graphs

The properties of relations that we have discussed in §3.13 and §4.1 are computable when the domain of the relation is finite. For instance, if such a relation is given in the form of a graph, we can determine whether the relation is reflexive by checking whether there is an arc in the graph from each vertex to itself:

```
(define (reflexive? graph)
  (for-all-in-set? (pipe (adapter 0 0) (related-by graph))
                   (vertices graph)))
```

An irreflexive relation is one that nothing bears to itself. We can determine whether a relation with a finite domain is irreflexive by looking through its arcs, stopping if we find one that has the same vertex as its head and tail:

```
(define (irreflexive? graph)
  (not (exists-in-set? (pipe (dispatch arc-tail arc-head) equal?)
                       (arcs graph))))
```

A symmetric relation, as we saw in §3.13, is one that a value *a* bears to a value *b* only if *b* also bears it to *a*. We can test for this property by reversing every arc in the graph and comparing the result to the original set of arcs. The two sets are equal if and only if the graph is symmetric:

```
(define (symmetric? graph)
  (let ((connections (arcs graph)))
    ((set-of= arc=?) connections
                     (fast-map-set reverse-arc connections))))
```

This definition of symmetric? requires the arc from *a* to *b* and the arc from *b* to *a* to be identically labeled (or both unlabeled) in order for the graph to count as symmetric. Changing 'arc=?' to 'same-endpoints?' in the third line removes this requirement (so that labels are ignored completely).

At the opposite extreme, a relation is *asymmetric* if there are *no* values *a* and *b* such that *a* bears the relation to *b* and *b* also bears the relation to *a*. In the graph of an asymmetric relation, no two arcs are antiparallel. Accordingly, we'll compare arcs with the same-endpoints? predicate to begin with this time:

```
(define (asymmetric? graph)
  (let ((connections (arcs graph)))
    ((set-disjointness same-endpoints?) connections
                                        (fast-map-set reverse-arc
                                                      connections))))
```

Note that asymmetry is not the same thing as connexity, although the two properties are related: A relation *R* is connected if and only if its complement (^not *R*) is asymmetrical. Thus we can define the predicate connected? as

```
(define connected? (pipe graph-complement asymmetric?))
```

A relation *R* is transitive, as we saw in §3.13, if, for any values *a*, *b*, and *c* in its domain such that *a* bears *R* to *b* and *b* bears *R* to *c*, *a* also bears *R* to *c*. The graph-product procedure gives us an easy way to compute this:

```
(define (transitive? graph)
  ((set-subsethood same-endpoints?) (arcs (graph-product graph graph))
                                    (arcs graph)))
```

At the opposite extreme, a relation is *intransitive* if there are *no* values a, b, and c in its domain such that a bears R to b, b bears R to c, and a also bears R to c. Again, we can compute this by determining whether the graph of R and its relational product with itself are *disjoint*:

```
(define (intransitive? graph)
  ((set-disjointness same-endpoints?) (arcs (graph-product graph graph))
                                       (arcs graph)))
```

Certain combinations of these properties are particularly significant, as we have seen:

```
(define equivalence-relation? (^and reflexive? symmetric? transitive?))
```

```
(define ordering-relation? (^et connected? transitive?))
```

Additional Graph Accessors

Because of the richness of graph structures and the diversity of algorithms operating on them, several more ways of accessing their components are in common use.

Sometimes, for instance, we'll want to consider only the arcs that originate at a specified vertex in a graph:

```
(define (arcs-leaving tail graph)
  (filter-set (pipe arc-tail (equal-to tail)) (arcs graph)))
```

or, conversely, those that terminate at a specified vertex:

```
(define (arcs-arriving head graph)
  (filter-set (pipe arc-head (equal-to head)) (arcs graph)))
```

In many graph algorithms, we need to compute the set of *neighbors* of a given vertex u—the vertices at the other ends of the arcs that begin at u. One approach would be to extract those arcs with `arcs-leaving` and then recover their heads by mapping `arc-head` over the resulting set:

```
(define slow-neighbors
  (pipe arcs-leaving (sect fast-map-set arc-head <>)))
```

However, as in the design of the `related-by` procedure above, a procedure that finds the neighbors of a vertex is often invoked repeatedly, for different vertices in the same graph. As a result, it is usually more efficient to curry the procedure, receiving the graph argument first, building its adjacency representation just once, and returning a procedure that looks up the vertex it receives in that adjacency representation:

```
(define (neighbors graph)
  (let ((adjacency (adjacency-representation graph)))
    (sect lookup <> adjacency)))
```

Again, sometimes we'll need to recover the label associated with a particular arc in a graph, given only its tail and head. The `label-lookup` procedure receives a graph and returns a procedure, specialized to the given graph, for carrying out this search. If the search is successful, the constructed procedure returns the arc's label; if not, it returns #f, or some alternative default value provided as an (optional) second argument to `label-lookup`.

As with `related-by` and `neighbors`, it's useful to build an intermediate data structure to speed up the search. Adjacency representations omit everything about labels, so they won't quite do the job; but we can construct a similar table, again with the tail vertices as keys, in which the entries, rather than being sets, are themselves tables, associating head vertices with arc labels.

The implementation for the procedure to build the new data structure is therefore almost identical to the code for the `adjacency-representation` procedure:

```
(define (label-structure graph)
  ((fold-set (create
               ((fold-set table
                          (sect fast-put-into-table <> (table) <>))
                (vertices graph)))
             (lambda (arc tab)
               (table-update (arc-tail arc)
                             (sect fast-put-into-table (arc-head arc)
                                                       (arc-label arc)
                                                       <>)

                             tab)))
   (arcs graph)))
```

The procedure that `label-lookup` constructs then provides the interface to this data structure, performing the two-stage lookup and returning the result if it is successful, the default value if it is not:

```
(define (label-lookup graph . optional)
  (let ((label-table (label-structure graph)))
    (lambda (tail head)
      (apply lookup head (lookup tail label-table) optional))))
```

The *out-degree* of a vertex in a graph is the number of arcs of which that vertex is the tail—the cardinality of the set of the vertex's neighbors. Since we'll generally want to compute the out-degrees of a number of vertices in the same graph, the `out-degree` procedure is curried:

```
(define (out-degree graph)
  (pipe (neighbors graph) cardinality))
```

Similarly, the *in-degree* of a vertex is the number of arcs leading to it—the number of arcs of which it is the head. In this case, the graph's adjacency representation is not so helpful, so we'll use the direct approach of folding over the set of arcs, counting the ones that have the given vertex as the head:

```
(define (in-degree graph)
  (lambda (head)
    ((fold-set (create 0)
               (conditionally-combine (pipe arc-head (equal-to head))
                                      (pipe >next add1)))
     (arcs graph))))
```

Undirected Graphs

When a graph is irreflexive and symmetric, we can notionally collapse each pair of arcs connecting the same two vertices—one from a to b and the other from b to a—into an unoriented *edge*. If there are labels, we think of them in this context as attached to the edges of the graph rather than to the underlying arcs.

Formally, we think of the *edge* type as being defined by the equation

$$edge(\alpha, \beta) \;=\; set(\alpha) \times \beta$$

with the side constraint that only sets of cardinality 2 are permitted.

An *undirected graph*[1] is one that represents an irreflexive and symmetric relation on its vertices. The predicate undirected? determines whether a given graph is undirected:

```
(define undirected? (^et irreflexive? symmetric?))
```

In order to preserve symmetry, we'll perform incremental operations on undirected graphs one edge at a time (rather than one arc at a time, as with graphs generally). The add-labeled-edge procedure receives two existing vertices (assumed to be distinct), the label for the edge connecting them, and the graph in which they are vertices, and returns a graph to which the edge has been added:

```
(define (add-labeled-edge end-0 end-1 label graph)
  (add-labeled-arc end-0
                   end-1
                   label
                   (add-labeled-arc end-1 end-0 label graph)))
```

The add-edge procedure adds an unlabeled edge:

```
(define add-edge (sect add-labeled-edge <> <> null <>))
```

---

[1]Some authorities apply the word "graph" only to what we are calling undirected graphs, using the term "digraph" or "directed graph" for what we are calling graphs.

Similarly, we can delete an edge from a graph by deleting the two underlying arcs, again preserving symmetry:

```
(define (delete-edge end-0 end-1 graph)
  (delete-arc end-0 end-1 (delete-arc end-1 end-0 graph)))
```

When considering an edge in isolation, we'll represent it as a tuple with two fields, respectively containing the set of its endpoints and its label. (The constructor is make-edge, the selectors are edge-endpoints, edge-label, and deedge, the classification predicate is edge?, and the equality predicate is edge=?.) As remarked above, the set occupying the endpoints field must have exactly two members.

```
(define-record-type edge
  (make-edge endpoints label)
  proto-edge?
  (endpoints edge-endpoints)
  (label edge-label))

(define deedge (dispatch edge-endpoints edge-label))

(define edge?
  (^et proto-edge?
       (pipe edge-endpoints
             (^et set? (pipe cardinality (sect = <> 2))))))

(define edge=?
  (^et (compare-by edge-endpoints set=?)
       (compare-by edge-label equal?)))
```

The ends selector returns the endpoints of an edge as separate values rather than as a set:

```
(define ends (pipe edge-endpoints deset))
```

The edges procedure constructs the set of edges of an undirected graph by running through the arcs of the underlying directed graph. As we encounter each one, we convert it into an edge and add it to the result, then remove both it and the reverse arc from further consideration:

```
(define (edges graph)
  ((rec (edger aro)
     (if (empty-set? aro)
         (set)
         (receive (chosen others) (take-from-set aro)
           (receive (end-0 end-1 label) (dearc chosen)
             (fast-put-into-set
               (make-edge (set end-0 end-1) label)
```

```
        (edger (remp (^et (pipe arc-tail (equal-to end-1))
                          (pipe arc-head (equal-to end-0)))
                     others)))))))
 (arcs graph)))
```

In an undirected graph, symmetry guarantees that the in-degree of each vertex is equal to its out-degree, and the neutral term degree applies to the number of edges of which a given vertex is an endpoint:

```
(define degree out-degree)
```

---

make-graph   (afp graphs)
$set(\alpha),\ set(arc(\alpha,\ \beta))\ \rightarrow graph(\alpha,\ \beta)$
verts   sagaro
Construct a graph with the members of verts as its vertices and the members of sagaro as its arcs.
Precondition: The endpoints of every member of sagaro are members of verts.

vertices   (afp graphs)
$graph(\alpha,\ any)\ \rightarrow set(\alpha)$
graph
Return a set containing the vertices of graph.

arcs   (afp graphs)
$graph(\alpha,\ \beta)\ \rightarrow set(arc(\alpha,\ \beta))$
graph
Return a set containing the arcs of graph.

make-arc   (afp graphs)
$\alpha,\quad \alpha,\quad \beta\qquad \rightarrow arc(\alpha,\ \beta)$
tail head label
Construct an arc with tail as its tail, head as its head, and label as its label.

arc-tail   (afp graphs)
$arc(\alpha,\ any)\ \rightarrow \alpha$
sago
Return the tail of sago.

arc-head   (afp graphs)
$arc(\alpha,\ any)\ \rightarrow \alpha$
sago
Return the head of sago.

arc-label   (afp graphs)
$arc(any,\ \alpha)\ \rightarrow \alpha$
sago
Return the label of sago.

dearc   (afp graphs)
$arc(\alpha,\ \beta)\ \rightarrow \alpha,\ \alpha,\ \beta$
sago
Return the components of sago, namely, its tail, head, and label, in that order.

arc?   (afp graphs)
$any\qquad \rightarrow Boolean$
something
Determine whether something is an arc.

arc=?   (afp graphs)
$arc(any,\ any),\ arc(any,\ any)\ \rightarrow Boolean$
left   right

Determine whether left and right are the same arc, that is, whether they have the same tail, the same head, and the same label.

same-endpoints?   (afp graphs)
arc(any, any), arc(any, any) → *Boolean*
left   right
Determine whether left and right have the same head and the same tail.

reverse-arc   (afp graphs)
arc(α, β) → *arc(α, β)*
revertend
Construct an arc similar to revertend, but with its endpoints reversed.

graph?   (afp graphs)
any   → *Boolean*
something
Determine whether something is a graph.

graph=?   (afp graphs)
graph(any, any), graph(any, any) → *Boolean*
left   right
Determine whether left and right are the same graph.

empty-graph   (afp graphs)
→ *graph(any, any)*
Construct an empty graph.

add-vertex   (afp graphs)
α,   graph(α, β) → *graph(α, β)*
new-vertex graph
Construct a graph similar to graph. except that it has new-vertex as a vertex.
Precondition: new-vertex is not a vertex of graph.

arcless-graph   (afp graphs)
set(α) → *graph(α, any)*
verts
Construct a graph with the members of verts as its vertices and no arcs.

add-labeled-arc   (afp graphs)
α,   α,   β,   graph(α, β) → *graph(α, β)*
tail head label graph
Construct a graph similar to graph, except that it includes an arc with tail, head, and label as its components.
Precondition: tail is a vertex of graph.
Precondition: head is a vertex of graph.
Precondition: graph contains no arc with tail as its tail and head as its head.

add-arc   (afp graphs)
α,   α,   graph(α, null) → *graph(α, null)*
tail head graph
Construct a graph similar to graph, except that it includes an unlabeled arc with tail as its tail and head as its head.
Precondition: tail is a vertex of graph.
Precondition: head is a vertex of graph.
Precondition: graph contains no arc with tail as its tail and head as its head.

delete-arc   (afp graphs)
α,   α,   graph(α, β) → *graph(α, β)*
tail head graph
Construct a graph similar to graph, but containing no arc with tail as its tail and head as its head.

replace-arc   (afp graphs)
α,   α,   β,   graph(α, β) → *graph(α, β)*
tail head label graph
Construct a graph similar to graph, but containing an arc with tail, head, and label as its

components, and no other arc with `tail` as its tail and `head` as its head.
Precondition: `tail` is a vertex of graph.
Precondition: `head` is a vertex of graph.

delete-vertex (afp graphs)
α, $graph(\alpha, \beta)$ → $graph(\alpha, \beta)$
delend graph
Construct a graph similar to graph, but not containing delend as a vertex, nor any arcs with delend as an endpoint.

restriction (afp graphs)
$set(\alpha)$, $graph(\alpha, \beta)$ → $graph(\alpha, \beta)$
keepers graph
Construct a graph similar to graph, but not containing any vertex that is not a member of keepers, nor any arc with an endpoint that is not a member of keepers.

relation-graph (afp graphs)
$set(\alpha)$, $(\alpha, \alpha \to Boolean)$ → $graph(\alpha, null)$
domain relation
Construct a graph with the members of domain as its vertices, having an unlabeled arc from one vertex to another if and only if those vertices (in that order) satisfy relation.
Precondition: relation can accept any members of domain.

adjacency-representation (afp graphs)
$graph(\alpha, \beta)$ → $table(\alpha, set(\alpha))$
graph
Construct the adjacency representation of the arcs of graph.

related-by (afp graphs)
$graph(\alpha, \beta)$ → $(\alpha, \quad \alpha \quad \to Boolean)$
graph $\qquad$ tail head
Construct a predicate that determines whether there is an arc from `tail` to `head` in graph.

complete-graph (afp graphs)
$set(\alpha)$ → $graph(\alpha, null)$
aro
Construct the complete graph on aro.

graph-converse (afp graphs)
$graph(\alpha, \beta)$ → $graph(\alpha, \beta)$
graph
Construct a graph similar to graph, but with all of its arcs reversed.

graph-complement (afp graphs)
$graph(\alpha, any)$ → $graph(\alpha, null)$
graph
Compute the complement of graph.

graph-product (afp graphs)
$graph(\alpha, any)$, $graph(\alpha, any)$ → $graph(\alpha, null)$
left $\qquad$ right
Compute the graph of the relational product of left and right.
Precondition: The vertices of left and the vertices of right are the same set.

reflexive? (afp graphs)
$graph(any, any)$ → $Boolean$
graph
Determine whether graph expresses a reflexive relation.

irreflexive? (afp graphs)
$graph(any, any)$ → $Boolean$
graph
Determine whether graph expresses an irreflexive relation.

symmetric? (afp graphs)
$graph(any, any)$ → $Boolean$
graph

Determine whether graph expresses a symmetric relation.

asymmetric?   (afp graphs)
graph(any, any) → Boolean
graph
Determine whether graph expresses an asymmetric relation, that is, whether no two arcs in graph have the same endpoints.

connected?   (afp graphs)
graph(any, any) → Boolean
graph
Determine whether graph expresses a connected relation.

transitive?   (afp graphs)
graph(any, any) → Boolean
graph
Determine whether graph expresses a transitive relation.

intransitive?   (afp graphs)
graph(any, any) → Boolean
graph
Determine whether graph expresses an intransitive relation.

equivalence-relation?   (afp graphs)
graph(any, any) → Boolean
graph
Determine whether graph expresses an equivalence relation.

ordering-relation?   (afp graphs)
graph(any, any) → Boolean
graph
Determine whether graph expresses an ordering relation on its vertices.

arcs-leaving   (afp graphs)
α,   graph(α, β) → set(arc(α, β))
tail graph
Construct the set of arcs in graph originating at tail.

arcs-arriving   (afp graphs)
α,   graph(α, β) → set(arc(α, β))
head graph
Construct the set of arcs in graph terminating at head.

neighbors   (afp graphs)
graph(α, β) → (α   → set(α))
graph   tail
Construct a procedure that, in turn, constructs the set of neighbors of tail in graph.
Precondition: tail is a vertex of graph.

label-structure   (afp graphs)
graph(α, β) → table(α, table(α, β))
graph
Construct a table in which the keys are the vertices of graph and the entries are themselves tables in which the keys are again the vertices of graph and the entries are the labels on the arcs in graph.

label-lookup   (afp graphs)
graph(α, β), β ...   → (α,   α   → β | Boolean)
graph   optional   tail head
Construct a procedure that searches for the label of an arc in graph that has tail as its tail and head as its head. If the search is successful, the procedure returns the label; otherwise, it returns the initial element of optional, or #f if optional is empty.
Precondition: tail is a vertex of graph.
Precondition: head is a vertex of graph.

out-degree   (afp graphs)

$graph(\alpha, any) \rightarrow (\alpha \rightarrow natural\text{-}number)$
graph   tail

Construct a procedure that computes the number of arcs in graph having tail as their tail.
Precondition: tail is a vertex of graph.

in-degree   (afp graphs)

$graph(\alpha, any) \rightarrow (\alpha \rightarrow natural\text{-}number)$
graph   head

Construct a procedure that computes the number of arcs in graph having head as their head.
Precondition: head is a vertex of graph.

undirected?   (afp graphs)

$graph(any, any) \rightarrow Boolean$
graph

Determine whether graph is undirected.

add-labeled-edge   (afp graphs)

$\alpha, \quad \alpha, \quad \beta, \quad graph(\alpha, \beta) \rightarrow graph(\alpha, \beta)$
end-0 end-1 label graph

Construct an undirected graph similar to graph, except that it includes an edge between end-0
and end-1, with label as its label.
Precondition: end-0 is a vertex of graph.
Precondition: end-1 is a vertex of graph.
Precondition: graph is undirected.
Precondition: graph contains no edge with end-0 and end-1 as its endpoints.

add-edge   (afp graphs)

$\alpha, \quad \alpha, \quad graph(\alpha, null) \rightarrow graph(\alpha, null)$
end-0 end-1 graph

Construct an undirected graph similar to graph, except that it includes an unlabeled edge
between end-0 and end-1.
Precondition: end-0 is a vertex of graph.
Precondition: end-1 is a vertex of graph.
Precondition: graph is undirected.
Precondition: graph contains no edge with end-0 as end-1 as its endpoints.

delete-edge   (afp graphs)

$\alpha, \quad \alpha, \quad graph(\alpha, \beta) \rightarrow graph(\alpha, \beta)$
end-0 end-1 graph

Construct an undirected graph similar to graph, but without any edge between end-0 and
end-1.
Precondition: graph is undirected.

make-edge   (afp graphs)

$set(\alpha), \quad \beta \rightarrow edge(\alpha, \beta)$
endpoints label

Construct an edge with the members of endpoints as its endpoints and label as its label.
Precondition: The cardinality of endpoints is 2.

edge-endpoints   (afp graphs)

$edge(\alpha, any) \rightarrow set(\alpha)$
edge

Return a set containing the endpoints of edge.

edge-label   (afp graphs)

$edge(any, \alpha) \rightarrow \alpha$
edge

Return the label of edge.

deedge   (afp graphs)

$edge(\alpha, \beta) \rightarrow set(\alpha), \beta$
edge

Return a set containing the endpoints of edge, and its label.

edge?   (afp graphs)

```
any          → Boolean
something
```
Determine whether something is an edge.

```
edge=?                                                            (afp graphs)
edge(any, any),  edge(any, any)  → Boolean
left           right
```
Determine whether left and right have the same endpoints and the same label.

```
ends                                                              (afp graphs)
edge(α, any)  → α, α
edge
```
Return the endpoints of edge, in either order.

```
edges                                                             (afp graphs)
graph(α, β)  → set(edge(α, β))
graph
```
Return a set containing the edges of graph.
Precondition: graph is undirected.

```
degree                                                            (afp graphs)
graph(α, any)  → (α       → natural-number)
graph              vert
```
Compute the degree of vert in graph.
Precondition: graph is undirected.
Precondition: vert is a vertex of graph.

Exercises

6.1–1   In the *diversity graph* for a set S, the vertices are the members of S and there is an arc from every vertex to every other vertex, but no arc from any vertex to itself. Define a procedure diversity-graph that constructs the diversity graph for a given set.

6.1–2   The *image* of a set S under a relation R is the set of values to which members of S bear R. Define a procedure image that receives a set and a graph and returns the image of the given set under the relation that the graph represents.

6.1–3   For any positive integer n, the $(n+1)$th *relational power* of a relation R is the relational product of R with its nth relational power. We take the first relational power of R to be R itself. Define a procedure graph-power that receives two arguments, the graph of a relation R with a finite domain and a positive integer n, and returns the graph of the nth relational power of R.

6.1–4   In the preceding exercise, would it be possible to extend the concept of a relational power to cover the case in which $n = 0$? If so, revise the definition of graph-power to allow this; if not, explain why it would be nonsensical. (Hint: Is there an identity for the operation of relational product?)

6.1–5   Prove that if a relation is both connected and intransitive, then its domain is the empty set.

6.1–6   Define a procedure pair-product-graph that receives two graphs, left and right, as its arguments and returns a graph in which the vertices are pairs comprising a vertex of `left` and a vertex of `right`, and the arcs connect pairs whose cars are connected by arcs in `left` and whose cdrs are connected by arcs in `right`.

6.1–7   An undirected graph is a *star graph* if there is one vertex (the *hub*) that has every other vertex as a neighbor, and each of the other vertices has the hub as its only neighbor (that is, there are no edges between non-hub vertices). Define a predicate `star-graph?` that determines whether a given undirected graph is a star graph.

6.2   Depth-First Traversal

Traversing Graphs

When our objective is simply to perform some operation on each vertex of a graph, folding or mapping over its vertices is adequate. Often, however, we wish to operate on those vertices in an order that depends on the graph's arcs, notionally moving from one vertex to another only when there is an arc from the former to the latter. To *traverse* a graph is to operate on its vertices while following the arcs in this way.

The generality of graphs as a data structure makes it difficult to formulate traversal algorithms. If a graph is not connected, it may be impossible to move from one vertex of a graph to another solely by following arcs. In the extreme case, of course, a graph may have no arcs at all, so that *every* vertex is cut off from every other one in this way. In other graphs, there may be several ways to move along arcs from one vertex to another. Some graphs contain *cycles*, so that we might start at a vertex, move along one or more arcs, and end up back at our starting point. In the execution of a traversal procedure, incautiously following arcs around a cycle can lead to unbounded recursion. Our traversal algorithms should avoid this pitfall.

To avoid unbounded recursion, we'll give each of the traversal procedures that we write an argument that specifies which vertices of the graph precede the current one in the ordering that the traversal is following. The natural data structure for this purpose is a set; let's call it `visited`. At the beginning of a traversal, `visited` is empty. As we encounter each vertex for the first time, we adjoin it to `visited` and pass the result into any recursive invocation as the new value of `visited`. If, having traversed an arc from one vertex to another, we find ourselves at a vertex that is a member of the `visited` set, we back up instead of operating on it again. Since the number of vertices is finite and we never operate on any vertex more than once, the recursion must eventually terminate.

We can initiate a traversal at any vertex of a graph. If it turns out to be impossible to reach all of the other vertices from our chosen starting point by moving along arcs, we'll visit as many as we can, and then reenter from a new starting point, choosing any vertex that is not yet in the `visited` set.

The Depth-First Order

Suppose that in the course of a traversal we follow an arc from one vertex, u, to another, v. In the *depth-first* order of traversal, the next step is to investigate the arcs leaving v, looking for an unvisited neighbor; we back up to consider other arcs leaving u only after we have visited all of the neighbors of v. (We'll study the alternative *breadth-first* traversal order, in which we visit each of the neighbors of u before proceeding to the neighbors of those neighbors, in §6.4.)

In a depth-first traversal, we backtrack to the tail of an arc after visiting its head (and all of the other vertices that can be reached through the head). This presents us with a choice in the timing of the operation to be performed on every vertex: We can either perform it as soon as we arrive at the vertex, before visiting its neighbors, or wait until we are about to backtrack to the tail of the arc by which we reached the vertex. In fact, there are some cases in which we want to do both, applying one procedure before visiting the vertex's neighbors and a different procedure afterwards. Thus our traversal procedures receive two arguments, `arrive` and `depart`, denoting the operations to be applied at arrival and departure.

When invoking a traversal procedure, if we choose not to perform an operation at one time or the other, we can express this choice by supplying the adapter `>all-but-initial` as a dummy operation. (Recall that this adapter discards its first argument, which in this case is the vertex to be visited, and returns all the others unchanged.)

To visit a vertex, then, we begin by checking whether the vertex has already been visited (that is, whether it is a member of the `visited` set). If so, we back out, returning the `visited` set (unchanged), along with any values that have been computed during the part of the traversal that has already been carried out. If, on the other hand, the new vertex has *not* previously been visited, we apply `arrive` to it and to the other results of the computation so far. We then compute the set of its neighbors and fold over that set, as if following an arc out to each one in turn. The values returned by the call to the folder (the procedure that `fold-set` constructs) reflect operations performed on those neighbors, their previously unvisited neighbors, and so on, along with a `visited` set that includes all of the now-visited vertices. Finally, we apply `depart` to the current vertex and the values just returned by the folder, and return the results along with the new `visited` set.

The procedure needs many arguments to carry all the necessary information: the current vertex, the `visited` set, all of the incoming values computed so far in the traversal, the `arrive` and `depart` procedures, and some way of figuring out what the neighbors of the current vertex are. For this last purpose, we'll rely on the caller to supply a procedure `nabes` that can be applied to any vertex of the graph to get the set of its neighbors. (The caller can, for instance, invoke `neighbors` to obtain such a procedure.) The `arrive`, `depart`, and `nabes` procedures are the same for all of the recursive calls that the procedure generates, so we shall lift them out, leaving the current vertex, `visited`, and the intermediate results of the computation as the parameters of the actual recursive procedure:

```
(define (depth-first-visit nabes arrive depart)
  (rec (visit vertex visited . so-far)
    (if (member? vertex visited)
        (apply values visited so-far)
        (receive after-arrival (apply arrive vertex so-far)
          (receive (new-visited . new-so-far)
                   ((fold-set (apply create (fast-put-into-set vertex
                                                               visited)
                                      after-arrival)
                              visit)
                    (nabes vertex))
            (receive after-departure (apply depart vertex new-so-far)
              (apply values new-visited after-departure)))))))
```

To traverse an entire graph, then, we fold over its vertices, trying each one in turn to ensure that none remains unvisited, and accumulating and finally returning the results of the arrive and depart operations:

```
(define (depth-first-traversal base arrive depart)
  (let ((new-base (receive starters (base)
                    (apply create (set) starters))))
    (lambda (graph)
      (receive (visited . finals)
               ((fold-set new-base (depth-first-visit (neighbors graph)
                                                      arrive
                                                      depart))
                (vertices graph))
        (delist finals)))))
```

Topological Sorting

To illustrate the use of the depth-first-traversal procedure, let's consider the problem of making a list of the vertices of a graph in such a way that, for any vertices u and v, if u precedes v on the list, then there is no arc from v to u in the graph. Because the order of the vertices in the list reflects the topology of the graph, the process of constructing such a list is called *topological sorting*.

Not every graph can be sorted topologically. If it contains a cycle—a sequence $\langle v_0, \ldots, v_k \rangle$ of two or more distinct vertices such that there is an arc in the graph from v_0 to v_1, an arc from v_1 to v_2, ..., an arc from v_{k-1} to v_k, and also an arc from v_k to v_0—then clearly there is no way to list the vertices so that all of the arcs in the cycle point forwards along the list. So it is a precondition of topological sorting that the graph to be sorted is *acyclic*, that is, free of cycles.

We can topologically sort any graph that satisfies this precondition by traversing it depth-first and prepending each vertex to an initially empty list as we depart from it. The first vertex that is prepended—the one that is last in the result of the topological sort—must be one that has no neighbors, since we leave it immediately after entering it. (It cannot have neighbors that have previously been visited, since the only vertices that have been visited when we reach it form a sequence that would contain a cycle if there were an arc back to one of them, which would violate the precondition that the graph has no cycles.) And at each subsequent stage, we prepend a vertex only after all of its neighbors have been added to the list (and so follow the vertex in the completed list):

```
(define topological-sort
  (depth-first-traversal list >all-but-initial prepend))
```

Reachable Vertices

We can repeat the approach that we used in `depth-first-visit` to develop a procedure that finds all of the vertices of a given graph that can be reached by starting from a given vertex of that graph and advancing along arcs—rather like `neighbors`, except that we'll permit multiple-arc connections, and also throw in the starting vertex itself (since it is trivial to reach a vertex if you start there). To emphasize the similarity with `neighbors`, and to allow for the common case in which we'll do many calls using the same graph, we'll curry the procedure, giving it the graph initially and the starting vertex separately:

```
(define (reachables graph)
  (let ((nabes (neighbors graph)))
    (let ((visit (rec (visit current visited)
                    (if (member? current visited)
                        visited
                        ((fold-set (create (fast-put-into-set current
                                                              visited))
                                   visit)
                         (nabes current))))))
      (sect visit <> (set)))))
```

Essentially, the `reachables` procedure computes the `visited` set that results from a depth-first traversal beginning with the starting vertex.

---

depth-first-visit   (afp depth-first-traversal)
$(\alpha \to set(\alpha))$, $(\alpha, \beta \ldots \to \beta \ldots)$, $(\alpha, \beta \ldots \to \beta \ldots) \to$
nabes   arrive   depart
$(\alpha, \quad set(\alpha), \quad \beta \ldots \quad \to \beta \ldots)$
vertex visited so-far

Construct a procedure that visits vertex, receiving as additional arguments the set of previously visited vertices (visited) and the results of the computations undertaken during those previous visits (so-far). If vertex is a member of visited, the constructed procedure returns visited and the elements of so-far; otherwise, the constructed procedure invokes arrive (giving it vertex and the elements of so-far as arguments), iteratively invokes itself for each of the neighbors of the vertex, as determined by nabes (giving itself the neighbor, the result of adding vertex to visited, and the results of the most recent visit as arguments), and finally invokes depart (giving it vertex and the results of the most recent visit as arguments). The constructed procedure returns the results of the final visit.

Precondition: nabes can receive vertex.

Precondition: nabes can receive any element of any result of nabes.

Precondition: arrive can receive vertex and the elements of so-far.

Precondition: arrive can receive any element of any result of nabes and the elements of so-far.

Precondition: arrive can receive any element of any result of nabes and the results of any invocation of depart.

Precondition: depart can receive vertex and the elements of so-far.

Precondition: depart can receive any element of any result of nabes and the elements of so-far.

Precondition: depart can receive any element of any result of nabes and the results of any invocation of depart.

depth-first-traversal   (afp depth-first-traversal)

$(\rightarrow \alpha \ldots)$, $(\beta, \alpha \ldots \rightarrow \alpha \ldots)$, $(\beta, \alpha \ldots \rightarrow \alpha \ldots)$ $\rightarrow$ $(graph(\beta, any) \rightarrow \alpha \ldots)$
base   arrive   depart   graph

Construct a procedure that traverses graph in depth-first order, starting from an arbitrarily chosen vertex, returning the results obtained by invoking a given base procedure to obtain some initial values, and then transforming these values by applying an "arrival procedure" to each vertex and the incoming values as the vertex is reached, and a "departure procedure" to the vertex and the derived values after all of the vertex's neighbors have been similarly visited.

Precondition: arrive can receive any vertex of graph and the results of any invocation of base.

Precondition: arrive can receive any vertex of graph and the results of any invocation of depart.

Precondition: depart can receive any vertex of graph and the results of any invocation of base.

Precondition: depart can receive any vertex of graph and the results of any invocation of depart.

topological-sort   (afp depth-first-traversal)

$graph(\alpha, any) \rightarrow list(\alpha)$
graph

Construct a list of the vertices of graph such that there is no arc in graph in which the head precedes (in the list) the tail.

Precondition: graph is acyclic.

reachables   (afp graphs)

$graph(\alpha, any) \rightarrow (\alpha \rightarrow set(\alpha))$
graph   vert

Construct a procedure that, in turn, constructs the set of vertices that can be reached from vert by following arcs in graph.

Exercises

6.2–1 Let G be the graph with the symbols a, b, c, and d as its vertices and arcs from a to b, from a to c, from b to d, and from c to d. In what orders could a depth-first traversal visit the vertices of G? (There is more than one order, because the traversal can make some choices arbitrarily: for instance, which vertex to visit first, and which of the neighbors of a to try first.)

6.2–2 Define a procedure traversal-graph that performs a depth-first traversal of a given graph and returns a graph with the same vertices, containing only

the arcs that the algorithm traversed in order to reach previously unvisited
vertices.

6.2–3   Define a procedure `acyclic?` that determines whether a given graph
contains any cycles.

6.2–4   Define a predicate `traversable?` that determines whether a given graph
contains at least one vertex from which all the graph's vertices are reachable.

6.2–5   Define a procedure `transitive-closure` that, given a graph G, constructs a graph with the same vertices as G, but with an arc from vertex u to
vertex v whenever v is reachable from u in G.

6.3   Paths

Formally, a *path* in a graph is a non-empty sequence of its vertices such that
for every pair v_i, v_{i+1} of vertices that are adjacent in the sequence, there is
an arc in the graph from v_i to v_{i+1}. (This definition counts every one-element
sequence, vacuously, as a path from the vertex in the sequence to itself.)

A depth-first strategy for finding a path from one given vertex in a graph
(the *origin*) to another (the *destination*) systematically advances from the origin
to one of its neighbors, and from there to a neighbor of the neighbor, and so
on, until the destination is found or a vertex is reached that has no unvisited
neighbors. In the latter case, we back out and try an alternative at the most
recently visited vertex that offers one. The search fails if we back up all the way
to the origin and run out of alternatives there.

The `depth-first-visit` procedure isn't quite the right mechanism to use in
implementing this strategy, since that procedure visits *all* of the vertices that
are reachable from the starting vertex, and in constructing a path we are often
able to reach the destination long before that exhaustive search is complete.
However, it still makes sense to keep track of a `visited` set, since it's pointless
to revisit a vertex that we have already encountered and either added to the
path or discarded as unhelpful.

In this case, however, we only need `visited` until we actually find the path;
at that point, our only objective is to return that path to the original caller as
quickly as possible. So our recursive `visit` procedure returns different values,
depending on whether or not it has found the path: If so, it returns #t and the
path it discovered; if not, it returns #f and the new `visited` set.

The recursive `try-neighbors` procedure, nested deep inside the main recursion, runs through the set of vertices adjacent to the current vertex and tries to
extend the path through each one in turn towards the destination. If any of the
attempts is successful, its results are returned immediately. Otherwise, when
the set of adjacent vertices is exhausted, `try-neighbors` returns #f, along with
a new `visited` set that now contains all of the adjacent vertices.

It turns out to be most convenient to construct the path in reverse order. The `path-finder` procedure therefore reverses the completed path just before returning it.

```
(define (path-finder graph)
  (let ((nabes (neighbors graph)))
    (lambda (origin destination)
      ((pipe (rec (visit vertex visited path-so-far)
                 (if (member? vertex visited)
                     (values #f visited)
                     (if (equal? vertex destination)
                         (values #t (reverse path-so-far))
                         ((rec (try-neighbors alternatives visited)
                               (if (empty-set? alternatives)
                                   (values #f visited)
                                   (receive (chosen others)
                                            (take-from-set alternatives)
                                       (receive (found result)
                                                (visit chosen
                                                       visited
                                                       (prepend chosen
                                                                path-so-far))
                                         (if found
                                             (values found result)
                                             (try-neighbors others result))))))
                          (nabes vertex)
                          (fast-put-into-set vertex visited)))))
             (^if >initial >next >initial))
       origin (set) (list origin)))))
```

Connected Components

A graph is *path-connected* if, for any vertices u and v of the graph, there is a path in the graph from u to v. When the graph is undirected, there is an easy way to test whether it is path-connected: Choose any vertex w and determine whether every vertex is reachable from it. If not, obviously the graph is not path-connected (since there is no path from w to an unreachable vertex); if so, the graph is connected, since you can get from u to v by going from u to w (reversing the path from w to u) and from there to v.

The following procedure implements this test (and therefore carries the precondition that `graph` is undirected):

```
(define (path-connected? graph)
  (let ((verts (vertices graph))
        (reach (reachables graph)))
    (or (empty-set? verts)
        (receive (chosen ignored) (take-from-set verts)
          (subset? verts (reach chosen))))))
```

In any non-empty undirected graph, one can partition the set of its vertices into subsets, so that there is a path from one vertex to another if and only if they belong to the same subset. If the graph is path-connected, the partition is trivial—there is only one subset, and it contains all of the vertices. The other extreme case occurs when each vertex can reach only itself, so that the partition consists of the unit sets of the vertices; this occurs when the graph has no edges. The subgraphs of a graph G that are formed by partitioning the edges along with the vertices that they connect are the *connected components* of G.

We can collect the connected components of an undirected graph by selecting any vertex, rounding up all of the vertices that are reachable from it, making them into one component, and then repeating the process with any vertex that has not yet been put into a component. We keep going until every vertex of the original undirected graph is in a component:

```
(define (connected-components graph)
  (let ((reach (reachables graph)))
    ((rec (detach verts)
       (if (empty-set? verts)
           (set)
           (receive (chosen others) (take-from-set verts)
             (let ((in-reach (reach chosen)))
               (fast-put-into-set (restriction in-reach graph)
                                  (detach (set-difference verts
                                                          in-reach)))))))
     (vertices graph))))
```

In the special case of the empty graph, this algorithm returns an empty set of components, in accordance with the general rule that the empty graph is not a component of any graph. With this convention, every graph has a unique decomposition into a set of connected components.

---

path-finder (afp paths)
graph(α, any) → *(α,*   *α*   → *list(α) | Boolean)*
graph   origin destination
Construct a predicate that attempts to find a path from origin to destination in graph. If the constructed procedure is successful, it returns the path; otherwise, it returns #f.
Precondition: origin is a vertex of graph.
Precondition: destination is a vertex of graph.

path-connected? (afp paths)
graph(any, any) → *Boolean*
graph
Determine whether there is a path from every vertex in graph to every other vertex in graph.
Precondition: graph is undirected.

connected-components (afp paths)
graph(α, β) → *set(graph(α, β))*
graph
Construct a set containing the connected components of graph.
Precondition: graph is undirected.

Exercises

6.3–1 A path is *cycle-free* if no two of its elements are the same vertex. Show that, if there is a path from vertex u to vertex v in a graph G, then there is a cycle-free path from u to v in G.

6.3–2 Using `depth-first-visit`, define a procedure `all-cycle-free-paths-finder` that is analogous to `path-finder`, except that the procedure it constructs returns a set containing *all* of the cycle-free paths from `origin` to `destination` in the given graph.

6.3–3 An undirected graph G has four connected components, each containing a different number of vertices. What is the least number of vertices that G could have? What is the least number of edges?

6.3–4 A *bottleneck* in an undirected graph is an edge whose deletion would increase the number of connected components of the graph. Define a procedure `bottlenecks` that computes the set of bottlenecks in a given undirected graph.

6.4 Breadth-First Traversal

Let's now turn to the alternative *breadth-first* method of traversing a graph. Choosing any vertex as our starting point, we first visit that vertex, and then all of the neighbors of that vertex, then all of the neighbors of those neighbors, and so on, skipping any vertex that we have previously visited by some other route, until we have visited all the vertices that can be reached from the starting point by traversing a sequence of arcs.

To carry out this plan, we must carefully maintain two data structures: the familiar `visited` set, comprising all of the vertices on which we have already operated, and a buffer containing the "waiting" vertices that make up the boundary between the visited and unvisited parts of the graph. Initially, the `visited` set is empty and the waiting buffer contains only one vertex, the chosen starting point for the traversal.

At each step in the traversal, we take a vertex from the buffer. If we have already visited it, we simply discard it. If not, we visit it, perform whatever computation is appropriate, and add it to the set of visited vertices and its neighbors to the waiting buffer. The traversal ends when the buffer is empty. This must happen eventually, because no vertex can be visited more than once; after each of the reachable vertices has been visited, the size of the buffer is reduced at each step. (Nothing is ever removed from the set of visited vertices.)

As usual, we can abstractly represent the computation performed during the visit to a vertex by requiring the caller to provide an `operate` procedure. (We don't split the operation into an `arrive` procedure and a `depart` procedure, as we did in depth-first traversal, because there is no occasion for backtracking or "returning through" a vertex in a breadth-first traversal.) We'll require the caller to supply a vertex as the first argument to operate and allow it to receive any number of additional arguments, representing the intermediate results of the computation at the current point in the traversal. From these arguments, operate constructs a new set of intermediate results, corresponding to the optional arguments that it receives.

The breadth-first-visit procedure constructs a procedure that can be invoked to traverse the part of a graph that can be reached from a designated vertex vertex, given a set visited of previously visited vertices and any number of additional values representing the initial state of the computation. The breadth-first-visit procedure itself receives as its arguments two procedures: nabes, which when applied to any vertex returns the set of neighbors of that vertex, and operate, which advances the computation as described above:

```
(define (breadth-first-visit nabes operate)
  (lambda (vertex visited . so-far)
    (apply (rec (visit visited waiting . so-far)
             (if (empty-buffer? waiting)
                 (apply values visited so-far)
                 (receive (chosen others) (take-from-buffer waiting)
                   (if (member? chosen visited)
                       (apply visit visited others so-far)
                       (receive new-so-far (apply operate chosen so-far)
                         (apply visit
                                (fast-put-into-set chosen visited)
                                ((fold-set (create others)
                                           put-into-buffer)
                                 (nabes chosen))
                                new-so-far))))))
           visited (buffer vertex) so-far)))
```

The recursive procedure here is the internal visit procedure, to which we initially pass the visited set and a one-element buffer containing our designed starting point, vertex. In each recursive call, visit checks whether the waiting buffer is empty and, if so, returns its final values; otherwise, it removes a vertex, chosen, from the buffer and determines whether chosen has been visited. If it has, the visit procedure is called again, with a waiting buffer that is shorter by one vertex; however, if chosen is new, visit invokes operate to deal with it, adds it to the visited set, adds its neighbors to the waiting buffer, and again invokes itself recursively.

A call to breadth-first-visit may or may not pick up all of the vertices in a graph. It will fail to do so if some vertices are not reachable from the chosen starting point. The full breadth-first-traversal algorithm therefore chooses such starting points repeatedly from the unvisited vertices until none are left:

```
(define (breadth-first-traversal base operate)
  (let ((new-base (receive starters (base)
                    (apply create (set) starters)))))
```

```
(lambda (graph)
  (receive (visited . finals)
           ((fold-set new-base (breadth-first-visit (neighbors graph)
                                                    operate))
            (vertices graph))
    (delist finals)))))
```

It's now clear why we need, specifically, a buffer as the data structure for the vertices on the boundary: A buffer preserves the "breadth-first" property that all of the starting vertex's neighbors must be visited before any of the neighbors of those neighbors, and they in turn before any of *their* neighbors, and so on. The first-in, first-out discipline of the buffer guarantees the correct visiting order.

---

breadth-first-visit   (afp breadth-first-traversal)
$(\alpha \rightarrow set(\alpha)), (\alpha, \beta \ldots \rightarrow \beta \ldots) \rightarrow (\alpha, \quad set(\alpha), \beta \ldots \rightarrow \beta \ldots)$
nabes   operate   vertex visited so-far
Construct a procedure that traverses part of a graph by visiting in succession each of the vertices that is reachable from vertex, starting with vertex itself and proceeding in breadth-first order through its neighbors (as determined by nabes), the neighbors of those neighbors, and so on. If vertex is a member of visited, the constructed procedure returns visited and the elements of so-far; otherwise, it invokes operate (giving it vertex and the results of computations undertaken in previous visits).
Precondition: nabes can receive vertex.
Precondition: nabes can receive any element of any result of an invocation of nabes.
Precondition: operate can receive vertex and the elements of so-far.
Precondition: operate can receive any element of any result of an invocation of nabes, along with the results of any invocation of operate.

breadth-first-traversal   (afp breadth-first-traversal)
$(\rightarrow \alpha \ldots), (\beta, \alpha \ldots \rightarrow \alpha \ldots) \rightarrow (graph(\beta, any) \rightarrow \alpha)$
base   operate   graph
Construct a procedure that traverses graph in breadth-first order, starting from an arbitrarily chosen vertex, returning the results obtained by invoking base to obtain some initial values, and then transforming these values by applying operate to each vertex and the results of previous such operations.
Precondition: operate can receive any vertex of graph and the results of any invocation of base.
Precondition: operate can receive any vertex of graph and the results of any invocation of operate.

Exercises

6.4–1 Let G be the graph with the symbols a, b, c, and d as its vertices and arcs from a to b, from a to c, from b to d, and from c to d. In what orders could a breadth-first traversal visit the vertices of G?

6.4–2 The *distance* from a vertex u to a vertex v in a graph is the least number of arcs in a path connecting u to v. Define a procedure distance that receives a graph and constructs a procedure that, in turn, computes the distance from any vertex to any vertex in that graph, provided that the second vertex is reachable from the first.

6.4–3 A vertex v is *antipodal to* a vertex u in a graph if no vertex of the graph has a greater distance from u. Define a procedure `antipodes` that receives a graph and constructs a procedure that, in turn, constructs the set of vertices antipodal to a given vertex of the graph.

6.5 Spanning Trees

A *spanning tree* for a path-connected undirected graph G is an acyclic, path-connected, undirected graph with the same vertices as G and a subset of G's edges. (Don't be misled by the word "tree"; for graph theorists, a tree is simply an undirected graph that does not contain any cycles. Unlike the trees that we discussed in §3.10, spanning trees are not hierarchical and don't have roots or subtrees.) Think of the spanning tree as a kind of skeleton of G, retaining just enough edges to hold the graph together (that is, to keep it path-connected). In a spanning tree, there is still a path from any vertex to any other, but every such path is unique; in effect, edges have been removed until all of the redundant paths have been eliminated.

For instance, in the simplest non-trivial case, G has three vertices, and there is an edge between each pair of them (three edges in all). Removing any one of the edges leaves a path-connected graph. Such a graph is a spanning tree for G, because removing another edge would leave the graph non-path-connected (the common endpoint of the two removed edges would no longer be reachable from either of the other vertices).

To construct a spanning tree for a given path-connected, undirected graph G, we can start with an edgeless graph with the same vertices and restore the edges of G one at a time, skipping over any whose endpoints are already connected by a path:

```
(define (slow-spanning-tree graph)
  ((fold-set (create (arcless-graph (vertices graph)))
            (lambda (edge spanner)
              (receive (end-0 end-1) (ends edge)
                (if (list? ((path-finder spanner) end-0 end-1))
                    spanner
                    (add-labeled-edge end-0 end-1 (edge-label edge)
                                      spanner)))))
   (edges graph)))
```

When the number of edges is large in comparison to the number of vertices, this algorithm is likely to complete the spanning tree early on and then waste a lot of time proving that all of the remaining edges have endpoints that are already connected by a path. Fortunately, there's an easy way to recognize that the spanning tree is complete.

The edgeless graph with which we begin has as many connected components as it has vertices. Every time we add an edge, it connects two components that

were previously separate (since there is no path between the endpoints until we
add the edge), so that the number of connected components is reduced by one.
Once we get the number of connected components down to one, we know that
no more edges will be added, because there is already a path between any two
vertices in the same connected component.

Thus the number of edges in any spanning tree for a path-connected, non-
empty, undirected graph G is one less than the number of vertices in G. So we
can compute the number of edges that we need and decrement it every time we
add an edge to the spanning tree as it develops, stopping when we get to zero.

Here's the code that results from this insight:

```
(define spanning-tree
  (run (dispatch
         (run vertices cardinality sub1 (sect max <> 0))
         (pipe vertices arcless-graph)
         edges)
       (iterate
         (pipe >initial zero?)
         (lambda (countdown spanner rest-of-edges)
           (receive (chosen others) (take-from-set rest-of-edges)
             (receive (termini label) (deedge chosen)
               (receive (end-0 end-1) (deset termini)
                 (if (list? ((path-finder spanner) end-0 end-1))
                     (values countdown spanner others)
                     (values (sub1 countdown)
                             (add-labeled-edge end-0 end-1 label
                                               spanner)
                             others)))))))
       >next))
```

When a path-connected, undirected graph G is labeled with numbers, a
minimum spanning tree for G is one in which the sum of the edge labels is less
than or equal to the sum of the labels in any other spanning tree for G. We can
adapt the spanning-tree algorithm so that it produces a minimum spanning
tree by preprocessing the set of edges, sorting them so that the lowest-weight
edges are tried first:

```
(define minimum-spanning-tree
  (run (dispatch
         (run vertices cardinality sub1 (sect max <> 0))
         (pipe vertices arcless-graph)
         (run edges
              set->bag
              (sect sort (compare-by edge-label <=) <>)))
       (iterate
         (pipe >initial zero?)
         (lambda (countdown spanner rest-of-edges)
           (receive (chosen others) (deprepend rest-of-edges)
```

```
(receive (termini label) (deedge chosen)
  (receive (end-0 end-1) (deset termini)
    (if (list? ((path-finder spanner) end-0 end-1))
        (values countdown spanner others)
        (values (sub1 countdown)
                (add-labeled-edge end-0 end-1 label spanner)
                others)))))))
>next))
```

To see that this algorithm always returns a minimum spanning tree, let T be its result, and let T^* be any minimum spanning tree for G. If T is the same graph as T^*, we're done. Otherwise, let e be the first edge not in T^* that the algorithm added to T, and let S be the graph with the same vertices and edges as T, except without edge e. Now, in the graph S, there is no path between the endpoints of e (because the only such path in T was the edge e itself, and that edge is not in S); S will thus have two connected components, S_0 and S_1, one for each endpoint of e.

However, since T^* is a spanning tree, there is a path in T^* that connects the endpoints of e, and that path must contain an edge e^* with one endpoint in S_0 and the other in S_1. Moreover, there can be only one such edge (otherwise there would be a cycle in T^*), and e^*'s label must be equal to that of e; for if it were less, the algorithm would have selected e^* rather than e when building T, while if it were greater, replacing e^* with e in T^* would yield a spanning tree with lower total weight than T^*, and we assumed that T^* was a minimum spanning tree.

Suppose, then, that we go ahead and replace e^* with e in T^*. The resulting graph T^{**} is still a minimum spanning tree for G (since its total weight is unchanged), and now it's more similar to T. We can now repeat this argument with T and T^{**}, and as often as necessary after that, until each of the differences has been found and eliminated. Then T will have been shown to be a minimum spanning tree.

An Alternative Method

An alternative strategy for building the minimum spanning tree is to add vertices, rather than edges, one by one. Taking any vertex as our initial seedling, we add to the developing spanning tree whichever vertex we can attach to it by an edge of minimum weight, and repeat until all of the vertices have been attached. At each step, the only edges we consider are those that have one endpoint already in the developing spanning tree and the other outside it. The proof presented just above can also be used to show that the tree we construct by this alternative method is a minimum spanning tree.

A *cut* is a partition of the vertices of a graph into two subsets—let's call them the *ins* and the *outs*. So the heart of this strategy is finding a minimum-weight edge that *crosses the cut*, connecting one of the ins to one of the outs. Such an edge is called a *light edge* across the cut.

We can begin by finding all the ways of crossing a cut. The `crossings` procedure returns a set of edges that cross a given cut in a given graph. For this application, we want to curry the procedure, since we'll consider several different cuts in the same graph as we add vertices to the developing spanning tree. We specify the cut by giving either its ins or its outs (as a set), whichever is convenient. The algorithm for this step is to compute the set of edges and filter out those with both endpoints on the same side of the cut:

```
(define (crossings graph)
  (let ((edge-set (edges graph)))
    (lambda (cut)
      (remp-set (pipe ends (compare-by (sect member? <> cut) boolean=?))
              edge-set))))
```

The procedure for finding a light edge across a cut in a given graph selects the crossing of minimum weight:

```
(define (light-edge graph)
  (pipe (crossings graph) (extreme-in-set (compare-by edge-label <=))))
```

The main algorithm for constructing a minimum spanning tree, then, repeatedly finds light edges and pulls their far endpoints across the cut into the spanning tree:

```
(define (alternative-minimum-spanning-tree graph)
  (let ((verts (vertices graph))
        (light-edge-finder (light-edge graph)))
    (if (empty-set? verts)
        (empty-graph)
        ((run take-from-set
              (~initial (sect add-vertex <> (empty-graph)))
              (iterate
                (pipe >next empty-set?)
                (lambda (spanner outs)
                  (let ((connector (light-edge-finder outs)))
                    (receive (termini label) (deedge connector)
                      (receive (end-0 end-1) (deset termini)
                        (let ((ligand (if (member? end-0 outs)
                                          end-0
                                          end-1)))
                          (values (add-labeled-edge
                                    end-0
                                    end-1
                                    label
                                    (add-vertex ligand spanner))
                                  (remove-from-set ligand outs)))))))))
          >initial)
         verts))))
```

Each of these algorithms can be further improved by maintaining and passing along a specialized data structure, designed to optimize either the determination of whether there is a path between two vertices (in the earlier algorithm) or the computation of light edges (in this one). The optimized versions are known respectively as *Kruskal's algorithm* and *Prim's algorithm*, after their inventors.

---

spanning-tree   (afp spanning-trees)
$graph(\alpha, \beta) \rightarrow graph(\alpha, \beta)$
graph
Construct a spanning tree for graph.
Precondition: graph is undirected.
Precondition: graph is path-connected.

minimum-spanning-tree   (afp spanning-trees)
$graph(\alpha, number) \rightarrow graph(\alpha, number)$
graph
Construct a minimum-weight spanning tree for graph.
Precondition: graph is undirected.
Precondition: graph is path-connected.

crossings   (afp spanning-trees)
$graph(\alpha, \beta) \rightarrow (set(\alpha) \rightarrow set(edge(\alpha, \beta)))$
graph   cut
Construct a procedure that, in turn, constructs the set of edges of graph that have exactly one endpoint that is a member of cut.
Precondition: graph is undirected.

light-edge   (afp spanning-trees)
$graph(\alpha, number) \rightarrow (set(\alpha) \rightarrow edge(\alpha, number))$
graph   cut
Construct a procedure that finds the edge in graph with the least label among those that have exactly one endpoint that is a member of cut.
Precondition: graph is undirected.

alternative-minimum-spanning-tree   (afp spanning-trees)
$graph(\alpha, number) \rightarrow graph(\alpha, number)$
graph
Construct a minimum-weight spanning tree for graph.
Precondition: graph is undirected.
Precondition: graph is path-connected.

Exercises

6.5–1 Let G be an undirected graph in which the vertices are the integers 2, 3, 4, 5, and 6, and there is an edge between two vertices if and only if neither of them is a divisor of the other. Show that G is path-connected and construct a spanning tree for G.

6.5–2 In the preceding exercise, label each edge with the product of its endpoints. What is the minimum spanning tree for G? In what order will minimum-spanning-tree add the edges in constructing this tree? Assuming that alternative-minimum-spanning-tree starts with vertex 4 on the "ins" side of the cut and vertices 2, 3, 5, and 6 on the "outs" side, in what order will it add the vertices?

6.5–3 Define a `maximum-spanning-tree` procedure that computes a *maximum* spanning tree for a given path-connected, undirected graph in which the edge labels are numbers. (The goal is for the sum of the edge labels in the spanning tree to equal or exceed the sum of the edge labels in any spanning tree for the same graph.)

6.6 Shortest Paths

If a graph is path-connected, and its arcs are labeled with positive numbers, it is often useful to determine the *shortest path* from one vertex to another, that is, the path for which the sum of the labels of the arcs that make up the path (which we'll call the *path sum*) is the least. Solving one shortest-path problem in a graph usually entails solving other such problems in the same graph, so we'll design the procedures that find shortest paths either as "all-pairs" algorithms (which find the shortest paths connecting all pairs of vertices in a given graph) or "single-source" algorithms (which find the shortest path to each vertex from a given starting vertex in a given graph).

The Bellman–Ford Algorithm

One approach to the single-source version of the problem is to run through all of the arcs of the graph, determining for each arc in turn whether it can be used to create or improve on a path from the starting vertex to the head of the arc. This will be true whenever (1) a path from the starting vertex (let's call it s) to the arc's tail is already known, and (2) either no path from s to the arc's head is known, or else the path sum of the best known path from s to the arc's head is greater than the sum of the arc's label and the path sum of the best known path from s to the arc's tail.

When these conditions are met, the arc is said to be *relaxable*, and the operation of creating or improving the path is called *relaxing the arc*.

Running through the arcs just once is insufficient, since that first pass will find only the optimal one-arc paths from s. However, if we run through the arcs k times in succession, we'll pick up the optimal k-arc paths from s. Since the shortest path cannot contain more than $n - 1$ arcs, where n is the number of vertices in the graph, we can be sure of finding all of the shortest paths by running through the arcs $n - 1$ times.

The *Bellman–Ford algorithm* implements this idea. It returns a table in which the keys are the vertices of the graph. The entry with which a key k is associated provides two pieces of information about the shortest path from s to k: its path sum and a list of the vertices that lie along the path. Theoretically, the path sum can be computed from the list of vertices and the graph, so it's redundant to keep it around as a separate item. During the execution of the algorithm, however, it is convenient to interleave the computation of the path sum with the determination of the path, since we constantly need partial path sums to determine whether arcs are relaxable. Accordingly, each entry in our table will be a pair, with the path sum from s to the associated key as its car and the list of vertices lying along the path as its cdr.

Another representational choice that simplifies the algorithm is to list the vertices of a path in reverse order, so that, in the entry associated with vertex k, the list of vertices begins with k and ends with s. Since paths are built up incrementally, vertex by vertex, starting from s, it is natural for the lists that represent them to reflect this incremental construction.

Given one arc from a graph and a partially constructed path table for that graph, the `relaxable?` procedure determines whether the arc can be relaxed:

```
(define (relaxable? sago path-table)
  (receive (tail head label) (dearc sago)
    (let ((path-to-tail (lookup tail path-table))
          (path-to-head (lookup head path-table)))
      (and (pair? path-to-tail)
           (or (not path-to-head)
               (< (+ (car path-to-tail) label) (car path-to-head)))))))
```

Note that the calls to `lookup` can fail. If the table has no entry for the arc's tail vertex, then there is no known path from s to that vertex. In that case, the arc is not relaxable and `#f` is returned immediately. If there is no entry for the head, then the arc *is* relaxable (any path is an improvement over no path). Otherwise, we compare the path sum for the path to the arc's tail and through the arc to the path sum for the shortest previously encountered path to the arc's head and return `#t` if the path sum for the new path is less, `#f` if it is not.

The `relax` procedure determines whether a given arc from a graph is relaxable (given also the partially constructed path table), and if so, returns a path table that contains the newly created or improved path. If the arc cannot be relaxed, the `relax` procedure returns the given path table, unchanged:

```
(define (relax sago path-table)
  (if (relaxable? sago path-table)
      (receive (tail head label) (dearc sago)
        (receive (path-sum path-vertices)
                 (decons (lookup tail path-table))
          (put-into-table head
                          (cons (+ path-sum label)
                                (prepend head path-vertices))
                          path-table)))
      path-table))
```

In the Bellman–Ford algorithm, we run through all of the arcs $n - 1$ times, where n is the number of vertices, relaxing at every opportunity. Initially, the partial path table contains only one entry, indicating that the shortest path from the start vertex s to itself has length 0 and consists of s alone:

```
(define (shortest-paths-from graph start)
  (let ((sagaro (arcs graph))
        (start-table (table (cons start (cons 0 (list start))))))
    ((fold-natural (create start-table)
                   (lambda (path-table)
                     ((fold-set (create path-table) relax) sagaro)))
     (sub1 (cardinality (vertices graph))))))
```

The Bellman–Ford algorithm yields correct answers even when arcs of the graph are allowed to have negative weights, provided that the graph contains no cycle of arcs with a negative path sum containing a vertex that is reachable from s. When such a cycle exists, there is no shortest path from s to any vertex that can be reached by going through any vertex in the cycle. We could go below the weight of *any* proposed path by going around and around the cycle enough times.

To detect the presence of such a cycle, we can examine the path table that the algorithm constructs. If one or more of the graph's arcs is still relaxable, relative to that path table, then the supposed "shortest path" to the head vertex of that arc contains $n + 1$ vertices. This implies that at least one vertex is repeated, so that the path contains a cycle. This cycle must have negative path weight, since otherwise the algorithm would have constructed a path with a smaller (or equally small) path sum by omitting the cycle.

The `safe-shortest-paths-from` procedure incorporates this after-the-fact test. It returns #f rather than a path table if the Bellman–Ford algorithm detects a cycle of arcs with a negative path sum:

```
(define (safe-shortest-path-from graph start)
  (let ((path-table (shortest-paths-from graph start)))
    (if (exists-in-set? (sect relaxable? <> path-table) (arcs graph))
        #f
        path-table)))
```

Dijkstra's Algorithm

An alternative method for computing shortest paths from a fixed starting vertex is to build the path table one vertex at a time, adding at each step whichever vertex has the shortest path from the origin, using only previously added vertices as intermediate steps. As we add each vertex, we try to relax all of the arcs leaving it, which has the effect of recalculating shortest paths to the target vertices of those arcs.

Given a non-empty set of vertices in a graph and a (partially completed) path table for that graph, the `nearest` procedure returns whichever of the vertices in the set is nearest to the implicit origin, according to the path table:

```
(define (nearest aro tab)
```

```
((extreme-in-set (compare-by (pipe (sect lookup <> tab) car) <=))
 aro))
```

Dijkstra's algorithm repeatedly chooses the nearest vertex and relaxes the arcs leaving it, terminating when no more vertices are accessible from the origin. As in the Bellman–Ford algorithm, the path table initially contains only the origin (with a path sum of 0, for a trivial path consisting of just the origin itself):

```
(define (shortest-paths-from graph start)
  ((pipe (iterate
            (pipe >initial empty-set?)
            (lambda (candidates tab remaining)
              (let ((chosen (nearest candidates tab)))
                (let ((new-tab ((fold-set (create tab) relax)
                                  (arcs-leaving chosen graph)))
                      (new-remaining (remove-from-set chosen remaining)))
                  (values (intersection new-remaining
                                          (table-keys new-tab))
                          new-tab
                          new-remaining)))))
         >next)
    (set start)
    (table (cons start (cons 0 (list start))))
    (vertices graph)))
```

For Dijkstra's algorithm, it is important to require that all of the arc labels be positive. If this condition is not met, it is possible to lower a path sum by extending the path. The algorithm presupposes that this cannot happen. In other words, Dijkstra's algorithm relies on the assumption that the shortest path from s to a given vertex includes the shortest path from s to any intermediate vertex, and this may not be true if any of the arc labels is negative.

Applying any algorithm for the single-source shortest-path problem to each vertex of a graph in succession yields an algorithm for the all-pairs version of the problem:

```
(define (all-shortest-paths graph)
  ((fold-set table
             (lambda (vertex tab)
               (put-into-table vertex
                                 (shortest-paths-from graph vertex)
                                 tab)))
    (vertices graph)))
```

The result returned by this procedure is a two-level table in which the keys are the vertices of the given graph and the corresponding data are path tables describing the shortest paths starting respectively at those vertices.

The Floyd–Warshall Algorithm

An alternative approach to the all-pairs shortest-path problem that is sometimes more efficient is the *Floyd–Warshall algorithm*. We begin with just the "trivial" paths—the zero-weight, single-vertex path from each vertex to itself, and the two-vertex path along each arc, from its tail to its head. We then consider each vertex in turn as a possible intermediary that might either open up a route from a starting vertex to a previously inaccessible goal (made by splicing together the previously known paths from the start to the intermediary and from the intermediary to the goal) or provide a shorter path than the best one that we were able to construct using only previously considered intermediaries. Once we have examined every possible intermediary, the shortest paths that we have constructed will be the shortest ones overall.

Given any graph, the `trivial-table` procedure constructs and returns a two-level path table containing only the trivial paths. The plan is first to run through the vertices, adding an entry for the zero-length path from each vertex to itself, and then to run through the arcs, adding an entry for the two-vertex path comprising each arc. Arcs in which the tail and head are identical are excepted, since the zero-length path is shorter than the two-vertex path in those cases, provided once again that none of the arc labels is negative:

```
(define (trivial-table graph)
  ((fold-set (create ((fold-set table
                        (lambda (vertex tab)
                          (put-into-table
                           vertex
                           (table (cons vertex
                                        (cons 0 (list vertex))))
                           tab)))
                      (vertices graph)))
           (lambda (arc tab)
             (receive (tail head label) (dearc arc)
               (if (equal? tail head)
                   tab
                   (table-update tail
                     (sect put-into-table
                           head
                           (cons label (list head tail))
                           <>)
                     tab)))))
   (arcs graph)))
```

The operation of splicing paths, combining two path-table entries into a path-table entry that describes the combined path, is straightforward: Add the path lengths and catenate the vertex lists, removing the extra copy of the vertex at which the splice occurs. In the catenation, the vertex list from the second given path comes first, because the vertex lists are in reverse order, with the origin of the path at the far end.

```
(define (splice-paths left right)
  (cons (+ (car left) (car right))
        (catenate (cdr right) (cdr (cdr left)))))
```

As described above, the repeated step in the Floyd–Warshall algorithm is comparing (1) the shortest known path from a starting vertex (the *origin*) to an ending vertex (the *goal*) and (2) a path obtained by combining the shortest known path from the origin to some intermediate vertex with the shortest known path from the intermediate vertex to the goal. The mechanics of this step are complicated by the potential absence of any or all of the three paths. Here is the fundamental logic:

(1) If all three paths (from origin to goal, from origin to intermediate, and from intermediate to goal) are known to exist, then we want to check whether using the intermediate vertex produces a shorter path. If so, we should splice the origin-to-intermediate and intermediate-to-goal paths and add the result to the new path table we're constructing for the origin; if not, we should copy the known origin-to-goal path into the new path table.

(2) If origin-to-intermediate and intermediate-to-goal paths are known, but no origin-to-goal path has previously been found, we should splice the origin-to-intermediate and intermediate-to-goal paths and add the result to the new path table. (In this case, there is nothing to which we could compare the length of the new path.)

(3) If an origin-to-goal path is known, but there is either no origin-to-intermediate path or no intermediate-to-goal path, then we should copy the known origin-to-goal path into the new path table.

(4) If no origin-to-goal path is known, and no path through the intermediate can be completed either (either because there is no origin-to-intermediate path, or because there is no intermediate-to-goal path, or both), then nothing should be added to the new path table, which instead should be returned unchanged.

The `test-connection` procedure implements this step. The first three parameters, `fore`, `aft`, and `direct`, are pairs respectively representing the origin-to-intermediate, intermediate-to-goal, and origin-to-goal paths (unless no such path is known, in which case the value of the parameter is #f). The `goal` parameter designates the goal vertex, and `tab` is the path table for the origin vertex:

```
(define (test-connection fore aft direct goal tab)
  (if (and (pair? fore) (pair? aft))
      (put-into-table goal
                      (if (and (pair? direct)
                               (< (car direct) (+ (car fore) (car aft))))
                          direct
```

```
                         (splice-paths fore aft))
                  tab)
       (if (pair? direct)
           (put-into-table goal direct tab)
           tab)))
```

The Floyd–Warshall algorithm has the structure of a triply nested loop, here implemented as calls to the fold-set procedure. Each loop runs through the vertices of the given graph; the outer loop considers each vertex in turn as a potential intermediate, while the inner loops run through all possible combinations of origin and goal. The test-connection procedure is invoked from the combiner procedure in the innermost call to fold-set once the various paths have been recovered from the appropriate path tables:

```
(define (all-shortest-paths graph)
  (let ((verts (vertices graph)))
    ((fold-set
      (create (trivial-table graph))
      (lambda (intermediate tab)
        (let ((mid-paths (lookup intermediate tab)))
          ((fold-set
            table
            (lambda (origin outer)
              (let ((origin-paths (lookup origin tab)))
                (let ((forepath (lookup intermediate origin-paths)))
                  (put-into-table
                   origin
                   ((fold-set
                     table
                     (lambda (goal new-tab)
                       (test-connection forepath
                                        (lookup goal mid-paths)
                                        (lookup goal origin-paths)
                                        goal
                                        new-tab)))
                    verts)
                   outer)))))
           verts))))
     verts)))
```

---

relaxable?   (afp paths)
arc(α, number), table(α, pair(number, list(α))) → Boolean
sago   path-table
Determine whether sago can be relaxed, relative to path-table.

relax   (afp paths)
arc(α, number), table(α, pair(number, list(α))) → table(α, pair(number, list(α)))
sago   path-table
Construct a path table similar to path-table, but with the entry for the head of sago revised if sago is relaxable.

shortest-paths-from   (afp shortest-paths Bellman-Ford)
graph(α, number), α $\rightarrow$ table(α, pair(number, list(α)))
graph   start
Construct a path table giving the shortest path from start to every vertex in graph that is
reachable from start.
Precondition: graph contains no cycle of arcs with a negative path sum containing a vertex
that is reachable from start.
Precondition: start is a vertex of graph.

safe-shortest-paths-from   (afp shortest-paths Bellman-Ford)
graph(α, number), α $\rightarrow$ table(α, pair(number, list(α))) | Boolean
graph   start
Construct a path table giving the shortest path from start to every vertex in graph that is
reachable from start; return #f if there is a cycle of arcs with a negative path sum containing
a vertex that is reachable from start.
Precondition: start is a vertex of graph.

nearest   (afp paths)
set(α), table(α, pair(number, list(α))) $\rightarrow$ α
aro   tab
Return the element of aro that has the least path sum (as reported by tab).
Precondition: aro is not empty.
Precondition: Every member of aro is a key in tab.

shortest-paths-from   (afp shortest-paths Dijkstra)
graph(α, number), α $\rightarrow$ table(α, pair(number, list(α)))
graph   start
Construct a path table giving the shortest path from start to every vertex in graph that is
reachable from start.
Precondition: Every arc in graph has a positive label.
Precondition: start is a vertex of graph.

all-shortest-paths   (afp shortest-paths Dijkstra)
graph(α, number) $\rightarrow$ table(α, table(α, pair(number), list(α)))
graph
Construct a two-level path table giving the shortest path from any vertex to any vertex in
graph.
Precondition: Every arc in graph has a positive label.

trivial-table   .   (afp shortest-paths Floyd-Warshall)
graph(α, number) $\rightarrow$ table(α, table(α, pair(number), list(α)))
graph
Construct a two-level path table containing the trivial (one-vertex and two-vertex) paths for
graph, along with their path sums.

splice-paths   (afp paths)
pair(number, list(α)), pair(number, list(α)) $\rightarrow$ pair(number, list(α))
left   right
Combine the path-table entries left and right, returning a path-table entry that describes a
path leading from the origin of left to the destination of right.
Precondition: The destination of left is the origin of right.

test-connection   (afp shortest-paths Floyd-Warshall)
(pair(number, list(α)) | Boolean), (pair(number, list(α)) | Boolean),
fore   aft
    (pair(number, list(α)) | Boolean), α,   table(α, pair(number, list(α))) $\rightarrow$
    direct   goal tab
                                                       table(α, pair(number, list(α)))
Return a path table similar to tab, but updated using information about three potential
paths within a graph: one (fore) connecting an "origin" vertex to some intermediate vertex,
a second (aft) connecting the intermediate vertex to a "goal" vertex (goal), and a third
(direct) connecting the origin to the goal directly. In place of any or all of these paths, the
value #f, signifying the absence of a path, may be received.

Precondition: If neither `fore` nor `direct` is `#f`, then the origin of `fore` is the origin of `direct`.
Precondition: If neither `fore` nor `aft` is `#f`, then the destination of `fore` is the origin of `aft`.
Precondition: If `aft` is not `#f`, then the destination of `aft` is `goal`.
Precondition: If `direct` is not `#f`, then the destination of `direct` is `goal`.
Precondition: `goal` is a key in `tab`.

`all-shortest-paths`   (afp shortest-paths Floyd-Warshall)
graph(α, number) $\rightarrow$ *table(α, table(α, pair(number), list(α)))*
graph
Construct a two-level path table giving the shortest path from any vertex to any vertex in graph.
Precondition: Every arc in graph has a positive label.

Exercises

6.6–1 Let G be a graph in which the vertices are the integers 2, 3, 4, 5, and 6, and there is an arc from u to v if either (a) u is a multiple of v and $v < u$, or (b) u is not a divisor of v and $u < v$. Label each arc with the product of its endpoints. Compute the two-level path table for G.

6.6–2 Define a variant of the `all-shortest-paths` procedure that accepts an unlabeled graph, treating each arc as having weight 1. (The shortest path from u to v in this case is the one that contains the fewest vertices.)

6.6–3 We could store information about the shortest paths in a graph in a different kind of table, one in which each key is a pair of vertices and each entry is a pair consisting of a path sum and a (reversed) vertex list. A key with u as its car and v as its cdr is associated with an entry describing the shortest path in the graph from u to v.

Define a variant of the `Floyd-Warshall` procedure that constructs and returns a table with this structure rather than a two-level path table.

6.7   Flow Networks

We can use graphs to model the movement of people, goods, or information within a transport network. Vertices represent the fixed nodes of the network (depots in a rail network, for instance, or workstations and routers in a computer network). Arcs represent the transport links connecting the nodes (tracks in the rail network, cables or wireless connections in the computer network).

In the *capacity graph* for a network, a label on each arc indicates the maximum amount of whatever is being transported that can move across the arc, from the node at its tail to the node at its head, in some fixed length of time. Any asymmetric graph containing two or more vertices in which all of the arcs are labeled with positive numbers qualifies as a capacity graph:

```
(define capacity-graph?
  (let ((positive-label? (pipe arc-label (^et number? positive?))))
    (^and asymmetric?
```

```
(run vertices cardinality (sect <= 2 <>))
(pipe arcs (sect for-all-in-set? positive-label? <>)))))
```

Two of these conditions reflect commonsense assumptions about the utility of
the model. Capacities are positive, because in the real world a zero-capacity
transport link would be useless and superfluous, and a negative-capacity transport link would be nonsensical. The graph has at least two vertices, because a
zero- or one-node network wouldn't actually amove anything anywhere.

The rationale for requiring the capacity graph to be asymmetric is less apparent. In some applications, it is either technically impossible or pointless to
transport things both from u to v and from v to u over the same network at
the same time, but there are other cases in which the existence of antiparallel
arcs in the capacity graph would seem entirely natural or even essential. However, several of the procedures introduced below can be formulated more clearly
and efficiently if they can rely on the asymmetry of the capacity graph as a
precondition, so we'll accept this limitation in practice.

Fortunately, we need not lose any generality by imposing it. When it seems
natural to model a transport network with a capacity graph that contains antiparallel arcs, we can force it to be asymmetric by deleting one of the arcs in
each such pair and, in its place, inserting a new vertex, with an incoming arc
from the tail of the now-deleted arc and an outgoing arc to its head. Each of
the new arcs should bear the same label as the now-deleted one. In other words,
we think of the transport link represented by the now-deleted arc as a sequence
of two links, with a node in the middle that does nothing but pass whatever is
being transported from the first link to the second.

Since the new vertices are entirely virtual, this operation has no effect on
the model's correctness or its ability to represent the transport network. It
does, however, ensure that our graph of the network is asymmetric, as required.
(Even an asymmetric graph can have antiparallel *paths*, provided that at least
one of those paths includes two or more arcs.)

In any actual use of the transport network, whatever is being transported
enters the network at one or more of its nodes, called the *origins*, and similarly
leaves the network at one or more nodes, called *destinations*. In our models,
we'll assume that there is only one origin and one destination, and that the two
are represented by different vertices in the graph.

Once again, we don't actually lose any generality in making this assumption.
If a network has two or more origins, we can model it in the capacity graph by
adding a "super-origin" vertex to the graph, with arcs connecting it to all of the
actual origins, labeled with the sum of the labels on the outgoing arcs from all of
the actual origins. Notionally, in the capacity graph, the material is transported
instantaneously from the super-origin to the nodes at which it enters the real-
world system. Similarly, at the other end, we can if necessary add a "super-
destination" vertex, with incoming arcs from all the actual destinations, labeled
with the sum of the labels of the incoming arcs at all of the actual destinations.
Like the strategy for removing antiparallel arcs, these preliminary adjustments

do not affect the model's correctness or flexibility.

A *flow graph* is a snapshot of a network, indicating how much of the available capacity is actually used in the course of some act of transportation. It has the same vertices and arcs as the network's capacity graph, but the labels on its arcs now signify the movement of whatever is being transported across the links that the arcs represent.

The label on an arc in a flow graph, therefore, is a number in the range from 0 to the label on the corresponding arc in the capacity graph for the network. If the label is 0, the transport link represented by that arc is not being used at all. If the label is equal to the label for the corresponding arc in the capacity graph, the full capacity of the link is being used. We'll assume that any intermediate value is also possible, representing partial use of the transport link within its capacity.

The `flow-in-range?` predicate determines whether each of the arcs in a graph has a label that is in the appropriate range, as specified by the capacity graph for the same network:

```
(define (flow-in-range? graph capacity-graph)
  (let ((capacity (label-lookup capacity-graph 0)))
    (for-all-in-set? (lambda (arc)
                       (receive (tail head label) (dearc arc)
                         (and (number? label)
                              (<= 0 label (capacity tail head)))))
                     (arcs graph))))
```

There is one further constraint on flow graphs: The net flow at any node other than the origin and the destination is 0. The idea is that any warehouses, overflow tanks, or storage devices anywhere in the interior of the network are omitted from the model as irrelevant. At any node other than the origin and the destination, whatever comes in must be balanced by an equivalent amount going out.

The `net-flow` procedure computes the net flow at a given vertex in a graph. The procedure constructed by the call to `fold-set` in the third line finds the sum of the labels of the arcs in a given set. To obtain the net flow, we subtract the sum of the labels of the incoming arcs from the sum of the labels of the outgoing arcs:

```
(define net-flow
  (run (dispatch arcs-leaving arcs-arriving)
       (~each (fold-set (create 0) (pipe (~initial arc-label) +)))
       -))
```

The `flow-conserved?` predicate determines whether the net flow is 0 at every vertex in a given graph except its origin and destination:

```
(define (flow-conserved? graph origin destination)
```

```
(for-all-in-set? (^or (equal-to origin)
                      (equal-to destination)
                      (pipe (sect net-flow <> graph) zero?))
                 (vertices graph)))
```

The `flow-graph?` predicate, which determines whether a given graph represents a flow (relative to a given capacity graph, with the origin and the destination specified), is the conjunction of the conditions specified above:

```
(define (flow-graph? candidate capacity-graph origin destination)
  (let ((verts (vertices candidate)))
    (and (set=? verts (vertices capacity-graph))
         ((set-of= same-endpoints?) (arcs candidate)
                                    (arcs capacity-graph))
         (flow-in-range? candidate capacity-graph)
         (member? origin verts)
         (member? destination verts)
         (not (equal? origin destination))
         (flow-conserved? candidate origin destination))))
```

The *value of a flow* is the amount of whatever it is that is being transported that the flow moves from the origin to the destination. It can be computed easily, given the origin of the flow and its graph, since the value of the flow is equal to the net flow at the origin.

```
(define flow-value net-flow)
```

For any capacity graph, with any choice of origin and destination vertices, there exists at least one flow graph—namely, the one with value 0, with no flow along any arc. The following `zero-flow` procedure can receive any capacity graph and returns a flow graph representing the zero flow through the same network:

```
(define (zero-flow graph)
  ((fold-set (create (arcless-graph (vertices graph)))
             (lambda (arc flow-graph)
               (add-labeled-arc (arc-tail arc) (arc-head arc) 0
                                flow-graph)))
   (arcs graph)))
```

Residual Networks and Maximum Flows

It is not necessary for a flow to use the full capacity of the transportation network or of any connection within it. However, in many applications, it is natural to inquire how much spare capacity there is in a flow network and whether it could be used to transport more from the origin to the destination.

A *residual network* is a graph that shows how much the amount being transported from one node to another in a flow network might be increased or decreased, while still remaining within the capacity of that connection. The residual network has the same vertices as a capacity graph or a flow graph. An opportunity for increasing the flow through an arc in the flow graph is represented by a corresponding arc in the residual network, labeled with the difference between the capacity and the existing flow through that arc; an opportunity for decreasing the flow through an arc is represented by an antiparallel (reversed) arc in the residual network, labeled with the existing flow.

When the label on an arc in the flow graph is equal to the corresponding label in the capacity graph, indicating that the transport link that it represents is being fully used, there is no opportunity for increasing the flow through that arc, so there is no corresponding arc in the residual network, only the antiparallel arc. Similarly, when the label on an arc in the flow graph is 0, there is no opportunity for decreasing the flow through that arc, and so there is no antiparallel arc in the residual network. However, both the forward and reversed arcs appear in the residual network when the flow is neither 0 nor equal to the capacity:

```
(define (residual-network capacity-graph flow-graph)
  (let ((capacity (label-lookup capacity-graph 0)))
    ((fold-set (create (arcless-graph (vertices flow-graph)))
               (lambda (arc residual)
                 (receive (tail head label) (dearc arc)
                   (let ((cap (capacity tail head)))
                     (if (zero? label)
                         (add-labeled-arc tail head cap residual)
                         (add-labeled-arc head tail label
                           (if (= label cap)
                               residual
                               (add-labeled-arc tail head (- cap label)
                                 residual)))))))))
     (arcs flow-graph))))
```

If there is a path in the residual network from the origin of a flow to its destination (an *augmenting path*), then we can construct a flow of greater value by increasing or decreasing the labels on the corresponding arcs in the flow graph. The "corresponding" arc in the flow graph is the one that has the same endpoints as an arc along the path in the residual network. We increase the label on that arc if it is directed in the same way as the arc in the residual network and decrease the label if it runs in the opposite direction. The amount by which the flow can be increased or decreased is the minimum of the labels on the arcs along the path (in the residual network).

The augment-flow procedure, then, receives a flow graph, a residual network, and a path in that residual network (which in our application will always be a path from the origin of the flow to the destination), and constructs a revised flow graph in which the arc labels have been adjusted to include the augmentation prescribed by the path. Note again that this may entail *decreasing* the flow across some arcs of the flow graph that are antiparallel to arcs along the augmenting path in the residual network.

We begin by drawing up a list of pairs of vertices that are adjacent along the path; these will be the endpoints of the arcs that we want to adjust in the flow graph. The label on each arc is to be increased or decreased by the same amount `delta`, which we compute as the minimum of the labels on the arcs along the path in the residual network. We then look up the corresponding arc in the flow graph. If it's present, we add `delta` to its arc label; otherwise, we subtract `delta` from the label on the arc with the same endpoints, but oriented in the opposite direction:

```
(define (augment-flow flow-graph residual path)
  (let ((adjs (adjacent-pairs path))
        (flow (label-lookup flow-graph)))
    (let ((delta ((extreme-in-list <=)
                  (map (pipe decons (label-lookup residual 0)) adjs))))
      ((fold-list
        (create flow-graph)
        (lambda (adj new-flow-graph)
          (receive (tail head) (decons adj)
            (let ((old-adj-flow (flow tail head)))
              (if (number? old-adj-flow)
                  (replace-arc tail head (+ old-adj-flow delta)
                               new-flow-graph)
                  (replace-arc head tail (- (flow head tail) delta)
                               new-flow-graph))))))
       adjs))))
```

By repeatedly invoking the `augment-flow` procedure until no more augmenting paths can be found, we obtain a *maximum flow* for the capacity graph—a flow of the greatest possible value. This is the *Ford–Fulkerson algorithm*:

```
(define (maximum-network-flow capacity-graph origin destination)
  ((rec (augment flow-graph)
     (let ((residual (residual-network capacity-graph flow-graph)))
       (let ((augmenting-path
              ((path-finder residual) origin destination)))
         (if (not augmenting-path)
             flow-graph
             (augment (augment-flow
                       flow-graph residual augmenting-path))))))
   (zero-flow capacity-graph)))
```

The absence of an augmenting path guarantees that the highest possible value for the flow has been achieved, since the residual network for the final flow effectively partitions the vertices of the capacity graph into two disjoint subsets—those that are reachable from the origin in the residual network and those that are not—with the destination in the second subset. All of the connections from vertices in the former of these sets to vertices in the latter are filled to capacity, and all of the connections in the opposite direction are empty (otherwise a vertex in the latter set would be reachable from the origin in the residual network). Thus no flow whatever could transport more from the vertices in the former set to the vertices of the latter set, and hence no flow whatever could transport more from origin to destination.

---

capacity-graph?   (afp flow-networks)
$graph(\alpha,\ any)\ \rightarrow\ Boolean$
graph
Determine whether graph is a capacity graph.

flow-in-range?   (afp flow-networks)
$graph(\alpha,\ any),\ graph(\alpha,\ number)\ \rightarrow\ Boolean$
graph   capacity-graph
Determine whether each of the arcs in graph has a label that is a number in the appropriate range, as specified by capacity-graph.
Precondition: The vertices of graph are the vertices of capacity-graph.
Precondition: Each arc in graph has the same tail and the same head as some arc in capacity-graph.
Precondition: capacity-graph is a capacity graph.

net-flow   (afp flow-networks)
$\alpha,\quad graph(\alpha,\ number)\ \rightarrow\ number$
vert graph
Compute the net flow through vert in graph.
Precondition: vert is a vertex of graph.

flow-conserved?   (afp flow-networks)
$graph(\alpha,\ number),\ \alpha,\quad\ \alpha\qquad\ \rightarrow\ Boolean$
graph   origin destination
Determine whether the net flow in graph is 0 at every vertex other than origin and destination.

flow-graph?   (afp flow-networks)
$graph(\alpha,\ any),\ graph(\alpha,\ number),\ \alpha,\quad\ \alpha\qquad\ \rightarrow\ Boolean$
graph   capacity-graph   origin destination
Determine whether graph is a flow graph, relative to capacity-graph, with zero net flow at every vertex except origin and destination.
Precondition: capacity-graph is a capacity graph.

flow-value   (afp flow-networks)
$\alpha,\quad graph(\alpha,\ number)\ \rightarrow\ number$
origin graph
Compute the value of the flow in graph, taking origin as its origin.
Precondition: graph is a flow graph with origin as its origin.

zero-flow   (afp flow-networks)
$graph(\alpha,\ number)\ \rightarrow\ graph(\alpha,\ number)$
graph
Construct a flow graph of value 0 relative to graph.
Precondition: graph is a capacity graph.

residual-network   (afp flow-networks)
$graph(\alpha,\ number),\ graph(\alpha,\ number)\ \rightarrow\ graph(\alpha,\ number)$
capacity-graph   flow-graph
Compute the graph of the residual network of flow-graph relative to capacity-graph.
Precondition: capacity-graph is a capacity graph.
Precondition: flow-graph is a flow graph relative to capacity-graph.

augment-flow   (afp flow-networks)

graph(α, number), graph(α, number), list(α) → *graph(α, number)*
flow-graph   residual   path
Construct a flow graph similar to flow-graph, except that the value of the flow from its origin
to its destination is greater, as a result of adjustments in the arc labels in flow-graph along
path in residual.
Precondition: residual is the residual network for flow-graph relative to some capacity graph.
Precondition: path is an augmenting path in residual.

maximum-network-flow   (afp flow-networks)
graph(α, number),   α,   α   → *graph(α, number)*
capacity-graph   origin destination
Construct a flow graph of maximum value in the network described by capacity-graph, with
origin as its origin and destination as its destination.
Precondition: capacity-graph is a capacity graph.
Precondition: origin and destination are distinct vertices in capacity-graph.

Exercises

6.7–1   Let G be a graph in which the vertices are the integers 2, 3, 4, 5, and 6,
and there is arc from u to v if either (a) u is a multiple of v and $v < u$, or (b) u
is not a divisor of v and $u < v$. Label each arc with the product of its endpoints.
Find a maximum flow from vertex 6 to vertex 5 in this graph, considered as a
flow network. Compute the residual network for this flow.

6.7–2   Prove that the value of the maximum flow from u to v in a capacity
graph G is equal to the value of the maximum flow from v to u in its converse.

6.7–3   On some graphs, we can improve the performance of the Ford–Fulkerson
algorithm by replacing the call to the procedure that path-finder constructs
with a call to a procedure that finds the shortest path from the origin to the
destination (that is, the path containing the fewest vertices). Define such a
procedure and adapt maximum-network-flow to use it.

Chapter 7

Sublist Search

The sublist-search problem is to find the positions at which copies of a given list p (the "pattern") occur within another (usually much longer) given list t (the "text"). For instance, p might be a list of nucleotides that can direct the construction of some particular protein, and t a list of nucleotides occurring along some strand of DNA; the position of a match might then indicate the location of some part of a gene. Alternatively, p might be a list of the characters in a word, and t a list of the characters in some long text; the results of the sublist search would then be the positions of the word in the text. It's useful to consider several algorithms for sublist search, since they have different strengths and weaknesses.

7.1 The Simple, Slow Algorithm

First, let's clarify the problem, and state more specifically what we want to obtain as an answer to any instance of it. We'll assume that `equal?` is a satisfactory criterion of sameness for the values occurring in p and t, so that a "copy" of p inside t is a section of t with the same elements as p, arranged in the same order as in p. We can identify the position of the copy by the number of elements of t that precede the matching section. (If p is not null, this will be the same as the index in t of the first element of the section that matches p.)

Using this convention, we require that the result of any sublist search be a list of natural numbers in ascending order, identifying the positions in t of the sections that are copies of p. (If there are no copies of p in t, the result is an empty list.)

For instance, if we search for the pattern (list 'foo 'bar 'foo) in the text (list 'foo 'foo 'foo 'bar 'foo 'bar 'foo 'foo 'bar 'bar 'foo 'bar 'foo 'foo 'bar), we find that one copy starts at position 2, another at position 4, and yet another at position 10, so the result of the sublist search is (list 2 4 10). Note that the copies can overlap one another, so that we must think of each

© Springer-Verlag GmbH Germany, part of Springer Nature 2018
J. D. Stone, *Algorithms for Functional Programming*,
https://doi.org/10.1007/978-3-662-57970-1_7

matching operation as independent. After finding one copy, it's not sufficient
to pick up where that copy leaves off. We must ensure that we find *every* copy
of the pattern, even the overlapping ones.

The data structures that we are given as inputs to the problem suggest a
few brute-force strategies. We could, for instance, use sections (from §5.2) to
get a list of all the sublists of the text that have the same length as the pattern,
and then find the positions in that list at which values that match the pattern
occur. Alternatively, we could fold over the natural numbers from 0 up to and
including the difference between the length of the text and the length of the
pattern, extracting the appropriate-length sublist of the text for each position
and comparing it to the pattern, and adding the position number to our result
if the lists match. Yet another possibility is an iteration in which we compare
the pattern to a prefix of the text at each step and then apply rest to the text
to advance to the next position, stopping when the remaining text is shorter
than the pattern.

The matches-prefix? predicate determines whether the entire pattern
matches a prefix of the text:

```
(define matches-prefix?
  (check (pipe >initial empty-list?)
         (pipe (~each first) equal?)
         (~each rest)))
```

If the pattern is the empty list, it matches immediately. Otherwise, we continue
only if the first elements of the pattern and the text are the same, and proceed
by supplying the rest of the pattern and the rest of the text as arguments to
the recursive call.

It is a precondition of the matches-prefix? predicate that the length of
the pattern is less than or equal to the length of the text. We can use
matches-prefix? in the definition of our brute-force sublist-search procedure,
but the recursion has to be arranged in a slightly unusual way in order to guarantee that the precondition is satisfied at each invocation of matches-prefix?:

```
(define (sublist-search pattern text)
  (let ((last-position (- (length text) (length pattern))))
    ((rec (searcher start remaining-text)
       (let ((rest-of-matches (if (= start last-position)
                                  (list)
                                  (searcher (add1 start)
                                            (rest remaining-text)))))
         (if (matches-prefix? pattern remaining-text)
             (prepend start rest-of-matches)
             rest-of-matches)))
     0 text)))
```

This algorithm is deplorably slow in the worst case, which occurs when the text and the pattern are both lists consisting almost entirely of copies of some value, except possibly with a different value right at the end of either or both. The `sublist-search` procedure shown above then invokes `matches-prefix?` at every possible position, and `matches-prefix?` has to work its way all the way to the end of the pattern before determining whether a match is present, so the total number of element comparisons is proportional to the product of the lengths of the pattern and text.

Even in less extreme cases, however, this simple `sublist-search` procedure is inefficient, because it does not store any information in the course of one invocation of `matches-prefix?` that it could use to simplify the next invocation, or to avoid even attempting invocations that cannot possibly succeed. In the remaining sections of this chapter, we shall develop a few ways to acquire and store such information.

Substring Search

Algorithms for sublist searching are often presented with string values for the pattern and text and with `char=?` instead of `equal?` as the criterion of sameness. The same general approaches are available, but strings have an advantage over lists that the algorithms commonly exploit: Scheme provides a built-in procedure `string-ref` that selects a character at a specified position in a string, just as `list-ref` selects a value at a specified position in a list. Unlike `list-ref`, however, `string-ref` takes a constant (small) amount of time regardless of which position is specified.

When dealing with string patterns and texts, therefore, it is usual to apply recursion guided by natural numbers to generate arguments to `string-ref`, instead of trying to pick strings apart with analogues of `first` and `rest` (which would be extremely slow).

For instance, here's the string analogue of `matches-prefix?`. It tests whether a copy of its first argument occurs within its second argument, beginning at a position specified by the third argument. (The `string-length` procedure, also predefined in Scheme, computes the number of characters in its argument, which must be a string.)

```
(define (occurs-at? pattern text shift)
  (let ((pattern-length (string-length pattern)))
    ((check (sect = <> pattern-length)
            (pipe (dispatch (sect string-ref pattern <>)
                            (pipe (sect + shift <>)
                                  (sect string-ref text <>)))
                  char=?)
            add1)
     0)))
```

The string analogue of the simple, slow `sublist-search` procedure, then, runs through the possible positions in the text, checking at each position for a copy of the pattern:

```
(define (substring-search pattern text)
  (let ((last-position (- (string-length text) (string-length pattern))))
    ((rec (searcher start)
       (let ((rest-of-matches (if (= start last-position)
                                  (list)
                                  (searcher (add1 start)))))
         (if (occurs-at? pattern text start)
             (prepend start rest-of-matches)
             rest-of-matches)))
     0)))
```

---

matches-prefix?   (afp lists)
list(α), list(α) → *Boolean*
pattern text
Determine whether each element of pattern is the same as the corresponding element of text.
Precondition: The length of pattern is less than or equal to the length of text.

sublist-search   (afp sublist-search simple-slow-sublist-search)
list(α), list(α) → *list(natural-number)*
pattern text
Construct a list of the positions in text at which sublists that match pattern begin, in ascending order.
Precondition: The length of pattern is less than or equal to the length of text.

occurs-at?   (afp strings)
string,   string,   natural-number → *Boolean*
pattern text   shift
Determine whether pattern is a substring of text that begins at position shift.
Precondition: The sum of shift and the length of pattern is less than or equal to the length of text.

substring-search   (afp sublist-search simple-slow-sublist-search)
string,   string → *list(natural-number)*
pattern text
Construct a list of the positions in text at which substrings that match pattern begin, in ascending order.
Precondition: The length of pattern is less than or equal to the length of text.

Exercises

7.1–1   If the pattern in an instance of sublist search is the empty list, and the text is a list of seven values, at how many positions (if any) will `simple-slow-sublist-search` detect a match?

7.1–2   Suppose that the pattern and text in a sublist search are both lists of integers, and we want to detect *approximate* matches, in which the disparity between corresponding elements of the pattern and text is less than or equal to, say, 16, as well as exact matches (in which, of course, the disparity is 0).

Adapt the matches-prefix? procedure to detect such approximate matches, then define a higher-order procedure prefix-matcher that receives a binary element-comparison procedure and returns a variation of the matches-prefix? procedure that uses it as the criterion of sameness for elements of the prefix and text.

7.1–3 Define a procedure first-sublist-match that receives two lists, a pattern and a text, and returns the *least* position in the text at which a sublist matching the pattern begins, or #f if there is no such position. The procedure should return this value as soon as it has computed it, without examining subsequent positions in the text.

7.2 The Knuth–Morris–Pratt Algorithm

One way to speed up the matching process is to skip a matching attempt when information that we have already acquired, in previous matching attempts, proves that it will fail. Instead of always advancing to the next position in the text and starting every matching attempt at the beginning of the pattern, we should *compute* the next position that might lead to a successful match, and skip element-to-element comparisons when we know that they will succeed. The Knuth–Morris–Pratt algorithm implements this strategy.

To get an idea of how the algorithm works, let's think more carefully about how and when to align the pattern against the text. Let m be the length of the pattern, and suppose that we have just finished comparing the element at position i in the text with the element at position j of the pattern. We need to advance to a new position in the text in two cases: (1) If the most recent element-to-element comparison failed, we need to "slide" the pattern along the text to the next position at which a match is possible. (2) If the most recent element-to-element comparison succeeded, and j is the position of the last element of the pattern (in other words, $j = m - 1$), all the other elements in the pattern having been previously matched to text elements, we want to add the current starting position of the sublist, $i - j$, to the result set, and in this case too we want to slide the pattern along the text to the next position at which a match is possible.

(In the remaining case, where the most recent comparison succeeded but we haven't yet reached the end of the pattern, no realignment is needed. Instead, we just move on to compare the next element of the pattern against the next element of the text.)

The hard part is calculating how far to slide. Let's consider case (1) first. If the mismatch occurs right at the beginning of the pattern (in other words, if $j = 0$), then we have no choice: Since we don't want to miss any possible matches, and the matching attempt at the current position doesn't tell us anything about what lies ahead, we cannot increase the advance more than one position farther down the text, and we have to start the pattern over again there. On the other hand, if we have already matched one or more text elements before encountering the mismatch, then it is pointless to try to match any of those text elements again, and so we can slide the pattern forwards along the text by the number of elements matched—*unless there is repetition within the pattern*, specifically, a sublist that is both a proper prefix and a proper suffix of the part of the pattern that we succeeded in matching. (A "proper" prefix or suffix is one that is not empty and does not comprise the entire list of which it is a part.)

If there is such a sublist, then there may be a match in which the copy at the beginning of the pattern is aligned with the part of the text where the copy at the end of the partial match used to be. If the repeated sequence is k elements long, then the starting point of this possible match is $i - k$, and we need to realign the pattern so that its first k elements correspond to the k most recently examined elements of the text (which they must match, since equal? is transitive).

For instance, suppose that the pattern is (list 'c 'o 'n 'c 'o 'r 'd) and the text is (list 'b 'a 'c 'o 'n 'c 'o 'n 'c 'o 'r 'd 'a 't). When we try position 2 as a starting point of the text, we can match the first five elements of the pattern with the next five elements of the text, but then the element n at position $i = 7$ in the text does not match the element r at position $j = 5$ in the pattern.

If there were no repetition within the part of the pattern that we had matched, then we would skip past all of the matched elements in the text and try to match the whole pattern again, comparing position 0 in the pattern with position 7 in the text, since in that case none of the starting positions between 2 and 7 in the text could possibly lead to a match. In the actual situation, however, there is a sublist, namely (list 'c 'o), that is both a proper prefix and a proper suffix of the part of the pattern that we have matched, (list 'c 'o 'n 'c 'o). So the next starting position in the text at which we might find a match is the one that aligns the first two elements of the pattern with the last two elements matched in the text—starting position $i - 2$, or 5. In this case, indeed, it turns out that this second match succeeds, so that our matcher will ultimately return (list 5).

In some cases, more than one sublist is both a proper prefix and a proper suffix of the matched part of the pattern. For instance, if we have matched (list 0 1 2 0 1 2 0), then of course (list 0) occurs both at the beginning and end ($k = 1$), but so does (list 0 1 2 0) ($k = 4$). To be sure of catching every possible match, we must use the largest possible value of k, so that the realignment does not move the pattern too far along the text.

After the realignment, however, we don't have to compare the repeated values in the pattern to the text again, since we know that they will match (they are the same values that matched before, at the same positions in the text). The matching process can proceed by comparing the element at position k of the pattern with the element at position i of the text—the one that caused the mismatch—and continue rightwards from there.

Now let's go back and consider case (2). This time, we've matched the entire pattern—m elements in all—to the text. If there is no repetition in the pattern, then the next starting position at which a match is possible is $i + 1$, because the element at position i of the text, having matched the element at position j of the pattern, won't match any of the earlier elements. So we can skip directly from starting position $i - j$ to starting position $i + 1$. On the other hand, if there is a sequence of k values that begins and ends the whole pattern, then again we might miss a match by taking such a large jump. Instead, we have to align the last k elements that we matched in the text to the first k elements of the pattern, and we do this by taking $i + 1 - k$ as the next shift. The next comparison, then, is between the element at position k of the pattern and the one at position $i + 1$ of the text.

Despite the need to calculate k, the length of the longest suffix of the matched part of the pattern that is also a prefix of the pattern, this approach is potentially much more efficient than `simple-slow-sublist-search`. Since k depends only on the pattern and the number of elements matched, the values of k for a given pattern can be computed in advance and stored (in, say, a list). Then, no matter how long the text is, we can skip through it, never performing the same element-to-element comparison twice, being guided by the appropriate stored value of k whenever we encounter a mismatch (case 0) or match the last element of the pattern (case 1).

To compute the list of the values of k, given a pattern, we could just do a separate brute-force search for every possible number of elements matched (from 1 to m) and collect the results. Within each search, we would try smaller and smaller values of k until we found one that worked. Such a search will always terminate, because $k = 0$ always works: The empty list occurs at the beginning and end of *any* sublist of the pattern.

But this approach, like the simple, slow algorithm for sublist search itself, is needlessly inefficient, and for a similar reason: The elements of the list are not independent of one another. We can do better by reusing the information that we collect while computing one value of k when computing later ones. Specifically, suppose that we have computed the appropriate list entries for prefixes of lengths 1 through i, and we want to compute the next shift number— the value of k to be used when $i + 1$ elements of the pattern have been matched in the text before a mismatch occurs. This new shift number is at most one greater than the previous one. It will be exactly one greater when the repeated sublist can be extended by one element both at the beginning of the pattern and at the end of the matched part of the pattern. Otherwise, we want to slide the pattern along itself in the same way that we slide it along the text during actual matching operations. We can compute how far to slide it by consulting the very list of shift numbers that we are constructing!

It turns out to be most convenient to maintain this list in reverse order, since it will be built up from right to left as we consider successive values of i, from 1 up to the length of the pattern.

The `next-prefix-length` procedure uses this method to compute the next

354 CHAPTER 7. SUBLIST SEARCH

shift number, given the pattern, the number of elements matched (called `index` in the code), and the list (called `prefix-lengths`) of shift numbers that have already been computed. The preconditions of this procedure are (1) that `index` is positive, but less than the length of `pattern`; (2) that the length of `prefix-lengths` is equal to `index`; and (3) that the element at each position p in `prefix-lengths` is a correctly computed shift number for `pattern`, namely, the length of the longest prefix of `pattern` that is also a proper suffix of the sublist comprising the first $index - p$ elements of `pattern`:

```
(define (next-prefix-length ls index prefix-lengths)
  ((rec (matcher matched)
     (if (equal? (list-ref ls matched) (list-ref ls index))
         (add1 matched)
         (if (zero? matched)
             0
             (matcher (list-ref prefix-lengths (- index matched))))))
   (first prefix-lengths)))
```

The idea is that `matched` keeps track of the number of elements from the beginning of `ls` that are known to match elements leading up to position `index`. Initially, we bind `matched` to the previous shift number. If the next element of `ls` matches the one at position `index`, we've identified the case in which the shift number is one greater than the preceding one, so we return `(add1 matched)`; otherwise, we need to try a smaller value for `matched`. If `matched` is already 0, however, there are no smaller values to try, so we give up and return 0 for the shift number; otherwise, we can check the `prefix-lengths` list for possible repetitions within the sublist of matched elements, and issue a recursive call with the value recovered from that list as the new value of `matched`, in the hope of being able to extend that shorter sublist.

By repeated calls to `next-prefix-length`, we can construct the entire list of shift numbers from the pattern alone. The `prefix-function` procedure receives the pattern, computes the list of shift numbers, and encapsulates it in a specialized procedure, to be used in the matching process, that receives the number of elements matched as an argument and returns the appropriate shift number:

```
(define (prefix-function pattern)
  (let ((len (length pattern)))
    (let ((prefix-function-list
            ((ply-natural
              (create (list 0))
              (lambda (index prefix-lengths)
                (prepend (next-prefix-length pattern
                                             index
                                             prefix-lengths)
                         prefix-lengths)))
             (sub1 len))))
      (pipe (sect - len <>) (sect list-ref prefix-function-list <>)))))
```

In the actual execution of the Knuth–Morris–Pratt algorithm, then, we examine the elements of the text one at a time, and compare at least one element of the pattern against that text element in an attempt to match it—possibly more than one, if there are several ways to align the pattern against the text that might lead to a match. Given the text and pattern for a matching operation, the KMP-stepper procedure constructs and returns a customized procedure that computes and tests alignments of the pattern against one particular element of the text, until it either finds one in which the pattern element matches the text element or runs out of possibilities. The customized procedure, when it is finally invoked, receives three arguments: the text element to be matched (element), its position in the text (index), and the number of pattern elements that are known to match elements at immediately preceding positions in the text (matched).

The customized procedure returns two values: a Boolean, indicating whether it has successfully matched the last element of the pattern against element (thus completing a match of the entire pattern), and a natural number, indicating how to realign the pattern against the text for the next step in the computation—more specifically, how many elements from the beginning of the pattern are known to match the most recently examined elements of the text.

To compute this second return value, we distinguish four cases:

- If the pattern element matches the text element, and it is the last element of the pattern, we can invoke the customized prefix function to compute the length of the longest proper prefix of the pattern that could lead to another match and return #t and that length.

- If the pattern element matches the text element, and it is not the last element of the pattern, then we add 1 to the number of previously matched elements of the prefix and return #f and the result.

- If the pattern element does not match the text element, and it is at position 0 in the pattern, then we have no more options and have to return #f and 0, so that at the next position in the text we'll start over at the beginning of the pattern.

- If the pattern element does not match the text element, but it is not at position 0 in the pattern, then again we can invoke the customized prefix function to give us another option. In this case, however, we don't want to advance to the next text element quite yet, since we may still find a matching element earlier on in the pattern. Accordingly, the procedure realigns the pattern internally and invokes itself recursively with the new alignment.

```
(define (KMP-stepper pattern)
  (let ((len (length pattern))
        (pf (prefix-function pattern)))
```

```
    (lambda (text-element matched)
      ((rec (matcher pattern-position)
         (if (equal? (list-ref pattern pattern-position) text-element)
             (let ((one-more (add1 pattern-position)))
               (if (= one-more len)
                   (values #t (pf one-more))
                   (values #f one-more)))
             (if (zero? pattern-position)
                 (values #f 0)
                 (matcher (pf pattern-position)))))
       matched))))
```

The sublist-search procedure itself calls KMP-stepper to obtain the appropriately customized procedure and invokes that procedure at every position in the text. If the first value it returns is #t, sublist-search computes the position at which the match started and adds it to its list of matches. Regardless of the first returned value, however, the second returned value contains the information needed to realign the pattern against the next element of the text so that there is no possibility of missing a match.

The empty pattern has to be treated as a special case, because it does not meet the precondition for KMP-stepper. Since the empty pattern matches at every position, we can just generate the result without even looking at the elements of the text in this case:

```
(define (sublist-search pattern text)
  (let ((text-length (length text)))
    (if (zero? (length pattern))
        ((unfold-list (equal-to (add1 text-length)) identity add1) 0)
        (let ((stepper (KMP-stepper pattern)))
          ((rec (searcher subtext position matched)
             (if (empty-list? subtext)
                 (list)
                 (receive (completed new-matched)
                          (stepper (first subtext) matched)
                   (let ((recursive-result (searcher (rest subtext)
                                                     (add1 position)
                                                     new-matched)))
                     (if completed
                         (prepend (- position matched) recursive-result)
                         recursive-result)))))
           text 0 0)))))
```

Since the Knuth–Morris–Pratt algorithm consistently advances through the text string, never backing up, it is particularly well adapted to applications in which the text string must be read in one character at a time from a device that permits only sequential access (as, for instance, when it is too large to fit into random-access memory and must be read in from a file on a hard disk) or generated from a source.

Substring Search

The Knuth–Morris–Pratt algorithm can also be used effectively to search for copies of a string pattern inside a string text. A few of the details are different, because of the difference between the random-access nature of strings and the sequential-access nature of lists.

The analogue of the `next-prefix-length` procedure differs only in that `string-ref` replaces `list-ref` when we access components of the pattern:

```
(define (next-string-prefix-length str index prefix-lengths)
  ((rec (matcher matched)
     (if (equal? (string-ref str matched) (string-ref str index))
         (add1 matched)
         (if (zero? matched)
             0
             (matcher (list-ref prefix-lengths (- index matched))))))
   (first prefix-lengths)))
```

The construction of the prefix function and the stepper procedure are essentially identical to their list counterparts:

```
(define (string-prefix-function pattern)
  (let ((len (string-length pattern)))
    (let ((prefix-function-list
            ((ply-natural
               (create (list 0))
               (lambda (index prefix-lengths)
                 (prepend (next-string-prefix-length pattern
                                                      index
                                                      prefix-lengths)
                          prefix-lengths)))
             (sub1 len))))
      (pipe (sect - len <>) (sect list-ref prefix-function-list <>)))))

(define (KMP-string-stepper pattern)
  (let ((len (string-length pattern))
        (spf (string-prefix-function pattern)))
    (lambda (text-element matched)
      ((rec (matcher pattern-position)
         (if (char=? (string-ref pattern pattern-position) text-element)
             (let ((one-more (add1 pattern-position)))
               (if (= one-more len)
                   (values #t (spf one-more))
                   (values #f one-more)))
             (if (zero? pattern-position)
                 (values #f 0)
                 (matcher (spf pattern-position)))))
       matched))))
```

In the main search procedure, the internal recursive procedure searcher can be simplified slightly, since we only need to keep track of position, not subtext:

```
(define (substring-search pattern text)
  (let ((text-length (string-length text)))
    (if (zero? (string-length pattern))
        ((unfold-list (equal-to (add1 text-length)) identity add1) 0)
        (let ((stepper (KMP-string-stepper pattern)))
          ((rec (searcher position matched)
             (if (= position text-length)
                 (list)
                 (receive (completed new-matched)
                          (stepper (string-ref text position) matched)
                   (let ((recursive-result (searcher (add1 position)
                                                     new-matched)))
                     (if completed
                         (prepend (- position matched) recursive-result)
                         recursive-result)))))
           0 0)))))
```

---

next-prefix-length   (afp sublist-search Knuth-Morris-Pratt)
list(any), natural-number, list(natural-number) → natural-number
ls   index   prefix-lengths
Compute the length of the longest prefix of ls that is also a proper suffix of the prefix of ls of length index, consulting prefix-lengths to obtain similar values for lesser values of index.
Precondition: index is less than or equal to the length of ls.
Precondition: The length of prefix-lengths is index.
Precondition: For every natural number n less than index, the element at position index$-n-1$ of prefix-lengths is the length of the longest prefix of ls that is also a proper suffix of the prefix of ls of length n.

prefix-function   (afp sublist-search Knuth-Morris-Pratt)
list(any) → (natural-number → natural-number)
pattern   index
Construct a procedure that computes the length of the longest prefix of pattern that is also a proper suffix of the prefix of pattern of length index.
Precondition: index is less than or equal to the length of pattern.

KMP-stepper   (afp sublist-search Knuth-Morris-Pratt)
list(α) → (α,   natural-number → Boolean, natural-number)
pattern   text-element matched
Construct a procedure that tests whether text-element occurs at position matched in pattern and, if so, whether position matched is the last position in pattern. If both conditions are met, the constructed procedure returns #t and the length of the longest proper prefix of pattern that is also a suffix of pattern; otherwise, the constructed procedure returns #f and, as a second result, either the successor of matched (if text-element was successfully matched to an element of pattern), or the length of the longest proper prefix of pattern that is also a suffix of the prefix of pattern ending just before position matched.
Precondition: pattern is not empty.
Precondition: matched is less than the length of pattern.

sublist-search   (afp sublist-search Knuth-Morris-Pratt)
list(α), list(α) → list(natural-number)
pattern text
Construct a list of the positions in text at which sublists that match pattern begin, in ascending order.
Precondition: The length of pattern is less than or equal to the length of text.

next-string-prefix-length   (afp sublist-search Knuth-Morris-Pratt)
string, natural-number, list(natural-number) → natural-number
str   index   prefix-lengths
Compute the length of the longest prefix of str that is also a proper suffix of the prefix of str
of length index, consulting prefix-lengths to obtain similar values for lesser values of index.
Precondition: index is less than or equal to the length of str.
Precondition: The length of prefix-lengths is index.
Precondition: For every natural number n less than index, the element at position index$-n-1$
of prefix-lengths is the length of the longest prefix of str that is also a proper suffix of the
prefix of str of length n.

string-prefix-function   (afp sublist-search Knuth-Morris-Pratt)
string   → (natural-number → natural-number)
pattern   index
Construct a procedure that computes the length of the longest prefix of pattern that is also
a proper suffix of the prefix of pattern of length index.
Precondition: index is less than or equal to the length of pattern.

KMP-string-stepper   (afp sublist-search Knuth-Morris-Pratt)
string   → (character,   natural-number → Boolean, natural-number)
pattern   text-element   matched
Construct a procedure that tests whether text-element occurs at position matched in pattern
and, if so, whether position matched is the last position in pattern. If both conditions are met,
the constructed procedure returns #t and the length of the longest proper prefix of pattern
that is also a suffix of pattern; otherwise, the constructed procedure returns #f and, as a
second result, either the successor of matched (if text-element was successfully matched to an
element of pattern), or the length of the longest proper prefix of pattern that is also a suffix
of the prefix of pattern ending just before position matched.
Precondition: pattern is not empty.
Precondition: matched is less than the length of pattern.

substring-search   (afp sublist-search Knuth-Morris-Pratt)
string,   string → list(natural-number)
pattern text
Construct a list of the positions in text at which substrings that match pattern begin, in
ascending order.
Precondition: The length of pattern is less than or equal to the length of text.

Exercises

7.2–1 The domain of the prefix function for the pattern (list 'alpha 'beta
'gamma 'delta 'alpha 'beta 'gamma 'alpha 'beta 'alpha) consists of the
natural numbers from 0 to 10. Compute, by hand, the value of the prefix
function for each argument in this domain.

7.2–2 Adapt the Knuth–Morris–Pratt substring-search procedure so that it
constructs a source that searches for a string pattern in a "text" that is a source
(possibly finite) of characters. When tapped, the source should return as its
first result a natural number indicating the position in the text source at which
the first occurrence of the pattern begins (or the end-of-source value, if the text
is a finite source containing no occurrence of the pattern). The second result, as
usual, should be a source that continues the search (or an empty finite source,
if the text is an empty finite source).

7.2–3 Under what conditions, if any, could the source-oriented version of the `substring-search` procedure developed in the preceding exercise fail to terminate?

7.2–4   Define a procedure `KMP-comparison-counter` that computes the number of times a pattern element is compared to a text element in the course of applying the Knuth–Morris–Pratt algorithm to a given pattern and a given text.

7.3   The Boyer–Moore Algorithm

Even the Knuth–Morris–Pratt algorithm does not use *all* of the information that is acquired during one matching attempt. When a mismatch occurs, the identity of the *text* element that fails to match can also be instructive, since it is pointless to attempt subsequent matches that would compare that mismatching text element with a pattern element that is already known not to match it.

The Boyer–Moore algorithm initially constructs a table in which each key is a value that occurs in the pattern, and the entry with which a key is associated is the greatest position in the pattern at which that value occurs in the pattern string. The algorithm then repeatedly tries to match the pattern against sections of the text of the same length. In each matching attempt, it compares corresponding values *from right to left* until either (1) the whole pattern been matched or (2) a mismatch occurs.

In case (1), the algorithm adds the starting position of the matching section of the text to the result list and advances to the next position in the text.

In case (2), the algorithm looks up the text element that caused the mismatch in the table derived from the prefix and computes the alignment of pattern against text that would bring the mismatching text value into alignment with its rightmost occurrence in the pattern. If this alignment would move the pattern backwards, the algorithm has already either tested it or determined that no match can succeed, so it again advances to the next sublist of the text. If, however, the alignment would move the pattern forwards, the algorithm implements it by advancing the appropriate distance down the text before starting the next matching attempt. Finally, if the text element that caused the mismatch is not in the pattern at all, we can slide the pattern completely beyond the point of the mismatch.

In any of these cases, having advanced through the text, the algorithm attempts another match, again comparing elements from right to left.

If the pattern is long, and many different values occur frequently in the text, a mismatch that occurs early in the element-by-element scan often results in a large increase in the shift. Consequently, the Boyer–Moore algorithm can often find all of the occurrences of the pattern within the text without looking, even once, at most of the elements of the text!

Since the element-by-element scan proceeds from right-to-left, this algorithm isn't helpful in sublist search, since we can't reach the rightmost element of a sublist without going through the elements that precede it, in which case we might just as well pause to inspect them. However, given a random-access structure such as a string, the use of a mismatch table often speeds up the search considerably. Accordingly, we'll implement the Boyer–Moore algorithm only for substring search.

Given a pattern string, the `rightmost-occurrence-finder` constructs the table of rightmost occurrences and returns a specialized procedure that serves as an interface to the table. The specialized procedure returns the rightmost position at which its argument occurs in the pattern, or -1 if it does not occur at all:

```
(define (rightmost-occurrence-finder pattern)
  (let ((len (string-length pattern)))
    ((rec (builder position tab)
       (if (= position len)
           (sect lookup <> tab -1)
           (builder (add1 position)
                    (put-into-table (string-ref pattern position)
                                    position
                                    tab))))
     0 (table))))
```

Given both a pattern and a text, the `Boyer-Moore-stepper` procedure returns a procedure that tries to match the pattern to a substring of the text that begins at a specified position, proceeding from right to left. The constructed procedure returns -1 if the match is completed successfully; if a mismatch is encountered, it returns the position (in the pattern) at which the mismatch occurs:

```
(define (Boyer-Moore-stepper pattern text)
  (let ((len (string-length pattern)))
    (lambda (start)
      ((rec (matcher remaining)
         (if (zero? remaining)
             -1
             (let ((next (sub1 remaining)))
               (if (char=? (string-ref pattern next)
                           (string-ref text (+ start next)))
                   (matcher next)
                   next))))
       len))))
```

The `substring-search` procedure, then, invokes `rightmost-occurrence-finder` to obtain a customized mismatch lookup procedure for the given pattern, and `Boyer-Moore-stepper` to obtain the customized step procedure for the given pattern and text. It then alternately invokes the step procedure to attempt matches and computes the appropriate number of positions to slide to get the next offset at which a match could occur. We stop the process when we reach a position in the text after which too few characters remain to accommodate the pattern:

```
(define (substring-search pattern text)
  (let ((find (rightmost-occurrence-finder pattern))
        (step (Boyer-Moore-stepper pattern text))
        (last-position (- (string-length text)
                          (string-length pattern))))
    ((rec (shifter position)
       (if (< last-position position)
           (list)
           (let ((step-result (step position)))
             (if (negative? step-result)
                 (prepend position (shifter (add1 position)))
                 (let ((pattern-position
                        (find (string-ref text
                                          (+ position step-result)))))
                   (shifter (+ position
                              (max 1 (- pattern-position
                                        step-result)))))))))
     0)))
```

---

rightmost-occurrence-finder   (afp sublist-search Boyer-Moore)
string   → *(character* → *integer)*
pattern   sought
Construct a procedure that computes the greatest position at which sought occurs within pattern, returning -1 if there is no such position.

Boyer-Moore-stepper   (afp sublist-search Boyer-Moore)
string, string → *(natural-number* → *natural-number)*
pattern text   start
Construct a procedure that tries to match pattern to the substring of text that begins at start, returning the greatest position in pattern at which a mismatch occurs, or -1 if the match is successful.
Precondition: The sum of start and the length of pattern is less than or equal to the length of text.

substring-search   (afp sublist-search Boyer-Moore)
string, string → *list(natural-number)*
pattern text
Construct a list of the positions in text at which substrings that match pattern begin, in ascending order.

Exercises

7.3–1   Determine how many invocations of char=? the Boyer–Moore algorithm performs in searching for occurrences of the pattern "gatonwgat" in the text "isgatonwgatngdenwgatonwgatonwgatnaffyualdegatonwgatnar".

7.3–2   One way to extend the utility of substring search is to allow the pattern to contain occurrences of a *wildcard character*, which can match any single character in the text. Adapt our implementation of the Boyer–Moore algorithm so that it treats a question mark in the pattern as a wildcard character.

7.4 The Rabin–Karp Algorithm

The Rabin–Karp algorithm is an alternative approach to speeding up the naive matching algorithm of §7.1. Instead of looking for ways to avoid redundant element matches, we can replace the call to `matches-prefix?` with a simpler and faster test that compares the whole pattern to the relevant prefix of the text as a unit.

The fundamental idea is to convert the pattern and the text prefix into natural numbers, which can be tested for equality with a single invocation of `=`. This conversion presupposes that the values in the pattern and text are taken from a fixed, finite set of potential elements. If we take the cardinality of this set as a base of numeration and regard the values in this set as digits in numerals in this base, then each list of a given length (specifically, the length of the pattern) numerically expresses a different natural number, as a sum of multiples of powers of the base.

For instance, if the pattern and text represent fragmentary sequences of nucleotide bases in a molecule of DNA, the set might consist of the four symbols A, C, G, and T, representing the four kinds of molecules that constitute those nucleotide bases (adenine, cytosine, guanine, and thymine). The Rabin–Karp algorithm assigns a digit value to each of the symbols—0 to A, 1 to C, 2 to G, and 3 to T, for instance. Let's encapsulate this assignment in a procedure:

```
(define nucleotide-value
  (let ((nucleotide-list (list 'A 'C 'G 'T)))
    (sect position-in <> nucleotide-list)))
```

A pattern such as `(list 'T 'A 'A 'C 'G 'T)` then corresponds to a base-four numeral, 300123. To compute the natural number that this numeral denotes, we would compute the sum of the products of the digits with the corresponding powers of the base of numeration (which in this case is four): $3 \cdot 4^5 + 0 \cdot 4^4 + 0 \cdot 4^3 + 1 \cdot 4^2 + 2 \cdot 4^1 + 3 \cdot 4^0$, which turns out to be the number that we express in our ordinary base-ten system of numeration as 3099 ($3 \cdot 10^3 + 0 \cdot 10^2 + 9 \cdot 10^1 + 9 \cdot 10^0$). The `dna-numeric-value` procedure defined below computes the natural number that corresponds to a list of the four nucleotides:

```
(define dna-numeric-value
  (process-list (create 0)
                (pipe (cross nucleotide-value (sect * <> 4))
                      +)))
```

However, if one is looking for a long pattern containing values taken from a large set, a procedure like `dna-numeric-value` can return natural numbers so large that it becomes noticeably less efficient to compute them or even to compare them. In most implementations of the Rabin–Karp algorithm, therefore, the numeric values are stored and operated on using *modular arithmetic*: Whenever a step in the computation of such a value equals or exceeds some upper bound (the *modulus*), it is divided by the modulus and replaced in subsequent computations by the remainder of the division. (Mathematicians use the notation "x mod y" to express the remainder resulting from the division of a natural number x by a positive integer y.)

Not all arithmetic operations on natural numbers have modular analogues, but addition and multiplication do. The identities

$$(a + b) \bmod m \ = \ ((a \bmod m) + (b \bmod m)) \bmod m,$$
$$(a \cdot b) \bmod m \ = \ ((a \bmod m) \cdot (b \bmod m)) \bmod m$$

enable us, in effect, to cast out multiples of the modulus m at any point in a sequence of additions and multiplications. Provided that we end with a division by the modulus, the final result will be the same no matter how many casting-out operations we perform along the way in order to keep the intermediate results small and manageable.

For instance, in many implementations of Scheme, addition and multiplication are faster if both the operands and the result can be represented internally as *fixnums*—integers small enough that they can be stored in a single memory location or in one of the registers of the central processing unit. For the particular sequence of operations required in one step of the `process-list` recursion in the `dna-numeric-value` procedure, one would have to guarantee that multiplying a number less than the modulus by 4 and adding the result to the numeric value of a nucleotide (which will always be less than 4) yields a fixnum.

An upper bound for the moduli that guarantee this property can be computed by dividing the successor of the largest natural number that can be represented as a fixnum (which depends on choices made by the Scheme implementer) by the base of numeration. For instance, in version 0.7.3 of the Chibi-Scheme processor, the largest natural number represented as a fixnum is 536870911 (which is $2^{29} - 1$). For our nucleotide lists, therefore, the number we choose for the modulus should not exceed (`div` (`add1` 536870911) 4), which is 134217728.

One disadvantage of using modular arithmetic is that it is possible for different strings to *collide*—that is, to be converted to the same numeric value, simply because their long-form, unreduced numeric values happen to differ by some multiple of the modulus. When the modulus is large, this will be a rare occurrence, but not rare enough to ignore. Since the numerical equality of the modular-arithmetic values of a pattern string and a substring of the text is a necessary, but not a sufficient, condition for their equality as strings, we are still obliged to do the character-by-character match if the numeric test using = succeeds. The advantage of the numeric test is that it detects *mismatches* more quickly in so many cases.

The number of collisions will generally be smaller if we choose some modulus that has no factors in common with the size of the character set. For instance, the upper bound 134217728 itself would be a poor choice, because it is itself a power of 4, so that any two lists of nucleotides that happened to have a sufficiently long common suffix would necessarily collide. A better choice would be the greatest prime number less than 134217728, which turns out to be 134217689. Here's how we can integrate the division by the modulus into the computation:

```
(define dna-modular-numeric-value
  (let ((modulus 134217689))
    (process-list (create 0)
                  (run (cross nucleotide-value (sect * <> 4))
                       +
                       (sect mod <> modulus))))))
```

Some collisions still occur, but they tend to involve nucleotide sequences that are otherwise unalike and will quickly be distinguished during the element-by-element match.

We can abstract the form of this computation from the particular numbers that occur in it, supplying them as arguments to a higher-order procedure, along with the procedure that computes the "digit value" of each element:

```
(define (modular-numeric-evaluator base digit-value modulus)
  (process-list (create 0)
                (run (cross digit-value (sect * <> base))
                     +
                     (sect mod <> modulus)))))
```

One further difficulty remains. We can compute the numeric value of the pattern once and for all, at the beginning of the match. However, as we work our way through the text, we'll need the numeric value of each section that is equal in length to the pattern. If we have to compute each one by invoking dna-modular-numeric-value, the process will take even longer than the element-by-element comparisons featured in the simple, slow string matcher.

The solution is to use dna-modular-numeric-value only for the prefix of the original text that has the same length as the pattern, and then to use a simpler transformation to obtain the numeric value of each subsequent section of the same length. Suppose, for instance, that the text is (list 'G 'G 'A 'T 'G 'T 'T 'A 'G 'G 'C 'G 'T 'C 'A 'A 'G 'T 'A 'A) and the pattern is a list of three nucleotides. If we call dna-modular-numeric-value to get the numeric value of (list 'G 'G 'A) (the prefix of the text that has the same length as the pattern), we can convert it into the numeric value of (list 'G 'A 'T) (the next section of the same length) without recalculating from scratch. All we have to do is subtract away the numeric value of the initial "digit" G, multiply the remainder by four, and add the value of the new final digit T. The multiplication basically scales up the values of the intervening digits to reflect the fact that each of them is being moved up into a position with a "place value" that is four times as large—from the units place to the fours place, from the fours place to the sixteens place, and so on.

Given the modulus that we have chosen, all three of these operations can be done within the range of fixnums, and they take a constant time, regardless

of the length of the pattern. The transformation essentially slides a window,
equal in length to the pattern, one position further along the text, converting
the numeric value of the old section into the numeric value of the new one.

We can separate out all the arithmetic involved by supplying a total of
six natural numbers to the `slide-text-window` procedure that implements the
transformation: the length of the pattern, the "base of numeration" (that is,
the cardinality of the set from which our list elements are drawn), the chosen
modulus, the number that represents the section of the text list that we're sliding
away from, the "digit value" of the element at the beginning of that section, and
the "digit value" of the new element that appears at the end of the section that
we're sliding to (that is, the next new element of `text`. In the application of
the algorithm, the first three of these numbers remain fixed throughout, while
the last three change as the window slides along the text, so we'll separate the
fixed arguments from the changing ones in the implementation:

```
(define (slide-text-window len base modulus)
  (let ((initial-weight ((fold-natural (create 1)
                                       (pipe (sect * <> base)
                                             (sect mod <> modulus)))
                         (sub1 len))))
    (lambda (current old new)
      (mod (+ (* (mod (- current (* old initial-weight)) modulus)
                 base)
              new)
           modulus))))
```

For this to work, the pattern cannot be the empty list, because then the
window into the text is also empty, and the proposed transformation becomes
nonsensical. The main algorithm must therefore deal with the empty pattern
as a special case.

The Rabin–Karp algorithm, then, has an overall structure similar to that of
the naive string matcher, but computes the numeric "signature" of each section
of the text and checks whether it matches the signature of the pattern before
invoking `matches-prefix?`:

```
(define (Rabin-Karp-sublist-searcher base digit-value modulus)
  (let ((evaluator
          (modular-numeric-evaluator base digit-value modulus)))
    (lambda (pattern text)
      (let ((pattern-length (length pattern))
            (text-length (length text)))
        (if (zero? pattern-length)
            ((unfold-list (equal-to (add1 text-length)) identity add1) 0)
            (let ((slider
                    (slide-text-window pattern-length base modulus))
                  (pattern-signature (evaluator pattern)))
              ((rec (searcher position subtext after-drop signature)
```

```
                    (let ((rest-of-matches
                           (if (empty-list? after-drop)
                               (list)
                               (searcher
                                 (add1 position)
                                 (rest subtext)
                                 (rest after-drop)
                                 (slider
                                   signature
                                   (digit-value (first subtext))
                                   (digit-value (first after-drop)))))))
                      (if (and (= signature pattern-signature)
                               (matches-prefix? pattern subtext))
                          (prepend position rest-of-matches)
                          rest-of-matches)))
            0
            text
            (drop text pattern-length)
            (evaluator (take text pattern-length)))))))))
```

The same basic algorithm can be used, with only minor modifications, for substring search. For strings, we can use a fixed base that depends on the character set. Scheme's predefined `char->integer` procedure maps characters to Unicode scalar values (as described in the *Revised*[7] *Report on the Algorithmic Language Scheme*), all of which are less than 1114112, so we'll take that as our base and use `char->integer` to compute the "digit values" of individual characters.

We might as well settle on a modulus as well. Implementations of the *Revised*[7] *Report on the Algorithmic Language Scheme* generally provide fixnums up to at least $2^{29} - 1$. Dividing 2^{29} by 1114112 yields 481, and the largest prime less than or equal to 481 is 479, so we'll take that as our modulus for substring comparisons. Using such a small modulus will cause many accidental collisions, but the `occurs-at?` procedure will almost always detect them by performing a single character comparison, an overhead which is preferable to the cost of arithmetic on integers that are not fixnums.

Since the values of `base`, `digit-value`, and `modulus` are fixed, we need only a single modular evaluator for strings, rather than a higher-order procedure. In the Rabin–Karp algorithm, we'll apply the evaluator not only to the entire pattern but also to a prefix of the text, so we'll give it an extra parameter so that we can tell it where the prefix ends:

```
(define (string-evaluate str len)
  (let ((base 1114112)
        (modulus 479))
    ((lower-ply-natural (create 0)
                    (run (cross (pipe (sect string-ref str <>)
                                      char->integer)
                                (sect * <> base))
```

```
                            +
                    (sect mod <> modulus)))
    len)))
```

Using the fixed values of base, digit-value, and modulus and string-evaluate, and changing the list operations to string operations, we obtain the following substring-search procedure:

```
(define substring-search
  (let ((base 1114112)
        (modulus 479))
    (lambda (pattern text)
      (let ((pattern-length (string-length pattern))
            (text-length (string-length text)))
        (if (zero? pattern-length)
            ((unfold-list (equal-to (add1 text-length)) identity add1) 0)
            (let ((slider
                    (slide-text-window pattern-length base modulus))
                  (pattern-signature
                    (string-evaluate pattern pattern-length)))
              ((rec (searcher position signature)
                 (let ((rest-of-matches
                         (if (<= text-length (+ position pattern-length))
                             (list)
                             (searcher
                               (add1 position)
                               (slider
                                 signature
                                 (char->integer
                                   (string-ref text position))
                                 (char->integer
                                   (string-ref text
                                               (+ position
                                                  pattern-length)))))))) 
                   (if (and (= signature pattern-signature)
                            (occurs-at? pattern text position))
                       (prepend position rest-of-matches)
                       rest-of-matches)))
               0
               (string-evaluate text pattern-length)))))))))
```

---

modular-numeric-evaluator   (afp sublist-search Rabin-Karp)

natural-number, ($\alpha \rightarrow$ natural-number), natural-number $\rightarrow$
base   digit-value   modulus
                                                       (list(α) $\rightarrow$ natural-number)
                                                         ls

Construct a procedure that computes the numeric value of ls modulo modulus, taking base as the base of numeration and applying digit-value to each element to determine its numeric value as a digit in that system of numeration.
Precondition: digit-value can receive any element of ls.

Precondition: digit-value returns a different result for every argument it can receive.
Precondition: Every value returned by digit-value is less than base.
Precondition: modulus is positive.

slide-text-window   (afp sublist-search Rabin-Karp)
natural-number, natural-number, natural-number →
len   base   modulus
              (*natural-number, natural-number, natural-number* → *natural-number*)
               current   old   new
Construct a procedure that computes the numeric value (modulo modulus) of a list of length
len consisting of all but the initial element of a list with old as the digit value of its initial
element and current as its numeric value (modulo modulus), followed by an element with new
as its digit value. The elements of the list are assumed to be drawn from a fixed, finite set of
cardinality base.
Precondition: len is positive.
Precondition: current is less than modulus.
Precondition: old is less than base.
Precondition: new is less than base.

Rabin-Karp-sublist-searcher   (afp sublist-search Rabin-Karp)
natural-number, (α → *natural-number), natural-number* →
base   digit-value   modulus
                 (*list(α), list(α)* → *list(natural-number)*)
                 pattern text
Construct a procedure that, in turn, constructs a list of the positions in text at which sublists
that match pattern begin, in ascending order.
Precondition: digit-value can receive any element of pattern.
Precondition: digit-value can receive any element of text.
Precondition: Every value returned by digit-value is less than base.
Precondition: digit-value returns a different result for every argument it can receive.
Precondition: modulus is positive.
Precondition: The length of pattern is less than or equal to the length of text.

char->integer   (rnrs base (6))
character → *natural-number*
ch
Return the Unicode scalar value corresponding to ch.

string-evaluate   (afp sublist-search Rabin-Karp)
string, natural-number → *natural-number*
str   len
Compute the numeric signature of the prefix of str of length len.
Precondition: len is less than or equal to the length of str.

substring-search   (afp sublist-search Rabin-Karp)
string, string → *list(natural-number)*
pattern text
Construct a list of the positions in text at which substrings that match pattern begin, in
ascending order.
Precondition: The length of pattern is less than or equal to the length of text.

Exercises

7.4–1 Compute (by hand) the signature of the pattern (list 5 7 12 4),
assuming that base is 16, digit-value is identity, and modulus is 359.

7.4–2 Find two English words of the same length for which string-evaluate
returns the same value.

7.4–3   Adapt the Rabin–Karp algorithm so that it receives a bag of values as its pattern argument and searches the text (which is still a list) for selections that have the values in the bag as their elements, returning a list of the starting positions of such selections.

Appendix A

Recommended Reading

For readers who wish to learn more about algorithms, functional programming, or both, I recommend the following works:

Bird, Richard. *Introduction to Functional Programming Using Haskell*, second edition. London: Prentice Hall Europe, 1998. ISBN 0-13-484346-0.

Bird, Richard. *Pearls of Functional Algorithm Design*. Cambridge: Cambridge University Press, 2010. ISBN 978-0-521-51338-8.

Bird, Richard, and Oege de Moor. *The Algebra of Programming*. London: Prentice Hall, 1997. ISBN 0-13-507245-X.

Cormen, Thomas H., Charles E. Leiserson, Ronald L. Rivest, and Clifford Stein. *Introduction to Algorithms*, third edition. Cambridge, Massachusetts: The MIT Press, 2009. ISBN 978-0-262-03384-8.

Dybvig, R. Kent. *The Scheme Programming Language*, fourth edition. Cambridge, Massachusetts: The MIT Press, 2009. ISBN 978-0-262-51298-5.

Knuth, Donald E. *The Art of Computer Programming*, so far comprising four volumes: *Fundamental Algorithms*, third edition (Reading, Massachusetts: Addison–Wesley, 1997; ISBN 0-201-89683-4); *Seminumerical Algorithms*, third edition (Reading, Massachusetts: Addison–Wesley, 1998; ISBN 0-201-89684-2); *Sorting and Searching*, second edition (Reading, Massachusetts: Addison–Wesley, 1998; ISBN 0-201-89685-0); and *Combinatorial Algorithms*, Part 1 (Upper Saddle River, New Jersey: Addison–Wesley, 2011; ISBN 978-0-201-03804-0).

Liao, Andrew M. "Three Priority Queue Applications Revisited." *Algorithmica* **7** (1992), pp. 415–427.

Okasaki, Chris. *Purely Functional Data Structures*. Cambridge: Cambridge University Press, 1998. ISBN 0-521-63124-6.

Rabhi, Fethi, and Guy Lapalme. *Algorithms: A Functional Programming Approach*. Harlow, England: Addison–Wesley, 1999. ISBN 0-201-59604-0.

© Springer-Verlag GmbH Germany, part of Springer Nature 2018
J. D. Stone, *Algorithms for Functional Programming*,
https://doi.org/10.1007/978-3-662-57970-1

Sedgewick, Robert. "Left-Leaning Red-Black Trees." Princeton, New Jersey, 2008. http://www.cs.princeton.edu/~rs/talks/LLRB/RedBlack.pdf.

Skiena, Steven S. *The Algorithm Design Manual*, second edition. New York: Springer, 2008. ISBN 978-1-84800-069-8.

Appendix B

The (afp primitives) Library

The (afp primitives) library exports the procedures and syntactic extensions that are used, but not otherwise defined, in *Algorithms for Functional Programming*. A great majority of them (fifty-nine of the seventy-one) are derived from the *Revised[7] Report on the Algorithmic Language Scheme* without change. To specify unambiguously how the remaining twelve work, and to enable readers who, for whatever reason, cannot access the author's Web site to explore and use the code developed here, I here include the source code for this library, with the comments deleted.

Experienced Scheme programmers will recognize much of this code as derived from Scheme Requests for Implementation 8 (receive), 26 (sect, which in the SRFI is called cut), and 31 (rec). I am indebted to Al Petrovsky for the careful formulations he contributed to SRFIs 26 and 31, which I have adapted here.

For fuller attributions and explanations, please see the online version of this library at

https://unity.homelinux.net/afp/code/afp/primitives.sld

```
(define-library (afp primitives)
  (export quote + - * / div-and-mod expt square lambda apply list values
          delist zero? positive? negative? even? odd? < <= = > >= boolean?
          not number? integer? char? string? symbol? procedure? boolean=?
          char=? string=? symbol=? equal? if and or define let rec
          receive map sect length natural-number? null null? pair? cons
          car cdr list? list-ref reverse append min max source
          end-of-source end-of-source? define-record-type char-ci=?
          string<=? char<=? string>=? char>=? string-ref string-length
          char->integer)
  (import (rename (scheme base) (expt r7rs-expt))
          (only (scheme char) char-ci=?))
  (begin
    (define (div-and-mod dividend divisor)
      (let-values (((near-quot near-rem) (floor/ dividend divisor)))
```

© Springer-Verlag GmbH Germany, part of Springer Nature 2018
J. D. Stone, *Algorithms for Functional Programming*,
https://doi.org/10.1007/978-3-662-57970-1

```
        (if (negative? near-rem)
            (values (+ near-quot 1) (- near-rem divisor))
            (values near-quot near-rem))))

(define (expt base exponent)
  (unless (integer? exponent)
    (error "expt: non-integer exponent"))
  (r7rs-expt base exponent))

(define (delist ls)
  (apply values ls))

(define-syntax rec
  (syntax-rules ()
    ((rec (name . variables) . body)
     (letrec ((name (lambda variables . body))) name))
    ((rec name expression)
     (letrec ((name expression)) name))))

(define-syntax receive
  (syntax-rules ()
    ((receive formals expression body ...)
     (call-with-values (lambda () expression)
                       (lambda formals body ...)))))

(define-syntax internal-sect
  (syntax-rules (<> <...>)
    ((internal-sect (slot-name ...) (proc arg ...))
     (lambda (slot-name ...) ((begin proc) arg ...)))
    ((internal-sect (slot-name ...) (proc arg ...) <...>)
     (lambda (slot-name ... . rest-slot)
       (apply proc arg ... rest-slot)))
    ((internal-sect (slot-name ...) (position ...) <> . cs)
     (internal-sect (slot-name ... x) (position ... x) . cs))
    ((internal-sect (slot-name ...) (position ...) const . cs)
     (internal-sect (slot-name ...) (position ... const) . cs))))

(define-syntax sect
  (syntax-rules ()
    ((sect . consts-or-slots)
     (internal-sect () () . consts-or-slots))))

(define (natural-number? something)
  (and (integer? something)
       (exact? something)
       (not (negative? something))))

(define null '())

(define-syntax source
```

```
    (syntax-rules ()
      ((_ body)
       (lambda () body))))

(define-record-type end-of-source-record
  (end-of-source)
  end-of-source?)))
```

Appendix C

Using the AFP Libraries

Scheme Language Processors

I have thoroughly tested the code in this book under the following implementations of the *Revised*[7] *Report on the Algorithmic Language Scheme* and can recommend them. Instructions for downloading and installing them are available at the cited Web sites, as is extensive documentation.

- Chibi-Scheme: http://synthcode.com/wiki/chibi-scheme
- Larceny: http://www.larcenists.org/
- Racket: https://www.racket-lang.org/

Racket does not come with an implementation of R[7]RS built in. Instead, after installing Racket, users must add on a separate r7rs package, from a different source:

- Racket R[7]RS: https://github.com/lexi-lambda/racket-r7rs

Downloading and Installing the Libraries

Libraries containing the procedures developed in this book are available on my Web site, beginning at

https://unity.homelinux.net/afp/code/

On this front-door page, you will find a link to each library, which you can explore online or download through your browser, as well as a link to a compressed archive file (.tgz format) containing all of those libraries.

The test programs that I wrote to validate the code are also available at that site, in the tests directory. There is also a support directory containing some additional scaffolding code.

© Springer-Verlag GmbH Germany, part of Springer Nature 2018
J. D. Stone, *Algorithms for Functional Programming*,
https://doi.org/10.1007/978-3-662-57970-1

If your computer is running GNU/Linux, you can download the archive file and install the files from the command line. You may find it helpful to begin by creating a new directory for them and making it the current working directory:

```
mkdir afp-work
cd afp-work
```

Then the commands

```
wget https://unity.homelinux.net/afp/afp-tarball.tgz
tar zxvf afp-tarball.tgz
```

download the archive file and unpack it, creating three subdirectories, afp, tests, and support. The procedure libraries are in afp; tests contains my test programs, and support contains some additional scaffolding for the test procedures (a pseudorandom-number generator, for instance).

You may also find it helpful to create at least one additional subdirectory of afp-work, for your programs. I'll assume that you have such a subdirectory and that it's called programs.

Finally, if you're using the Racket implementation of the *Revised*[7] *Report on the Algorithmic Language Scheme*, you may find it convenient to place a copy of the afp subdirectory, or a symbolic link to it, in one of the directories on the Racket collection path. In version 6.1 of Racket for Debian GNU/Linux, which I used when preparing this book, the directories on the collection path were ~/.racket/6.1/collects/ for an individual user's libraries and /usr/share/racket/collects/ for libraries available to all users of the system. (You'll need the privileges of a system administrator to copy the afp libraries into the latter directory.) This step also simplifies the use of the graphical program-development environment that Racket supplies.

Creating Program Files

The first few lines of a Scheme program that uses the AFP procedure libraries look something like this:

```
(import (afp primitives)
        (afp lists)
        (afp sorting mergesort))
```

The import-expression lists the libraries containing the definitions that your program needs, usually because it invokes the procedures that they define. The Scheme program processor finds the libraries in the afp directory, where (in this example) it will find primitives.sls, lists.sls, and a nested subdirectory sorting that in turn has mergesort.sls within it.

The import list can also include some or all of the standard libraries specified in the *Revised*[7] *Report on the Algorithmic Language Scheme*, which define many procedures that (afp primitives) lacks:

```
(import (scheme base)
        (afp tables)
        (afp permutations)
        (scheme write))
```

The Scheme program processor will find the standard libraries in the directories in which they were originally installed, so you won't need copies of them in your afp-work directory.

If you try to import different definitions of the same identifier (from different libraries), the Scheme program processor reports an error. Since (afp primitives) duplicates many of the procedures in (scheme base), you will get this error if you try to import both (afp primitives) and (scheme base), in full, in the same program. Usually, however, you need only a few of the definitions in (afp primitives), ones that don't conflict with any of the standard libraries. You can use an only-clause in an import-expression to select those particular definitions:

```
(import (scheme base)
        (only (afp primitives) rec receive sect))
```

Only the three specified definitions are brought in from (afp primitives) in this case, and they don't conflict with any definitions in (scheme base).

To create files containing Scheme programs that use the AFP libraries, you · can use a text editor. GNU Emacs would be a good choice. It has a Scheme mode that supports many common programming operations, tailored to the syntax of Scheme. In addition, GNU Emacs is well documented, configurable, and extensible. (Its powerful extension language, Emacs Lisp, has some strong similarities to Scheme.)

Racket is packaged with a graphical program-development environment, Dr-Racket, which combines an editor with an interactive language processor in a single graphical interface. DrRacket also provides helpful facilities for debugging.

Executing Programs

If your current working directory is the one in which you extracted the files from the tarball (the directory called afp-work above), and you created a subdirectory called programs and created a Scheme program using the AFP libraries in a file called, say, frogs.ss in the programs directory, you can direct the Scheme language processor that you are using to execute the program from the command line.

If you are using the Chibi-Scheme implementation, the command is

```
chibi-scheme -I . programs/frogs.ss
```

The `-I` `.` option directs Chibi-Scheme to look in subdirectories of the current working directory for libraries.

If you are using the Larceny implementation, the command is

```
larceny -r7rs -path . -program programs/frogs.ss
```

If you are using the command-line version of the Racket implementation, the command is

```
racket --search . programs/frogs.ss
```

The option `--search` `.` is not needed if you have copied the AFP libraries into one of the directories that is already on the Racket collection path.

If you are using DrRacket, you can run a program by opening the file containing it and clicking on the word Run on the toolbar, just above the text field in which the source code is displayed. Output from the program will appear in a separate text field below the one containing the source code.

Limitations

In testing the AFP libraries, I encountered some quirks and limitations in each of the various implementations of the *Revised*[7] *Report on the Algorithmic Language Scheme* that I used. (The full set of test programs is available at the AFP Web site mentioned above.)

In Chibi-Scheme and Larceny, the `expt` procedure returns inexact values even when both arguments are exact integers, if the second argument is negative. Consequently, some of the tests that I wrote to validate the code in the AFP libraries failed in these implementations.

In Larceny, it is possible for there to be two values of the same record type that do not satisfy `equal?` even though all of their respective fields do. The *Revised*[7] *Report on the Algorithmic Language Scheme* permits this behavior, but it seems counterintuitive, in that it makes records behave differently from Scheme's other data structures (pairs, lists, vectors, strings, and bytevectors). For instance, this is why I couldn't define `arc=?`, in §6.1, simply as `equal?`.

In Larceny, and in Racket with the `r7rs` package, the keyword `else` is not recognized as a syntactic keyword in `guard`-expressions, as the standard requires. No `guard`-expressions are used in this book, but my test programs have some. I had to replace the keyword `else` with `#t` to make them work.

Racket treats integer division by zero as an unrecoverable error that cannot be handled in a `guard`-expression. This invalidates some of my tests, and I had to comment them out in order to run the full test suite under Racket.

Racket with the `r7rs` package requires all libraries to have names containing at least two components. (For instance, `(afp primitives)` is OK, but just (primitives) is not.) All of the libraries introduced in this book meet this condition.

Racket with the r7rs package requires each program and library file to begin with the language directive #!r7rs (or #lang r7rs). I used a short shell script to add this directive at the top of each file in order to test with Racket.

Racket requires all libraries to be in files bearing the filetype extension .rkt. The same shell script that added the directive also changed the extension on the Racket version of the file.

Index

© Springer-Verlag GmbH Germany, part of Springer Nature 2018
J. D. Stone, *Algorithms for Functional Programming*,
https://doi.org/10.1007/978-3-662-57970-1

Printed in the United States
By Bookmasters